TRENDS IN SMOKING
AND HEALTH RESEARCH

TRENDS IN SMOKING AND HEALTH RESEARCH

J. H. OWING
EDITOR

Nova Biomedical Books
New York

For permission to use material from this book please contact us:
Telephone 631-231-7269; Fax 631-231-8175
Web Site: http://www.novapublishers.com

NOTICE TO THE READER

The Publisher has taken reasonable care in the preparation of this book, but makes no expressed or implied warranty of any kind and assumes no responsibility for any errors or omissions. No liability is assumed for incidental or consequential damages in connection with or arising out of information contained in this book. The Publisher shall not be liable for any special, consequential, or exemplary damages resulting, in whole or in part, from the readers' use of, or reliance upon, this material.

This publication is designed to provide accurate and authoritative information with regard to the subject matter covered herein. It is sold with the clear understanding that the Publisher is not engaged in rendering legal or any other professional services. If legal or any other expert assistance is required, the services of a competent person should be sought. FROM A DECLARATION OF PARTICIPANTS JOINTLY ADOPTED BY A COMMITTEE OF THE AMERICAN BAR ASSOCIATION AND A COMMITTEE OF PUBLISHERS.

LIBRARY OF CONGRESS CATALOGING-IN-PUBLICATION DATA:
Available Upon Request

ISBN 1-59454-391-7

Published by Nova Science Publishers, Inc. ✦ New York

Contents

Preface

Smoking is a greater cause of death and disability than any single disease, says the World Health Organisation. According to their figures, it is responsible for approximately five million deaths worldwide every year. Tobacco smoking is a known or probable cause of approximately 25 diseases including cancer, heart attacks and strokes. The WHO says that its impact on world health is still not fully assessed. This new book offers leading edge research from around the globe.

Lung cancer is the leading cause of cancer deaths in both developing and developed countries, and one of the most important 'avoidable' causes of death worldwide. At present more men than women die each year from lung cancer, but in recent years a rapid increase in lung cancer mortality has been observed among women in developed countries, compared with a leveling off or decrease among men. Few data are available to explain the ongoing increase in lung cancer incidence and mortality among women. While in the male population the occurrence of lung cancer is related mainly to the past and current prevalence of tobacco smoking, results of some studies among women suggest a nonnegligible role of other factors acting either as independent risk factors or as modifiers of the effect of smoking. The results of some studies suggest that women might be more susceptible than men to tobacco carcinogens, however, several recent cohort studies found no measurable excess of lung cancer among female smokers compared with male smokers, once amounts smoked have been controlled. The relative importance and contribution of each factor may vary with geographic area, lifestyle, and socioeconomic conditions.

To obtain insight into the role of tobacco and some other known or suspected lifestyle and environmental factors, a case-control study among women was conducted at the Charles University Hospital Na Bulovce, Prague, Czech Republic. In 1998-2002, personal interviews were done with 451 female cases and 1710 controls, using a structured questionnaire, after obtaining the examinees' informed consent. The data collected by trained interviewers were analyzed using unconditional logistic regression. Results of the case-control study presented in chapter I support the claim that cigarette smoking is far and away the most strongly active risk factor of lung cancer among Czech women, while cofactors may have a contributory role. Among nonsmoking women, a positive association with lung cancer risk was found for red meat, and an inverse association with black tea. Among smokers only, the personal history of tuberculosis or previous cancer, or family history of lung cancer among first degree relatives were associated with significant increases in risk, while inverse associations appeared for vegetables, apples, milk/dairy products, coffee, wine, and physical exercise. To obtain more specific results, further studies, with updated design, are needed. Recommendations derived from the study include strengthening primary prevention, the basic approach to the control of lung cancer. Avoiding tobacco, consuming a healthful diet, and staying physically active are important, mutually correlated principles in primary prevention of lung cancer, all amenable to change by modification of life style.

Many of the published data on the relationship of cigarette smoking with systolic and diastolic blood pressures (SBP and DBP, respectively), serum high-density lipoprotein cholesterol (HDL-C) subfractions is based on studies of middle-aged individuals. The data on young women are scarce. Chapter II examined the relationship of cigarette smoking with SBP, DBP and HDL-C subfractions in Japanese collegiate women. Thirty current smokers were individually matched for physical activity scores, age and body mass index (BMI) with 30 nonsmokers. There were no significant differences between smokers and nonsmokers in the mean nutrient intakes. The smokers had significantly lower mean SBP, DBP, HDL-C and HDL$_2$-C. Furthermore, when the subjects were divided into 3 groups by smoking habits: 30 nonsmokers and subjects who smoked 2-12 (n=15) and 13-20 (n=15) cigarettes/day, SBP, DBP, HDL-C and HDL$_2$-C showed dose-dependent relationships. In univariate analyses, number of cigarette smoking a day significantly negatively correlated with SBP, DBP, HDL-C, HDL$_2$-C and TC. Duration of cigarette smoking significantly negatively correlated with SBP, DBP and HDL$_2$-C and positively with TG. Waist significantly negatively correlated with HDL-C and HDL$_2$-C. Dietary fiber significantly positively correlated with HDL-C and HDL$_2$-C. When number of cigarette smoking a day, duration of cigarette smoking, waist and dietary fiber were included in the forward stepwise multiple regression analyses, there were negative relationships of cigarette smoking to SBP, DBP, HDL-C and HDL$_2$-C. Also, there were positive relationship of duration of cigarette smoking to TG. These results suggest that the known associations in older adults of cigarette smoking with blood pressure and HDL-C subfractions are already apparent in young women.

As outlined in chapter III, substantial numbers of women continue to smoke during pregnancy despite increased knowledge of the adverse health effects. Worldwide, the crude estimate of the number of women who smoked during pregnancy in 1995 was between 12-14 million. Smoking is considered the single most modifiable cause of adverse pregnancy outcomes in the US and other Western countries. Research has shown that women who have not been motivated to or able to quit on learning of their pregnancy can benefit from targeted smoking cessation interventions. Typically, such interventions can achieve a two or three-fold increase above the cessation rates achieved by women without help or in response to the basic level of advice and information typically provided as part of usual antenatal care.

Chapter IV explores the association between hypertension in pregnancy and smoking during pregnancy in Japanese women. A description of how maternal smoking during pregnancy may contribute to developing PE is also included. The importance of providing good control for the possible effects of bias and confounding factors, which are two of the problems inherent in various epidemiological studies, is also discussed.

In chapter V the authors highlight the most common adverse effects of smoking during pregnancy and, in the second part, explain how smokers can be helped to quit.

Chapter VI has the following structure: **Objective:** The association between maternal smoking in pregnancy and offspring's overweight and obesity was observed by chance at first. Overweight and obesity tend to increase in their prevalences. Childhood obesity often persists throughout adulthood. Therapeutic interventions are far from satisfactory results.

Therefore, prevention of overweight and obesity is a major public health issue. For effective prevention strategies exact identification of modifiable risk factors is required. In order to assess the impact of intrauterine tobacco exposure on overweight and obesity, 3 cross sectional studies were performed. **Setting:** Southern Germany. **Participants:** n=8,765 (survey I), n= 6,483 (survey II) and n=4,974 (survey III) German children aged 5.0 to 6.9 years. **Main outcome measures:** Overweight and obesity at school entry was defined as body mass index (weight in kilograms divided by squared height in meters) >90th percentile and >97th percentile (survey I and II) or according to sex- and age-specific body mass index cutpoints proposed by the International Obesity Task Force (survey III). Questions on maternal smoking differentiated between smoking in pregnancy vs. non-smoking in pregnancy (survey I and II) and additionally smoking in early pregnancy or smoking throughout pregnancy (survey III). **Results:** Offspring of mothers who smoked in pregnancy had higher prevalences of overweight and obesity in all 3 surveys. These associations could not be explained by confounding due to a number of constitutional, sociodemographic and lifestyle factors. The adjusted odds ratios for smoking in pregnancy and offspring's obesity indicated a risk for offspring of smoking mothers twice as much compared to offspring of non-smoking mothers. Smoking in early pregnancy yielded similar odds ratios for childhood overweight and obesity compared to smoking throughout pregnancy. **Conclusions:** The association between maternal smoking in pregnancy and offspring's overweight and obesity could be reproducibly observed in 3 surveys. Since adjustment for a wide range of potential confounders could not explain this association and smoking after pregnancy was not associated with childhood obesity, intrauterine exposure rather than family lifestyle factors associated with smoking appears to be instrumental. The first trimester has been identified as the critical period. Women of reproductive age should be advised to quit smoking prior to pregnancy.

As explained in chapter VII environmental tobacco smoke (ETS) exposure continues to be a major health concern for children. During pregnancy, ETS exposure is linked with obstetric complications, premature deliveries and fetal growth retardation. In children, ETS exposure results in negative respiratory health effects including an increase in lower respiratory tract infections, asthma exacerbation, reduced lung function, and an increased risk of sudden infant death syndrome (SIDS). ETS exposure in children is also considered to be an important risk factor for neurodevelopmental and behavioral problems and is associated with some childhood cancers. The major source of ETS for young children is from their smoking parents or other household members. Children are particularly vulnerable to the effects of ETS and suffer involuntarily as they usually have no control over their exposure. From a population level perspective, large numbers of children experience these risks because of the high prevalence of ETS exposure both in the home and in public places. Future studies employing longitudinal study designs and changes in exposure classifications will further explain the negative health effects. In addition, research in countries where maternal smoking is rare will help distinguish between the effects of ETS exposure among young children who have experienced in utero exposure versus postnatal exposure versus in utero and postnatal exposure. Reducing ETS exposure provides a number of policy challenges: regulating ETS exposure in the home and in public places. A research agenda that would guide the choice of policy options will be considered.

Despite wide-spread publicity and knowledge that tobacco use poses serious health risks, adolescent tobacco use is increasing in the United States and worldwide. Every day more than

4000 children under the age of 18 begin smoking in the United States alone (CDC, 2003; SMA, 2002). Of these children, one third eventually will die from smoking-related causes. In addition, the fact that 90% of adult smokers began smoking before age 20 indicates that adolescence is a critical target period for tobacco prevention. Susceptibility to tobacco use in adolescents includes social, psychological, environmental, and biobehavioral factors that influence tobacco initiation and maintenance. Chapter VIII provides an overview of adolescent tobacco use. It begins with a summary of the magnitude of this situation and the relevant epidemiology. It then discusses reasons why adolescence is a vulnerable phase in life for tobacco initiation and reviews the psychosocial, psychobiological, and environmental factors that influence tobacco initiation and maintenance. Next, this chapter discusses the physical and mental health effects of adolescent smoking. The chapter ends by reviewing intervention and cessation strategies to reduce adolescent smoking and how current findings may be used to develop prevention programs to deter adolescent smoking or treatment strategies to decrease adolescent smoking.

Chapter IX briefly discusses the incidence, presentation, and associated complications of an aneurysmal subarachnoid hemorrhage (aSAH). Subsequently, the effects of cigarette smoking on aneurysm formation, growth, and eventual rupture as well as the influence of cigarette smoking on the delayed development of cerebral vasospasm following aSAH will be examined.

Although the relationship between cigarette smoking and bone loss during adulthood is well established, the effect of smoking and second-hand-smoke on bone mass in adolescents is unknown. Because of the high prevalence of smoking among the adults living in China and the adolescent period being a critical time for both smoking initiation and bone accretion, the objective of the study in chapter X was to address the role of smoking and second-hand-smoke on adolescent bone mass in China. We measured cortical (forearm) and trabecular (os calcis) bone mineral content (BMC) and density (BMD) using dual energy x-ray absorptiometry (DXA) in 466 girls and boys (ages 12-16 yr). In 166 girls, forearm BMC was best predicted by BMI (24%), age (5%), and menarche (2%) for a combined variance of 31%, while 8% of the variance in os calcis BMC was predicted by BMI alone with no contribution by age or menarche. In 300 boys, a total of 24% of the variance in forearm BMC was explained by BMI (18%) and age (6%); os calcis BMC was only predicted by BMI (21%). The addition of cigarette smoking and second-hand-smoke into the multiple linear regression models did not make significant contributions to the variances in either girls or boys. The reasons may have been due to the low levels and duration of tobacco use and exposure among the adolescents we studied. Selecting an older sample of adolescents who smoke more frequently and for a long duration may have uncovered a different relationship. Nevertheless, this was the first study that investigated the role of smoking and second-hand-smoke on bone mass during adolescence.

In: Trends in Smoking and Health Research
Editors: J. H. Owing, pp. 1-33

ISBN: 1-59454-391-7
© 2005 Nova Science Publishers, Inc.

Chapter I

Lung Cancer among Women

Antonín K. Kubík[*,1], *Petr Zatloukal*[1], *Norbert Pauk*[1] *and Ladislav Tomášek*[2]

[1]Department of Pneumology and Thoracic Surgery, Charles University, 3rd Faculty of Medicine, University Hospital Na Bulovce, and Postgraduate Medical Institute, Prague, Czech Republic; [2]National Radiation Protection Institute, Prague, Czech Republic

Abstract

Lung cancer is the leading cause of cancer deaths in both developing and developed countries, and one of the most important 'avoidable' causes of death worldwide. At present more men than women die each year from lung cancer, but in recent years a rapid increase in lung cancer mortality has been observed among women in developed countries, compared with a leveling off or decrease among men. Few data are available to explain the ongoing increase in lung cancer incidence and mortality among women. While in the male population the occurrence of lung cancer is related mainly to the past and current prevalence of tobacco smoking, results of some studies among women suggest a nonnegligible role of other factors acting either as independent risk factors or as modifiers of the effect of smoking. The results of some studies suggest that women might be more susceptible than men to tobacco carcinogens, however, several recent cohort studies found no measurable excess of lung cancer among female smokers compared with male smokers, once amounts smoked have been controlled. The relative importance and contribution of each factor may vary with geographic area, lifestyle, and socioeconomic conditions.

To obtain insight into the role of tobacco and some other known or suspected lifestyle and environmental factors, a case-control study among women was conducted at the Charles University Hospital Na Bulovce, Prague, Czech Republic. In 1998-2002, personal interviews were done with 451 female cases and 1710 controls, using a structured questionnaire, after obtaining the examinees´ informed consent. The data collected by trained interviewers were analyzed using unconditional logistic regression.

---

[*] University Hospital Na Bulovce, Budinova 2, CZ-18081 Prague, Czech Republic. Phone +420 266082593, Fax +420 284840840; E-mail address: kubika@email.cz.

Results of our case-control study support the claim that cigarette smoking is far and away the most strongly active risk factor of lung cancer among Czech women, while cofactors may have a contributory role. Among nonsmoking women, a positive association with lung cancer risk was found for red meat, and an inverse association with black tea. Among smokers only, the personal history of tuberculosis or previous cancer, or family history of lung cancer among first degree relatives were associated with significant increases in risk, while inverse associations appeared for vegetables, apples, milk/dairy products, coffee, wine, and physical exercise. To obtain more specific results, further studies, with updated design, are needed. Recommendations derived from the study include strengthening primary prevention, the basic approach to the control of lung cancer. Avoiding tobacco, consuming a healthful diet, and staying physically active are important, mutually correlated principles in primary prevention of lung cancer, all amenable to change by modification of life style.

Part 1. Review of Recent Advances in the Epidemiology of Lung Cancer among Women

Introduction

Early in the twentieth century, lung cancer was a rare disease [Franceschi and Bidoli 1999]. Now, it is the most frequently diagnosed major cancer in the world and is also the most common cause of cancer deaths in males and females in the United States and worldwide [Travis *et al.* 1996]. At present, more men than women die each year from lung cancer, but in recent years a rapid increase in lung cancer mortality has been observed among women in developed countries, compared with a leveling off or decrease among men.

Trends in Lung Cancer

The epidemic of lung cancer was first noted in males in the United States and in a number of European countries during the 1940s. In the 1950s and 1960s, epidemiological studies provided evidence that cigarette smoking was the predominant cause of lung cancer [Doll and Hill 1950, Levin *et al.* 1950, Wynder *et al.* 1950, US Department of Health, Education and Welfare, 1964].

It was not until 1980 that the Surgeon General's Report concluded that increased smoking by women was accompanied by a steep increase in the number of female lung-cancer cases [U.S. Department of Health and Human Services 1980]. In March 2001, the Surgeon General noted that smoking-related diseases have become "epidemic" among women, with almost four of each 10 smoking-related deaths now occurring in women, a proportion that is more than double that in 1965 and largely due to disproportionate rise in lung cancer mortality among women [US Department of Health and Human Services 2001]. In the US in 2003, lung cancer is estimated to have accounted for 68,800 deaths in women, a number which was only slightly lower than the corresponding one for men, 88,400 [American Cancer Society 2004]. The incidence of lung cancer in women has continued to increase, so that as of 1987 in the US the number of deaths from lung cancer among women has been higher than that from breast cancer [Henschke and Miettinen 2004]. In the 1990s, the lung cancer incidence and mortality rates in US women were increasing much less steeply than before [Quinn 2003].

In Europe, among males, three major patterns are discernible in lung cancer mortality [La Vecchia *et al*.1998]. One, observed in Finland and the UK, started from high rates (65/100,000 males in Finland, 70/100,000 in the UK), and showed steady declines to reach 46/100,000 in Finland and 54/100,000 in the UK.

A second one, including most Northern and Central Europe, showed stable or inconsistent trends over time, though with appreciably different absolute values. Of particular interest were the low and only moderately upwards rates in Norway (around 30/100,000 males) and even more the low and steady ones in Sweden (around 24/100,000 males).

The third pattern involves Portugal, Spain and Greece in Southern Europe, and chiefly eastern European countries, which showed substantial rises in male lung cancer rates. Thus, in the early 1990s, Hungary (84/100,000 males) and Poland (71/100,000 males) had lung cancer rates higher than those of the UK or Finland in the early 1980s, i.e. around the peak of their epidemic, and, at least in Hungary, rates were still increasing. The overall rise in Hungary over the 12-year period considered was +42% in males and +73% in females. In Hungarian women, acceleration in the rate of increase of lung cancer mortality was observed since the end of the 1970s and beginning of the 1980s, in contrast to a significant reduction in the rate of increase of mortality in males [Tyczynski *et al*. 2004].

Lung cancer mortality rates in European women were upwards, but still relatively low in most countries, i.e. generally below 10/100,000, except in Hungary where overall female rates reached 18/100,000, the UK (21/100,000) and Denmark (25/100,000). Female lung cancer in the UK is predicted to increase, until by 2015 the numbers will almost equal those in men [Parsons and Somervaille 2000].

The trends in lung cancer rates in Eastern Europe reflect a major impact of the tobacco-related disease epidemic, as well as an unfavorable impact of diet, other environmental factors, and possibly other risk factors in Eastern Europe [Boyle 1992, Kubik *et al*. 1995].

In the recent phase of the lung cancer epidemic in the Czech Republic, a turn for the better has been taken in men: A decreasing trend in lung cancer mortality has been observed since the late 1980s. In the female population, further increase in lung cancer mortality can be expected for the first decade of the 21st century [Kubik *et al*. 1995, Kubik *et al*. 1999].

Trends in developing countries have been less well documented and the absence of authentic data on both the use of tobacco and lung cancer incidence and mortality make it more difficult to assess patterns in detail [Pandey 1999]. Available evidence suggests that increasing rates of cigarette smoking in developing countries will in time be reflected in lung cancer mortality. China is leading the world in tobacco production at 2.559700 metric tons produced each year (nearly half the total tobacco produced in the world) [Jablons *et al*. 2003].

Gender Differences in Lung Cancer Risk

Increasing lung cancer deaths among women have substantially altered the male: female ratio in this disease and produced a need to understand differences between men and women in lung cancer risk and how they relate to sex and gender.

Sex-linked factors are those which stem from biological differences between men and women, thus sex refers mainly to health risks relating to hormones or the reproductive system.

Gender-linked factors are those which result from socially constructed differences between men and women relating to different patterns of behavior, in particular smoking, which have their explanation in social and cultural constructions of femininity and masculinity. However, sex and gender factors may interact in their influence on health [Krieger and Zierler 1995, Krieger 2000].

Smoking and Lung Cancer in Women

The causal relationship between active smoking and lung cancer has been established on the basis of early case-control and prospective cohort studies. The odds ratios for developing lung cancer in smokers compared to never smokers have been very similar in different populations and clear dose-response relationship between the tobacco exposure and the risk of developing cancer has been shown [Doll and Peto 1976, Hammond 1966]. It is at present estimated that in most Western countries the proportion of lung cancers attributable to smoking is around 90% for males and 80% for females. The risk of developing lung cancer is already raised in those who smoke < 5 cigarettes.day per day and increases with the amount of cigarettes smoked daily [U.S. Department of Health and Human Services 1982].

In contrast to the past, new smokers are just as likely to be female as male. Recent studies indicate that teenagers experience more symptoms of nicotine dependence than adults, and that women experience more symptoms of nicotine dependence than men, while smoking the same number or fewer cigarettes per day [Kandel DB, Chen K 2000].

So for both females and males, the risk for developing lung cancer is associated with increasing daily cigarette consumption and duration of smoking, and decreases with number of years since quitting smoking [Fiore 1992, Peto et al. 2000]. However, this association appears to be stronger for females than for males. For an estimated lifetime tobacco-exposure of 40 pack-years, Risch et al. [1993] reported that the odds ratio for women was 28 (95%CI 15-52) compared with 10 (95% CI 6-16) for men. Furthermore, female lung cancer cases reported lower average numbers of cigarettes smoked per day over their smoking careers than their male counterparts, while comparison of increasing usage categories, i.e. number of cigarettes smoked per day, showed that the risk for lung cancer increased faster for females than for males.

Evidence from two other recent studies have also suggested that women's risk of lung cancer was higher than men's, not only at every level smoking, but also for both low-tar and high-tar cigarettes [Schriver et al. 2000, Zang and Wynder 1996]. Several recent cohort studies found no measurable excess of lung cancer among female smokers compared with male smokers, once amounts smoked have been controlled [Blot and McLaughlin 2004].

Differences in Smoking Habits

In particular, smokers switching from high to low tar brands have a tendency to compensate for the decrease in nicotine yield by increasing the number of puffs and the depth of inhalation, thereby changing the part of lungs most affected by smoking [Augustine et al. 1989]. The explanation for this phenomenon could be the one proposed by Wynder and

Hoffman [1994] that changes in smoking habits with increasing consumption of low-yield filter-tipped cigarettes causes changes in histopathology of lung cancer over time. Smokers of low-yield filter-tipped cigarettes have to take both more frequent and larger puffs to fulfil their needs for nicotine than smokers of high-yield non-filter tipped cigarettes do. That allows the cigarette smoke to reach the distant branches of the bronchioalveolar tree where adenocarcinoma usually occurs.

There are a number of possible explanations for the apparent higher relative risk for lung cancer in female ever-smokers compared with male ever-smokers.

Firstly, there may be more current smokers and fewer exsmokers among females than among males.

Secondly, female smokers could have greater daily tobacco consumption than male smokers. However, this has not been observed in any study so far.

Thirdly, there may be male-female differences in ways of smoking. If women take more puffs and inhale more deeply, they may have a higher risk for lung cancer, than what would be expected from their estimated life-time tobacco exposure. In other words, compensatory smoking behavior may be more pronounced among women than among men. This could also explain the higher frequency of adenocarcinoma among women [Levi et al. 1997, Zang and Wynder 1998].

Women smoke for different reasons than men, as women seem more likely to use cigarettes as buffer against negative feelings [Gritz et al. 1996, Jacobson 1981, Payne 2001, Zuckerman et al. 1990].

The age at which an individual begins their smoking career seems to be an independent risk factor for later development of lung cancer. Evidence from a study by Hegmann et al. [1993] suggest that for men, the relative risk (RR) is higher for those who begin to smoke before aged 19 years, whereas, for women, the increased risk appears to last 6 years longer, up to aged 25 years, which means that women who start to smoke up to this age have a higher RR than those who start smoking later in life. These findings may implicate both behavioral and biological differences between females and males in relation to risk for lung cancer.

Fourthly, women may be more susceptible to lung cancer for a given life-time tobacco exposure. This assumption is supported by the findings reported from the study by Risch et al. [1993], and similar observation have been reported from other recent case- control studies [Brownson et al.1989, Osann et al.1993, Schoenberg et al.1992]

A case control study by Morabia and Wynder [1991] did not reveal any gender difference in risk of lung cancer.

In a large prospective Danish population study comprising more than 30,000 subjects, the rate ratio, adjusted for pack-years and age, between female and male smokers for developing lung cancer was not different from unity (0.8, 95% CI 0.3-2.1) [Prescott et al. 1998].

In countries like Denmark, where it is, unfortunately, fully socially acceptable to smoke, under-reporting of tobacco consumption is unlikely, which supports the validity of the findings by Prescott et al. [1998].

Risk Factors other than Tobacco Smoking in Women

According to recent estimates, greater than 20% of this increasing disease among U.S. women has been due to causes other than active smoking [Mason 1994], and for at least 25%

female lung cancer cases in France indoor pollution, diet, and history of previous respiratory diseases have been important risk factors [Quoix 1999]. The relative importance and contribution of each factor can vary with geographic area and socioeconomic conditions.

Adenocarcinoma of the lung, which shows a weaker association with tobacco smoking than other types of lung cancer, is also found predominantly in women, suggesting a possible role for female hormones in this form of the disease [Baldini and Strauss 1997, Kirsh *et al.* 1982, Kubik *et al.* 2002]. Among female never-smokers in the Czech Women's Lung Cancer Study, almost one-half (47.9%) were adenocarcinomas [Kubik *et al.* 2002]. Adenocarcinomas has always represented the majority of lung cancer among nonsmokers of both genders, and increased, as a proportion, with increased duration of smoking cessation [Francesci and Bidoli 1999]. A trend was observed in the Czech Study: among recent quitters (less than 10 years ago), the proportion of adenocarcinomas was 25.7%, in contrast to 40.6% for the subgroup of ex-smokers with a longer duration of smoking cessation (quit 10 or more years ago) [Kubik *et al.* 2002].

What determines who will develop lung cancer? Lung cancer is often cited as an example of a malignancy that is solely determined by the environment. However, in addition to smoking and other environmental agents such as asbestos and radon, evidence is accumulating that genetic factors determine an individual's risk of developing lung cancer. Women may have an underlying predisposition to lung cancer.

Genetic Risk Factors

In addition to smoking and other environmental agents such as asbestos and radon, evidence is accumalating that genetic factors determine an individual's risk of developing lung cancer. Tokuhata and Lilienfeld [1963] established some of the early evidence of the familial aggregation of lung cancer. Interestingly, this was particularly true for females.

Horwitz *et al.* [1988], in a case-control study, demonstrated a statistically significant linear trend of increasing risk of lung cancer in women: Never-smokers with a family history of lung cancer had an OR of 5.7 in comparison to no family history of lung cancer. Smokers without a family history of lung cancer had an OR 15.1 versus OR 29.8 for smokers with a family history of lung cancer. At present, it is well accepted that both family history and smoking history are important risk factors for lung cancer. However, perhaps the familial aggregation of lung cancer reflects an increased susceptibility to tobacco carcinogens, particularly in women.

Schwartz *et al.* [1999] proceeded to examine the potential for susceptibility genes that may be common to breast or lung cancer, such as CYP1A1 and CP1B1, both involved with oestrogen metabolism and expressed in the lung.

CYP1A1 is a cytochrome P450 that is found in human lung but not liver, and codes for an enzyme responsible for the activation of polycyclic aromatic hydrocarbons (PAH) to reactive epoxides, which can lead to increased DNA adducts in the lung. These DNA adducts are believed to not only be a marker for carcinogen exposure, but are probably also part of the initiation of the malignant process. Mollerup *et al.* [1999] have demonstrated significantly higher levels of CYP1A1 expression in the nontumor lung tissue of currently smoking female lung cancer cases as compared with males. This increase in CYP1A1 expression was significantly correlated with elevated levels of DNA adducts which were highly related to smoking history. Ryberg *et al.* [1994] has previously shown that subjects with increased levels of DNA adducts develop lung cancer after lower smoking doses and/or shorter smoking history.

Dresler *et al.* [2000] demonstrated a significantly increased OR for polymorphic CYP1A1 (exon 7) in females with a smoking history as compared with wild-type CYP1A1 (OR 4.98, 95% CI 1.50- 16.39). In males, there was no increased risk for having polymorphic CYP1A1. Although the ORs between males and females for having a polymorphic CYP1A1 with a lung cancer diagnosis were not significantly different (4.98 versus 1.37, p=0.15), the result may suggest that the presence of a polymorphism in CYP1A1 does confer an increased risk for lung cancer in females. How sex steroids affect this increased expression of CYP1A1 remains unclear, but CYP1A1 is one of the enzymes responsible for the 2-hydroxylation of oestradiol to 2-OH-oestradiol, a catechol oestrogen.

Another mechanism that may be involved with an increased susceptibility in women has been examined by determining the expression of the gastrin-releasing peptide receptor (GRPR), the gene for which is located on the X chromosome [Shriver *et al.*2000] Gastrin-releasing peptide has been demonstrated to be an important growth factor in lung cancer and has differential levels in the urine of smokers versus nonsmokers. The frequency of the gene expression was greater in women and increased relative to the extent of tobacco-exposure history. This study concluded that because women expressed GRPR more frequently than men and generally had a lower pack-year smoking history, they might be more susceptible to tobacco smoke and potentially more vulnerable to developing lung cancer.

A higher frequency of a specific mutation, G to T transversion, was found in the p53 gene in lung tumors of women than those of men together with a higher concentration of carcinogen adducts in lung tissue, even though the women had experienced less tobacco exposure than the men [Kure *et al.* 1996]. A higher level of DNA adducts in lung tissue from female patients has also been reported [Ryberg *et al.* 1994]. There is also a recent report that DNA repair capacity is substantially lower in female lung-cancer patients than in their male counterparts [Wei *et al.* 2000]. The K-RAS mutation was also found to be more common in non-small-cell lung tumours from female smokers than male smokers [Nelson *et al.* 1999]. Other genes that might increase the carcinogenic effects of cigarette smoke in women are those that encode the carcinogen-metabolizing enzymes. Increased expression of the CYP1A1 isozyme has been reported in the lungs of females when compared to males [Mollerup *et al.* 1998]. This excess could lead to increased local activation of polycyclic hydrocarbons to carcinogenic intermediates in female lung. Nicotine can be converted to a carcinogenic nitrosamine, and nicotine is metabolized more slowly in women than in men, leading to higher overall nitrosamine exposure in women [Beckett *et al.* 1971, Benowitz and Jacob 1984].

Other Risk Factors of Lung Cancer in Women

Radon, indoor fumes from cooking and heating stoves, and ETS are three potential lung carcinogens to which women could be selectively exposed as a result of spending more time in the home than men. In comparison to smoking, radon is a relatively weak carcinogen and is unlikely to be the cause of much of the risk of lung cancer in female lifetime non-smokers. There are also an increasing number of studies which show that women's domestic work can put them at greater risk of lung cancer in areas of the world reliant on burning coal or other smoke-producing fuel for cooking, and this is perhaps the most important gender-linked factor after smoking. In China, in particular, where few women currently smoke, women's lung cancer is significantly associated with indoor fuel pollution and responsibility for cooking [Du *et al.* 1996, Luo *et al.* 1996]. Cooking with oil at high temperature has been associated with high levels of lung cancer amongst women [Gao *et al.* 1987].

Cooking fumes and vapours from heating stoves clearly have a role in lung-cancer incidence in non-smoking women in Asian countries, but are not normally a problem in western nations.

Environmental Tobacco Smoke and Risk of Lung Cancer in Women

Environmental tobacco smoke (ETS) is a complex mixture of irritant gases and particulate materials. The epidemiological link between domestic ETS exposure and bronchogenic carcinoma has been established, but the risk attributable to direct active smoking among women has increased to dwarf that of household ETS [Ernster 1996]. Two recently published meta-analyses concluded that exposure to ETS is a cause of lung cancer [Hackshaw *et al.* 1997, Zhong *et al.* 2000]. In most of the studies reporting results on different histological types of lung cancer and passive smoking, the increase in risk of adenocarcinoma was reported to be smaller than that of squamous- or small-cell carcinomas [Boffeta *et al.* 1998, Boffeta *et al.* 1999, Fontham *et al.* 1994].

The ETS contains essentially all the same carcinogenic and toxic/irritating agents as mainstream smoke inhaled by smokers. Attention was first directed to potential carcinogeneity of ETS by two studies which showed that there was an increased risk of lung cancer in nonsmoking females married to smoking males [Hirayama 1981, Trichopoulos *et al.* 1981]. The argument has been advanced that non-smoking women marry smoking men, but not vice versa. The topic has since been the subject of a number of epidemiological investigations and has been under continuous review. It has been concluded that passive smoking causes some increase in the risk of lung cancer [Burns 1991]. This conclusion is also supported by a recent meta-analysis calculating that marriage to a smoker increased the risk of lung cancer by 26% [Reynolds 1999]. However, men, especially in previous decades, are very likely to have experienced ETS exposure in the workplace, possibly in combination with other carcinogens such as asbestos, coal dust, or metals. Workplace ETS exposure is comparable to spousal ETS in contributing to lung-cancer risk [Reynolds 1999].

It is also important to consider the cumulative impact of ETS both in workplace and in the home. Various studies have suggested that the combined risks of smoking and working in an environment which is hazardous for lungs may be greater than the sum of risk attaching to either alone [Du *et al* 1996, Mant and Silagy 1998].

Diet and Risk of Developing Lung Cancer in Women

Diet can affect lung cancer risk. A large body of epidemiological evidence together with data from experimental studies, support the relationship between dietary constituents and the risk of specific cancers.

There are over 200 studies on the association between vegetables and fruits and lung cancer. The inverse relationship between intake of vegetables and fruits and risk of lung cancer has been considered to represent one of the best established associations in the field of nutritional epidemiology [Willett 1998].

There are two kinds of factors- those which may protect against the risk of lung cancer, and those which might act to increase the risk. These factors are socially distributed, but such distribution is related to gender.

There is some, as yet inconclusive, evidence that diet is a factor which can exert both negative and positive effects and which might influence lung cancer incidence, mortality or survival. In a large prospective study, the European Prospective Investigation into Cancer and Nutrition, carried out in 10 European countries, there was a significant inverse association between fruit consumption and lung cancer, however, no association between vegetable consumption or vegetable subtypes and lung cancer risk [Miller *et al.* 2004]. Using the Danish prospective cohort study "Diet, Cancer and Health" Skuladottir *et al.* [2004] found an inverse association between lung cancer risk and high intake of fruit, vegetables and total plant food.

Inconsistent results have been reported on the role of meat in lung cancer risk. Some studies showed an association between meat consumption and lung cancer risk [Sinha *et al.* 1998] while others did not [Axelsson 1996]. In a Japanese case-control study [Takezaki *et al.* 2001] of 240 female cases with adenocarcinoma and 1198 controls, frequent intake of cooked or raw fish was associated with decreased OR for adenocarcinoma (OR = 0.48, 95% CI 0.24-0.94) and the same was true in a parallel study among men (OR = 0.51, 95% CI 0.31- 0.84). In a recent Czech study [Zatloukal *et al.* 2003], no decrease in risk of adenocarcinoma for women consuming fish daily or several times per week, compared to women admitting no intake of fish, was found (OR = 1.59, 95% CI 0.94 – 2.67). The inconsistencies in studies across continents might be due, in part, to different cooking methods. In Western countries, there is a tradition to fry meat and fish at high temperatures, while in Japan, raw and steamed fish is consumed more often.

Hormones and Lung Cancer in Women

Siegfried [2001] stated that the oestrogen status is a recognized factor in lung cancer risk among women. However, as stated by Kabat [1996], the existing evidence for a role of hormones in adenocarcinoma of the lung in women is limited and circumstantial.

Oestrogens could act as lung-tumor promoters, through a receptor-mediated mechanism, and have also been implicated as a cause of lung cancer without receptor activation. Taioli and Wynder [1994] provided evidence that exogenous and endogenous oestrogens may be involved in the development of lung cancer, particularly adenocarcinoma, in women. They examined the histories of 180 women with lung adenocarcinoma. For each women with lung cancer, they assessed history of smoking and hormonal or oestrogen replacement therapy (ORT). For nonsmokers, ORT posed no additional risk.

Some studies demonstrate that women who smoke are relatively oestrogen deficient, due to altered pathways of oestrogen metabolism [Baron *et al.* 1990]. (71). Cigarette smoking induces an increase in oestradiol 2 -hydroxylation (active catechol oestrogen metabolite), which results in a decrease in the 16-alpha hydroxylation (16 alpha-hydroxy-estrones or oestriols) pathway. Decreased urinary levels of products from this 16- alpha hydroxylase pathway have been demonstrated in postmenopausal smokers versus nonsmokers [Key *et al.* 1996, Michnowicz et al. 1986]. Oestrogen metabolism and its effects on carcinogenesis or cancer growth remains a very active area of research. However, it is probable that this process differs between smoking and nonsmoking women [Dressler and Gritz 2003].

Why should oestrogen and/or its metabolites be of concern in lung tissue?

Both cytochrome P450 enzymes 1B1 and 1A1 are found in pulmonary tissue. These enzymes are responsible for oestradiol metabolism to catechol oestrogens or oestrons, which are considered carcinogenic. Beattie *et al.* [1985] demonstrated a significant incidence of oestrogen receptors in normal adult lung parenchyma and in bronchogenic carcinomas, which suggest that oestrogen continues to influence adult lung function. Kaiser *et al.* [1996] studied both cancer cell lines and human tumour tissues to identify the presence of sex hormones by binding assays and imunohistochemistry. Their results were not conclusive, but suggested that adenocarcinomas in females preferentially expressed sex-steroid hormones. A recent paper identified oestrogen receptors in pulmonary adenocarcinomas in both men and women [Dabbs et al. 2002]. Thus, the presence of oestrogen receptors may or may not be related to potential oestrogen-related carcinogenicity in pulmonary tissue.

In a hospital based case-control study of 176 nonsmoking Singapore Chinese women with lung cancer and 663 age-matched controls, a significant inverse relationship between three or more livebirths (OR = 0.65, 95% CI 0.44-0.96), a menstrual cycle length of more than 30 days (OR = 0.46, 95% CI 0.25-0.84), and the risk of lung cancer was observed [Seow et al. 2002]. In recent Czech case-control study [Zatloukal et al. 2003], statistically significant inverse associations of the risk of squamous-, small- and large-cell cancers combined with the quantity of menstrual flow (OR = 0.63, 95% CI 0.40-0.99), and pains or mental tension related to menses (OR = 0.61, 95% CI 0.42- 0.89) was observed. Gao *et al.* [1987] found an association of short menstrual cycle, and late age at menopause with the risk of adenocarcinoma of the lung among Chinese women in Shanghai.

Viruses and Lung Cancer in Women

A recent report documents the presence of human papilloma virus in lung tumor tissues from many non-smoking women in Taiwan. The association of this virus with lung cancer in non-smokers was seen in females but not in males [Chen *et al.* 2001]. Whether this virus is important in female lung-cancer in Europe is not known.

Lung Cancer and Respiratory Disorders

Both restrictive and obstructive lung disease have been associated with an increased risk of lung cancer. Patients with diffuse pulmonary fibrosis have a higher risk of pulmonary neoplasms, especially adenocarcinoma. This is independent of the origin of the fibrosis i.e. whether it has been caused by mineral fibers like asbestos or silica, or is idiopathic like idiopathic pulmonary fibrosis. Local fibrosis and scarring, following lung tuberculosis is associated with a higher risk of lung cancer among never smokers [Hinds *et al.* 1982, Howe *et al.* 1979]. The association of COPD with lung cancer is not surprising, as tobacco smoking is the main cause of both diseases. Chronic obstructive pulmonary disease affects more non-smoking women than men. Occurrence in the female non-smoking population was reported to be about twice that of the male non-smoking population [Chen *et al.* 2000].

Results of Treatment Strategy of Lung Cancer in Women

Surgery offers the best chance for cure in patients with localized nonsmall cell lung cancer. Radiotherapy is a commonly used treatment option in nonsmall cell lung cancer when nonoperable, and chemotherapy is the preferred treatment for small cell lung cancer.

Radzikowska *et al.* [2001] examined patients with all types of cancer and compared treatments in those aged above and below 50 years. She found younger age to be a predictor of better survival. The prevalence of females was higher in the younger age group (female:male ratio 3:1) versus older age group (1:6.8), as a result of gender differences in past smoking habits. Multivariate analyses revealed that males had an independent increased relative risk of mortality (RR 1.18). Other studies [Ferguson *et al.* 1990, McDuffie *et al.* 1987, Radzikowska and Glaz 2000] confirmed the observation that women had a better outcome with lung cancer.

A study specifically addressing lung surgery [Alexiou *et al.* 2002] showed that female gender exerts a significant positive effect on survival following lung resection for nonsmall cell lung cancer, which already started with higher operative mortality in males than females (4.6 versus 1.2). This effect was most pronounced when the disease was at an early stage and persisted after adjusting for important differences in the clinical, histopathological features, and extent of pulmonary resection. This study included a large number of patients, and took coexisting cardiovascular disease, respiratory and other conditions into account.

A few studies have specifically investigated small cell lung cancer [Argiris and Murren 2001, Spiegelman *et al.* 1989, Wolf *et al.* 1991], and also found women to have a better outcome, specifically the younger ones. Thus regardless of the type of lung cancer, women seem to have a better prognosis. However, it is not yet clear why this is so.

Concluding Remarks to the Review Part

Presently, tobacco use is the single largest and most preventable cause of premature adult death throughout the world. In the developed world, smoking is linked with an affluent lifestyle, and many, especially young, women, fuelled by aggressive tobacco marketing, are likely to take up smoking. Unfortunately, the prevalence of smoking among women increases even in developing countries. These trends, with a latency period of 2-3 decades, will translate into a rapid worldwide increase of new lung cancer cases.

The available evidence suggests that there are some very important differences between women and men in the web of relationships between lung cancer and biology, behavior and external factors. More should be done, in terms of integrating different approaches to advance a model which reflects the complexity of biology and gender as influences on risks of lung cancer. By now, strong tobacco control efforts are clearly needed in both developed and developing countries to decrease tobacco use among women.

Part 2: The Czech Women's Lung Cancer Case-Control Study

Few data are available to explain the on-going increase in lung cancer mortality among women in the Czech Republic, a Central European country with a population of over 10 million, 5726 deaths from lung cancer (of these, 1246 in women), and a per caput sale of 1882 cigarettes in the year 2000

While tobacco smoke has been found to be one of the major causes of lung cancer among the female population of many developed countries, various types of epidemiological research, including ecological, case-control, prospective studies, and randomized controlled trials, have indicated that diet, physical activity and other cofactors may play a non-negligible role in the cause of lung cancer [Alberg and Samet 2003, Fabricius and Lange 2004, Miller *et al.* 2004, Samet 1994]. However, the relative importance and contribution of some cofactors to the risk of cancer may vary with geographic area and socioeconomic conditions.

Our case control study has been conducted in the Czech Republic, where the population has been consuming a typical Central European diet, rich in foods from animal sources and lacking in fresh fruit and vegetables, in the second half of the past century [Bobak and Marmot 1996, Filiberti *et al.* 1995, Ginter 1998].

In the present hospital-based case-control study, we tried to examine the relationship between dietary factors physical activity and other cofactors and the risk of lung carcinoma among women in the Czech Republic, and compare the differences between the two groups of study participants with highly contrasting lung cancer risk: Nonsmokers (OR=1.00) vs. Smokers (OR=6.61).

Methods

Study Sample and Data Collection

A hospital-based case-control study of lung cancer among women was conducted in Prague University Hospital Na Bulovce, Departments of Pneumology, Thoracic Surgery, and Internal Medicine. To be included as a case, a female lung cancer patient had to be admitted between April 1998 and November 2002. Controls were all women, and were spouses, relatives, or friends of other patients of the departments, with conditions unrelated to smoking. Both cases and controls had to be aged 25-89 years, and reside within the catchment area covering the north-eastern sectors of Prague and the adjacent Central Bohemia Region (10 administrative districts). Personal interviews were completed with 451 cases (89% of those eligible) and 1,710 controls (response rate 79%). The reasons for non-participation among 507 eligible cases included patient's inability to cooperate during interview as a result of severe physical or mental disability (34 patients, 6.7%), refusal to be interviewed (5 subjects, 1.0%), or death shortly after admission (17 patients, 3.3%). Nonresponse among controls was due to 'no time for interview' (256 women, 11.8%), refusal to be interviewed (188 women, 8.7%), and a language barrier or mental incompetence (11 persons, 0.5%). Informed consent was obtained from all interviewed cases and controls. The interviewers were trained extensively to standardize data collection and coding techniques and to minimize inter-interviewer variation.

Questionnaire and Definitions

The questionnaire has been described previously elsewhere [Kubik *et al.* 2001, Kubik *et al.* 2002]. In brief, the questionnaire included a basic structured section on demographic characteristics; place of residence; type of house, occupation and workplace; further, a complete smoking history. Subjects were defined as current smokers if they smoked, at the time of the survey, either daily or occasionally. A daily smoker is someone who smokes at least one cigarette a day for at least three months, i.e., a total of approximately 100 cigarettes and over. An occasional smoker is someone who smokes, but not every day. Never smokers either have never smoked at all or have smoked less than 100 cigarettes in their lifetime. Ex-smokers are people who were formerly smokers but currently have not smoked for at least six months. In ex-smokers, the time since quitting was recorded. In this report, we present results for two groups of cases and controls: Group 1, called "Nonsmokers", including never smokers + long-term ex-smokers (quit 20 or more years ago); and Group 2, called "Smokers", containing current smokers + short-term ex-smokers (quit less than 10 years ago) (Table 1).

The questionnaire included sections on exposure to environmental tobacco smoke (passive smoking), physical activity (hours per week); preexisting lung disease or cancer (diagnosed by a physician at least 2 years before interview); family history of cancer among first degree relatives (parents and siblings); and menstrual and pregnancy history. Information on dietary habits was collected with 9 food items (red meat, poultry, fish, milk/dairy products, fat-rich foods, vegetables, apples, citrus fruit, other fruit); four non-alcoholic beverage items (black tea, green tea, herbal tea, coffee), and three alcoholic beverage categories (beer, wine, and spirits). The subjects were asked to try to estimate the best fitting answer reflecting the usual consumption in most years within the past 10-year period. One of four frequency estimates of consumption was to be selected: 1. Never, 2. Monthly or less, 3. Weekly or less, but more than once per month, or 4. Daily or several times per week. After completion of the questionnaire, the trained interviewer took basic anthropometric measures, such as standing height and weight. For subjects interviewed in 2000-2002, additional questions were asked concerning physical activity 1 and 20 years before the interview.

Table 1. Smoking habits and the risk of lung cancer.
Czech Women's Lung Cancer Study

Cases/ Controls	All study subjects 451/ 1710				
Smoking habits	Never smokers	Ex-smokers			Current smokers
		Quit 20 or more yrs ago	Quit 10-19 yrs ago	Quit <10 yrs ago	
Cases/ Controls	111/ 933	19/ 89	32/ 117	114/ 157	175/ 414
Odds ratio (OR)[a]	1.00	1.68	2.90	8.66	6.24
95%CI[b]	Referent	0.96-2.94	1.80-4.66	6.07-12.35	4.56-8.53
Study Groups	Group 1 "Nonsmokers"			Group 2 "Smokers"	
Cases/ Controls	130/ 1022			289/ 571	
Odds ratio (OR)[a]	1.00			6.61	
95%CI[b]	Referent			5.02-8.71	

[a]OR, odds ratio, adjusted for age, residence, and education.
[b]CI, confidence interval.

Statistical Methods

Descriptive statistics were used to characterize the study population. Statistical analyses were done using the unconditional logistic regression which provides results in the form of adjusted odds ratios. As the controls were not matched to cases, adjustment was done for age (in 5-year categories), residence, and education (as in Table 3). All adjusting variables were entered in the logistic regression as multiplicative and categorical factors. Tests for linear trend in tables were performed in equidistant categorical levels (1,2,…), even for numerical variables.

Results

The variation in lung cancer risk by smoking habits is shown in Table 1. After adjusting for age, residence, and education, the odds ratios were 6.24 for current smokers, 8.66 for ex-smokers who stopped smoking less than 10 years ago, 2.90 for ex-smokers who stopped 10-19 years ago, and 1.68 (95%CI 0.96-2.94) for ex-smokers who quit 20 or more years ago, all compared to never smokers. As evident, among ex-smokers, an inverse trend in the relative risk (OR) can be noted with years since quitting. High risk of lung cancer was observed among current smokers and ex-smokers who quitted less than 10 years ago. In contrast, the risk among women who stopped smoking 20 or more years ago was much lower, and not significantly different from that in never smokers.

Consequently, in the following part of this report, we present results for two groups of cases and controls: Group 1 "Nonsmokers" includes never smokers + long-term ex-smokers (quit 20 or more years ago); and Group 2 "Smokers", contains current smokers + short-term ex-smokers (quit less than 10 years ago). The risk estimate (OR) for "Smokers" was 6.61 times higher than among "Nonsmokers". The intermediate subgroup of ex-smokers who quit 10-19 years ago has not been included in either of the compared two groups because of their significant difference from either of them (Table 1, Fig. 1).

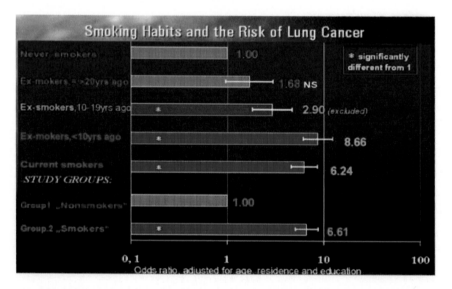

Figure 1. Smoking habits and the risk of lung cancer in women. Czech Women's Lung Cancer Study.

The mean age of "Nonsmokers" was higher than that of smoking women, both among cases and controls (Table 2). As expected, among 130 nonsmoking cases, adenocarcinoma was the predominant cell type (49.2%), followed by squamous cell (20.2%) and small cell cancers (10.5%). Among 289 smoking cases, adenocarcinoma was diagnosed in 29.3%, followed by small cell (28.2%), and squamous cell cancers (27.5%) (Table 2).

Using odds ratios adjusted for age, risk estimates appeared elevated for rural residence among both "Nonsmokers", and "Smokers", however, inversely associated with levels of education for "Smokers" only, but not for "Nonsmokers" (Table 3).

Table 2. Distribution of cases and controls by smoking habits, age-groups, and cell types. Czech Women's Lung Cancer Study

Variables	Cases		Controls	
	Group 1 "Nonsmokers"	Group 2 "Smokers"	Group 1 "Nonsmokers"	Group 2 "Smokers"
Population	130	289	1022	571
Mean age (SD[a])	67.2 (10.2)	61.4 (10.3)	59.5 (13.5)	52.6 (10.9)
Age groups (yrs)	No. (%)	No. (%)	No. (%)	No. (%)
25-34	- -	3 (1.0)	45 (4.4)	36 (6.3)
35-44	2 (1.5)	12 (4.1)	89 (8.7)	78 (13.7)
45-54	17 (13.1)	61 (21.1)	234 (22.9)	234 (41.0)
55-64	22 (16.9)	97 (33.6)	265 (25.9)	147 (25.7)
65-74	56 (43.1)	90 (31.2)	237 (23.2)	54 (9.5)
75-84	31 (23.9)	24 (8.3)	137 (13.4)	22 (3.8)
85-89	2 (1.5)	2 (0.7)	15 (1.5)	- -
Cell types	No. (%)	No. (%)		
Adenocarcinoma	61 (49.2)	82 (29.3)		
Squamous cell	25 (20.2)	77 (27.5)		
Small cell	13 (10.5)	79 (28.2)		
Large cell	7 (5.6)	19 (6.8)		
Carcinoma NOS[b]	18 (14.5)	23 (8.2)		
Microscopically confirmed	124 (100,0)	280 (100.0)		
Clinical diagnosis	6 .	9 .		

[a] SD, standard deviation.
[b]NOS, not otherwise specified.

Table 3. Some socio-demographic variables and the risk of lung cancer, by smoking history. Czech Women's Lung Cancer Study

	Group 1 "Nonsmokers"				Group 2 "Smokers"			
Variables	Cases	Controls	OR[a]	95%CI[b]	Cases	Controls	OR[a]	95%CI[b]
Residence								
Rural (≤100,000)	68	347	1.00	Referent	116	164	1.00	Referent
Urban (>100,000)	62	675	0.41	0.28 - 0.61	173	407	0.42	0.30 - 0.59
Education								
Elementary	31	192	1.00	Referent	94	104	1.00	Referent
Secondary (ordinary)	55	314	1.30	0.80 - 2.12	102	194	0.59	0.40 - 0.89
Secondary (advanced)	36	387	0.90	0.52 - 1.54	80	225	0.46	0.31 - 0.69
University	8	129	0.69	0.30 - 1.60	13	48	0.31	0.15 - 0.62
Test for trend				P=0.287				P<0.001

[a] OR, odds ratio, adjusted for age.
[b] CI, confidence interval.

Excess lung cancer risk was associated with more than monthly consumption of red meat among "Nonsmokers" (OR=2.20, 95%CI 1.07-4.51), however, no significant increase in risk was found among "Smokers" (OR=1.07, 95%CI 0.65-1.76) (Table 4, Fig.2).

Among "Nonsmokers" only, a protective effect was apparent for more than monthly drinking of black tea (OR=0.67, 95%CI 0.46-0.99).

Among "Smokers" only, protective effects were observed for several times per week or daily consumption of vegetables (OR=0.61, 95%CI 0.39-0.96), apples (OR=0.67, 95%CI 0.48-0.95), milk/dairy products (OR=0.54, 95%CI 0.32-0.93), coffee (OR=0.56, 95%CI 0.34-0.91), and wine (OR=0.69, 95%CI 0.49-0.98) (Table 4, Fig.2).

Table 4. Diet, alcohol consumption and the risk of lung cancer, by smoking history. Czech Women's Lung Cancer Study

Variables	Group 1 "Nonsmokers"				Group 2 "Smokers"			
	Cases	Controls	OR[a]	95%CI[b]	Cases	Controls	OR[a]	95%CI[b]
Red meat [d]	121	874	2.20	1.07 - 4.51	256	509	1.07	0.65 - 1.76
Poultry [d]	123	992	0.68	0.28 - 1.67	281	553	1.61	0.64 - 4.05
Fish [d]	88	705	1.09	0.72 - 1.65	202	369	1.33	0.94 - 1.88
Milk, dairy products [c]	123	959	1.29	0.56 - 2.96	258	522	0.54	0.32 - 0.93
Fat-rich foods [d]	54	501	0.88	0.60 - 1.30	143	336	0.81	0.59 - 1.12
Vegetables [c]	117	907	1.19	0.63 - 2.27	233	507	0.61	0.39 - 0.96
Apples [c]	106	827	1.02	0.62 - 1.67	182	425	0.67	0.48 - 0.95
Citrus fruits [c]	85	678	0.96	0.64 - 1.44	184	361	1.00	0.72 - 1.39
Other fruits [d]	121	957	1.01	0.48 - 2.13	256	532	0.60	0.34 - 1.04
Black tea [d]	69	631	0.67	0.46 - 0.99	163	293	1.22	0.89 - 1.67
Green tea [e]	40	372	0.88	0.58 - 1.34	87	175	1.16	0.82 - 1.64
Herbal tea [c]	89	670	1.13	0.75 - 1.71	169	317	1.04	0.76 - 1.43
Coffee [c]	91	761	0.90	0.59 - 1.38	246	521	0.56	0.34 - 0.91
Beer [e]	48	406	0.83	0.56 - 1.23	116	221	1.14	0.82 - 1.57
Wine [e]	29	355	0.65	0.41 - 1.03	80	241	0.69	0.49 - 0.98
Spirits [e]	8	130	0.55	0.25 - 1.18	42	101	0.82	0.53 - 1.27

[a] OR, odds ratio, adjusted for age, residence and education.
[b] CI, confidence interval.
[c] Daily or several times per week
[d] (Weekly or less, but more than once per month)+(Daily or several times per week)
[e] (Monthly or less)+(Weekly or less)+(Daily or several times per week).

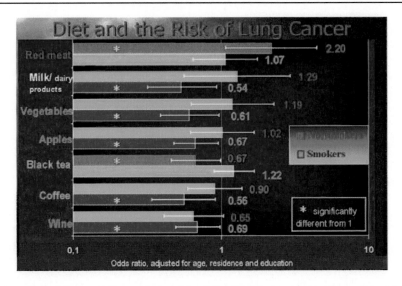

Figure 2. Diet, alcohol consumption and the risk of lungcancer in women, by smoking habits. Czech Women's Lung Cancer Study.

Among "Smokers" only, personal history of tuberculosis (OR=2.63, 95%CI 1.11-6.22), and previous cancer of any site (OR=2.36, 95%CI 1.21-4.60), or family history of lung cancer among first degree relatives (OR=1.78, 95%CI 1.10-2.87) were associated with significant increases in risk., however, not apparent for nonsmoking women (Fig.3).

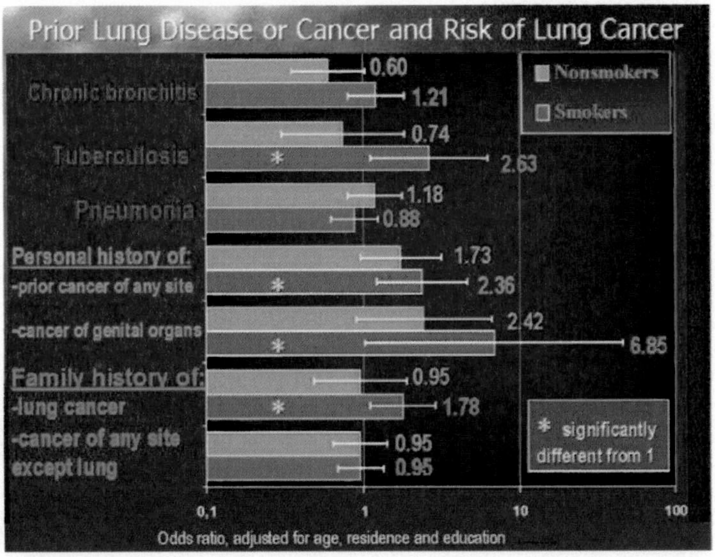

Figure 3. Prior lung disease, personal or family history of cancer and the risk of lung cancer in women. Czech Women's Lung Cancer Study.

Physical exercise (or sport, walking, within the recent ten years) was inversely associated with lung cancer risk among "Smokers". In smoking subjects, for the category of physical exercise (or sport, walking) more than 6 hours per week compared to 0-2 hours, the odds ratio was 0.48 (95%CI 0.32-0.71). For "Nonsmokers", the odds ratio (OR) was 0.74 (95%CI 0.45-

1.22, for more than 6 hours per week compared to 0-2 hours), the difference was not statistically significant (Table 5, Fig.4).

Table 5. Physical activities[a, b] , and the risk of lung cancer, by smoking history. Czech Women's Lung Cancer Study

Variables	Group 1 "Nonsmokers"				Group 2 "Smokers"			
	Cases	Controls	OR[c]	95%CI[d]	Cases	Controls	OR[c]	95%CI[d]
Physical exercise[a] (within recent 10 years)								
0-2 *hours/week*	40	280	1.00	Referent	126	167	1.00	Referent
3-6 *hours/week*	51	357	1.08	0.67-1.73	89	180	0.70	0.47-1.03
>6 *hours/week*	39	385	0.74	0.45-1.22	74	224	0.48	0.32-0.71
Test for trend				P=0.210				P<0.001
Other physical activities[b] (within recent 10 years)								
0-2 *hours/week*	48	389	1.00	Referent	128	217	1.00	Referent
3-6 *hours/week*	24	268	0.83	0.48-1.44	68	145	0.82	0.54-1.25
>6 *hours/week*	58	365	1.22	0.77-1.92	93	209	0.71	0.49-1.04
Test for trend				P=0.358				P=0.074
Physical exercise[a] (1 year before interview)								
0-2 *hours/week*	39	228	1.00	Referent	89	137	1.00	Referent
3-6 *hours/week*	28	188	1.00	0.57-1.77	39	101	0.78	0.46-1.31
>6 *hours/week*	21	166	1.01	0.54-1.86	36	114	0.63	0.37-1.05
Test for trend				P=0.980				P=0.069
Physical exercise[a] (20 years before interview)								
0-2 *hours/week*	20	122	1.00	Referent	48	84	1.00	Referent
3-6 *hours/week*	25	155	1.06	0.53-2.11	50	101	0.89	0.51-1.55
>6 *hours/week*	43	305	1.04	0.56-1.94	66	167	0.73	0.44-1.23
Test for trend				P=0.914				P=0.227

[a] Physical exercise, or sport, walking.
[b] Other non-occupational physical activities (e.g., in the garden, house).
[c] OR, odds ratio, adjusted for age, residence and education.
[d] CI, confidence interval.

Body mass index was significantly inversely associated with lung cancer risk. The odds ratio for the highest quartile (compared to the lowest quartile) was 0.44 (95%CI 0.25-0.78) among "Nonsmokers", and 0.27 (95%CI 0.17-0.44) among "Smokers". A significant trend was found with decreasing risk at higher levels of body mass index (P=0.022 for "Nonsmokers", and P<0.001 for "Smokers") (Table 5, Fig.4).

Inverse associations emerged for one or more deliveries among "Nonsmokers" (OR=0.50, 95%CI 0.27-0.94), for late onset of menopause (over 50 years) among "Smokers" only (OR=0.51, 95%CI 0.33-0.78), and long duration of menstrual flow (more than 6 days) among "Nonsmokers" only (OR=0.55, 95%CI 0.32-0.93) (Fig 5).

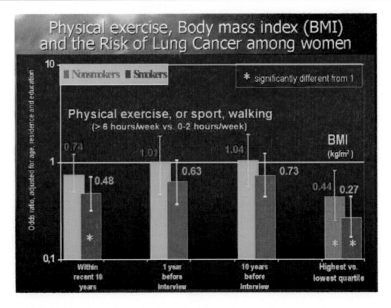

Figure 4. Physical exercise, body mass index (BMI) and the risk of lung cancer in women. Czech Women's Lung Cancer Study.

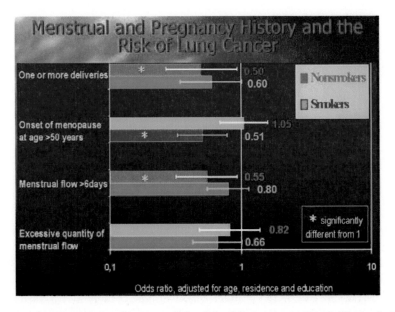

Figure 5. Menstrual and pregnancy history and the risk of lung cancer. Czech Women's Lung Cancer Study.

Among "Nonsmokers", the result of statistical analysis was suggestive of a weak elevation in the risk for exposure to environmental tobacco smoke (ETS) in childhood (before age 16) compared to no exposure (OR=1.40, 95%CI 0.95-2.05), however, the difference was not statistically significant. No elevation in risk could be traced for exposure to ETS in adult age or both in childhood and adult age (Fig 6).

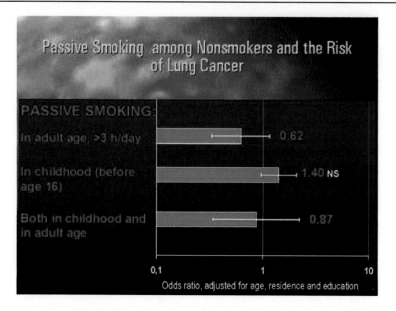

Figure 6. Exposure to environmental tobacco smoke (passive smoking) and the risk of lung cancer in women nonsmokers. Czech Women's Lung Cancer Study.

Discussion

The risk of lung cancer can be conceptualized as reflecting the joint consequences of the interrelationship between exposure to etiologic (or protective) agents and the individual susceptibility to these agents [Alberg and Samet 2003]. Genetic susceptibilities play a large role in lung cancer risk. They govern smoking behavior (affecting dopamine reward mechanisms due to nicotine and nicotine metabolism), carcinogen metabolisms and detoxification, DNA repair, cell cycle control and other cellular responses [Shields 2002].

Tobacco is the strongest epidemiologic risk factor for the development of lung cancer. Smoking has been shown to cause each of the major histologic types of lung cancer, the association between smoking and lung cancer appeared to be stronger for squamous/small cell cancers than for adenocarcinoma of the lung [Alberg and Samet 2003, Wu-Williams and Samet 1994]. Changes in the cigarette design and smoking behavior are supposed to be responsible for the most of the changing epidemiologic patterns in lung cancer by histologic types [Janssen-Heijnen and Coebergh 2001, Stellman et al. 1997]. Recently, the changing picture of lung cancer and the causes of these changes were summarized in an invited commentary by Hansen [2002], and in two reviews by Janssen-Heijnen and Coebergh [2001] and Alberg and Samet [2003].

It has been hypothesized that women are more susceptible to tobacco carcinogens than are men [Henschke and Miettinen 2004], however, several recent cohort studies found no measurable excess of lung cancer among female smokers compared with male smokers, once amounts smoked have been controlled [Blot and McLaughlin 2004]. The overwhelming contribution of cigarette smoking as a cause of lung cancer, imposes challenges to detecting the role that other lifestyle factors may play in the etiology of lung cancer [Alberg and Samet 2003]. Many factors associated with increase in the trend of female lung cancer have not yet been completely elucidated. For women, a more important role of factors other than smoking has been presumed than in men, such as diet, physical activity, nonmalignant lung disease, radon in dwellings, some occupational factors [Alavanja *et al.* 1995], exposure to environmental tobacco smoke, factors related to the endocrine, particularly oestrogen [Siegfried 2001].

Our report presenting results of a hospital based case-control study on the relationship between diet and other cofactors and the risk of lung carcinoma among Czech women has certain potential limitations which should be considered before conclusions are drawn. The exposures of interest were based on self report, therefore, some recall bias is of concern. In evaluating factors of life style, potential confounding from other factors cannot be ruled out. While smoking is known to be closely associated with less healthful diets [Morabia and Wynder 1990], the associations between dietary factors and lung cancer are likely to be very weak in comparison to smoking. Therefore, it may be difficult to discern whether the dietary factors have truly been disentangled from the effects of smoking [Alberg and Samet 2003)]. Merely controlling statistically for smoking may not be adequate, because nuances of smoking habits or susceptibility to cigarette smoke are not taken in account.

In our study, smoking habits were collected from subjects by in-person interviews, and several characteristics of smoking were recorded. Our estimate of tobacco exposure was based on pack-years of cigarettes, which were categorized in analyses into four classes. Generally, misclassification in smoking can affect the ability to control confounding, particularly when associations with other exposures are weak. Present findings were in addition checked by using continuous pack-years in logistic regression. As no substantial departure from present results emerged, we believe that residual confounding is minimal.

The results of studies on the role of meat in lung cancer risk have been inconsistent. Some studies showed an association between meat consumption and lung cancer risk [Sinha *et al.* 1998] while others did not [Axelsson *et al.* 1996]. In a case-control study of 234 nonsmoking female lung cancer cases and 535 controls in Germany [Kreuzer *et al.* 2002], a non-significantly 1.6 fold increased lung cancer risk was associated with daily consumption of meat (OR=1.61,95%CI 0.90-2.89). In the present study, we found a significantly increased risk of lung cancer for women in group 1 "Nonsmokers" (OR=2.20, 95%CI 1.07-4.51) consuming red meat at a higher frequency than once per month, however, not for group 2 "Smokers" (OR=1.07, 95%CI 0.65-1.76). In a recent multicenter case-control study of 506 non-smoking lung cancer cases and 1045 controls in 8 centers in Europe [Brennan *et al.* 2000], excess risk associated with meat consumption was restricted to squamous and small cell carcinomas, but was not apparent for adenocarcinomas. In a recent hospital-based case-control study of 200 male lung adenocarcinoma cases and 600 controls in Uruguay [De Stefani *et al.* 2002], increased risk of adenocarcinoma was significantly associated with high intake of red meat (OR=1.92, 95%CI 1.27-2.90), however, not of white meat (i.e., poultry and fish) (OR=0.91, 95%CI 0.60-1.39). In a Japanese case-control study [Takezaki *et al.* 2001] of 240 female cases with adenocarcinoma and 1198 controls, frequent intake of cooked or raw fish was associated with decreased OR for adenocarcinoma (OR=0.48, 95%CI 0.24-0.94), and the same was true in a parallel study among men (OR=0.51, 95%CI 0.31-0.84). In our study, we found no relationship between frequent intake of fish and the risk of lung cancer both among smoking and nonsmoking women. The inconsistencies in studies across continents might be due, in part, to different cooking methods. In Western countries, there is a tradition to fry meat and fish at high temperatures, while in Japan, raw and steamed fish is consumed more often. Burning or charring food is known to create many substances that are mutagenic. In meats cooked at high temperatures, several heterocyclic amines were found, however, the intake of some of them was not associated with lung cancer risk, while 2-amino-3,8-dimethylimidazo[4,5f]quinoxaline was associated with increased risk of lung cancer for nonsmokers and light/moderate smokers, but not for heavy smokers [Sinha *et al.* 2000].

In the present study, we found an inverse relationship between frequent (daily or several times per week) intake of milk/dairy products and the risk of lung cancer for women in group 2 "Smokers"(OR=0.54, 95%CI 0.32-0.93) however, not for group 1 "Nonsmokers" (OR=1.29, 95%CI 0.56-2.96). In the German study of 234 nonsmoking female lung cancer cases and 535 controls, protective effects with high intakes of cheese, milk and other dairy products were observed, showing a statistically significant trend with consumption of cheese [Kreuzer *et al.* 2002]. Information on the type of milk (whole, or reduced-fat) was not available in the German or our studies. In a case-control study of 569 lung cancer cases (of these, 214 women) and 569 matched controls in Buffalo, subjects reporting consumption of whole milk 3 or more times daily had a 2-fold increase in lung cancer risk compared to those who reported never drinking whole milk. The same frequency of intake reduced-fat milk was associated with a significant protective effect [Mettlin 1989]. In a population-based study of 413 matched case-control pairs of nonsmoking subjects in New York State, consumption of greens, fresh fruits and cheese was associated with a significant dose-dependent reduction in risk for lung cancer, whereas consumption of whole milk was associated with a significant dose-dependent increase in risk [Mayne *et al.* 1994].

The inverse relationship between intake of vegetables and fruits and risk of lung cancer represents one of the best established associations in the field of nutritional epidemiology [Willett 1998]. In a review of over 200 studies that examined the relationship between fruit and vegetable intake and 10 types of cancer, including lung cancer, a statistically significant protective effect of fruit and vegetable consumption was found in 128 of 156 dietary studies in which results were expressed in terms of relative risk [Block *et al.* 1992]. In a prospective study of 77 283 women in the Nurses' Health Study and 47 778 men in the Health Professionals' Follow-up Study higher fruit and vegetable intakes were associated with lower risks of lung cancer in women but not in men [Feskanich *et al.* 2000]. In a hospital-based case-control study on women in Barcelona, Spain, a reduction in risk, adjusted for smoking habits, was found for the intake of yellow/orange vegetables (mainly carrots) and tomatoes [Agudo 1997]. In a population-based case-control study of non-smoking 124 cases and 235 controls (of these, more than two thirds were women) in Stockholm, Sweden, a protective effect was suggested for vegetables, mediated primarily by carrots, and non-citrus fruits [Nyberg *et al.* 1998]. In the present study, we found significant inverse relationships between the risk of lung cancer and frequent intake (daily or several times per week) of vegetables (OR=0.61, 95%CI 0.39-0.96) and apples (OR=0.67, 95%CI 0.48-0.95), and a statistically nonsignificant inverse association with intake of other non-citrus fruits (OR=0.60, 95%CI 0.34-1.04) for group 2 "Smokers" only, no such protective effects were apparent among "Nonsmokers".

Data on risk of lung cancer among tea drinkers are scanty. In a review of the epidemiological evidence Blot *et al.* [1996] quoted 3 case-control, and 4 cohort studies, however, in all of them except one no association was noted. The one significant association reported came from a cohort study of British men, showing rising risks of lung cancer with increasing consumption [Kinlen *et al.* 1988]. Most of this trend, however, seems related to confounding factors, especially the rising prevalence of cigarette smoking with rising tea intake. In a case-control study among never smoking women in eight Canadian provinces (161 cases and 483 population controls) a significant inverse association was found between consumption of tea and the risk of lung cancer [Hu *et al.* 2002]. In a population based case-control study among women in Shanghai, China (649 cases 675 controls) the consumption of green tea was associated with reduced risk of lung cancer among nonsmoking women (OR=0.65, 95%CI 0.45-0.93), and the risk decreased with increasing consumption, however, little association was found among women who smoked (OR=0.94, 95%CI 0.40-2.22) [Zhong *et al.* 2001]. In the present study, black tea drinking, at a higher frequency than once per month, was inversely associated with lung cancer risk among "Nonsmokers" (OR=0.67, 95%CI 0.46-0.99), while no significant association was found among "Smokers" (OR=1.22, 95%CI 0.89-1.67).

Studies on association between coffee drinking and lung cancer risk are scarce [Tavani *et al.* 2000]. In a Norwegian cohort study of 43,000 subjects, some increase in lung cancer risk among men, but not in women was found [Stensvold *et al.* 1994]. In our study, coffee drinking daily or several times per week was significantly inversely associated with the risk of lung cancer among "Smokers" (OR=0.56, 95%CI 0.34-0.91), while no significant association was observed among "Nonsmokers" (OR=0.90, 95%CI 0.59-1.38).

Alcoholic beverages have been classified as carcinogenic to humans by the International Agency for Research on Cancer [IARC 1988], however, evidence is accumulating that drinking low to moderate amount of alcohol (1-2 drinks per day) might also have beneficial effects, mainly on cardiovascular disease, while data for cancer are still inconclusive [Bianchini *et al.* 2003]. In a meta-analysis of 16 cohort studies, the lowest mortality for all causes was observed for men consuming 1-2 drinks per day and for women consuming one drink per day [Holman *et al.* 1996]. Differential effects of specific alcoholic beverages have been hypothesized. The cancer preventive effect appears more pronounced with wine, and it is speculated that resveratrol, a natural component specifically present in red wine, may be the main component responsible for this effect [Bianchini *et al.* 2003]. In a pooled cohort study in Denmark, the risk of lung cancer in men much decreased by consumption of over 13 drinks of wine per week (RR=0.44), while consumption of corresponding amounts of beer and spirits increased the risk [Prescott *et al.* 1999]. In the group "Smokers" of our study, a significant protective effect was observed for wine (OR=0.69, 95%CI 0.49-0.98).

Previous studies on the role of personal history of chronic respiratory illnesses among non-smokers have been recently reviewed by Brownson et al. [1998]. A multicenter population-based case-control study among lifetime nonsmoking women in the United States provided evidence of association of asthma, chronic bronchitis, emphysema, and for age groups younger than 55 years tuberculosis and pneumonia with lung cancer risk [Wu *et al.* 1995]. In another large case-control study among nonsmoking women [Alavanja *et al.* 1992], each type of lung disease, except chronic bronchitis, showed some elevation in risk of adenocarcinoma, although effect estimates were not always statistically significant. Associations of lung cancer risk with emphysema, chronic bronchitis, and asthma were found among female never and former smokers in a population based case-control study in New York State [Mayne *et al.* 1999]. Some studies have reported an inverse association between asthma or hay fever and lung cancer in women [Osann 1991].

In a review of scientific evidence on physical activity and cancer prevention, Friedenreich and Orenstein [2002] identified 11 studies examining physical activity as a risk factor of lung cancer, of which 8 found a risk reduction. In the report of the IARC Working

Group on the Evaluation of Cancer Preventive Strategies [2002], five cohort studies and two case-control studies have been listed. In all of the cohort studies, a lower risk of lung cancer was associated with physical activity. The largest studies were the Harvard Health Alumni Study [Lee *et al.* 1999], and a population-based cohort study in Norway [Thune and Lund 1997]. The Norwegian scientists measured both recreational and occupational activity, and found a 30% decreased risk when these activities were combined into a total activity variable for the male study subjects, but no comparable risk decrease was observed for females. In our study, an inverse association was found between lung cancer risk and time (hours/week) devoted to physical exercise among smoking women, while no significant decrease in risk appeared among nonsmokers.

In a prospective study of 25 994 men aged 20-75 years in Finland, a significant inverse gradient between body mass index and the incidence of lung cancer was found [Knekt *et al.* 1991]. A similar inverse association was observed in some studies [Kark *et al.* 1995, Kabat 1996, Swanson *et al.* 1997], including the present investigation. Olson *et al.* [2002] reported that women in the upper BMI quintile were at decreased risk of all lung cancer subtypes. In contrast, in a case-control study conducted in New York State from 1982 to 1985, a positive relation between body mass index and lung cancer risk was found for both never smokers (188 case-control pairs) and former smokers (224 pairs) [Rauscher *et al.* 2000].

Several lines of suggestive evidence supporting the possibility that endocrine factors may play a role in the genesis of lung cancer in women were summarized by Kabat [1996] and Brownson *et al.* [1998]. In a hospital based case-control study of 176 nonsmoking Singapore Chinese women with lung cancer and 663 age-matched controls, a significant inverse relationship between 3 or more livebirths (OR=0.65, 95%CI 0.44-0.96), a menstrual cycle length of more than 30 days (OR=0.46, 95%CI 0.25-0.84), and the risk of lung cancer was observed [Seow *et al.* 2002]. In the present study, we found statistically significant inverse associations of the risk of lung cancer with long duration of menstrual flow (more than 6 days) and one or more deliveries among "Nonsmokers" only, and with late onset of menopause (over 50 years of age) among "Smokers" only. Gao *et al.* [1987] found an association of a short menstrual cycle, and late age at menopause with the risk of adenocarcinoma of the lung among Chinese women in Shanghai. In a review of possible lung cancer risk factors, Siegfried [2001] stated that the oestrogen status is a recognized factor in lung cancer risk among women. Taioli and Wynder [1994] provided evidence that exogenous and endogenous oestrogens may be involved in the development of lung cancer, particularly adenocarcinoma, in women, acting as lung tumor promoters through a receptor-mediated mechanism. However, as stated by Kabat [1996], the existing evidence for a role of hormones in carcinoma of the lung is limited and circumstantial. Further studies are needed that would obtain in-depth information on the possible role of reproductive and endocrine factors.

Two meta-analyses concluded that exposure to environmental tobacco smoke (ETS) is a cause of lung cancer [Hackshaw *et al.* 1997, Zhong *et al.* 2000]. A recent updated meta-analysis of more than 50 studies evaluated involuntary smoking and the risk of lung cancer in never smokers and compared the risk for spouses of smokers with risk for spouses of non-smokers [Vineis *et al.* 2004]. The risk among exposed subjects was approximately 25% greater than expected for women (based on data from 46 studies that included 6257 lung cancer case subjects) and 35% greater for men (based on data from 11 studies that included 442 lung cancer case subjects).

Conclusions

While active tobacco smoking has been recognized to be the main determinant of lung cancer risk among women in most developed countries, diet, prior lung disease, physical activity and other cofactors may be associated with increases or decreases in lung cancer risk. These associations may be different in smokers and nonsmokers. To obtain more specific results, further studies, with updated design, are needed. Along with tobacco use, dietary intake and physical activity are important risk factors for cancer that can be modified through lifestyle change [Byers et al. 2002]. To reduce lung cancer risk among women, public health efforts should include both tobacco control activities and recommendations concerning diet, physical activity and other cofactors.

Acknowledgements

Supported by the Internal Grant Agency (IGA) of the Ministry of Health of the Czech Republic grant # NR/8411-3, the International Association for the Study of Lung Cancer and the Cancer Research Foundation of America.

References

Agudo A, Esteve MG, Pallares C, Martinez-Ballarin I, Fabregat X, *et al.* (1997). Vegetable and fruit intake and the risk of lung cancer in women in Barcelona, Spain. *Eur J Cancer* **33**: 1256-61.

Alavanja MC, Brownson RG, Benichou J, *et al.*(1995). Attributable risk of lung cancer in lifetime nonsmokers and long-term ex-smokers (Missouri, United States). *Cancer Causes Control* **6**:209-16.

Alavanja MCR, Brownson RC, Boice JD Jr, *et al.* (1992) Preexisting lung disease and lung cancer among nonsmoking women. *Am J Epidemiol* **136**: 623-32.

Alberg AJ, Samet JM (2003). Epidemiology of lung cancer. *Chest* **123***: 21S-49S.*

Alexiou C, Onyeaka CVP, Beggs D*, et al.*(2002) Do women live longer following lung resection for carcinoma? *Eur J Cardiothorac Sur* **21**: 319-25.

American Cancer Society (2004). *Statistics 2003. Cancer Facts and Fig*ures. Available from: URL: http://www.cancer. org/docroot/STT/stt_0_2003.asp.

Argiris A, Murren JR (2001). Staging and clinical prognostic factors for small-cell lung cancer. *Cancer* **7**: 228-35.

Augustine A, Harris RE, Wynder EL (1989) Compensation as a risk factor for lung cancer for lung cancer in smokers who switch from nonfilter to filter cigarettes. *Am J Public Health* **79**: 188-91.

Axelsson G, Liljeqvist T, Andersson L, Bergman B, Rylander R (1996). Dietary factors and lung cancer among men in west Sweden. *Int J Epidemiol* **25**: 32-39.

Baldini EH, Strauss GM (1997). Women and lung cancer: waiting to exhale. *Chest* **112**: 229S-234S.

Baron JA, LaVecchia C, Levi F (1990). The antiestrogenic effect of cigarette smoking women. *Am J Obstet Gynecol* **162**: 502-14.

Beattie CW, Hansen NW, Thomas PA (1985). Steroid receptors in human lung cancer. *Cancer Res* **45**: 4206-14.

Beckett AH, Gorrod JW and Jenner P (1971). The effect of smoking on nicotine metabolism in vivo in man. *J Pharm Pharmacol* **23**(suppl): 62S-67S.

Benowitz NL, Jacob P (1984). Daily intake of nicotine during cigarette smoking. *Clin Pharmacol Ther* **35**: 499-504.

Bianchini F, Vainio H (2003). Wine and resveratrol: mechanisms of cancer prevention? *Eur J Cancer Prevention* **12**: 417-25.

Block G, Patterson B, Subar A.(1992). Fruit, vegetables and cancer prevention: a review of the epidemiological evidence. *Nutr Cancer* **18**: 1-29.

Blot WJ, Chow W-H, McLaughlin JK (1996). Tea and cancer: a review of the epidemiological evidence. *Eur J Cancer Prevention* **5**: 425-38.

Blot WJ, McLaughlin JK (2004). Are women more susceptible to lung cancer? *J Natl Cancer Inst* **96**: 812-3.

Bobak M, Marmot M (1996). East-West mortality divide and its potential explanations: proposed research agenda. *Br Med J* **312**:421-5.

Boffeta P, Agudo A, Ahrens W, Benhamou E, Benhamou S, Darby SC, et al.(1998). Multicenter case-control study of exposure to environmental tobacco smoke and lung cancer in Europe. *J Natl Cancer Inst* **90**: 1440-50.

Boffeta P, Ahrens W, Nyberg F, Mukeria A, Bruske-Hohlfeld I, Forte C, et al.(1999). Exposure to environmental tobacco smoke and risk of adenocarcinoma of the lung. *Int J Cancer* **83**: 635-9.

Boyle P (1992). Epidemiology in Central and Eastern Europe. *Epidemiology* **3**: 91-4.

Brennan P, Fortes C, Butler J, Agudo A, Benhamou S, Darby S, *et al.* (2000). A multicenter case-control study of diet and lung cancer among non-smokers. *Cancer Causes Control* **11**: 49-58.

Brownson RC, Alavanja MCR, Caporaso N, Simoes EJ, Chang JC (1998). Epidemiology and prevention of lung cancer in nonsmokers. *Epid Rev* **20**: 218-36.

Brownson RC, Chang JC, Davis JR (1992). Gender and histologic type variations in smoking-related risk of lung cancer. *Epidemiology* **70**: 69-76.

Burns DM (1991). The scientific rationale for comprehensive community-based smoking control strategies in smoking and tobacco control. Smoking and tobacco control monographs. No 1. Strategies to Control Tobacco Use in the United States. *NIH publication* No. 92-3316, pp. 1-31.

Byers T, Nestle M, McTiernan A, Doyle C, Currie-Williams A, Gansler T, Thun M, *et al.* (2002). American Cancer Society guidelines on nutrition and physical activity for cancer prevention: Reducing the risk of cancer with healthy food choices and physical activity. *CA Cancer J Clin* **52**: 92-119.

Chen Y, Breithaupt K, Muhajarine N (2000). Occurrence of chronic obstructive pulmonary disease among Canadians and sex-related risk factors. *J Clin Epidemiol* **53**: 755-61.

Chen YW, Chiou HL, Sheu GT, *et al* (2001). The association of human papilloma virus 16/18 infection with lung cancer among nonsmoking Taiwanese women. *Cancer Res* **61**: 2799-803.

Dabbs DJ, Landreneau RJ, Liu Y, *et al.* (2002). Detection of estrogen receptor by immunohistochemistry in pulmonary adenocarcinoma. *Ann Thorac Surg* **73**: 403-6.

De Stefani E, Brennan P, Boffetta P, et al. (2002). Diet and adenocarcinoma of the lung: a case-control study in Uruguay. *Lung Cancer* **35**:43- 51.

Doll R, Hill AB (1950). A study of etiology of carcinoma of the lung. *Br Med J* **2**: 740-8.

Doll R, Peto R (1976). Mortality in relation to smoking: 20 years observation on male British doctors. *Br Med J* **2**: 1525-36.

Dresler CM, Fratelli C, Babb J, Everly L, Evans AA, Clapper ML (2000). Gender difference in genetic susceptibility for lung cancer. *Lung Cancer* **20**: 153-60.

Dressler CM, Gritz ER (2003). Women and lung cancer: potential mechanisms of greater susceptibility to tobacco smoke. *Eur Respir Mon* **25**: 146-51.

Du YX, Cha Q, Chen XW, Chen YZ, Huang LF, Feng ZZ, Wu XF, Wu JM (1996). An epidemiological study of risk factors for lung cancer in Guangzhou, China. *Lung Cancer* **14**(Suppl 1): S9-S37.

Ernster VL (1996). Female lung cancer. *Ann Rev Public Health* **17**: 97-114.

Ferguson MK, Skosey C, Hoffman PC, Golomb HM (1990). Sex associated differences in presentation and survival in patients with lung cancer. *J Clin Oncol* **8**: 1402-7.

Feskanich D, Ziegler RG, Michaud DS, Giovannucci EL, Speizer FE, Willett WC, *et al.* (2000). Prospective study of fruit and vegetable consumption and risk of lung cancer among men and women. *J Natl Cancer Inst* **92**: 1812-23.

Filiberti R, Kubik A, Reissigova J, *et al.*(1995). Cancer, cardiovascular mortality, and diet in Italy and the Czech Republic. *Neoplasma* **42**:275-83.

Fiore MC (1992). Trends in cigarette smoking in the United States- the epidemiology of tobacco use. *Med Clin North Am* **76**: 289-303.

Fontham ET, Correa P, Reynolds P, Wu-Williams A, Buffler PA, Greenberg S, *et al.* (1994). Environmental tobacco smoke and lung cancer in nonsmoking women. A multicenter study. *JAMA* **271**: 1752-9.

Francesci S, Bidoli E (1999). The epidemiology of lung cancer. *Ann Oncol* **10**(Suppl 5): S3-S6.

Friedenreich CM, Orenstein MR (2002). Physical activity and cancer prevention: etiologic evidence and biological mechanisms. *J Nutr* **132**(11Suppl): 3456S-64S.

Ginter E (1998). Cardiovascular disease prevention in eastern Europe. *Nutrition* **14**: 452-7.

Gao YT, Blot WJ, Zheng W, Ershow AG, Hsu CW, Levin LI, *et al.* (1987). Lung cancer among Chinese women. *Int J Cancer* **40**: 604-9.

Gritz ER, Nielsen IR, Brooks LA (1996). Smoking cessation and gender. The influence of physiological, psychological, and behavioural factors. *J Am Medical Womens Ass* **51**: 35-42.

Hackshaw AK, Law MR, Wald NJ (1997). The accumulated evidence on lung cancer and environmental tobacco smoke. *Br Med J* **315**: 980-8.

Hammond EC (1966). Smoking in relation to the death rates of one million men and women. *Natl Cancer Inst Monogr* **19**: 127-204.

Hansen HH (2002). Lung cancer – a changing picture. *Curr Oncol Rep* **4**:97-8.

Hegmann KT, Frase AM, Keaney RP, *et al.* (1993). The effect of age at smoking initiation on lung cancer risk. *Epidemiology* **4**: 444-8.

Henschke CI, Miettinen OS (2004). Women's susceptibility to tobacco carcinogens. *Lung Cancer* **43**:1-5.

Hinds MW, Cohen HI, Kolonel LN (1982). Tuberculosis and lung cancer risk in nonsmoking women. *Am Rev Respir Dis* **125**: 776-8.

Hirayama T (1981). Nonsmoking wives of heavy smokers have a higher risk of lung cancer: a study from Japan. *Br Med J* **282**: 183-5.

Holman CD, English DR, Milne E, *et al.*(1996). Meta-analysis of alcohol and all-cause mortality: a validation of NHMRC recommendations. *Med J Aust.* **164**: 141-5.

Horwitz RI, Smaldone LF, Viscoli CM (1988). An ecogenetic hypothesis for lung cancer in women. *Arch Intern Med* **148**: 2609-12.

Howe GR, Lindsay J, Coppock E, Miller AB (1979). Isoniazide exposure in relation to cancer incidence and mortality in a cohort a tuberculosis patients. *Int J Epidemiol* **8**: 305-12.

Hu J, Mao Y, Dryer D, White K, *et al.* (2002). Risk factors for lung cancer among Canadian women who have never smoked. *Cancer Detect Prev* **26**: 129-38.

IARC (1988). *Alcohol Drinking. Monographs on the Evaluation of Carcinogenic Risks to Humans, Volume 44*. International Agency for Research on Cancer, Lyon.

IARC Working Group on the Evaluation of Preventive Strategies (2002). *Weight Control and Physical Activity. International Agency for Research on Cancer Handbooks of Cancer Prevention Volume 6*. IARC Press, Lyon.

Jablons DM, Cheng SJ, Carolyn Clary-Macy RN, Hirsch FR (2003). 1st International Lung Cancer Conference in Beijing, October 27-30, 2002. *Lung Cancer* **41**:237-44.

Jacobson B (1981). The ladykillers: why smoking is a feminist issue. London, Pluto press.

Janssen-Heijnen MLG, Coebergh J-WW (2001). Trends in incidence and prognosis of the histological subtypes of lung cancer in North America, Australia, New Zealand and Europe. *Lung Cancer* **31**:123-37.

Kabat GC (1996). Aspects of the epidemiology of lung cancer in smokers and nonsmokers in the United States. *Lung Cancer* **15**: 1-20.

Kaiser U, Hofmann J, Schilli M, *et al.* (1996). Steroid- hormone receptors in cell lines and tumor biopsies of human lung cancer. *Int J Cancer* **67**: 357-64.

Kandel DB, Chen K (2000) Extent of smoking and nicotine dependence in the United States: 1991-1993. *Nicotine Tob Res* **2**: 263-74.

Kark JD, Yaari S, Rasooly I *et al.*(1995). Are lean smokers at increased risk of lung cancer? The Israel Civil Servant Cancer Study. *Arch Intern Med* **155**: 2409-16.

Key TJA, Pike MC, Brown JB, Hermon C, Allen DS, Wang DY (1996). Cigarette smoking and urinary oestrogen excretion in pre-menopausal and post-menopausal women. *Br J Cancer* **8**: 1313-16.

Kinlen LJ, Willows AN, Goldblatt P, Yudkin J (1988). Tea consumption and cancer. *Br J Cancer* **58**: 397-401.

Kirsh MM, Tashian J, Sloan H (1982). Carcinoma of the lung in women. *Ann Thorac Surg* **34**: 34-9.

Knekt P, Heliovaara M, Rissanen A, *et al.*(1991). Leanness and lung cancer risk. *Int J Cancer* **49**: 208-13.

Kreuzer M, Heinrich J, Kreienbrock L, Rosario AS, Gerken M, *et al.* (2002). Risk factors for lung cancer among nonsmoking women. *Int J Cancer* **100**: 706-13.

Krieger N (2000). Refiguring "race": Epidemiology, racialized biology, and biological expressions of race relations. *Int J Health Serv* **30**: 211-6.

Krieger N, Zierler S (1995). Accounting for the health of women. *Curr Issues in Public Health* **1**: 251-6.

Kubik A, Parkin DM, Plesko I, *et al.*(1995). Patterns of cigarette sales and lung cancer mortality in some Central and Eastern European countries, 1960-1989. *Cancer* **75**: 2452-60.

Kubik A, Zatloukal P, Boyle P, Robertson C, Gandini S, Tomasek L , Gray N, Havel L (2001). A case-control study of lung cancer among Czech women. *Lung Cancer* **31**: 111-122.

Kubik A., Zatloukal P, Kriz J (1999). Trends in lung cancer mortality in the Czech Republic, 1950-1995, and prediction up to 1999. *Cas Lek ces* **138**: 310-5 (in Czech).

Kubik AK, Zatloukal P, Tomasek L, Petruzelka L (2002). Lung cancer risk among Czech women: A case-control study. *Prev Med* **34**: 436-44.

Kure EH, Ryberg D, Hewer A, *et al.* (1996). p53 mutations in lung tumours: relationship to gender and lung DNA adducts levels. *Carcinogenesis* **17**: 2201-5.

La Vecchia C, Levi F, Lucchini F, Negri E (1998). Trends in mortality from major diseases in Europe. *Eut J Epidemiol* **14**: 1-8.

Lee IM, Sesso HD, Paffenbarger RS Jr. (1999) Physical activity and risk of lung cancer. *Int J Epidemiol* **28**: 620-5.

Levi F, Franceschi S, LaVecchia C, Randimbison L, Van-Cong Te (1997). Lung carcinoma trends by histologic type in Vaud and Neuchatel, Switzerland, 1974-1994. *Cancer* **79**: 906-14.

Levin ML, Goldstein H, Gerhardt PR (1950). Cancer and tobacco smoking: A preliminary report. *JAMA* **143**: 336-8.

Luo RX, Wu B, Yi YN, Huang ZW, Lin RT (1996). Indoor burning coal air pollution and lung cancer- a case control study in Fuzhou, China. *Lung Cancer* **14** (Suppl): S113-9.

Mant D, Silagy C (1998). The epidemiology of men's health. In T. O′Dowd, D. Jewell (Eds.). *Men's health* , Oxford: Oxford University Press.

Mason TJ (1994). The descriptive epidemiology of lung cancer. In: Samet JM, editor. *Epidemiology of lung cancer.* New York: Dekker, p. 51-69.

Mayne ST, Buenconsejo J, Janerich DT (1999). Previous lung disease and risk of lung cancer among men and women nonsmokers. *Amer J Epidemiol* **149**: 13-20.

Mayne ST, Janerich DT, Greenwald P, Chorost S, Tucci C, Zaman MB, *et al.* (1994). Dietary beta carotene and lung cancer risk in U.S. nonsmokers. *J Natl Cancer Inst* **86**: 33-8.

McDuffie HH, Klaasen DJ, Dosman JA (1987). Female-male differences in patients with primary lung cancer. *Cancer* **59**: 1825-30.

Mettlin C (1989). Milk drinking, other beverage habits and lung cancer risk. *Int J Cancer* **43**: 608-12.

Michnovicz JJ, Hershcopf RJ, Naganuma H, Bradlow HL, Fishman J (1986). Increase 2-hydroxylation of estradiol as a possible mechanism for the anti-estrogenic effect of cigarette smoking. *N Eng J Med* **315**: 1305-9.

Miller AB, Altenburg H-P, Bueno-de-Mesquita B, *et al.* (2004). Fruits and vegetables and lung cancer: Findings from the European Prospective Investigation into Cancer and Nutrition. *Int J Cancer* **108**: 269-76.

Mollerup S, Ryberg D, Hewer A, *et al.* (1998) Gender differences in CYP1A1 expression among lung cancer patients. *Proc Am Assoc Cancer Res* **39**: 337.

Mollerup S, Ryber D, Hewer A, Phillips DH, Haugen A (1999). Sex differences in lung cyp1A1 expression and DNA adduct levels among lung cancer patients. *Cancer Res* **59**: 3317-20.

Morabia A, Wynder EL (1990). Dietary habits of smokers, people who never smoked, and exsmokers. *Am J Clin Nutr* **52**:933-7.

Morabia A, Wynder EL (1991). Cigarette smoking and lung cancer cell types. *Cancer* **68**: 2074-8.

Nelson HH, Christiani DC, Mark EJ, *et al* (1999). Implications and prognostic value of K-ras mutation for early-stage lung cancer in women. *J Natl Cancer Inst* **91**: 2032-8.

Nyberg F, Agrenius V, Svartengren K, Svensson C, Pershagen G. (1998) Dietary factors and risk of lung cancer in never smokers. *Int J Cancer* **78**: 430-6.

Olson JE, Yang P, Schmitz K, *et al.* (2002). Differential association of body mass index and fat distribution with three major histologic types of lung cancer: evidence from a cohort of older women. *Am J Epidemiol* **156**: 606-15.

Osann KE (1991). Lung cancer in women: the importance of smoking, family history of cancer, and medical history of respiratory disease. *Cancer Res* **51**:4893-7.

Osann KE, Anton-Culver H, Kurosaki T, Taylor T (1993). Sex differences in lung cancer risk associate with cigarette smoking. *Int J Cancer* **54**: 44-8.

Pandey M. Mathew A, Nair MK (1999). Global perspective of tobacco habits and lung cancer: A lesson for third world countries. *Eur J Cancer Prevention* **8**: 271-9.

Parsons NR, Somervaille L (2000). Estimation and projection of population lung cancer trends (United Kingdom). *Cancer Causes Control* **11**: 467-75.

Payne S (2001). Smoke like a man, die like a man? : A review of the relationship between gender, sex, and lung cancer. *Soc Sci Med* **53**:1067-80.

Peto R, Darby S, Deo H, *et al.* (2000). Smoking, smoking cessation, and lung cancer in the UK since 1950: combination of national statistics with two case-control studies. *BMJ* **321**: 323-9.

Prescott E, Osler M, Hein HO, *et al* (1998). Gender and smoking-related risk of lung cancer. *Epidemiology* **9**: 79-83.

Prescott E, Gronbaek M, Becker U, *et al.* (1999). Alcohol intake and the risk of lung cancer: influence of type of alcoholic beverage. *Am J Epidemiol* **149**:463-70.

Quinn MJ (2003). Cancer trends in the United States – A view from Europe. *J Natl Cancer Inst* **95**: 1258-61.

Quoix E (1999). Specific features of bronchial cancer in women. *Rev Pneumol Clin* **55**: 290-5 (in French).

Radzikowska E, Roszkowski K, Glaz P (2001). Lung cancer in patients under 50 years old. *Lung Cancer* **7**: 203-11.

Radzikowska E, Glaz P(2000). The role of sex as a prognostic factor in lung cancer. *Pneumol Alergol Pol* **68**: 25-33.

Rauscher GH, Mayne ST, Janerich DT (2000). Relation between body mass index and lung cancer risk in men and women never and former smokers. *Am J Epidemiol* **152**:506-13.

Reynolds P (1999). Epidemiologic evidence for workplace ETS as a risk factor for lung cancer among nonsmokers: specific risk estimates. *Environ Health Perspect* **107** (Suppl 6): 865-72.

Risch HA, Howe GR, Jain M, Burch JD, Holowaty EJ, Miller AB (1993). Are female smokers at higher risk for lung cancer than male smokers? A case control analysis by histologic type. *Am J Epidemiol* **138**: 281-93.

Ryberg D, Hewer A, Phillips DH, Haugen A (1994). Different susceptibility to smoking induced DNA damage among male and female lung cancer patients. *Cancer Res* **54**: 5801-3.

Samet JM (1994). *Epidemiology of lung cancer*. New York, NY: Marcel Dekker.

Schoenberg JB, Wilcox H, Mason T, Bill J, Stemhagen A (1989). Variation in smoking-related lung cancer risk among New Jersey women. *Am J Epidemiol* **130**: 688-95.

Schriver SP, Bourdeau HA, Gubish CT, *et al.* (2000). Sex-specific expression of gastrin-releasing peptide receptor: Relationship to smoking history and risk of lung cancer. *J Natl Cancer Inst* **92**: 24-33.

Schwartz AG, Siegfried JM, Weiss L (1999). Familial aggregation of breast cancer with early onset lung cancer. *Genetic Epidemiol* **17**: 274-84.

Seow A, Poh WT, Teh M, *et al.* (2002). Diet, reproductive factors and lung cancer risk among Chinese women in Singapore: evidence for a prospective effect of soy in nonsmokers. *Int J Cancer* **97**: 365-71.

Shields PG (2002). Molecular epidemiology of smoking and lung cancer. *Oncogene* **21**:6870-6.

Siegfried JM (2001). Women and lung cancer: does oestrogen play a role? *Lancet Oncol* **2**: 506-13.

Sinha R, Kulldorff M, Curtin J, Brown CC, Alavanja MCR, Swanson CA (1998). Fried, well-done red meat and risk of lung cancer in women (United States). *Cancer Causes Control* **9**: 621-30.

Sinha R, Kulldorff M, Swanson CA, Curtin J, Brownson RC, Alavanja MC (2000). Dietary heterocyclic amines and the risk of lung cancer among Missouri women. *Cancer Res* **60**: 3753-6.

Skuladottir H, Tjoenneland A, Overvad K, Stripp C, Christensen J *et al.* (2004). Does insufficient adjustment for smoking explain the preventive effects of fruit and vegetables on lung cancer? *Lung Cancer* **45**: 1-10.

Spiegelman D, Maurer LH, Ware JH, *et al.* (1989). Prognostic factors in small-cell carcinoma of the lung: an analysis of 1521 patients. *J Clin Oncol* **7**: 344: 54.

StellmanSD, Muscat JE, Thompson S, Hoffmann D, Wynder EL (1997). Risk of squamous cell carcinoma and adenocarcinoma of the lung in relation to lifetime filter cigarette smoking. *Cancer* **80**:382-8.

Stensvold I, Jacobsen BK (1994). Coffee and cancer: A prospective study of 43,000 Norwegian men and women. *Cancer Causes Control* **5**: 401-8.

Swanson CA, Brown CC, Sinha R, *et al.* (1997). Dietary fats and lung cancer risk among women: the Missouri Women's Health Study (United States). *Cancer Causes Control* **8**: 883-93.

Taioli E, Wynder EL (1994). Endocrine factors and adenocarcinoma of the lung in women. *J Natl Cancer Inst* **84**: 869-70.

Takezaki T, Hirose K, Inoue M, Hamajima A, Yatabe Y, Mitsudomi T, *et al.* (2001). Dietary factors and lung cancer risk in Japanese: with special reference to fish consumption and adenocarcinomas. *Br J Cancer* **84**:1199-206.

Tavani A, La Vecchia C (2000). Coffee and cancer: a review of epidemiological studies, 1990-1999. *Eur J Cancer Prevention* **9**: 241-56.

Thune I, Lund E (1997). The influence of physical activity on lung cancer risk. A prospective study. *Int J Cancer* **70**: 57-62.

Tokuhata GK, Lilienfeld AM (1963). Familial aggregation of lung cancer among hospital patients. *Public Health Rep* **78**: 277-83.

Travis WD, Lubin J, Ries I., Devesa S. (1996). United States lung carcinoma incidence trends: Declining for most histologic types among males, increasing among females. *Cancer* **77**: 2464-70.

Trichopoulos D, Kalandidi A, Sparros L, MacMahon B (1981). Lung cancer and passive smoking. *Int J Cancer* **27**: 1-4.

Tyczynski JE, Bray F, Aareleid T, Dalmas M, Kurtinaitis J, *et al.* (2004). Lung cancer mortality patterns in selected Central, Eastern and Southern European countries. *Int J Cancer* **109**: 598-610.

Ulrik CS (2003). Smoking and mortality in women: smoke like a man, die (at least) like a man. *European Repir Mon* **25**: 103-17.

US Department of Health, Education and Welfare (1964). *Smoking and Health: A report of the Advisory Committee to the Surgeon General of the Public Health Service.* Washington, DC: US Government Printing Office, DHEW Publication No. 1103.

US Department of Health and Human Services (1980). *The Health Consequences of Smoking for Women. A Report of the Surgeon General.* Washington, DC: U.S. Department of Health and Human Services, PublicHealth Service, Office of the Assistant Secretary for Health, Office on Smoking and Health.

U.S. Department of Health and Human Services (1982). *The health consequences of smoking: cancer. A report of the Surgeon General.* 1982. DHHS Publication No. (PHS) 82- 50179, Washington, D.C., US Government Printing Office.

US Department of Health and Human Services (2001). *Women and smoking: a report of the Surgeon General 2001.* Washington, DC: US Department of Health and Human Services, Center for Disease Control and Prevention, National Center for Chronic Disease, Prevention and Health Promotion., Office on Smoking and Health.

Vineis P, Alavanja M, Buffler P, *et al.* (2004). Tobacco and cancer: Recent epidemiological evidence. *J Natl Cancer Inst* **96**: 99-106.

Wei Q, Cheng L, Amos CI, *et al.* (2000). Repair of tobacco carcinogen-induced DNA adducts and lung cancer risk: a molecular epidemiologic study. *J Natl Cancer Inst* **92**: 1764-72.

Willett W (1998). *Nutritional epidemiology,* 2nd edition. New York: Oxford Univ Press.

Wolf M, Holle R, Hans K, Drings P, Havemann K (1991). Analysis of prognostic factors in 766 patients with small cell lung cancer (SCLC): the role of sex as a predictor for survival. *Br J Cancer* **63**: 987-92.

Wu AH, Fontham ETH, Reynolds P, *et al.* (1995). Previous lung disease and risk of lung cancer among lifetime nonsmoking women in the United States. *Amer J Epidemiol* **141**: 1023-32.

Wu-Williams AH, Samet JM (1994). Lung cancer and cigarette smoking. In: Samet JM, ed. *Epidemiology of lung cancer.* New York, Marcel Dekker, pp.71-108.

Wynder EL, Graham EA (1950). Tobacco smoking as a possible etiologic factor in bronchogenic carcinoma: A study of six hundred and eighty-four proved cases. *JAMA* **143**:329-46.

Wynder EL, Hoffman D (1994). Smoking and lung cancer: Scientific Challenges and Opportunities. *Cancer Res* **54**: 5284-95.

Zang EA, Wynder EL (1996). Differences in lung cancer risk between men and women: Examination of the evidence. *J Natl Cancer Inst* **88**: 183-92.

Zang EA, Wynder EL (1998). Smoking trends in the United States between 1969 and 1995 based on patients hospitalized with non-smoking related diseases. *Prev Med* **27**: 854-61.

Zatloukal P, Kubik A, Pauk N, Tomasek L, Petruzelka L (2003). Adenocarcinoma of the lung among women: risk associated with smoking, prior lung disease, diet and menstrual and pregnancy history. *Lung Cancer* **41**: 283-93.

Zhong L, Goldberg MS, Gao YT, Hanley JA, Parent ME, Jin F (2001). A population-based case-control study of lung cancer and green tea consumption among women living in Shanghai, China. *Epidemiology* **12**: 695-700.

Zhong L, Goldberg MS, Parent M-E, Hanley JA (2000). Exposure to environmental tobacco smoke and the risk of lung cancer: a meta-analysis. *Lung Cancer* **27**: 3-18.

Zuckerman M, Ball S, Black J (1990). Influences of sensation seeking, gender, risk appraisal, and situational motivation on smoking. *Addict Behav* **15**: 209-20.

In: Trends in Smoking and Health Research
Editors: J. H. Owing, pp. 35-49

ISBN: 1-59454-391-7
© 2005 Nova Science Publishers, Inc.

Chapter II

Cigarette Smoking, High-Density Lipoprotein Cholesterol Subfractions and Blood Pressure in Japanese Collegiate Women

Hiroyuki Imamura[*], *Reika Masuda and Noriko Miyamoto*

Laboratory of Nutrition and Exercise Physiology, Department of Nutritional Sciences,
Nakamura Gakuen University, Fukuoka, Japan

Abstract

Many of the published data on the relationship of cigarette smoking with systolic and diastolic blood pressures (SBP and DBP, respectively), serum high-density lipoprotein cholesterol (HDL-C) subfractions is based on studies of middle-aged individuals. The data on young women are scarce. This chapter examined the relationship of cigarette smoking with SBP, DBP and HDL-C subfractions in Japanese collegiate women. Thirty current smokers were individually matched for physical activity scores, age and body mass index (BMI) with 30 nonsmokers. There were no significant differences between smokers and nonsmokers in the mean nutrient intakes. The smokers had significantly lower mean SBP, DBP, HDL-C and HDL_2-C. Furthermore, when the subjects were divided into 3 groups by smoking habits: 30 nonsmokers and subjects who smoked 2-12 (n=15) and 13-20 (n=15) cigarettes/day, SBP, DBP, HDL-C and HDL_2-C showed dose-dependent relationships. In univariate analyses, number of cigarette smoking a day significantly negatively correlated with SBP, DBP, HDL-C, HDL_2-C and TC. Duration of cigarette smoking significantly negatively correlated with SBP, DBP and HDL_2-C and positively with TG. Waist significantly negatively correlated with HDL-C and HDL_2-C. Dietary fiber significantly positively correlated with HDL-C and HDL_2-C. When number of cigarette smoking a day, duration of cigarette smoking, waist and dietary fiber were included in the forward stepwise multiple regression analyses, there were negative

[*]   PhD; Laboratory of Nutrition and Exercise Physiology, Department of Nutritional Sciences, Nakamura Gakuen University, 5-7-1 Befu, Jonan-ku, Fukuoka 814-0198, Japan; TEL (092) 851-5964 FAX (092) 851-5964; Email address: Imamura@nakamura-u.ac.jp

relationships of cigarette smoking to SBP, DBP, HDL-C and HDL$_2$-C. Also, there were positive relationship of duration of cigarette smoking to TG. These results suggest that the known associations in older adults of cigarette smoking with blood pressure and HDL-C subfractions are already apparent in young women.

Key words: cigarette smoking; blood pressure; serum lipids and lipoproteins, women

Introduction

Cigarette smoking is one of the major risk factors for coronary heart disease [1]. It has been shown that plasma high-density lipoprotein cholesterol (HDL-C) concentrations are inversely correlated with coronary heart disease risk factors [2]. Cigarette smoking is associated with a lower concentration of HDL-C [3], which can explain in part the increased risk of coronary heart disease in smokers. The lower HDL-C concentrations in smokers compared with nonsmokers have been attributed to lowered HDL$_2$-C [4-6], HDL$_3$-C [7], or to both subfractions [8]. However, these data are based on studies of middle-aged or older individuals. The data on young women are scarce. One study found that cigarette smoking was significantly negatively related to HDL-C in white girls. However, this study did not measure HDL subfractions [9]. In a recent study [10], we reported that smokers had significantly lower mean HDL$_2$-C than nonsmokers in collegiate women. However, we did not examine the dose-response relationship of cigarette smoking with HDL subfractions.

The relationship between cigarette smoking and blood pressure has been reported by Green et al. [11], who examined the results of 15 published studies and stated that a negative association between smoking and blood pressure was consistent over a wide range of cross-sectional epidemiological studies. However, only limited studies [11-18], have specifically examined the dose-dependent relationship between cigarette smoking and blood pressure. Among these, the dose-dependent relationship between cigarette smoking and blood pressure has been demonstrated in men [12-14]. However, a dose-dependent relationship was not clearly demonstrated in women [11, 15, 16], although cigarette smokers, as a group, had lower blood pressure than non-smokers in two studies [11, 15]. One study [17] in both men and women demonstrated a dose-dependent relationship between cigarette smoking and blood pressure independent of drinking status and gender. However, men and women were not shown separately in this study.

Japanese people have quite different dietary habits than those of people living western countries. The traditional Japanese dietary habits are characterized by high salt and carbohydrate intakes along with low fat, protein and calcium intakes [19]. Despite the fact that Japan has experienced westernization of dietary habits over the past few decades, especially in young people, the Japanese diet still retains its traditional character [20]. The smoking rate in Japan is still high in men (52.7%) but low in women (10.6%). The rate is the highest in both young men (60.9%) and women (16.9%) aged 20 to 29 years and declines with increasing age [20]. The purpose of this study was to examine the dose-dependent relationship of cigarette smoking with HDL subfractions and blood pressure in Japanese collegiate women.

Methods

Subjects and Self-Administered Questionnaire

Collegiate women were recruited from one university and consented to the procedure after explanation of the purpose of the study. To be included in the study, they had to meet the following criteria: 1) they were menstruating at normal intervals, ranging from 26-31 days, which fell within the normally accepted range [21]; 2) they drank alcohol less than once a week and even then only had a small amount; 3) they were not on any medication at the time of their participation in the study; and 4) they had never taken birth control pills. Smokers were eligible if they smoked at least for one year. Thirty current smokers volunteered, who were individually matched for physical activity scores, age and body mass index (BMI) with 30 nonsmokers who had never smoked. The study protocol was approved by the Ethics Committee of the Nakamura Gakuen University and informed consent was obtained from each subject.

Information on smoking, physical activity habits, and coffee consumption was obtained via a self-administered questionnaire. Accuracy of the questionnaire was checked through individual interviews. Smokers were asked to indicate how many cigarettes a day (number of cigarette smoking) and how many years did they smoke (duration of cigarette smoking). The frequency, duration and mode of physical activity were questioned, and scores 1-5 were given according to Young and Steinhardt [22]. Coffee consumption, how many cups of coffee a day, week, or month was questioned.

Measurements

The body weight and height were measured with the subjects in underwear to the nearest 0.1 kg and 0.1cm, respectively. The BMI was expressed as weight/height^2 (kg/m^2).

Maximal oxygen uptake was measured with a continuous multistage exercise test to volitional exhaustion on a Monark bicycle ergometer. The test was conducted in air-conditioned facilities with a temperature set at 25°C. After resting for 10 min, each subject began unloaded cycling at a rate of 50 per min. The duration of each stage was set at three minutes. The first work load was set at 50-W. Thereafter, the work rate was increased in 25-W increments until volitional exhaustion or until subject was unable to maintain the pedaling rate. Ventilatory measurements were made by standard open-circuit calorimetry (Wyvern Software Physiologic Exercise Testing System; P.K. Morgan Instruments, Inc., Andover, MA, USA) with 30 second sampling intervals. The subject wore noseclips and breathed through a Hans Rudolph low-resistance low-dead-space valve that was connected to a mixing chamber via lightweight tubing. The system was calibrated against a known mixture of gases (Sumitomo Seika, Chiba, Japan) before each experiment. The electrocardiogram, using a bipolar CM5 lead configuration, was monitored via radio telemetry (NIHON KODEN). Exercise heart rate was determined during the final minute of each stage. The primary criterion for attainment of maximal oxygen uptake was the subject's inability to keep up with pedaling at a rate of 50 per min despite urging by testing staff and a plateau of oxygen uptake, despite an increase in the workload [23].

Dietary information was collected using a 3-weekday diet record. Each diet was analyzed by means of a computer program. Each food item was coded according to the Tables of the Japanese foodstuff Composition [24].

Physical exercise was not allowed 48 hours, and beverages other than water and cigarette smoking were not allowed 24 hours prior to the blood pressure measurements and blood sampling. Subjects arrived at the laboratory by 08:00 h. The temperature of the laboratory was set at 25°C. The resting systolic and fifth phase diastolic blood pressures (SBP and DBP, respectively) were recorded as the mean of three measurements. The measurements were made by a trained nurse using a cuff and mercury sphygmomanometer after the subject had been sitting for more than 20 minutes. After blood pressure was measured, fasting (12 hour) blood samples were drawn from the antecubital vein.

Blood Analysis

All blood samples were taken between days 7 and 9 of the menstrual cycle when estrogen levels were relatively low [21]. The samples were immediately stored on ice, and kept on ice until centrifuged within 10 minutes in a refrigerated centrifuge at 4°C. The serum collected for total cholesterol (TC) and triglycerides (TG) analyses were frozen immediately after centrifugation and stored at -80°C. The serum collected for high-density lipoprotein cholesterol (HDL-C), HDL_2-C, HDL_3-C, and low-density lipoprotein cholesterol (LDL-C) analyses were refrigerated at 4°C. Samples were analyzed within 10 days.

TC (L type Total Cholesterol kit, Wako Pure Chemical Industries, Ltd, Tokyo, Japan) [25] and TG (L type TG·H kit, Wako Pure Chemical Industries, Ltd, Tokyo, Japan) [26] were analyzed by enzymatic methods using a Hitachi Autoanalyzer 7170. HDL-C (HDL-C Auto Daiichi kit, Daiichi Chemical Company, Tokyo, Japan) [27] was analyzed by direct assay with selective inhibition method using a Hitachi Autoanalyzer 7170. HDL_2-C and HDL_3-C (Sterozyme auto 545, Fuji Rebio, Inc., Tokyo, Japan) [28] were analyzed by ultracentrifugation method using a Beckman Ultracentrifuge type L8-56 and a Hitachi Autoanalyzer 7070. LDL-C (Determiner TC555, Kyowa Medics, Tokyo, Japan) [29] was analyzed by hepalin and citrate precipitation method using a Hitachi Autoanalyzer 7150. All measurements were duplicated.

The coefficients of variation for intra-assay and inter-assay were 0.54% and 2.71% for TC, 4.16% and 7.34% for TG, 0.91% and 1.73% for HDL-C, 7.18% and 8.71% for HDL_2-C, 7.27% and 7.33% for HDL_3-C, 1.37% and 3.70% for LDL-C, respectively.

Statistical Analysis

The results are expressed as mean±SD. The differences in proportions between smokers and nonsmokers were tested using the Chi-square (χ^2) test. The t-test was used to compare the mean values between smokers and non-smokers. The mean differences among the three groups divided by smoking habits were determined by analysis of variance techniques. The Scheffe's method was used to identify specific significant differences when significant F values were identified. Pearson correlation coefficients were used to examine simple correlations between two variables in 30 smokers. Stepwise multiple regression analyses were performed with HDL-C, HDL_2-C, HDL_3-C, LDL-C, TC and TG as the dependent variables. Because of the small sample size (n=60), the number of independent variables included in each model was limited to number of cigarette smoking a day, duration of cigarette smoking and other variables which showed significant correlation in the univariate analyses (p<0.05) with serum lipids and lipoproteins and blood pressure.

Results

The smokers currently smoked 12.1±6.8 (2 to 20) cigarettes per day and had been smoking for 2.6±1.4 (1.0 to 8.5) years. For each physical activity score from 1 to 5, there were 22, 1, 1, 4 and 2 smokers and nonsmokers, respectively. Number of subjects who do not consume coffee, drink every day, 2-4 cups a week, and 2-4 cups a month were 6, 7, 16, and 1 for smokers and 7, 3, 20, and 0 for nonsmokers. There were no significant differences in the distribution of subjects between the two groups.

The mean characteristics and biochemical values are shown in Table 1. The smokers had significantly lower mean SBP, DBP, HDL-C and HDL_2-C than nonsmokers. There were no significant differences between smokers and nonsmokers in the mean nutrient and foodstuff intakes (Table 2). When the subjects were divided into 3 groups by smoking habits: 30 non-smokers and subjects who smoked 2-12 (n=15) and 13-20 (n=15) cigarettes/day, SBP, DBP, HDL-C and HDL_2-C showed dose-dependent relationships (Table 3).

Table 1 Mean (SD) characteristics and biochemical values

		Nonsmoker (n=30)			Smoker (n=30)			
Age	(years)	20.8	±	0.9	20.8	±	0.7	
Height	(cm)	159.2	±	4.7	159.5	±	6.3	
Weight	(kg)	52.4	±	5.8	52.2	±	6.5	
BMI	(kg/m^2)	20.7	±	2.0	20.7	±	2.1	
VO_2max	$(ml·kg^{-1}·min^{-1})$	37.9	±	7.8	41.2	±	6.6	
SBP	(mmHg)	100.2	±	9.4	92.8	±	7.9	†
DBP	(mmHg)	65.4	±	9.4	58.0	±	6.9	†
HDL-C	(mg/dl)	69.0	±	15.9	60.4	±	11.3	*
HDL_2-C	(mg/dl)	50.5	±	15.9	40.1	±	10.3	†
HDL_3-C	(mg/dl)	17.1	±	2.4	17.2	±	2.7	
LDL-C	(mg/dl)	96.5	±	22.7	101.2	±	20.1	
TC	(mg/dl)	186.7	±	22.3	175.8	±	22.3	
TG	(mg/dl)	67.7	±	28.5	80.8	±	34.0	

Values are the mean ± SD. *p<0.05, †p<0.01

Abbreviations: SBP, systolic blood pressure; DBP, diastolic blood pressure;

BMI, body mass index; VO_2max, maximal oxygen uptake;

HDL-C, high-density lipoprotein cholesterol;

LDL-C, low-density lipoprotein cholesterol;

TC, total cholesterol; TG, triglycerides.

Table 2. Nutrient and foodstuff intakes of the subjects

		Nonsmoker (n=30)			Smoker (n=30)		
Energy	(kcal)	1572	±	378	1643	±	495
Protein	(g)	55.1	±	11.4	56.0	±	17.3
Fat	(g)	52.9	±	20.8	56.8	±	23.9
Carbohydrate	(g)	212.3	±	47.7	215.0	±	66.1
Potassium	(mg)	1892	±	626	1921	±	825
Calcium	(mg)	407	±	138	435	±	222
Magnesium	(mg)	198	±	42	193	±	81
Phosphorus	(mg)	823	±	175	835	±	287
Iron	(mg)	6.9	±	2.5	6.2	±	2.5
Zinc	(mg)	6.7	±	1.9	6.6	±	2.5
Copper	(mg)	0.9	±	0.3	0.8	±	0.3
V.A	(µgRE)	678	±	427	470	±	250
V.D	(µg)	5.3	±	3.8	5.3	±	5.9
V.E	(mgα-TE)	7.2	±	2.7	6.6	±	2.6
V.K	(µg)	154.0	±	99.4	154.7	±	143.9
V.B$_1$	(mg)	0.74	±	0.24	0.91	±	0.76
V.B$_2$	(mg)	0.99	±	0.28	1.12	±	0.42
V.C	(mg)	68	±	37	78	±	61
Fiber	(g)	10.4	±	5.1	8.4	±	3.8
Salt	(g)	6.9	±	2.1	7.4	±	3.0
Fruits	(g)	44.0	±	46.7	60.0	±	82.7
GV	(g)	67.3	±	47.9	54.4	±	68.3
OV	(g)	98.3	±	52.7	86.4	±	90.9
S	(g)	14.7	±	6.1	18.9	±	13.9
P	(g)	11.6	±	4.4	12.1	±	8.7

Values are the mean ± SD.

Abbreviations: V, vitamin; GV, green vegetables; OV, other vegetables;
S, saturated fat; P, polysaturated fat.

In univariate analyses, number of cigarette smoking a day significantly negatively correlated with HDL-C, HDL$_2$-C, TC, SBP and DBP. Duration of cigarette smoking significantly negatively correlated with HDL$_2$-C, SBP, DBP and positively with TG. Waist significantly negatively correlated with HDL-C and HDL$_2$-C. Dietary fiber significantly positively correlated with HDL-C and HDL$_2$-C (Table 4). The age, dietary habits such as intakes of cholesterol, total fat, saturated fat, polyunsaturated fat , fruit, vegetables and coffee consumption, maximal oxygen uptake in ml·kg^{-1}·min^{-1} and physical activity scores did not significantly correlate with any serum lipids, lipoproteins and blood pressure (data not shown).

Table 3. Biochemical and blood pressure values when the subjects were divided into three groups by smoking habits

		Nonsmoker			Smoker (2-12)			Smoker (13-20)		
HDL-C	(mg/dl)	69.0	±	15.9	63.8	±	12.4	56.9	±	9.2	*
HDL$_2$-C	(mg/dl)	50.5	±	15.9	43.4	±	11.6	36.8	±	7.8	*
HDL$_3$-C	(mg/dl)	17.1	±	2.4	17.2	±	2.4	17.3	±	3.1	
LDL-C	(mg/dl)	96.5	±	22.7	105.0	±	18.1	97.3	±	21.8	
TC	(mg/dl)	186.7	±	22.3	184.0	±	19.4	167.6	±	22.5	*
TG	(mg/dl)	67.7	±	28.5	93.1	±	39.6 *	68.5	±	22.3	
SBP	(mmHg)	100.2	±	9.4	94.7	±	8.3	91.0	±	7.3	*
DBP	(mmHg)	65.4	±	9.4	59.1	±	5.9	56.9	±	7.8	*

Values are the mean ± SD.
*$p<0.05$ when compared with nonsmoker.
Abbreviations: HDL-C, high-density lipoprotein cholesterol; LDL-C, low-density lipoprotein cholesterol; TC, total cholesterol; TG, triglycerides; SBP, systolic blood pressure; DBP, diastolic blood pressure.

Thus, we entered the number of cigarette smoking a day, duration of cigarette smoking, waist, dietary fiber and TG into the stepwise multiple regression analyses as independent variables. As results, there were negative relationships of number of cigarette smoking a day with HDL-C, HDL$_2$-C, TC, SBP and DBP. Also, there was positive relationship of duration of cigarette smoking with TG (Table 5).

Discussion

Confounding Factors

Smokers tend to be less active than non-smokers [30]. Less active people in comparison with active people tend to show higher TC and TG and/or lower HDL-C [31-33]. It has been reported that physical activity was positively associated with HDL-C [34] and negatively associated with blood pressure [35]. It has also been reported that physical training lowers blood pressure [36-40].

Smokers are often leaner than non-smokers [41]. Lean subjects, in comparison with their counterparts, tend to show lower TC, TG, SBP and DBP [42]. It has been reported that percent body fat showed a significant positive correlations with SBP and DBP and negative correlation after adjusting for the effects of age and maximal oxygen uptake [43, 44].

Smokers show higher intakes of energy, total fat, saturated fat, cholesterol and lower intakes of polyunsaturated fat, fiber, vitamin C, vitamin E and β-carotene than nonsmokers [45]. Saturated fatty acids, cholesterol and excess caloric intake raise serum LDL [46]. Consumption of fruit and vegetables is inversely related to LDL [47]. It has also been suggested that diets higher in fruits and vegetables and lower in meats (except fish) may reduce the risk of developing high blood pressure [48].

Table 4. Pearson Correlation Coefficients Between Selected Variables

	HDL-C	HDL$_2$-C	HDL$_3$-C	LDL-C	TC	TG	SBP	DBP
NCS	-0.36 †	-0.40 †	0.07	0.06	-0.31 *	0.05	-0.41 †	-0.37 †
DCS	-0.22	-0.29 *	0.14	0.24	-0.04	0.26 *	-0.28 *	-0.27 *
Waist	-0.34 †	-0.26 *	-0.03	0.19	-0.05	0.20	0.08	-0.02
Fiber	0.34 †	0.29 *	0.04	0.00	0.21	0.04	0.16	0.12
TG	-0.25	-0.29 *	-0.06	0.35 †	0.24		-0.03	-0.26 *

*P<0.05, †P<0.01

Abbreviations: NCS, number of cigarettes smoked/day; DCS, duration of cigarette smoking;
TG, triglycerides; HDL-C, high-density lipoprotein cholesterol;
LDL-C, low-density lipoprotein cholesterol; TC, total cholesterol;
SBP, systolic blood pressure; DBP, diastolic blood pressure.

Table 5. Standaedized Partial Regression Coefficients of Serum lipids and lipoproteins and blood pressure with Selected Independent Variables

	HDL-C	HDL$_2$-C	HDL$_3$-C	LDL-C	TC	TG	SBP	DBP
NCS	-0.31 *	-0.39 †			-0.32 *		-0.41 †	-0.37 †
DCS						0.26 *		
Waist	-0.30 *							
Fiber								
TG		-0.27 *		0.35 †	0.25 *			
R^2	0.21	0.23		0.13	0.16	0.07	0.17	0.14

*p<0.05, †p<0.01; Abbreviations same as Table 4.

Smokers show higher intake of alcohol [30, 49]. It has been reported that alcohol consumption was positively associated with HDL, HDL_2, HDL_3, SBP, and DBP [50, 51]. One study investigated the effects of alcohol consumption on the lipoprotein profiles of 34 premenopausal women. Subjects' diet and various other potentially confounding variables including phase of the menstrual cycle were controlled. Although these observations are limited to a single phase of the menstrual cycle, with alcohol intake, HDL, HDL_2, and HDL_3 increased and LDL-C decreased [52].

In addition to these confounding factors, menstrual cycle can also influence lipid metabolism. Estradiol increases TG and HDL_2 [53]. Increase of HDL-C at ovulation in healthy women has been reported [21, 54].

In the present study, smokers were individually matched for physical activity scores, age and BMI with nonsmokers. In addition, maximal oxygen uptake in $ml \cdot kg^{-1} \cdot min^{-1}$ and dietary habits such as intakes of cholesterol, total fat, saturated fat, polyunsaturated fat, fruit, vegetables and coffee consumption did not differ significantly between smokers and nonsmokers. Also, these variables did not correlated with any of the serum lipids and lipoproteins and blood pressure. Furthermore, to avoid confounding influence of the acute effects of cigarette smoking [55], menstrual cycle phase and alcohol intake on these parameters, the smokers were refrained from cigarette smoking for 24 hours before blood pressure measurement and blood sampling, which were taken between days 7 and 9 of the menstrual cycle, and only collegiate women who drank alcohol less than once a week were admitted to the study.

Relationship of Cigarette Smoking with HDL-C Subfractions in Women

Vangent et al. [56] reported that smokers had significantly lower HDL-C than nonsmokers, irrespective of contraceptive use. However, these authors did not specifically examine the dose-dependent relationships. Førde et al. [57] reported that smokers had significantly lower HDL-C than non-smokers, after adjusting for age, relative body weight and leisure time physical activity. Willett et al. [58] also reported the similar results. These authors examined dose-dependent relationships, but such relationships were not observed. Chen et al. [59], on the other hand, did not find any relationship between cigarette smoking and HDL-C. In contrast, 2 studies [16, 60] have reported dose-dependent negative relationship between cigarette smoking and HDL-C after adjusting for age, obesity, alcohol intake and/or exercise.

The lower HDL-C concentrations in smokers compared with nonsmokers have been attributed to lowered HDL_2-C [4-6], HDL_3-C [7], or to both subfractions [8]. However, these data are based on studies of middle-aged or older individuals. The data on young women are scarce. In a recent study [10], we reported that smokers had significantly lower mean HDL_2-C than nonsmokers in collegiate women. However, we did not examine the dose-response relationship of cigarette smoking with HDL subfractions. In the present study, HDL-C and HDL_2-C showed dose-dependent relationships. In univariate analyses, number of cigarette smoking a day significantly negatively correlated with HDL-C and HDL_2-C. Duration of cigarette smoking significantly negatively correlated with HDL_2-C. When number of cigarette smoking a day, duration of cigarette smoking, waist and dietary fiber were included in the forward stepwise multiple regression analyses, there were negative relationships of cigarette smoking with HDL-C and HDL_2-C.

In the present study, smokers showed significantly lower HDL_2-C. The magnitude of difference in HDL_2-C was 14.2%, which was slightly smaller than the differences reported by others, ranging from 16.7% to 26.2% [4-6, 8]. The divergent results obtained in these studies could be due to the differences in age, gender, physical activity, obesity and/or other confounding factors as aforementioned.

Although the mechanisms whereby cigarette smoking decrease HDL_2-C observed in the present study using young women is not known, it is possible that they could be indirectly and/or directly caused by the gas phase of cigarette smoke, which possesses a variety of components (eg, free radicals and aldehydes) capable of damaging lipids and proteins [61-63], and causing endothelial dysfunction [64]. It is also possible that they could be caused by an increase in hepatic lipase activity [4, 65]. Hepatic lipase converts the large, TG-rich HDL_2, back into small TG- and cholesteryl ester-poor HDL_3-C [65]. Thus, the increase in hepatic lipase activity would be expected to increase HDL_3-C and decrease HDL_2-C. It has been reported that plasma hepatic lipase activity was significantly higher in smokers than in nonsmokers [4]. However, this study used acute myocardial infarction patients. Thus, the effects of smoking on plasma hepatic lipase activity need to be investigated in young normolipidemic women.

Relationship of Cigarette Smoking to Blood Pressure in Women

The stability of the blood pressure values can be improved by stabilizing the conditions in which the measurements are done and also by increasing the number of measurements for each subject. In the present study, blood pressure was measured three times in the morning.

Brischetto et al. [16] did not find any relationship between cigarette smoking and blood pressure. Gofin et al. [15] reported that both SBP and DBP were significantly lower in smokers than in non-smokers in middle-aged women after adjusting for the effects of age, body mass, ethnic origin and season. Savdie et al. [17] demonstrated negative dose-dependent relationships of cigarette smoking to both SBP and DBP independent of drinking status and sex. However, men and women were not shown separately in the data. Havlik et al. [66] reported the negative relationships of cigarette smoking to SBP and DBP. However, in their study, only standardized regression coefficients for the multivariate regression analyses were presented, the mean values were not presented, and young and middle-aged women were not shown separately in the data. Ribeiro [67] examined the joint effects of biological and social dimensions on BP by means of identifying an internally homogenous subgroup of subjects and reported that lean and young smokers had significantly lower DBP than the lean and young nonsmokers. Green et al. [11] reported both SBP and DBP were significantly lower in smokers than in nonsmokers in the older women, but not in the younger women. In a recent study [49] using women aged 20-39 years, we reported that the light and moderate smokers had significantly lower mean SBP, and all smokers had significantly lower mean DBP than nonsmokers. Our previous study as well as the study by Green et al. [11], examined dose-dependent relationships, but such relationships were not observed. In contrast, in the present study using collegiate women, SBP and DBP showed dose-dependent relationships.

In the present study, subjects who smoked 2-12 and 13-20 cigarettes/day had significantly lower mean SBP (5.5 and 9.2 mmHg) and DBP (6.3 and 8.5 mmHg) than nonsmokers, respectively. Although it has been suggested that a 2 mmHg reduction in DBP would result in a 17% decrease in the prevalence of hypertension as well as a 6% decrease in reduction in the risk of coronary heart disease [68], these results need to be cautiously approached because, as noted by Gofin et al. [15], it does not offset the substantial increase in coronary risk associated with smoking.

It has been reported that smoking acutely increase blood pressure [69]. However, the mechanisms by which chronic cigarette smoking decreases blood pressure are unclear. Three explanations have been proposed: 1) the alleviation of stress by cigarette smoking may contribute to the lowering of blood pressure [12]; 2) regular smokers who do not smoke before and during their examination may experience a downward rebound of blood pressure due to the short-term absence of a nicotine stimulus [66]; and 3) there may be substances in cigarette smoke, other than nicotine, which have hypotensive action [17].

In conclusion, the smokers had significantly lower mean HDL-C, HDL_2-C, TC, SBP and DBP than nonsmokers. Furthermore, when the subjects were divided into 3 groups by smoking habits, HDL-C, HDL_2-C, SBP and DBP showed dose-dependent relationships. These results suggest that the known associations in older adults of cigarette smoking with HDL-C subfractions and blood pressure are already apparent in young women.

References

[1] Friedman, G. D., Dales, L. G. & Ury, H. K. (1979). Mortality in middle-aged smokers and nonsmokers. *N Eng J Med*, 300:213-217.

[2] Gordon, T., Castelli, W. P., Hjortland, M. C., Kannel, W. B. & Dawber, T. R. (1977). High density lipoprotein as a protective factor against coronary heart disease. *Am J Med*, **62**:707-714.

[3] Craig, W. Y., Palomaki, G. E. & Haddow, J. E. (1989). Cigarette smoking and serum lipid and lipoprotein concentrations: an analysis of published data. *Br Med J*, **298**: 784-788.

[4] Moriguchi, E. H., Fusegawa, Y., Tamachi, H. & Goto, Y. (1990). Effects of smoking on HDL subfractions in myocardial infarction patients: effects on lecithin-cholesterol acyltransferase and hepatic lipase. *Clin Chim Acta*, **195**:139-144.

[5] Freeman, D. J., Griffin, B. A., Murray, E., Lindsay, G. M., Gaffeney, D., Packard, C. J. & Shepherd, J. (1993). Smoking and plasma lipoproteins in man: effects on low density lipoprotein cholesterol levels and high density lipoprotein subfraction distribution. *Eur J Clin Invest,* **23**:630-640.

[6] Shennan, N. M., Seed, M. & Wynn, V. (1985). Variation in serum lipid and lipoprotein levels associated with changes in smoking behaviour in non-obese Caucasian males. *Atherosclerosis*, **58**:17-25.

[7] Haffner, S. M., Applebaum-Bowden, D. & Wahl, P. W. (1985). Epidemiological correlates of high density lipoprotein subfractions, apolipoproteins A-I, A-II, and D, and lecithin cholesterol acyltransferase: effects of smoking, alcohol, and adiposity. *Arteriosclerosis*, **5**:169-177.

[8]   Ito, T., Nishiwaki, M., Ishikawa, T. & Nakamura, H. (1995). CETP and LCAT activities are unrelated to smoking and moderate alcohol consumption in healthy normolipidemic men. *Jpn Circ J*, **59**:541-546.

[9]   Voors, A. W., Srinivasan, S. R., Hunter, S. M., Webber, L. S., Sklov, M. C. & Berenson, G. S. (1982). Smoking, oral contraceptives, and serum lipid and lipoprotein levels in youth. *Preventive Med*, **11**:1-12.

[10] Imamura, H., Teshima, K., Miyamoto, N. & Shirota, T. (2002). Cigarette smoking, high-density lipoprotein cholesterol subfractions, and lecithin:cholesterol acyltransferase in young women. *Metabolism*, **51**:1313-1316.

[11] Green, M. S., Jucha, E. & Luz, Y. (1986). Blood pressure in smokers and nonsmokers: Epidemiologic findings. *Am Heart J*, **111**: 932-940.

[12] Handa, K., Tanaka, H., Shindo, M., Kono, S., Sasaki, J. & Arakawa, K. (1990). Relationship of cigarette smoking to blood pressure and serum lipids. *Atherosclerosis*, **84**:189-193.

[13] Berglund, G. & Wilhelmsen, L. (1975). Factors related to blood pressure in a general population sample of Swedish men. *Acta Med Scand*, **198**: 291-298.

[14] Goldbourt, U. & Medalie, J. H. (1977). Characteristics of smokers, non-smokers and ex-smokers among 10,000 adult males in Israel. II. Physiologic, biochemical and genetic characteristics. *Am J Epidemiol*, **105**: 75-86.

[15] Gofin, R., Kark, J. D. & Friedlander, Y. (1982). Cigarette smoking, blood pressure and pulse rate in the Jerusalem lipid research clinic prevalence study. *Isr J Med Sci*, **18**: 1217-1222.

[16] Brischetto, C. S., Connor, W. E., Connor, S. L. & Matarazzo, J. D. (1983). Plasma lipid and lipoprotein profiles of cigarette smokers from randomly selected families: Enhancement of hyperlipidemia and depression of high-density lipoprotein. *Am J Cardiol*, **52**: 675-680.

[17] Savdie, E., Grosslight, G. M. & Adena, M. A. (1984). Relation of alcohol and cigarette consumption to blood pressure and serum creatinine levels. *J Chron Dis*, **37**: 617-23.

[18] Jenkins, C. D., Zyzanski, S. J. & Rosenman, R. H. (1973). Biological, psychological, and social characteristics of men with different smoking habits. *Health Serv Rep*, **88**: 834-43.

[19] Hirota, T., Nara, M., Ohguri, M., Manago, E. & Hirota, K. (1992). Effect of diet and lifestyle on bone mass in Asian young women. *Am J Clin Nutr*, **55**:1168-73.

[20] The Ministry of Health and Welfare (Ed.) (1998). Present intake of nutrients in Japanese. Tokyo: Daiichi Press. (in Japanese).

[21] Lyons Wall, P. M., Choudhury, N., Gerbrandy, E. A. & Truswell, A. S. (1994). Increase of high-density lipoprotein cholesterol at ovulation in healthy women. *Atherosclerosis*, **105**:171-178.

[22] Young, D. R. & Steinhardt, M. A. (1993). The importance of physical fitness versus physical activity for coronary artery disease risk factors: a cross-sectional analysis. *Res Q Exerc Sport* **64**:377-384.

[23] Imamura, H., Katagiri, S., Uchida, K., Miyamoto, N., Nakano, H. & Shirota, T. (2000). Acute effects of moderate exercise on serum lipids, lipoproteins, and apolipoproteins in sedentary young women. *Clin Exp Pharm Physiol*, **27**:975-979.

[24] The Resources Council of the Science and Technology Agency (Ed.) (1987). The 4th Revised Edition of Tables of Japanese Foodstuff Composition, Tokyo: Ishiyaku Press (in Japanese).

[25] Richmond, W. (1973). Preparation and properties of a cholesterol oxidase from nocardia sp. and its application to the enzymatic assay of total cholesterol in serum. *Clin Chem*, **19**:1350-6.

[26] Spayd, R. W., Bruschi, B., Burdick, B. A., Dappen, G. M., Eikenberry, J. N., Esders, W., Figueras, J., Goodhue, C. T., LaRossa, D. D., Nelson, R. W., Rand, R. N. & Wu, T.-W. (1978). Multilayer film elements for clinical analysis: applications to representative chemical determinations. *Clin Chem*, **24**:1343-1350.

[27] Fukui, I. (1981). Determination methods and clinical significance of HDL-cholesterol. *Jpn J Clin Pathol*, **29**:1071-1078 (in Japanese).

[28] Hata, Y., Ueno, T. & Ogishima, K. (1983). Fractionation of serum lipoproteins into VLDL, LDL, HDL, HDL_2 and HDL_3 by one-step ultracentrifugation using Beckman Lp-42 Ti Rotor. *Jpn J Clin Pathol*, **31**:634-640 (in Japanese).

[29] Wieland, H. & Seidel, D. (1983). A simple specific method for precipitation of low density lipoproteins. *J Lipid Res*, **24**:904-909.

[30] Imamura, H., Tanaka, K., Hirae, C., Futagami, T., Yoshimura, Y., Uchida, K., Tanaka, A. & Kobata, D. (1996). Relationship of cigarette smoking to blood pressure and serum lipids and lipoproteins in men. *Clin Exp Pharm Physiol*, **23**: 397-402.

[31] Wood, P. D. & Haskell, W. L. (1979). The effect of exercise on plasma high density lipoproteins. *Lipids*, **14**:417-427.

[32] Nishimura, C., Imamura, H., Komatsu, Y., Tanaka, K., Hirae, C., Futagami, T., Yoshimura, Y. & Shirota, T. (1995). Physical fitness, blood properties, and nutritional intake of female college soccer players. *J Exercise Sports Physiol*, **2**:159-166 (in Japanese).

[33] Suter, E. & Hawes, M. R. (1993). Relationship of physical activity, body fat, diet, and blood lipid profile in youths. *Med Sci Sports Exerc*, **25**:748-754.

[34] Yao, M., Lichtenstein, A. H., Roberts, S. B., Ma, G., Gao, S., Tucker, K. L. & McCrory, M. A. (2003). Relative influence of diet and physical activity on cardiovascular risk factors in urban Chinese adults. *Int J Obe*, **27**:920-932.

[35] Forrest, K. Y.-Z., Bunker, C. H., Kriska, A. M., Ukoli, F. A. M., Huston, S. L. & Markovic, N. (2001). Physical activity and cardiovascular risk factors in a developing population. *Med Sci Sports Exerc*, **33**:1598-1604.

[36] Moreau, K. L., Degarmo, R., Langley, J., McMahon, C., Howley, E. T., Bassett, D. R. & Thompson, D. L. (2001). Increasing daily walking lowers blood pressure in postmenopausal women. *Med Sci Sports Exerc*, **33**:1825-1831.

[37] Kang, H.-S., Gutin, B., Barbeau, P., Owens, S., Lemmon, C. R., Allison, J., Litaker, M. S. & Le, N.-A. (2002). Physical training improves insulin resistance syndrome markers in obese adolescents. *Med Sci Sports Exerc*, **34**:1920-1927.

[38] Koga, M., Ideishi, M., Matsusaki, M., Tashiro, E., Kinoshita, A., Ikeda, M., Tanaka, H., Shindo, M. & Arakawa, K. (1992). Mild exercise decreases plasma endogenous digitalislike substance in hypertensive individuals. *Hypertension* [suppl II]: II-231-II-236.

[39] Tashiro, E., Miura, S., Koga, M., Sasaguri, M., Ideishi, M., Ikeda, M., Tanaka, H., Shindo, M. & Arakawa, K. (1993). Crossover comparison between the depressor effects

of low and high work-rate exercise in mild hupertension. *Clin. Exp. Pharm. Physiol.* **20**:689-696.

[40] Urata, H., Tanabe, Y., Kiyonaga, A., Ikeda, M., Tanaka, H., Shindo, M. & Arakawa, K. (1987). Antihypertensive and volume-dependent effects of mild exercise on essential hypertension. *Hypertension*, **9**:245-252.

[41] Erikssen, J. & Enger, S. C. (1978). The effect of smoking on selected coronary heart disease risk factors in middle-aged men. *Acta Med Scand*, **203**,27-30.

[42] Ortlepp, J. R., Metrikat, J., Albrecht, M., Maya-Pelzer, P., Pongratz, H. & Hoffmann, R. (2003). Relation of body mass index, physical fitness, and the cardiovascular risk profile in 3127 young normal weight men with an apparently optimal lifestyle. *Int J Obe*, **27**:979-982.

[43] Imamura, H., Matsubara, M., Minayoshi, M., Imai, M., Kunikata, K., Nakamura, S., Kobata, D. & Morii, H. (1992). A criterion for evaluation of obesity based on the relationship between percent body fat and medical examination parameters. *Jpn J Phys Fitness Sports Med* **41**:70-78 (in Japanese).

[44] Imamura, H., Matsubara, M., Minayoshi, M., Kunikata, K., Imai, M., Nakamura, S., Kobata, D. & Morii, H. (1992). A criterion for evaluation of obesity in men based on the relationship between percent body fat and medical examination parameters. *Jpn J Phys Fitness Sports Med*, **41**:322-329 (in Japanese).

[45] Dallongeville, J., Marecaux, N., Fruchart, J.-C. & Amouye, P. (1998). Cigarette smoking is associated with unhealthy patterns of nutrient intake: a meta-analysis. *J Nutr*, **128**:1450-1457.

[46] Grundy, S. M. & Denke, M. A. (1990). Dietary influences on serum lipids and lipoproteins. *J Lipid Res*, **31**:1149-1172.

[47] Djoussé, L., Arnett, D. K., Coon, H., Province, M. A., Moore, L. L. & Ellison, R. C. (2004). Fruit and vegetable consumption and LDL cholesterol: the National Heart, Lung, and Blood Institute Family Heart Study. *Am J Clin Nutr*, **79**:213-217.

[48] Miura, K., Greenland, P., Stamler, J., Liu, K., Daviglus, M. L. & Nakagawa, H. (2004). Relation of vegetable, fruit, and meat intake to 7-year blood pressure change in middle-aged men. *Am J Epidemiol*, **159**:572-580.

[49] Imamura, H., Uchida, K. & Kobata, D. (2000). Relationship of cigarette smoking with blood pressure, serum lipids and lipoproteins in young Japanese women. *Clin. Exp. Pharm. Physiol*, **27**:364-369.

[50] Gaziano, J. M., Buring, J. E., Breslow, J. L., Goldhaber, S. Z., Rosner, B., VanDenbrugh, M., Willett, W. & Hennekens, C. H. (1993). Moderate alcohol intake, increased levels of high-density lipoprotein and its subfractions, and decreased risk of myocardial infarction. *N Engl J Med*, **329**:1829-1834.

[51] Russell, M., Cooper, M. L., Frone, M. R. & Welte, J. W. (1991). Alcohol drinking patterns and blood pressure. *Am J Public Health*, **81**:452-457.

[52] Clevidence, B. A., Reichman, M. E., Judd, J. T., Muesing, R. A., Schatzkin, A., Schaefer, E. J., Li, Z., Jenner, J., Brown, C. C., Sunkin, M. S., Campbell, W. S. & Taylor, P. R. (1995). Effects of alcohol consumption on lipoproteins of premenopausal women: a controlled diet study. Arterioscler Thromb, *Vasc Biol* **15**:179-184.

[53] Bunt, J. C. (1990). Metabolic actions of estradiol: significance for acute and chronic exercise responses. *Med Sci Sports Exerc*, **22**:286-290.

[54] Azogui, G., Ben-Shlomo, I., Zohar, S., Kook, A., Presser, S. & Aviram, M. (1992). High density lipoprotein concentration is increased during the ovulatory phase of the menstrual cycle in healthy young women. *Gynecol Endocrinol*, **6**:253-257.

[55] Swank, A.M. & Fell, R.D. (1990). Effects of acute smoking and exercise on high-density lipoprotein-cholesterol and subfractions in black female smokers. *Metabolism*, **39**;343-348.

[56] Van Gent, C.M., Van Der Voort, H. & Hessel, L.W. (1978). High-density lipoprotein cholesterol, monthly variation and association with cardiovascular risk factors in 1000 forty-year-old Dutch citizens. *Clin Chim Acta*, **88**:155-62.

[57] Førde, O. H., Thelle, D. S., Arnesen, E. & Mjøs, O. D. (1986). Distribution of high density lipoprotein cholesterol according to relative body weight, cigarette smoking and leisure time physical activity. *Acta Med Scand*, **219**: 167-171.

[58] Willett, W., Hennekens, C. H., Castelli, W., Rosner, B., Evans, D., Taylor, J. & Kass, E. H. (1983). Effects of cigarette smoking on fasting triglyceride, total cholesterol, and HDL-cholesterol in women. *Am Heart J*, **105**: 417-421.

[59] Chen, H., Zhuang, H. & Han, Q. (1983). Serum high density lipoprotein cholesterol and factors influencing its level in healthy Chinese. *Atherosclerosis*, **48**: 71-79.

[60] Criqui, M. H., Wallace, R. B., Heiss, G., Mishkel, M., Schonfeld, G. & Jones, G. T. L. (1980). Cigarette smoking and plasma hight-density lipoprotein cholesterol: The lipid research clinics program prevalence study. *Circulation*, **62** (suppl IV): IV-70-IV-76.

[61] 61 McCall, M.R., van den Berg, J. J. M, Kuypers, F. A., Tribble, D. L., Krauss, R. M., Knoff, L. J. & Forte, T. M. (1994). Modification of LCAT activity and HDL structure: new links between cigarette smoke and coronary heart disease risk. *Arterioscler Thromb*, **14**:248-253.

[62] Church, D. F. & Pryor, W. A. (1985). Free-radical chemistry of cigarette smoke and its toxicological implications. *Environ Health Perspect*, **64**:111-126.

[63] Reznick, A. Z., Cross, C. E., Hu M-L, Suzuki, Y. J., Khwaja, S.,Safadi, A., Motchini, P. A., Packer, L. & Halliwell, B. (1992). Modification of plasma proteins by cigarette smoke as measured by protein carbonyl formation. *Biochem J*, **286**:607-611.

[64] Cai, H. & Harrison, D. G. (2000). Endothelial dysfunction in cardiovascular diseases: the role of oxidant stress. *Circ Res*, **87**:840-844.

[65] Franceschini, G., Maderna, P. & Sirtori, C. R. (1991). Reverse cholesterol transport: physiology and pharmacology. *Atherosclerosis*, **88**:99-107.

[66] Havlik, R. J., Garrison, R. J., Feinleib, M., Padget,t S., Castelli, P. M. & McNamara, P. M. (1980). Evidence for additional blood pressure correlates in adults 20-56 years old. *Circulation*, **61**: 710-715.

[67] Ribeiro, M. B. D. (1983). Hypertension among female workers in Sao Paulo, Brazil: Predictors and joint effects. *Hypertension*, **5** (supp V):V-144-V-148.

[68] Cook, N. R., Cohen, J., Hebert, P. R., Taylor, J. O. & Hennekens, C. H. (1995). Implications of small reductions in diastolic blood pressure for primary prevention. *Arch. Intern. Med*, **155**: 701-709.

[69] Cryer, P. E., Haymond, M. W., Santiago, J. V. & Shah, S. D. (1976). Norepinephrine and epinephrine release and adrenergic mediation of smoking-associated hemodynamic and metabolic events. *N Engl J Med*, **295**:573-577.

In: Trends in Smoking and Health Research
Editors: J. H. Owing, pp. 51-68
ISBN: 1-59454-391-7
© 2005 Nova Science Publishers, Inc.

Chapter III

Smoking During Pregnancy

Katherine Everett
Chronic Diseases of Lifestyle Unit,
Medical Research Council, South Africa

Abstract

Substantial numbers of women continue to smoke during pregnancy despite increased knowledge of the adverse health effects. Worldwide, the crude estimate of the number of women who smoked during pregnancy in 1995 was between 12-14 million. Smoking is considered the single most modifiable cause of adverse pregnancy outcomes in the US and other Western countries. Research has shown that women who have not been motivated to or able to quit on learning of their pregnancy can benefit from targeted smoking cessation interventions. Typically, such interventions can achieve a two or three-fold increase above the cessation rates achieved by women without help or in response to the basic level of advice and information typically provided as part of usual antenatal care.

Prevalence of Smoking During Pregnancy

Substantial numbers of women continue to smoke during pregnancy despite increased knowledge of the adverse health effects. Worldwide, the crude estimate of the number of women who smoked during pregnancy in 1995 was between 12-14 million [1]. Smoking is considered the single most modifiable cause of adverse pregnancy outcomes in the US and other Western countries. In the US, 19% of pregnant women smoked during pregnancy in 2000 [2]. In Australia, three studies [3] of women attending public antenatal clinics, reported 35%-38% of pregnant women continued to smoke during pregnancy and in New Zealand, approximately 25% of women smoke during pregnancy, with disproportionately higher rates for Maori and lower socio-economic groups [4]. In the UK, smoking during pregnancy remained fairly consistent in the 1990s, with 27% of pregnant women currently smoking in 1992 and 30% in 1999 [5]. Smoking prevalence among the lower income groups has been consistently about three times higher than women in higher income groups. Prevalence has remained especially high among young women from lower income groups, with 51% reporting that they currently smoked in 1999. These surveys have also shown that a minority of women quit smoking (28%), compared to the number of women who reduce their smoking (43%) and that most women who quit, tend to do so in the first trimester of pregnancy. Sweden is one country where there have been dramatic improvements in smoking rates among pregnant women. A sustained national campaign, carried out in maternity health clinics during the 1990s, succeeded in halving the number of women who smoked during pregnancy from 31% in 1983 to 12% in 2000 [6]. A survey of pregnant women in four South African cities showed that 21 % of pregnant women overall smoked, with marked differences between socio-economic and ethnic groups [7]. Little is known about the smoking rates among pregnant women in other developing countries. Such surveys are likely to underestimate the prevalence of smoking as non-disclosure of smoking during pregnancy is higher than in population surveys because of the greater social desirability of the non-smoking response.

Surveys have shown distinct differences between women who smoke during pregnancy and those who do not. Continued smoking and high daily tobacco consumption have shown strong associations with socio-economic disadvantage, high parity, being single, living in a smoking household and attending public health services [8]. The perception of risk increases with increasing education and having a partner who smokes appears to be a particularly influential factor in women continuing to smoke and in quitters relapsing postpartum [9]. Pregnant women who continue to smoke also tend to have more psychological and emotional problems than non-smokers. Depression, high levels of work stress and little perceived social support, particularly from the partner, are also associated with continued smoking [9-11]. Some women report that smoking actually helps them cope with the stresses and strains induced by the pregnancy [12]. A survey in South Africa showed that unplanned pregnancy was associated with continued smoking in pregnancy [13]. Women who are having their first baby are more likely to stop smoking, possibly because they are less sceptical of the risks than women who have smoked during previous pregnancies with no obvious negative consequence [14]. Some studies have shown a stronger intervention effect among women entering antenatal care early [15,16]. These women may be more prevention orientated, more open to cessation earlier, or simply receive more exposure to the intervention. Concern about weight gain also appears to be an important consideration for pregnant women [17].

In some cases, cultural differences appear to play a more important role than social inequality. For example, in the US, African American women and Hispanic women have a lower prevalence of smoking in pregnancy than white women [18]. Immigrants from Asia or the Middle East who settle in Northern Europe, North America or Australia retain a lower prevalence of smoking, despite relative socio-economic disadvantage [19]. In South Africa, women of mixed race have very high rates of smoking during pregnancy – 47% compared to 4% of African women, who constitute the majority and the least advantaged group [7].

Women are more likely to make an attempt to stop smoking before or during their pregnancy than at any other time of their lives, providing a unique window for health care providers to intervene. The only other groups shown to have comparable cessation rates are patients with pulmonary or cardiac diseases and subjects in intensive risk factor intervention trials [20]. About 25% - 33% of women who smoke before pregnancy, quit on their own on learning of their pregnancy [21]. This group, termed 'spontaneous quitters', tends to be of higher socio-economic and educational status, smoke less heavily, have a non-smoking partner, perceive more positive support for quitting, experience more nausea and have stronger beliefs about the risks of smoking during pregnancy than those women who continue smoking [22, 23]. They quit primarily for the health of the baby rather than for themselves. While most of these women (85%) are able to maintain abstinence throughout their pregnancy, over 70% relapse within 6 months to a year after delivery [24, 25], implying that their intentions were to suspend smoking rather than give up permanently. This points to the need to include spontaneous quitters in smoking cessation programmes for pregnant women. As a group, they are often excluded because they define themselves as not smoking. Shifting their motivation for quitting, to include both the baby and their own health and teaching coping skills may be important in preventing spontaneous quitters women from returning to smoking.

Research has shown that women who have not been motivated to or able to quit on learning of their pregnancy can benefit from targeted smoking cessation interventions. Typically, such interventions can achieve a two or three-fold increase above the cessation rates achieved by women without help or in response to the basic level of advice and information typically provided as part of usual antenatal care.

Smoking Cessation Interventions with Pregnant Women: A Review of the Evidence

Numerous randomised control trials have demonstrated that smoking cessation interventions for pregnant women can significantly improve normal cessation rates during pregnancy. Many studies have also demonstrated that such programmes can produce decreases in the incidence of low birth weight and premature birth [8, 21, 26-31].

Effectiveness has been most clearly documented for cognitive behavioural interventions[*], consisting of brief, structured, individual counselling from a trained provider and the provision of self-help quit materials [32]. Randomised control trials, rated as high quality trials, have produced quit rates on average 8-12% higher than the rates of control groups receiving usual care [8,27]. Studies have documented the behavioural impact of such best practice interventions in optimal clinical conditions (efficacy evaluations) and with large representative samples of pregnant smokers under normal practice-program conditions, (effectiveness evaluations), thus supporting internal and external validity [33]. They have also been conducted in public health care settings, where clients are predominantly of lower income, as well as among private patients in relatively more privileged circumstances. The trials involving private clients have been found to have a stronger effect than those involving public clients, producing quit rates on average ranging from 22-25% [34].

A variety of maternity care providers have been found to be effective in delivering smoking cessation programmes for pregnant women, including doctors, nurses, midwives and health education specialists [21,28]. The most efficacious type of counsellor may vary from

---

[*] This category generally involves individualised counselling and the provision of information and self help materials, which assist the smoker in making practical plans to quit, reviewing past experiences, identifying potential problems and enlisting support from family and friends. It typically also includes the teaching of coping and problem solving skills. Most programmes that have been tested have been eclectic, involving many different components. This kind of support is provided to those smokers who are willing to make a quit attempt and would like help in doing so.

setting to setting and by socio-cultural environment. Midwives and nurses are seen as a particularly appropriate group as they usually spend more time with patients and see health education as an important aspect of their work. Surveys have shown that nurses and midwives generally have more positive attitudes than medical staff towards smoking cessation. Compared with midwives, antenatal medical staff tend to give a lower priority to smoking cessation and believe that they have inadequate skills in the area [35,36].

The success of home visits by nurses in improving a number of health behaviours has been documented [37], suggesting that they may be helpful. In a controlled trial, Old and colleagues demonstrated significant, biochemically validated reductions in smoking among women receiving home visits by a nurse compared to controls [38]. However, such interventions are more costly than brief, clinic-based interventions and are therefore less frequently implemented and studied. Addressing the teaching and learning needs of staff and including them in the development of interventions has shown to be key to their acceptance and sustainability within primary maternity care[39].

There have been very few studies on the use of peer counsellors in smoking cessation programmes for pregnant women, even though they have been used to positive effect in other aspects of prenatal care, such as the promotion of breastfeeding. One intervention, which used peer educators, failed to enhance quit rates even though it was a replication of an intervention that had proved efficacious in other trials [40]. The author's argued that one plausible reason for the failure of their trial could have been because they used peer educators rather than professional counsellors, as was the case in the other interventions. However, another study [41], found that peer counselling significantly reduced daily smoking and increased infant birthweight, despite its failure to effect cession, suggesting that peer counselling intervention programmes may be worthwhile. The key advantage of using peer counsellors in health education is that they have the ability to disseminate information in a way that is easily understood by their peers. In addition, because women can identify more closely with them, they have the potential for positive role modelling and increasing perceived social support.

Peer group cessation programmes for pregnant women have been very poorly attended in virtually all trials where they were planned and are therefore not recommended [8, 42]. As yet, there is insufficient evidence to draw any conclusions as to whether the use of interactive software or feedback based on ultrasound and other biochemical measures are particularly useful or not [27, 43]. It seems that only a small minority of women take up offers of referral to specialist support, but there is evidence that it can be effective [29].

While risk information alone has the potential to increase cessation, the addition of intervention components, which teach cessation skills, significantly increase quit rates [44]. Numerous self-help quit materials including guides, booklets and videos have been tested and shown to work with pregnant women from various demographic groups. It is clear that these materials need to be tailored specifically to pregnancy, as where general smoking cessation materials have been used they have failed [16, 28, 32]. It has also been demonstrated there is a greater acceptance and use of intervention methods if materials are further tailored to the concerns and barriers to behavioural change of the specific target group [21]. For example, Lowe et al 1998, found that a self help manual, which had proven to be effective in a number of settings in the US, was poorly accepted by pregnant women in Brisbane in Australia [45].

Importantly, education materials appear to be effective when used as an adjunct to personal advice given by a health care provider and are seldom effective on their own [46]. Moore at al (2002), for example, suggest that their self-help intervention, consisting of a series of 5 booklets mailed to pregnant women at various intervals, failed because of a lack of verbal reinforcement [47]. In a study by Pullon et al (2003) [39], women commented that they responded to an educational resource only when a midwife introduced it to them during the course of an antenatal visit.

More resource intensive behavioural interventions, which have used brief counselling at first prenatal visit, followed by additional support either by telephone, post or further personal contact have been found to yield larger benefits in some studies [26, 28, 29, 48, 49] but not in others [30, 50]. For instance, Ershoff et al (1999) [51], found that neither a computerised telephone cessation programme, nor the provision of motivational counselling by nurse educators improved cessation rates over a tailored self help book delivered within the context of advice from prenatal care providers. And Windsor et al 1993 [52] found that the additions of a chart reminder, medical letter and social support methods did not increase quit rates in their study.

Some researchers have advocated Motivational Interviewing (MI) as a means of improving consultations about smoking cessation in pregnancy [26, 51, 53-55]. MI is a patient-centred counselling method tailored to women's stage of readiness to change, which has emerged as an alternative to direct persuasion in counselling people with addictive problems. When using this approach, health care providers provide an open and non-threatening context for discussion of stigmatised behaviours and focus on helping clients explore and resolve their feelings of ambivalence about behavioural change [55]. Motivational interviewing has been used to positive effect by midwives in Sweden as one component of their nationwide smoking cessation programme for pregnant women [56] and a recent study in the US, demonstrated the effectiveness of an intervention which used usual care providers to deliver a low intensity intervention based on MI principles [57]. The intervention was significantly associated with both sustained quitting during pregnancy and with long term smoking abstinence. In another study [49], a 15 minute, follow up phone call based on MI principles, was found to be a useful adjunct to a basic intervention. However, in a pilot study in Glasgow, four MI sessions, delivered by a trained midwife at the woman's home, failed to have any positive impact on smoking behaviour, prompting the researchers to argue for definitive randomised control trials to prove whether proactive, opportunistic MI can effectively help pregnant women stop smoking or not [53]. While it was not found to be the case in these interventions, other researchers have reported that the main obstacle to using MI in the context of the primary care consultation is the amount of time it requires [54, 55].

Development of Evaluation Research among Pregnant Women

Several reviews and meta-evaluations have made important contributions to advancing the methodological rigour of smoking cessation evaluation research among pregnant women. These include the two meta-evaluations published by Windsor and Orleans in 1986 [58] and Windsor, Boyd and Orleans in 1998 [21] and the following reviews: Walsh and Redman 1993 [27], Floyd et al 1993 [26], Walsh et al 2001 [32], Dolan-Mullen et al in 1994 [28], the Cochrane review by Lumley et al in 2004 [8] and Windsor 2000 [59] and 2003 [33]. These papers provide a complete assessment of this area of evaluation research to date and show a positive trend in methodological standards over time.

Poor measurement of smoking status was a major methodological weakness in much of the research conducted in the 1980s and early 1990s. While population surveys of smoking status among adults may produce valid self reports, societal pressure for pregnant women not to smoke has been found to strongly influence self reports of smoking status during pregnancy in both experimental and control groups. Three studies which have assessed deception rates, reported them to be 24% [59], 30% [52] and as high as 50% [60]. For this reason, biochemical validation of smoking status is now an essential requirement for establishing the internal validity of evaluation trials of smoking cessation programmes for pregnant women. All self-reports should be confirmed biochemically at baseline, mid and end of pregnancy and it has been recommended that studies assess the levels of non-disclosure. Several biochemical measures have been used, including expired air carbon monoxide and tests for cotinine in urine and saliva. Cotinine, a metabolic by product of nicotine, has greater specificity and sensitivity than CO and is thus used more widely. The most practical way to measure cotinine during pregnancy is to test the urine samples that are routinely taken at every antenatal care visit. Studies not using biochemical corroboration of self reports should be assumed to reflect substantial non-disclosure and a deception rate of at least 25% should be used to adjust self- report data. Patients lost to follow up and patients for whom no biochemical tests are available should be classified as smokers. Multiple early studies produced inflated quit rates because they failed to include patients lost to follow up in their denominator to calculate end of pregnancy quit rates. A full description of patients who drop out or refuse to participate are important for assessing selection bias and generalisability.

Rates of disclosure among self reported smokers can be improved by using questions which allow a greater range of responses. Mullen et al showed that the use of a multiple choice question improved disclosure at the first antenatal visit by 40% above the simple question: "Do you smoke: Yes or No" [61].

Reviews [21, 26, 27] have also pointed to the need to conduct more "effectiveness evaluations", which rely on usual care providers to deliver programmes in the context of routine antenatal care. Earlier studies tended to use designated providers whose specific job was to deliver the intervention. There are now several studies that have documented the success of minimal smoking cessation interventions using existing providers in normal practice conditions. One of the most important being the Smoking for Cessation or Reduction in Pregnancy Trial (SCRIPT) by Windsor et al 2000 [59], which documented the feasibility and effectiveness of an intervention disseminated to Medicaid recipients in 10 maternity clinics in Alabama, USA. They reported a cotinine validated quit rate of 17.3% in the experimental group and 8.8% in the control group. However, such studies often encounter difficulties, such as recruitment of women [62], provider compliance problems and contamination of controls [63] incomplete documentation of implementation and uneven exposure of women to the intervention [60], system barriers to implementing the intervention [64], high rates of loss to follow up [40] and selection bias [65].

A general lack of process evaluation data in reported randomised control trials was pointed out by Walsh and Redman in 1993 [27], Windsor, Boyd and Orleans in 1998 and more recently reiterated by Lumley, Oliver and Waters in 2004 [8]. This becomes even more important as research in this area moves beyond efficacy trials to effectiveness trials. They emphasised the importance of documenting the levels of provider compliance and patient exposure to the various intervention components, as well as the personal experiences and perceptions of acceptability of both staff and women who participate in such programmes. They also argued for more detailed descriptions of the nature of interventions and usual care. Such information is essential in reaching conclusions about behavioural impact and internal validity and is helpful to future researchers who may wish to replicate successful interventions in other settings. Research methods such as provider completed checklists, exit interviews with patients, focus groups and direct observation of the quality of interaction between patient and provider by using video or audiotape are all appropriate in evaluating the process of interventions. Multiple methods are recommended as each method has its own limitations: health care providers tend to overstate their level of preventive care, smokers over report receiving smoking advice and direct observation is intrusive and may produce a degree of reactivity [63].

Recently, the relative lack of research documenting women's views, concerns and experiences of smoking cessation interventions has been raised as an issue. Interventions have also been criticised for rarely involving or consulting women in the development of programmes and for not taking into account the possible negative effects of smoking cessation interventions may have on pregnant women's psychological well being [66]. Of particular concern is that women who continue to smoke, especially those with high risk pregnancies, may experience increased guilt and anxiety, which could possibly have a detrimental effect on their relationships with their partners and antenatal care providers. One study, which did examine this issue, found that almost three quarters of experimental respondents agreed that the antismoking advice they had received had made them feel guilty. However, a greater proportion of these women reported that, nonetheless, they were pleased to receive this advice [63].

Best Practice Smoking Cessation Interventions for Pregnant Women

An important consensus on best practice interventions for pregnant women was reached at a workshop convened by the Health Resources and Services Administration and Centres for Disease Control in 1998 [67]. The workshop recommended that all prenatal health care providers adopt the evidence based procedures for brief smoking cessation interventions as outlined in the Agency for Health Care Policy and Research's (AHCPR) clinical guideline (which has since been updated and published as a US Public Health Service Report, entitled "Treating Tobacco Use and Dependence") [68]. The guideline provides specific recommendations for providing brief, tobacco cessation interventions in the clinical context based on a rigorous review of empirical smoking cessation research. It suggests that even those clinicians who face severe time constraints can effectively implement tobacco cessation strategies. Whilst intensive interventions are more successful, there is substantial evidence that structured interventions as brief as 3 minutes can still significantly increase cessation rates. It also recommends that health care systems should make institutional changes to ensure the systematic identification of and intervention with smokers.

The review conducted for the workshop confirmed that these guidelines are effective with pregnant women and that when delivered by a trained provider with the provision of self help materials tailored specifically for pregnancy, they can achieve significantly higher quit rates than those achieved with usual care. A single counselling session of 5-15 minutes, using the guideline procedures, was found to achieve a modest but clinically significant effect on cessation rates across 16 evaluation studies, with an average risk ratio of 1.7 and a 95% confidence interval of 1.3 to 2.2), suggesting a 70% improvement in cessation and that the outcome of cessation was at least 30% higher in the treated versus the untreated groups [69]. It appeared that this brief, structured intervention was as effective with ethnic minority women as with white women, but that almost all the benefits of brief counselling occurred in light to moderate smokers. In their review, Melvin et al (2000) [30] conclude that these guidelines are appropriate to use with pregnant women during routine prenatal visits and feasible to implement in most clinic settings without inhibiting other important aspects of prenatal care or disrupting patient flow.

The American College of Obstetricians and Gynaecologists has since adapted and promoted these guidelines for use with pregnant women who smoke [70]. It is suggested that physicians, general practitioners, midwives, nurses, nutritionists, social workers and lay health educators, after appropriate training, can perform all 5 steps (the 5As) outlined in the Guideline with pregnant women who smoke. Alternatively, doctors may provide *ask-advise-assess* and then refer the women to a midwife or nurse for steps *assist and arrange*.

As in the original guideline, the key intervention strategies for pregnant women are based on the following 5 steps: Ask, Advise, Assess, Assist and Arrange [70]. Each step is designed to take about 1 minute of the clinician's time, except for Step 4, which is estimated to take 3 minutes or more. The recommended steps are outlined below:

Step 1) A*sk* about, and document smoking status on the clinic record. If the woman stopped smoking before or as she found out she was pregnant, the clinician is advised to congratulate her on her decision to quit, review the benefits of quitting and encourage her to stay quit. If the woman is still smoking, clinicians are advised to proceed with the following steps.

Step 2) *Advise* the patient to quit in a clear, strong, personalised manner. For pregnant women, this should include discussion of the multiple risks of smoking to the pregnancy, fetus and infant and the benefits of quitting for both the woman and the baby. Advice should be tailored to the woman's existing level of knowledge.

Step 3) A*ssess* the willingness of the women to quit within the next 30 days. If the woman is ready to make a quit attempt, the provider can proceed to the next step. If not, it is suggested that the patient be given information to build motivation and confidence in making a quit attempt in the future and that the situation be reassessed during subsequent visits.

Step 4) A*ssist* the patient in preparing to quit by offering practical counselling on quit strategies, prompting the smoker to seek social support from partners, family and friends and providing pregnancy specific self-help materials, such as booklets or videos. Such resources can save precious counselling time, can teach patients problem solving and coping skills related to cessation and can help them prepare a personal plan for quitting. It is recommended that women are encouraged to set a definite quit date, as this will make it more likely that they will make a serious quit attempt.

Step 5) A*rrange* for a follow up contact, during which smoking status is reassessed and ongoing support is offered.

Smoking Cessation Intervention for Pregnant Patients
ASK – 1 minute
Ask the patient to choose the statement that best describes her smoking status:
A.   I have NEVER smoked or have smoked LESS THAN 100 cigarettes in my lifetime.   †
B.   I stopped smoking BEFORE I found out I was pregnant, and I am not smoking now.   †
C.   I stopped smoking AFTER I found out I was pregnant, and I am not smoking now.   †
D.   I smoke some now, but I have cut down on the number of cigarettes I smoke SINCE I found out I was pregnant.   †
E.   I smoke regularly now, about the same as BEFORE I found out I was pregnant.   †
If the patient stopped smoking before or after she found out she was pregnant (B or C), reinforce her decision to quit, congratulate her on success in quitting, and encourage her to stay smoke free throughout pregnancy and postpartum.
If the patient is still smoking (D or E), document smoking status in her medical record, and proceed to Advise, Assess, Assist, and Arrange.
ADVISE – 1 minute
Provide clear, strong advice to quit with personalized messages about the benefits of quitting and the impact of smoking and quitting on the woman and fetus.   †
ASSESS – 1 minute
Assess the willingness of the patient to attempt to quit within 30 days.   †
If the patient is ready to quit, proceed to Assist.
If the patient is not ready, provide information to motivate the patient to quit and proceed to Arrange.
ASSIST – 3 minutes +
Suggest and encourage the use of problem-solving methods and skills for smoking cessation (e.g. identify "trigger" situations).   †
Provide social support as part of the treatment (e.g. "we can help you quit").   †
Arrange social support in the smoker's environment (e.g. identify "quit buddy" and smoke-free space).   †
Provide pregnancy-specific, self-help smoking cessation materials.   †
ARRANGE – 1 minute +
Assess smoking status at subsequent prenatal visits and, if patient continues to smoke, encourage cessation.
Data from Melvin C, Dolan Mullen P, Windsor RA, Whiteside HP, Goldenberg RL. Recommended cessation counselling for pregnant women who smoke: a review of the evidence. Tobacco Control 2000; 9: 1-5.

Figure 1. Counselling procedures for pregnant smokers recommended by American College of Obstetricians and Gynaecologists

It is emphasised that such motivational interventions are most likely to be successful when the clinician is empathetic, promotes patient autonomy and choice, avoids pressurising or judging the woman in any negative way and supports patient self-efficacy, for example, by identifying previous successes in efforts to change behaviour. Clinicians also need to be sensitive to concerns women may have about quitting.

Practitioners are urged to continue to encourage women to quit smoking throughout their pregnancy. Although quitting early in pregnancy yields the greatest benefits, quitting at any point can be beneficial. Some studies have suggested that smoking in the third trimester is particularly detrimental [71]. It is therefore recommended that smoking status be monitored throughout pregnancy, providing opportunities health care providers to support success, reinforce steps taken towards quitting and continue to motivate those still in the pre- and contemplation phase of behavioural change.

The Guideline indicates that the type of behavioural counselling described above may not be sufficient for pregnant women who are heavy smokers. Only about 4% of patients who smoke more than 20 cigarettes a day typically quit with these methods, compared to 16% of light smokers and 12% of moderate smokers [33]. Clinicians are advised to refer heavy smokers for more intensive counselling if brief counselling proves ineffective. If this fails, it is suggested that the use of NRT be judiciously evaluated with patient.

Table 1 represents a synopsis of the behavioural impact of 8 evaluation studies representing "best practice" methods derived from the US Public Service Clinical Practice guideline. The average effect size was 7.7% (cotinine confirmed) and the effect size range was 4.0 % to 15.7%.

These best practice methods have been derived from and evaluated in North America, Europe and Australia. There is pressing need to adapt and evaluate these methods in other settings, particularly in developing countries in South America, Africa and Asia.

Table 1. Behavioural impact of smoking cessation methods representing the Guideline [33]

Evaluation Study	Measure	E Group		C Group		Effect Size (E-C)
		N	%	N	%	
Windsor, et al – 2000 *	S-COT	139	17.3+	126	8.8	+8.5
Gebauer, et al – 1998 *	S-COT	84	15.5	94	0.0	+15.5
Hartmann, et al – 1996 *	CO	107	20.0	100	10.0	+10.0
Valbo, et al (Nor) – 1996	CO	107	27.0	105	11.4	+15.7
Windsor, et al – 1993 *	S-COT	400	14.2	414	8.4	+5.8
O'Connor, et al (Can) – 1992	U-COT	90	13.3	84	6.0	+7.3
H Jalmarson, et al (Swe) – 1991	SCN	444	12.6	209	8.6	+4.0
Windsor, et al – 1985 *	SCN	102	13.7	104	1.9	+11.8
U.S. Studies * Total			15.4		6.9	+8.5
Non U.S. Studies Total			15.0		-8.8	+6.2
Total			15.2		7.5	+7.7

Effect Size Range = 4.0% to 15.7% + = Multiple systems changes –reduced rate

Use of Nicotine Replacement Therapy with Pregnant Smokers

In the general population of smokers, nicotine replacement therapy, used as an adjunct to counselling has been shown to increase cessation rates [68]. However, to date there have been too few studies on the use of pharmocotherapies, such as nicotine replacement therapy (NRT) or bupropion, in pregnant women to clearly establish their safety and efficacy during pregnancy. Furthermore, guidelines for doses with pregnant smokers are lacking in the medical and pharmacokinetic literature [72].

There are some studies that have suggested that the benefits of NRT in helping pregnant women quit outweigh the risks of continuing to smoke. A 1991 study by Wright et al [73], found that the daily dose of nicotine and peak blood levels of nicotine in women using NRT gum or a patch were lower than those of smokers who continued to smoke a pack a day. On this basis, plus the fact that quitting would eliminate fetal exposure to carbon monoxide and the other 4000 toxic substances in cigarettes, the authors concluded that NRT would be less harmful for smokers who smoke more than twenty cigarettes a day [74]. Two other, small studies on the use of NRT during pregnancy found no adverse effects on the mother or fetus compared to smokers [73,75]. A recent trial of NRT in pregnancy reported no difference between the quit rates of the intervention and placebo control groups, but found the mean birthweight difference was 186grams higher in the NRT group [76].

On the basis of current, limited evidence it is recommended that the use of pharmocotherapies only be considered when a 'best practice' intervention has failed, if the woman is highly motivated to quit and smokes more than 10 cigarettes a day.

Harm Reduction

Although less than the ideal outcome, significant reduction in the number of cigarettes smoked has been shown to produce small, but meaningful health gains for pregnant women and their newborns [77].

A significant reduction in smoking, especially among heavier smokers, has been found to be a valid measure of the behavioural impact of interventions in a number of evaluation studies [59, 78, 79] and appears to offer some measure of protection for the fetus [79]. However, the value of harm reduction approaches is still under debate. An early study by Hebel et al in 1988 [80], found that the benefits of decreased smoking for the outcome measure of birthweight were almost entirely limited to those women who had quit completely during pregnancy. However, Windsor et al (1999) [78] have recently recommended biochemical measurements as indicators of harm reduction in pregnant smokers, on the basis of their finding of a 92g increase in mean birthweight for babies of women who showed a reduction of 50% or more in the baseline saliva cotinine levels established at trial entry. In an Australian trial [65], whilst researchers did not find any significant effect on quit rates, they did find that babies born to women in the intervention group were on average 84g heavier than those in the control group, suggesting that reduced tobacco consumption during pregnancy can have a beneficial effect. In several other studies, it was clear that smoking reduction took place to a greater extent in the intervention group, with a positive effect on birthweight [8]. In the most recent Cochrane review [8], it was suggested that harm minimisation, as well as quitting, be given due attention in smoking cessation programmes and that new measures of reliably measuring levels of daily tobacco consumption need to be developed. For those women who continue to smoke in the last trimester, it may be worthwhile to encourage them to stop or reduce consumption just prior to delivery and to increase other health protection behaviours like vitamins and exercise [81].

Postpartum Relapse

Although women are more likely to quit smoking during pregnancy, both spontaneously and with assistance, than at any other time, many unfortunately, relapse during pregnancy or post partum. This is especially true with public health populations [21]. The return to smoking appears to be related to stress, lack of sleep, concerns about weight gain and the ability to protect the baby from environmental tobacco smoke [81]. Few interventions have focused on this critical transition period. A recent trial, with the goal of reducing relapse after delivery, mailed videos and newsletters to women and their partners during the final weeks of the pregnancy and the first 6 weeks after birth. Results showed significantly greater abstinence in the intervention group over the entire follow up period and at 12 months after delivery (55% v 45%), supporting the notion that it is possible to reduce postpartum relapse among some women [82].

Greater attention needs to be given to assisting women to continue to abstain from smoking after delivery. Importantly, smoking cessation programmes need to include spontaneous quitters as a target group. Shifting the focus of their motivation to protecting their own health, as well as the baby's and broadening the focus to include the woman's partner and family may be helpful strategies. A women's partner appears to play a critical role in both continued smoking in pregnancy and postpartum relapse [81]. It has been recommended that future trials in this area need a relapse prevention component and need to conduct follow up research during the at least the first 3 to 6 months of the post partum period. Preventing relapse after delivery has the additional benefit of protecting the infant from environmental tobacco smoke, which has been linked to SIDS, respiratory infections, reduced lung function and otitis media [83]. It also has the potential to encourage and extend the duration of breastfeeding. Studies have consistently shown that women who smoke are less likely to start breastfeeding than nonsmokers and tend to wean their infants earlier [84]. Relapse prevention methods may be at least as cost effective as attempts to increase quit rates of smokers[21].

Conclusion

The scientific basis for smoking cessation during pregnancy is definitive. If implemented widely, best practice interventions have the potential to achieve important reductions in adverse maternal, infant and pregnancy outcomes and to reduce associated, excess health care costs. Smoking cessation interventions confer immediate health gains for both mothers and babies and given the substantial savings associated with averting pregnancy complications and low birth weight deliveries, they have also proven to be highly cost effective, with an estimated $6 saved for every dollar invested [85,86]. The accumulation of evidence in support of smoking cessation interventions for pregnant women is now sufficiently strong to warrant the highest category recommendation by the US Preventative Services Task Force (Category A). This is higher that the recommendation given to other common clinical activities such as routine screening for anaemia in pregnancy or for gestational diabetes mellitus (US Preventive Task Force 1996) [87].

There are now clear guidelines for clinicians regarding the delivery of best practice cessation interventions for pregnant women. It remains for policymakers to promote such evidence-based procedures and for clinicians to take responsibility for integrating these methods into clinical practice. Future evaluation research is needed to determine the barriers to the dissemination and adoption of best practice interventions in diverse settings. Obstacles include limited staff time, competing priorities, pessimism about the effectiveness of interventions and a lack of training, confidence and counselling skills. However, a study by Windsor and colleagues in 2000, showed encouraging results in integrating the "5A best practice" methods into diverse Medicaid care services. They attributed their success to carefully building consensus with health service staff at a policy, management and practice level, conducting patient flow analyses to determine how practices could be reorganised to incorporate the new methods without adding significant consultation time and to providing specific practice guidance and staff training. This study also demonstrated that the philosophy of providing "best clinical practice" methods is an important theme to use in persuading professional staff and primary care health educators to participate in quality improvement initiatives [33].

References

[1] Windsor, R. A. Smoking during pregnancy. In *Women and the Tobacco Epidemic, Challenges for the 21*[st] *century.* World Health Organisation. WHO/NMH/TFI/01.

[2] National Household Survey of Drug Abuse. Rockville (MD) Substance and Mental Health Services Administration, Office of Applied Studies, 1990 to 2000.

[3] Walsh, R. A., Redman, S., Brinsmead, M., & Fryer, J. L. (1997) Predictors of smoking in pregnancy and attitudes and knowledge of risk of pregnant smokers. *Drug Alcohol Rev*, **16**, 41-67.

[4] Ministry of Health. (1999) Taking the pulse: The 1996/97 New Zealand Health Survey. Ministry of Health, Wellington.

[5] Health Education Authority UK report (1999). Smoking and Pregnancy: *Survey of knowledge, attitudes and behaviour* 1992-1999. HEA.

[6] Smoke Free Children – a report.(2003). *The First Ten Years*. Published by Cancerfonden, Stockholm, Sweden.

[7] Steyn, K., Yach, D., Stander, I., & Fourie, J. (1997). Smoking in urban pregnant women in South Africa. *South African Medical Journal, 87*, 460-463.

[8] Lumley, J., Oliver, S., & Waters, E. (2004). Interventions for promoting smoking cessation during pregnancy (Cochrane Review). In *The Cochrane Library,(Issue 1).* Chichester, UK: John Wiley and Sons Ltd.

[9]   McBride, C. M., Curry, S. J., Grothaus, L. C., et al. (1998). Partner smoking status and pregnant smoker;s perceptions of support for and the likelihood of smoking cessation. *Health Psychol,* **17,** 63-69.

[10] Dejin-Karlsson, E., Hanson, B.S., Ostergren, P., Ranstam, J., Isacsson, S.O., & Sjoberg, N.O. (1996). Psychosocial resources and persistent smoking in early pregnancy – a population study of women in their first pregnancy in Sweden. *J Epidemiol Comm Health,* **50,** 33-39.

[11] Wergeland, E., Strand, K., & Bjerkedal, T. (1996). Smoking in pregnancy: a way to cope with excessive workload. *Scan J Prim Health Care,* **14,** 21-28.

[12] Van Lieshout, F., Everett, K., Steyn, K. & Petersen, Z. Interviews with pregnant women about smoking during pregnancy. *Unpublished paper.* Medical Research Council, South Africa.

[13] Petersen, Z., Steyn, K., & Everett, K. Survey of knowledge, attitudes and beliefs of coloured pregnant women. *Unpublished paper.* Medical Research Council, South Africa.

[14] Baric, L., MacArthur, C., & Sherwood, M. (1976). A study of health education aspects of smoking in pregnancy. *J Health Education,* **19** *(2),* 1-16.

[15] Mayer, J. P., Hawkins, B., & Todd, R. (1990). A randomised evaluation of smoking cessation interventions for pregnant women at a WIC clinic. *Am J Public Health,* **80** *(1),* 76-78.

[16] Windsor, R., Cutter, G., Morris, J., Reese, Y., Manzella, V., et al. (1985). The effectiveness of smoking cessation methods for smokers in public health maternity clinics: A randomised trial. *Am J Public Health,* **75,** 1389-92.

[17] Klesges, R.C., Meyers, A.W., Klesges, L. M., et al. (1986). Smoking, body weight and their effects on smoking behaviour. A Comprehensive review of the literature. *Psych Bulletin.* **106,** 204-230.

[18] Bergen, A.W., & Caporosa, N. (1999). Cigarette smoking. *J Nat Cancer Institute,* **91,** 1365-1375.

[19] Potter, A., Lumley, J., & Watson, L. (1996). The new risk factors for SIDS: is there an association with ethnic differences and place of birth differences in incidence in Victoria? *Early Hum Development,* **45,** 119-131.

[20] Schwartz, J.L. (1987). Review and Evaluation of smoking cessation methods: The US and Canada, 1978-1985. *NIH Publication, no* 87-2940. US Dept of Health and Human Services, Public Health Services, National Institutes of Health, Bethesda, Maryland.

[21] Windsor, R.A., Boyd, N.R., & Orleans, C.T. (1998). A meta evaluation of smoking cessation intervention research among pregnant women: improving the science and the art. *Health Ed Res* Vol 13 (no. 3), 419-438.

[22] Quinn, V.P., Mullen, P.D., & Ershoff, D.H. (1991). Women who stop spontaneously prior to prenatal care and predictors of relapse before delivery. *Addictive Behaviours,* **6,** 153-160.

[23] Ryan, P., Booth, R., Coates, D., Chapman, A., & Healy, P. (1980). Experiences of pregnancy. Pregnant Pause campaign. *Health Commission of New South Wales*, Division of Drug and Alcohol Services.

[24] Fingerhut, L., Kleinman, J.,C., & Kendrick, J.S. (1990). Smoking before, during and after pregnancy. *Am J Public Health,* **80,** 541-44.

[25] Mullen, P.D., Richardson, M.A., Quinn, V.P., & Ershoff, D. H. (1997). Postpartum return to smoking: who is at risk and when. *Am J Health Promotion,* **11,** 323-330.

[26] Floyd, R., Rimer, B., Giovino, G., Mullen P., & Sullivan, S. (1993). A review of smoking in pregnancy: effect on pregnancy outcomes and cessation efforts. *Annual Review of Public Health, 14,* 379-411.

[27] Walsh, R., & Redman, S. (1993). Smoking Cessation in pregnancy: do effective programmes exist?" *Health Promotion Internationa,l Oxford University Press,* vol 8 *(*no. 2), 111-127.

[28] Dolan-Mullen, P., Ramirez, G., & Groff, J. (1994). A meta-analysis of randomised trials of prenatal smoking cessation interventions. *Am J Obstet Gynecol.* vol 171 *(*no.5), 1328-1334.

[29] Raw, M., McNeill, A., & West, R. (1998). Smoking cessation guidelines for health professionals – a guide to effective smoking cessation interventions for the health care system. *Thorax, 53 (*Supplement 5), S1-S18 Dec.

[30] Melvin, C.L,, Dolan-Mullen, P., Windsor, R. A., Whiteside, H.P., & Goldenberg, R.L. (2000). Recommended cessation counselling for pregnant women who smoke: a review of the evidence. *Tobacco Control,* 9 (Supp 3), iii80-84.

[31] Messecar, D. C. (2001). Smoking cessation interventions for pregnant women to prevent low birth weight: what does the evidence show? *J Am Acad Nurse Practice, April.* **13** (4), 171-7.

[32] Walsh. R., Lowe, J.B., & Hopkins. (2001). Quitting smoking in Pregnancy. *eMJA Clinical Practice,* **175,** 320-323. The Medical Directory of Australia.

[33] Windsor, R. A. (2003). Smoking Cessation or Reductions in Pregnancy Treatment Methods (SCRIPT): A meta- evaluation of the impact of dissemination. *Am J of Med Sciences,* **326** (4), 216-222.

[34] Ershoff, D., Mullen, P.D., & Quinn, V.P. (1989). A randomised trial of serialised self help smoking cessation programme for pregnant women in an HMO. *Am J Pub Health,* **79** (2), 182-87.

[35] Walsh, R.A., Redman, S., Brinsmead, M.W., & Arnold, B. (1995). Smoking cessation in pregnancy: a survey of medical and nursing directors of public health antenatal clinics in Australia. *Australian and New Zealand Journal of Obstetrics and Gyneacology,* **35,** 144-150.

[36] Clasper, P. & White, M. Smoking cessation interventions in pregnancy: practice and views of midwives, GPs and obstetricians. (1995). *Health Education Journal,* **54,** 150-162.

[37] American Academy of Pediatrics. (1998). The role of home-visitation programmes in improving health outcomes for children and families. *Pediatrics, 10,* 486-489.

[38] Olds, D.L., Henderson, C. R., Tatelbaum, R., et al. (1986). Improving the delivery of prenatal care and outcomes of pregnancy: a randomised trial of nurse home visitation. *Pediatrics, 77,* 16-28.

[39] Pullon, S., Mcleod, D., Benn, C., Viccars, A., White, S., Cookson, T., Dowell, A., & Green R. Smoking cessation in New Zealand: Education and resources for use by midwives for women who smoke during pregnancy. *Health Promotion International,* **18,** (4), 315-325.

[40] Gielen, A. C., Windsor, R., Faden, R. R., O'Campo, P., Repke, J., & Davis, M. (1997). Evaluation of a smoking cessation intervention for pregnant women in an urban prenatal clinic. *Health Education Research,* **12,** 247-54.

[41] Malchodi, C. S., Oncken, C., Dornelas, E. A., Caramanica, L., Gregonis, E. & Curry, S. (2003). The effect of peer counselling on smoking cessation and reduction. *Obstet Gynecol,* **101**, 504-10.

[42] West, R. (1994). Smoking cessation interventions in pregnancy: guidance to purchasers and providers. London: Heatlh Education Authority.

[43] Goldenberg, R. L., Klerman, L.V., Windsor, R. A., & Whiteside, H.P. (2000). Smoking in Pregnancy: Final thoughts. *Tobacco Control, 9* (Supp III), iii 85-86.

[44] Mayer, J.P, Hawkins, B., & Todd, R. (1990). A randomised evaluation of smoking cessation interventions for pregnant women at a WIC clinic. *Am J Public Health,* **80** (1), 76-78.

[45] Lowe, J.B., Balanda, K.P., & Clare, G. (1998). Evaluation of antenatal smoking cessation programmes for pregnant women. *Aus NZ J Public Health,***22**, 55-59.

[46] Fitzmaurice, D.A. (2001). Written information for treating minor illness. *BMJ,* **322**, 1193-4.

[47] Moore, L., Campbell, R., Whelan, A., Mills, N., Lupton, P., Misselbrook, E., & Frohlich, J. (2002). Self help smoking cessation in pregnancy: a cluster randomised control trial. *BMJ,* Vol 325, Dec, 1-6, bmj.com

[48] Kottke, T., Battista, R., DeFriese, G., & Brekke, M. (1988). Attributes of successful smoking cessation interventions in medical practice. *JAMA.,* May, vol 259 (no19), 2883-2889.

[49] Manfredi, C., Crittenden, K. S., Young, I. C., Engler, J., & Warnecke, R. (2000). The effect of a structured smoking cessation programme. Independent of exposure to existing interventions. *Am J Public Health,* May, vol 90 (no 5), 751-756.

[50] Secker Walker, R. H., Solomon, L. J., Flynn, B. S., Skelly, J. M., & Mead, P.B. (1998). Reducing smoking during pregnancy and post-partum: physician;s advice supported by individual counselling. *Prev Med.,* **27**, 422-30.

[51] Ershoff, D. H., Quinn, V. P., Boyd, N.R., Stern, J., Gregory, M., & Wirtschafter, D. (1999). The Kaiser Permanente Prenatal Smoking Cessation Trial. When more isn't better, what is enough? *Am J Prev Med.,* **17**, (3), 161-168.

[52] Windsor, R. A, Lowe, J,, Perkins, L., Smith-Yoder, D., Artz, L., Crawford, M., Amburgy, K., & Boyd, N. (1993). Health education for pregnant smokers: its behavioural impact and cost benefit. *Am J of Public Health,* **83**, (2): 201-206.

[53] Tappin, D. M., Lumsden, M. A., McIntyre, D., Mckay, C., Gilmour, W. H., Webber, R., Cowan, S., Crawford, F., & Currie, F. (2000). A pilot study to establish a randomised trial methodology to test the efficacy of a behavioural intervention. *Health Ed Res., Aug* **15** (4), 491-502.

[54] Velasquez, M., Hecht, J., Quinn, V., Emmons, K., DiClemente, C., & Dolan Mullen, P. (2000). Application of motivational interviewing to prenatal smoking cessation: training and implementation issues. *Tobacco Control, 9* (Supp III), iii 36-40.

[55] Rollnick, S., Butler, C., & Stott, N. (1997). Helping smokers make decision: the enhancement of brief intervention for medical practice. *Patient Education and Counselling,* **31**, 191-203.

[56] Cancerfonden. Smoke Free Pregnancy. Motivational interviewing – A guide for Midwives. Swedish Cancer Society. www.cancerfonden.se.

[57] Valanis, B., Lichtenstein, E., Mullooly, J. P., & Labuhn, K. (2001). Maternal smoking cessation and relapse prevention during health care visits. *Am J Prev Med.,* **20** (1), 1-8.

[58] Windsor, R. & Orleans, C. (1986). Guidelines and methodological standards for smoking intervention research among pregnant women: improving the science and the art. *Health Education Quarterly,* **13**, (2), 131-161.

[59] Windsor, R., Woodby, L., Miller, T., Hardin, M., Crawford, M., DiClemente, C. (2000). Effectiveness of Agency for Health Care Policy and Research clinical practice guideline and patient education methods for pregnant smokers in Medicaid maternity care. *Am J Obstet Gynecol.*, **182**, 68-75.

[60] Kendrick, J. S., Zahniser, C., Miller, N., Salas, N., Stine, J., Gargiullo, P. et al. (1995). Integrating smoking cessation into routine public prenatal care: the Smoking Cessation in Pregnancy Project. *American Journal of Public Health,* **85**, (20), 217-222.

[61] Mullen, P. D, Carbonari, J. P., Tabak, E., Glenday, M. (1991). Improving disclosure of smoking by pregnant women. *Am J Obstet Gynecol.*, **65**, 409-13.

[62] Hajek, P., West, R., Lee, A., Foulds, J., Owen, L., Eiser, J. R., Main, N. (2001).Randomised controlled trial of a midwife delivered brief smoking cessation intervention in pregnancy. *Addiction,* **96**, 485-494.

[63] Walsh, R., Redman, S., Byrne, J., Melmeth, A., & Brinsmead, M. (2000). Process measures in an antenatal smoking cessation trial: another part of the picture. *Health Ed Research: theory and practice,* **15**, (no 4), 469-483.

[64] Dolan-Mullen, P., DiClemente, C.C., Velasquez, M.M., Timpson, S.C., Groff, J.Y., Carbonari, J.P., & Nicol, L. (2000). Enhanced prenatal case management for low income smokers. *Tobacco Control,* **9** (iii), iii75-iii77.

[65] Panjari, M., Bell, R., Bishop, S., Astbury, J., Rice, G. & Doery, J. (1999). A randomised controlled trial of smoking cessation intervention during pregnancy. *Aust NZ Obstet Gynaecol,* **39**, 312-317.

[66] Oliver, S., Oakley, L., Lumley, J., & Waters, E. (2001). Smoking cessation programmes in pregnancy: systematically addressing development, implementation, women's concerns and effectiveness. *Health Ed J.,* **60**, (4), 362-370.

[67] Consensus workshop on Smoking Cessation during Pregnancy. Sponsored by the Robert Wood Johnson Foundation and the Smoke Free Families Program in collaboration with the Health Resources and Services Administration and the Centres for Disease Control and Prevention. Rockville, *Maryland*, 9-10 April 1998.

[68] Fiore, M. A clinical practice guideline for treating tobacco use and dependence. A US Public Health Service Report. (2000). *JAMA,* Vol 283, (no. 24), 3244-3252.

[69] Mullen, P. D. (1999). Maternal smoking during pregnancy and evidence based intervention to promote cessation. In: Spangler JG, ed. *Primary care: clinics in office practice(tobacco use and cessation).* Philadelphia: WB Saunders, 26:577-589.

[70] American College of Obstetricians and Gynaecologists. ACOG educational bulletin, (2001). *International Journal of Gynecology and Obstetrics,* **75**, 345-348.

[71] US Dept of Health and Human Services. (1990). The health benefits of quitting. US Dept of Health and Human Services, Public Health Service, Centers for Disease Control, Center for Chronic Disease Prevention and Health Promotion, *Office on Smoking and Health,* DHHS publication no (CDC) 90-8416.

[72] Little, B. (1999). Pharmacokinetics during pregnancy: evidence based maternal dose formulation. *Obstet Gynecol.,* **93**, 858-868.

[73] Wright, L. N., Thorp, J. M., Kuller, J. A. et al. (1997). Transdermal nicotine replacement in pregnancy: maternal pharmacokinetics and fetal effects. *Am J Obstet Gynecol.,* **176** (5), 1090-1094.

[74] Benowitz, N. (1991). Nicotine replacement therapy during pregnancy. *JAMA,* **266** (22), 3174-3177.

[75] Ogburn, P. L., Hurt, R. D., Croghan, I. T. et al. (1999). Nicotine patch use in pregnant smokers: nicotine and cotinine concentrations and fetal effects. *Am J Obstet Gynecol.,* **181**, 736-734.

[76] Wisborg, K., Henriksen, T. B., Jespersen, L. B., Secher, N. J. (2000). Nicotine patches for pregnant smokers: a randomised controlled study. *Obstet Gynecol.,* **96**, 967-971.

[77] US Dept of Health and Human Services. (1990). The Health benefits of smoking cessation.. USDHHS, PHS, CDC. Centre for Chronic Disease Prevention and Health Promotion. *Office on Smoking and Health.*

[78] Windsor, R. A., Qing Li., C., Boyd, N. R., & Hartmann, K. E. (1999). The use of significant reduction rates to evaluate health education methods for pregnant smokers:a new harm reduction behavioural indicator? *Health Ed Behav;* **26**, 48-662.

[79] Qing Li, C., Windsor, R. A., Perkins, L., Goldenberg, R. L., & Lowe, J. B. (1993). The impact of infant birth weight and gestational age of cotinine validated smoking reduction in pregnancy. *JAMA,* **269**, 1519-24

[80] Hebel, J. R., Fox, N. L., & Sexton, M. (1988). Dose response of birth weight to various measures of maternal smoking during pregnancy. *J Clinical Epidemiology,* **41**, 483-489.

[81] DiClemente, C. C., Dolan Mullen, P., & Windsor, R. (2000). The process of pregnancy smoking cessation: implications for interventions. *Tob Control,* **9** (suppl 3), iii16-iii21.

[82] Mullen, P. D., DiClemente, C. C., & Bartholomew, L. K. (2000). Theory and context and project PANDA: a program to help postpartum women stay off cigarettes. In Bartholomew, L. K., Parcel, G. S., Kok, G., & Gottlieb, H. *Designing theory and evidence based health promotion programmes.* Mountain View, California: Mayfield Publishers, 453-477.

[83] Charlton, A. (1994). Children and Passive smoking: a review. *J Fam Pract,* **38**, 267-77.

[84] US Dept of Health and Human Services & Centers for Disease Control and Prevention. (2001). Women and Smoking. *A Report of the US Surgeon General.* National Centre for Chronic Disease Prevention and Health Promotion. Office on Smoking and Health. www.cdc.gov/tobacco.

[85] Orleans, T., Barker, D., Kaufmann, N. J., & Marx, J. (2000). Helping pregnant smokers: meeting the challenge of the next decade. *Tobacco Control,* **9**, (Supp III), iii-iii11.

[86] Marks, J. S., Koplan, J. P., Hogue, C. J. R., et al. (1990). A cost benefit /cost effectiveness analysis of smoking cessation for pregnant women. *Am J of Preventive Medicine,* **6**, 282-91.

[87] US Preventative Task Force. (1996). Guide to clinical Preventive Service Task Force. *Guide to clinical preventive services,* 2nd ed. Baltimore: Williams and Williams.

In: Trends in Smoking and Health Research
Editors: J. H. Owing, pp. 69-77

ISBN: 1-59454-391-7
© 2005 Nova Science Publishers, Inc.

Chapter IV

Does Smoking Really Prevent Hypertension in Pregnancy? A Case-Control Study of Pregnant Women in Japan

Gen Kobashi[*]

Division of Preventive Medicine, Hokkaido University Graduate,
School of Medicine, Sapporo, Japan

Abstract

This paper explores the association between hypertension in pregnancy and smoking during pregnancy in Japanese women. A description of how maternal smoking during pregnancy may contribute to developing PE is also included. The importance of providing good control for the possible effects of bias and confounding factors, which are two of the problems inherent in various epidemiological studies, is also discussed.

Introduction

Hypertension in pregnancy (HP), a major contributor to maternal, fetal and neonatal morbidity and mortality, occurs in about 5-10% of pregnancies. HP includes gestational hypertension (GH), which is nonproteinuric hypertension of pregnancy, and preeclampsia (PE), which is hypertension with proteinuria and edema. HP is considered a multifactorial syndrome with various mechanisms of pathogenesis[1].

Smoking during pregnancy is known to have adverse effects on pregnancy outcomes. It increases the risk of intrauterine growth retardation, premature labor, placenta previa,

[*] Gen Kobashi, M.D., Ph.D. Division of Preventive Medicine, Hokkaido University Graduate School of Medicine, N15W7, Sapporo 060-8638, Japan. TEL: +81-11-706-5079; FAX: +81-11-706-7374; E-mail address: genkoba@med.hokudai.ac.jp

abruptio placentae, and some fetal anomalies[2,3] In the past decade, however, some researchers have reported new findings about the association between HP/PE and smoking during pregnancy. Some studies in Caucasians[4-8] showed that maternal smoking during pregnancy is associated with a reduced risk of HP, although those results have yet to be confirmed. The authors of those studies hypothesized that this protective effect was due to relaxation of smooth muscle due to an increased release of nitric oxide induced by nicotine, and to a decrease of the hemoglobin concentration caused by smoking, in heterogeneous clinical manifestations of HP.

This paper explores the association between HP and smoking during pregnancy in Japanese women. A description of how maternal smoking during pregnancy may contribute to developing PE is also included. The importance of providing good control for the possible effects of bias and confounding factors, which are two of the problems inherent in various epidemiological studies, is also discussed.

A Case-Control Study in Japanese Women

In the present study, 107 patients with HP were recruited, while 214 parity and age–matched controls were randomly selected from women who delivered babies at the University Hospital and its affiliated hospitals between 1994 and 1995. A self-administered questionnaire including questions about maternal smoking status before and during pregnancy was answered by the subjects 1 to 6 months after delivery. Clinical data such as family history of hypertension and prepregnancy BMI were obtained from medical records. The diagnostic criteria used for HP followed the recommendations of the National High Blood Pressure Education Program Working Group (1990, USA)[9], and accordingly, HP was diagnosed both of the following both criteria were met: (1) blood pressure ≥140/90 mmHg after 20 weeks of gestation, (2) proteinuria ≥30 mg/dl (1+ on dipstick) in a random determination. Women with blood pressure ≥140/90 mmHg and proteinuria prior to 20 weeks of gestation or at 4 weeks after delivery were excluded from the HP subjects, because they may have had latent hypertensive or renal disease. The normal controls were women who had not experienced hypertension, proteinuria, or edema during their pregnancy and for the first month after delivery. Women with HELLP (hemolysis, liver dysfunction, low platelets) syndrome, renal disease, diabetes mellitus, amniotic volume abnormalities, or fetal anomalies were excluded. Statistical analysis was carried out using the chi-squared test (df = 1). Yates' correction for continuity was used when an observed number was ≤5. All statistical analyses were conducted by use of a statistical analysis system package (SAS Institute Inc., Cary, NC).

The characteristics and outcomes of the pregnancies of the subjects are shown in Table 1. Mean maternal ages were 28.5±0.6 years in HP and 28.6±0.3 years in controls, and there was no significant difference between them. Both rate of possessing family history of hypertension and mean prepregnancy body mass index (BMI), well known risk factors for HP, in HP (35.5% and 22.6±0.4, respectively) were significantly higher than those in controls (14.9% and 20.7±0.2, respectively).

Smoking rates before pregnancy were 40.2% both in patients with HP and in controls, and during pregnancy were 19.6% in HP and 16.8% in controls. There were no significant differences between women with HP and the controls (Table 2). However, the classification of subjects based on whether they have "family history of hypertension" or not revealed a significant association between maternal smoking before pregnancy and HP in women without a family history of hypertension (47.8% in HP and 32.4% in controls, p<0.05) (Table 3). The classification of subjects based on whether or not they have "prepregnancy high body mass (BMI≧24)" revealed a significant association between maternal smoking before pregnancy and HP in women with a prepregnancy high body mass (53.2% in HP and 23.8% in controls, p<0.05) (Table 4).

Table 1. Clinical characteristics of Hypertension in Pregnancy & controls

	Hypertension in Pregnancy (n=107)	Controls (n=214)
Maternal age (years)	28.6±0.5	28.6±0.3
Frequency of primiparas (%)	82/107 (76.6)	164/214 (76.6)
Family history of hypertension (%)	38/107 (35.5)***	32/214 (14.9)
Prepregnancy body mass index (mean±SE)	22.6±0.4**	20.7±0.2

**p<0.01, ***p<0.001

Table 2. Maternal smoking status in Hypertension in Pregnancy & controls

		maternal smoking					
		before pregnancy			during pregnancy		
	n	Non-smokers	Smokers	% of Smokers	Non-smokers	Smokers	% of Smokers
HP	107	64	43	40.2	86	21	19.6
Controls	214	143	71	33.1	178	36	16.8

HP: Hypertension in Pregnancy

Table 3. Maternal smoking status in Hypertension in Pregnancy & controls according to family history of hypertension

		maternal smoking					
		before pregnancy			during pregnancy		
	n	NS	S	% Smokers	NS	S	% Smokers
Family history of hypertension (-)							
HP	69	36	33	47.8*	54	15	21.7
Controls	182	123	59	32.4	150	32	17.6
Family history of hypertension (+)							
HP	38	28	10	26.3	32	6	15.8
Controls	32	20	12	37.5	28	4	12.

*p<0.05

HP: Hypertension in Pregnancy, NS: Non-Smokers, S: Smokers

Table 4. Maternal smoking status in Hypertension in Pregnancy & controls according to prepregnancy Body Mass Index

		maternal smoking					
		before pregnancy			during pregnancy		
	n	**NS**	**S**	**% Smokers**	**NS**	**S**	**% Smokers**
Prepregnancy BMI<24							
HP	75	49	26	34.7	62	13	17.3
Controls	193	127	66	34.2	159	34	17.6
Prepregnancy BMI≥24							
HP	32	15	17	53.2 *	24	8	25.0
Controls	21	16	5	23.8	19	2	9.5

*p<0.05

HP: Hypertension in Pregnancy, BMI: Body Mass Index

NS: Non-Smokers, S: Smokers

The present study, which was conducted among Japanese pregnant women, reveals that smoking is a risk factor of HP in women with obesity as well as in those with a family history of hypertension. The smoking rate, which has recently increased in the younger generations[2,10], is estimated to be about 14% in Japanese women in average. In Hokkaido, it is higher than 16%, which is the highest rate in all prefectures in Japan. The rate of 20-29-year-old women reaches approximately 23%, which is also higher than that of any other age groups. In addition, recent data in a local newspaper confirm that the smoking rate of 20-29-year-old women exceeds 30% in Hokkaido. The rates of smokers before and during pregnancy found here were concordant with the results of our previous population survey, carried out for mothers in the babies' health check-up in the city of Sapporo, 34.3% and 18.5%, respectively (unpublished data).

Factors Contributing to Inconsistent Findings Across Studies

Studies on the association between HP and smoking have provided inconsistent findings. Some researchers have found a negative association while others have found no association at all between HP and smoking. There are several factors contributing to such inconsistent findings across studies.

Racial Differences

In general, the studies carried out among Caucasian women are more likely to report a negative association between HP and smoking compared to the studies carried out among Japanese women. This is due to the genetic differences between the two groups. In other words, there are some marked differences between the two groups in the frequency of some of the single nucleotide polymorphisms (SNPs) that are considered the principal risk factors of HP[11]. For example, the frequency of angiotensinogen T235, which is associated with abnormal physiological changes of the decidual spiral arteries, is about 40% among the Caucasians[12] which is lower than about 75% among the Japanese[13]. The frequency of the Asp298 variant of the endothelial nitric oxide synthase (NOS3) gene is about 40% among the Caucasians[14], which is higher than about 5% among the Japanese[15], respectively. The frequency of the factor V Leiden mutation (A1691) (i.e. mutation in the blood coagulation factor V gene) is 10% among the Caucasians[16], and 0% among the Japanese[17]. Due to such genetic differences between the Japanese and the Caucasians, the comparison between them (for example through meta analysis) in order to assess the health impact of smoking can be very problematic.

Effect of Obesity

The risk of diabetes, obesity and hyperlipemia is believed to be associated with oxidative stress[18,19]. Therefore, prepregnancy obesity is likely to make women more susceptible to oxidative stress. In other words, obese women are more likely than their non-obese counterparts to be affected by smoking. However, prepregnancy smoking usually causes women to lose weight. This means that prepregnancy smokers who are overweight are even more susceptible to smoking because it is highly likely that they would be even more overweight if they did not smoke before pregnancy.

Obesity is caused by genetic as well as environmental factors. The frequency of obesity, however, differs across races. As a result, it is necessary to carry out studies that not only include individuals from diverse racial backgrounds but also provide good control for the possible effects of BMI.

Multifactorial Nature of HP

No single explanation can account for the various aspects of etiology and pathogenesis of HP[1]. What is clinically termed HP is actually a multifactorial syndrome. For example, the pathogenesis of HP may vary across individuals. Some may have coagulation-fibrinolysis abnormalities, while others may have a predisposition to hypertension, and yet others may have placental insufficiency. All these symptoms are often commonly referred to as HP, regardless of their severity, presence/absence of proteinuria, timing of their onset (i.e. early vs. late), and whether or not they accompany intrauterine growth retardation.

In short, smoking could be a risk factor or a protective factor for HP, depending on the symptoms of HP. Furthermore, prevalence of each type of HP may differ across population groups and races.

Underestimation of the Prevalence of HP Due to Premature Labor and Threatened Premature Labor

Some reports suggest that smoking during pregnancy increases the risk of premature labor by 6% regardless of parity (i.e. primiparous or multiparous). Premature labor can potentially lead to the underestimation of the prevalence of HP because any of the symptoms of HP that normally occur during the late pregnancy will no longer occur if premature labor takes place. On the other hand, pregnant women with a diagnosis of threatened premature labor are likely to be advised to rest or undergo tocolytic therapy. Rest by itself is a protective factor for PE. Furthermore, a patient with a diagnosis of threatened premature labor is not often diagnosed with HP even when the mild symptoms of HP are evident in the patient, since the tocolytic agents tend to increase blood pressure. In fact, the majority of the studies on HP exclude patients with a diagnosis of threatened premature labor. All these factors potentially contribute to bias, thus leading to the underestimation of the prevalence of HP.

Association with Nausea and Vomiting

Smell of cigarette is often nauseating for those women who are experiencing nausea and vomiting in early pregnancy (NVP). This makes it easier for them to quit smoking. While many potential confounding factors are probably related to smoking during pregnancy, it is highly likely that those women who continue smoking during pregnancy have relatively mild cases of NVP. There are several studies reporting on the association between NVP and HP/PE[20]. Thus, it is justifiable to assume that women who are at a lower risk of developing HP are more likely than others to continue smoking during pregnancy.

Significant Differences in Large-Scale Studies

There are several reasons to believe that studies carried out among pregnant women are more likely to be large-scale prospective studies compared to those carried out among the general public or individuals in certain professions. Firstly, it takes less than 10 months to obtain certain pregnancy outcomes. Secondly, pregnant subjects are often selected from women receiving regular prenatal checkups provided by individual local governments, and the percentage of eligible women actually receiving the health-checkups tends to be quite high because pregnant women are health-conscious. However, in studies with large sample size, very small differences will be detected as statistically significant. In some cases, such differences may merely be the result of 'noise', or errors in the data. In view of these facts, particular care should be taken to select appropriate sample size and adjust for as many potential confounding factors as possible. For example, several factors should be taken into account when examining the association between HP and smoking during pregnancy, such as maternal age, parity, obesity, family history of hypertension, severity of NVP, incidence of premature labor and diagnosis of threatened premature labor.

Reliability of Data Obtained from Patient Record and Questionnaires

Information bias is inherent in self-reported smoking status obtained from pregnant women[21]. Because it is commonly understood that smoking during pregnancy can cause serious health problems to an unborn child, it is highly possible that some pregnant women may choose to lie about their smoking status. Urinary cotinine levels or hair nicotine consentration may provide more accurate measures of exposure to smoking[21,22]. However, these measurements may not be cost effective, and it may impose an excessive burden on the study subjects.

Conclusion

Figure 1 illustrates the effects of maternal smoking on HP. Smoking could be a protective factor or a risk factor of HP, depending on the symptoms of HP (i.e. susceptibility to oxidative stress and risk of intrauterine growth retardation). The true mechanism by which maternal smoking contributes to the development of HP may someday become clear through a number of high-quality epidemiological studies that provide good control for possible effects of bias and confounding factors. From the viewpoint of clinical medicine and public health, and in order to ensure the well-being of the mother and the baby, all women should be encouraged to avoid smoking before as well as during pregnancy, regardless of their racial backgrounds.

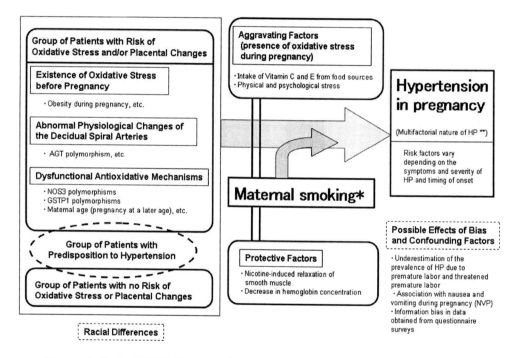

Figure 1. Potential Effects of Maternal Smoking on the Development of Hypertension in Pregnancy (HP)

Note: * Maternal Smoking could be a risk factor or protective factor for HP, depending on the effects of other risk factors. ** HP is a multifactorial syndrome. To date, researchers have been trying to provide a better classification for HP based on the specific combination of symptoms, severity, and timing of onset.

References

[1] Chesley LC. History and epidemiology of preeclampsia-eclampsia. *Clin Obstet Gynecol* **27**: 801-820, 1984

[2] Cnattingius S. The epidemiology of smoking during pregnancy:smoking prevalence, maternal characteristics, and pregnancy outcomes. *Nicotine Tob Res 6 Suppl* **2**: S125-140, 2004

[3] Littele J, Cardy A, Arslan MT, Gilmour M, Mossey PA. Smoking and orofacial clefts: a United Kingdom-based case-control study. *Cleft Palate Craniofac J* **41**:381-386, 2004

[4] Conde-Agudelo A, Althabe F, Belizan JM, Kafury-Goeta AC. Cigarette smoking during pregnancy and risk of preeclampsia: a systematic review. *Am J Obstet Gynecol.* 1999; 181: 1026-1035

[5] Newman MG, Lindsay MK, Graves W. Cigarette smoking and pre-eclampsia: their association and effects on clinical outcomes. *J Matern Fetal Med* 2001 Jun;10(3):166-70

[6] Odegard RA, Vatten LJ, Nilsen ST, Salvesen KA, Austgulen R. Risk factors and clinical manifestations of pre-eclampsia. *BJOG* 2000 Nov;107(11):1410-6

[7] Martin CL, Hall MH, Campbell DM. The effect of smoking on pre-eclampsia in twin pregnancy. *BJOG* 2000 Jun;107(6):745-9

[8] Slome J. Smoking and preeclampsia: is there a relationship? *J Midwifery Womens Health* 2000 Jul-Aug;45(4):351

[9] National High Blood Pressure Education Program Working Group. Report on high blood pressure in pregnancy (Consensus Report). *Am J Obstet Gynecol* **163**:1689-1712, 1990

[10] *Journal of Health and Welfare Statistics.* ed. by Health and Welfare Statistics Association (Tokyo) 81□83□2003. (in Japanese)

[11] Kobashi G, Shido K, Hata A, Yamada H, Kato EH, Kanamori M, Fujimoto S, Kondo K: Multivariate analysis of genetic and acquired factors: T235 variant of angiotensinogen gene as a potent independent risk factor for preeclampsia. *Semin Thromb Hemost* 2001;27:143-147.

[12] Ward K, Hata A, Jeunemaitre X, Helin C, Nelson L, Namikawa C, Farrington PF, Ogasawara M, Suzumori K, Tomoda S, Berrebi S, Sasaki M, Corvol P, Lifton RP, Lalouel JM: A molecular variant of angiotensinogen associated with preeclampsia. *Nat Genet* 1993;4:59-61.

[13] Kobashi G, Hata A, Shido K, Kato EH, Yamada H, Fujimoto S, Kishi R, Kondo K: Association of a variant of the angiotensinogen gene with pure type of hypertension in pregnancy in the Japanese: implication of a racial difference and significance of an age factor. *Am J Med Genet* 1999;86:232-236

[14] Poirier O, Mao C, Mallet C, Nicaud V, Herrman SM, Evans A, Ruidavets JB, Arveiler D, Luc G, Tiret L, Soubrier F, Cambien F. Polymorphisms of the endothelial nitric oxide synthase gene – no consistent association with myocardial infarction in the ECTIM study. *Eur J Clin Invest* 29:284-290,1999

[15] Kobashi G, Yamada H, Kato EH, Ebina Y, Ohta K, Fujimoto S: Glu298Asp variant of the endotherial nitric oxide synthase gene (NOS3) and hypertension in pregnancy. *Am J Med Genet* 2001;103:241-244.

[16] Grandone E, Margaglione M, Colaizzo D, Cappucci G, Paladini D, Martinelli P, Montanaro S, Pavone G, Di Minno G: Factor V Leiden, C>T MTHFR polymorphism and genetic susceptibility to preeclampsia. Thromb. *Haemost*. 1997;77:1052–1054

[17] Kobashi G, Yamada H, Asano T, Nagano S, Hata A, Kishi R, Kondo K, Fujimoto S: The factor V Leiden mutation is not a common cause of pregnancy-induced hypertension in Japan. *Semin Thromb Hemost* 1999;25:487-489

[18] Skrha J. Pathogenesis of angiopathy in diabetes. *Acta Diabetol 40 Suppl* **2**: S324-329, 2003

[19] Correeia ML, Haynes WG. Leptin, obesity and cardiovascular disease. *Curr Nephrol Hypertens* **13**:215-223,2004

[20] Zhang J, Cai WW. Severe vomiting during pregnancy: antenatal correlates and fetal outcomes. *Epidemiology* **2**:454-457, 1991

[21] Britton GR, Brinthaupt J, Stehle JM, James GD. Comparison of self reported smoking and urinary cotinine levels in a rural pregnant population. *J Obstet Gynecol Neonatal Nurs* **33**:306-311, 2004

[22] Klein J, Blanchette P, Koren G. Assessing nicotine metabolism in pregnancy - a novel approach using hair analysis. *Forensic Sci Int* **145**: 191-194, 2004

In: Trends in Smoking and Health Research
Editors: J. H. Owing, pp. 79-103

ISBN: 1-59454-391-7
© 2005 Nova Science Publishers, Inc.

Chapter V

Cigarette Smoking during Pregnancy

Hein Odendaal
Medical Research Council of South Africa

Abstract

In this article the authors highlight the most common adverse effects of smoking during pregnancy and, in the second part, explain how smokers can be helped to quit.

Introduction

Smoking of cigarettes is a major health problem. There are more than 1.2 billion cigarette smokers in the world. This habit is causing the death of about 5 million people per year.[1] More than 4000 chemicals, of which at least 60 are known carcinogens, are contained in the smoke from tobacco in cigarettes. The most harmful components are nicotine and carbon monoxide. In addition, nicotine is highly addictive, causing both stimulation and euphoria. [2-4]

In 1997, smoking caused the death of about 165,000 women in the U.S.A. Although much is done to educate the public about the adverse effects of cigarette smoking, 22 per cent of women in the U.S.A. smoked in 1998.[5] In the same country, lung cancer now accounts for 25 per cent of all cancer deaths among women. Since 1950, there has been a 600 per cent increase in women's death rates from lung cancer.[5] The number of women smokers between the ages of 18 and 21 tripled between 1911 and 1925 and again by 1939. [6]

Although the prevalence of smoking in adult women in the U.S.A. has declined in recent years, it is of great concern that so many young people smoke. In 2000, 29.7 per cent of high school senior girls reported having smoked within the previous 30 days.[7]

It is of great concern that many women from specific societies in developing countries smoke during pregnancy. In South Africa, for example, a study found that 47 % of colored women smoked, in contrast to 4 % and 3 % of black and Indian women respectively.[8]

The problem of tobacco smoking is a multidisciplinary issue. The issue extends far beyond medicine and related disciplines. It involves economic, socio-cultural, agricultural, environmental and international trade concerns.[9] The goal should therefor be to prevent young women to start smoking and to teach and support smokers how to quit, especially during pregnancy.[10]

In this article we will highlight the most common adverse effects of smoking during pregnancy and, in the second part, explain how smokers can be helped to quit.

The Clinical Problem

The most common general adverse health effects of cigarette smoking are lung cancer, heart disease, atherosclerotic vascular disease, laryngeal, oral and oesophageal cancer, chronic obstructive pulmonary disease, asthma, and respiratory infections.[11] According to a recent meta-analysis, maternal smoking during pregnancy is associated with intrauterine growth restriction, preterm labor, abruptio placentae, placenta praevia and premature rupture of membranes.[12 13] This confirms the findings of a previous meta-analysis. However, an increased risk of ectopic pregnancy was also found in this meta-analysis.[14] Ten per cent of perinatal mortality and 18 % of low birth weight infants are caused by cigarette smoking.[15] Studies suggest that infants of women who stop smoking by the first trimester of pregnancy have body measurements and birth weights comparable to those of babies born to non-smokers; on the other hand, smoking in the third trimester is particularly harmful.[11]

The Cigarette

Composition of Tobacco Smoke

In some parts of the world e.g. Germany and the U.S.A., tobacco companies add ingredients to tobacco products, either to impart a specific taste, flavor or aroma to the product, or for a specific technological purpose such as increasing the moisture-holding capacity of the tobacco. In other countries, e.g. the U.K., Australia and Canada, flavor ingredients are not generally used in cigarettes. There are 482 different tobacco ingredients, comprising of 462 flavors, 1 flavor/solvent, 1 solvent, 7 preservatives, 3 humectants, 5 binders, 1 filler and 2 process aids (one of which is water). The casing ingredients are added at levels of up to 68 mg on the cigarettes.[16 17] A recent overview found that commonly used tobacco ingredients do not change the toxicity of smoke as measured in specified assays and that ingredients have no effect on the levels of most smoke constituents that may be relevant to smoking-related diseases.[18] Although discussion of the carcinogenic effects of cigarette smoking is beyond the aims of this article, it is important to note that there are more than 50 carcinogens in tobacco smoke, of which the most potent are the polycyclic aromatic hydrocarbons and tobacco specific nitrosamines.[19]

Addiction

Nicotine is the primary agent responsible for the behavior of tobacco users. It is extremely addictive and causes dependence by producing centrally mediated reinforcing effects. Abstinence from tobacco after prolonged use causes withdrawal symptoms in the form of unpleasant sensations which usually peak within 1-2 weeks but may continue for as long as 3-4 weeks.[20]

Possible Mechanisms for Adverse Effects of Cigarette Smoking during Pregnancy

There are several ways in which cigarette smoking can affect pregnancy adversely (Table I). Each of these will be discussed in the following section.

Table I. Possible mechanisms for adverse effects of cigarette smoking during pregnancy

Increase in carbon monoxide
Adverse effects of nicotine
Endothelial damage to uterine and placental vessels
Lower folate levels

Carbon Monoxide

Carbon monoxide (CO) is a vital molecule in health and disease as it has many effects on different systems and functions.[21] It contributes to smoking-induced cardiovascular disease. In addition, environmental CO is associated with increased cardiovascular mortality and morbidity.[22] As far as the reproductive system is concerned, it inhibits the release of corticotropin releasing hormone, acts as a vasorelaxant and regulates uterine tone. In addition, it has an effect on placental function and development. According to these findings, CO seems to be protective of adverse pregnancy outcome but it has been shown that prolonged exposure to high levels of environmental CO is associated with growth restricted newborns.[23] Cigarette smoking is also associated with various deformities of the fetus.[24] It is most likely that the damage is caused by the hypoxia that follows carboxyhaemoglobinaemia, as similar defects are observed after CO poisoning. The fetus suffers from chronic hypoxic stress as indicated by higher haematocrit levels in the newborns of smokers.[25]

Nicotine

Nicotine is a potent, naturally occurring liquid alkaloid. It stimulates nicotine acetylcholine receptors localized peripherally at autonomic ganglia in the adrenal medulla and chemoreceptors of the carotid bodies and aortic body. It has powerful effects on the human body, particularly when administered rapidly or at high doses.[26] The effect of tobacco smoke on fetal growth is due to an accumulation of the effects of carbon monoxide and nicotine. The adverse effect of nicotine is through its vasoconstrictive effects on the uterine and potentially also on the umbilical artery.[27] Nicotine readily crosses the placenta. Fetuses of mothers who smoke are exposed to relatively higher levels of nicotine than their mothers. It is of great concern that nicotine can activate nicotine receptors in the fetal brain as this may affect brain development.[28]

Endothelial Effects

The endothelium, as we know now, plays a much greater role in health and disease than was ever thought to be the case ten years ago. It has been shown that the free radical components of cigarette smoke cause much of the enddothelial damage.[29] Even passive smoking is associated with abnormal endothelial function.[30] As far as the specific effect on the endothelium is concerned, it seems that smoking during pregnancy is associated with reduced cellular fibronectin and increased intracellular adhesion molecule-1.[31] In addition, it has been found that cigarette smoking is associated with increased circulating levels of lipid peroxidation products, which may contribute to endothelial damage. Endothelial injury may also be caused by increased circulating levels of von Willebrand's factor and catecholamines or lower prostacyclin production.[32] Using vital capillary microscopy, Zhang et al. assessed blood cell flow velocity in the nail bed circulation after cigarette smoking. Marked decrease in microcirculatory blood flow was noticed in 23 of the 24 subjects, one to five minutes after smoking.[33] Within minutes cigarette smoking also induces leukocyte adhesion to the vascular wall and formation of intravascular leukocyte-platelet aggregates.[34]

Folic Acid Metabolism

Folic acid is essential for normal cell function. It plays an essential role in the prevention of chromosome breakage and hypomethylation of DNA.[35] In addition, folate plays a vital role in the conversion of dietary folylpolyglutamates to monoglutamates, intestinal absorbtion, receptor and carrier-mediated transport across cell membranes and cellular transport.[36] A cross-sectional study demonstrated that pregnant women who smoked, had significantly lower concentrations of serum folate than pregnant women who did not smoke. Their red cell folate levels were also lower. No difference was found between the diet intake of folates between the two groups.[37] The lower serum folate levels may contribute to higher prevalence of miscarriages, intrauterine death and abruptio placentae in smokers.

Effects on Pregnancy

Early Pregnancy

Cigarette smoking has far reaching effects on many aspects of reproductive health (Table II), from gamete production and function and ovulation through poor implantation and placentation to adverse effects in late pregnancy.[12 38-42] The effects of cigarette smoking on the reproductive system are really extensive; cotinine, the major metabolite of nicotine, is even detectable in the follicular fluid of passive smokers.[43] The adverse effects of cigarette smoking on the reproductive system extend far beyond pregnancy. For example it is causing impotence, infertility and carcinoma of the cervix.[44-45]

Effects on Ovarian Function and Fertility

Van Voorhis et al. studied the effects of smoking on ovarian function and fertility in a cohort of 499 women involved in an assisted reproduction programme.[46] When women smoked during their treatment cycle there was about a 50 % reduction on implantation rate and ongoing pregnancy rate compared to those who never smoked. Cigarette smoking was also associated with a prolonged adverse effect, which was dose-dependent, on the ovarian function. The effect seemed to be toxic in nature as current smokers were affected but not past smokers. Fortunately the adverse effects of cigarette smoking on implantation are more reversible than the effects on ovarian function.[47] The harmful effects on early pregnancy are most likely due to the effects of smoking on invasive and villous trophoblasts, reduced angioblastic response in the endometrium and a modified maternal response to decidual remodelling.

Table II. Adverse reproductive effects of cigarette smoking

Reduction in sperm quality
Suppression of ovarian function
Reduction in reproductive capacity
Poor implantation of the embryo
Degeneration and aging of the placenta
Increase in ectopic pregnancy

Effects on the Placenta

Smoking is associated with extensive aging and degenerative changes in the placenta.[48] The aging is characterized by increased syncytial buds and degenerative changes, by increased amounts of collagen in the chorionic villi and an increased thickness of subtrophoblast basal membrane. One of the basic effects on the placenta seems to be that hypoxia and nicotine upregulates cytotrophoblast expression, changing the balance between proliferation and differentiation.[49] Cigarette smoking also affects the placental vasculature as the volume and surface area and calculated lengths for villous capillaries are significantly reduced in smokers.[50] Placentas of smokers are lighter at delivery when compared to non-smokers.[51-54]

Abortion

As little as one ounce of absolute alcohol, as infrequently as twice per week, doubles the risk of abortion.[55] These risks may further increase with the smoking of cigarettes in early pregnancy. In a study of nearly 15,000 young women, miscarriage was found to be increased in smokers.[56] Another recent study, in 970 women, also found an association between abortion and cigarette smoking and caffeine use.[57] In addition, an association between maternal smoking and spontaneous abortion was found in a case-control study, involving 782 cases of spontaneous abortion and 1543 controls.[58]

Makrydimas et al.[59] approached the problem from a different angle. They followed 866 pregnancies where the fetus was alive at 6-10 weeks gestation. In the 668 singleton pregnancies, where the fetus was alive at the time of the scan and where there was a complete follow up of the pregnancy, losses occurred in 7.5 % of pregnancies. The incidence of cigarette smoking was higher in mothers who later had fetal losses. Even passive smoking has been associated with second trimester spontaneous abortion.[60] The decrease in the number of spontaneous abortions was also confirmed in pregnancies conceived by in vitro fertilization.[61]

However, not all studies agree that maternal smoking is associated with spontaneous abortion. In a large recent study, in more than 24,000 pregnancies, adjusting for all possible conditions possibly associated with abortion, no increased risk was found in smokers.[62] These findings were supported by another study which found an association between abortion and the use of alcohol and caffeine intake.[63] The reason for the apparent controversy is that caffeine use is increased among smokers. The risk of abortion is increased by the consumption of caffeine/coffee but it may appear to be caused by smoking.[64] It therefore seems that the adverse effects of cigarette smoking on abortion are increased by the intake of caffeine.

Ectopic Pregnancy

The meta-analysis of Castles et al.[14] found 9 case-control studies on the association of smoking with ectopic pregnancy. The studies were published between 1982 and 1992. A total of 2,831 cases were compared. Odds ratios ranged between 0.88 and 2.5. Lower 95 % CIs were below one in only two studies. For the whole meta-analysis, the pooled odds ratio was 1.77 (95 % CI 1.31-2.22). However, when smoking was strictly defined at conception, as was done in five studies, the odds ratio declined to 1.51 (95 % CI 0.88-2.15). When they controlled for one or more other risk factors of ectopic pregnancy, such as a history of ectopic pregnancy, intrauterine devices inserted or pelvic inflammatory disease, the odds ratios varied between 1.60 and 1.93. All lower ranges of the 95 % CI were above one for the individual pooled
odds ratios.

A very recent case-control study addressed 803 cases of ectopic pregnancy and 1,683 deliveries as controls, between 1993 and 2000.[65] In the analysis, great care was taken to adjust for known risk factors for ectopic pregnancy. The number of cigarettes smoked per day had a significant effect on the frequency of ectopic pregnancy. The relationship found was regarded as causal as it was clearly dose-related and as smoking cessation reduced the risks to a level halfway between that of women who never smoked and that of present smokers. It is important to note that the effects of smoking were similar to that of infection. It has been said that some of the effects attributed to smoking of cigarettes, may be caused by sexually transmitted diseases. However, the effects of sexually transmitted diseases on tubal function are often permanent. This is in contrast to the study of Bouyer, which found an improvement after cessation of smoking and a direct dosage effect (Table III). It is therefore likely that smoking has a direct, but transient effect on tubal function.

Table III. Effects of Cigarette smoking on ectopic pregnancy (from Bouyer et al.[65])

	Adjusted OR	95 % CI	p-value
Never	1		<0.001
Past smoker	1.5	1.1-2.2	
1-9 cigarettes per day	1.7	1.2-2.4	
10-19 cigarettes per day	3.1	2.2-4.3	
≥ 20 cigarettes per day	3.9	2.6-5.9	

Another large recent study showed similar effects.[66] This case-control study involved 208 cases and 781 postpartum controls, from 1999-2000. After multivariate analysis, four independent risk factors for ectopic pregnancy remained, namely multiple sexual partners, pelvic inflammatory disease, smoking and infertility. The odds ratio for cigarette smoking was 2.49 (95 % CI 1.36-4.55).

Perinatal Complications

Several review articles and meta-analyses addressed the perinatal complications of tobacco use during pregnancy.[12 14 67] It was found that about 15-20 % of women smoke during pregnancy. Smoking is responsible for about 15 % of all preterm births, 20-30 % of all infants with low birth weights and a 150 % increase in overall perinatal mortality. The most common complications are listed in Table IV.

Table IV. Common perinatal complications of cigarette smoking during pregnancy

Placenta praevia
Abruptio placentae
Premature rupture of membranes
Preterm delivery
Low birth weight
Intrauterine growth restriction
Perinatal complications in pre-eclampsia
Sudden infant death syndrome
Unexplained intrauterine deaths
Intrapartum asphyxia

Placenta Praevia

The incidence rate of placenta praevia is 4 to 5 cases per 1000 pregnancies. Naeye was the first to report the association between cigarette smoking and placenta praevia.[68] Several years later Castles et al.[14] reviewed four case-control and two cohort studies on the association of smoking with placenta praevia. These six studies were published between 1986 and 1994 and involved 32,444 study patients. Odds ratios ranged between 1.17 and 3.19. In two of the studies the 95 % confidence intervals included one. Pooled data of the six studies gave an OR of 1.58 (95 % CI 1.04-2.12). As increased parity and a previous caesarean section are strongly associated with placenta praevia, four of the studies used multiple regressions to adjust for these confounders. For these studies the pooled OR was 1.54 (95 % CI 0.81-2.27). However, this uncertainty about the association between cigarette smoking and placenta praevia was cleared up in two recent studies. In the first, Fiaz and Ananth[69] performed a systematic review of the literature between 1966 and 2000. A total of 58 studies were identified. Meta-analysis confirmed the association between smoking and placenta praevia. In the second study a relative risk range between 1.5 and 3.0 was reported.[70]

No explanation for the higher frequency of placenta praevia could be found in the early studies. In a later report Handler et al. mentioned that both nicotine (through vasoconstriction) and CO (through carboxyhaemoglobinaemia) could cause placental hypoxaemia, leading to placental hypertrophy.[71] Williams et al.[72] as well as Handler et al. referred to a previous study which found that the placentas of smokers were thinner but larger than that of nonsmokers.[73] As could be expected, a placenta with an increased diameter has a better chance of partially or completely covering the cervical os.

Abruptio Placentae

Separation of a normally positioned placenta before delivery is a very serious condition and a leading course cause of maternal morbidity. In Cape Town, it is the most common cause of intrauterine death.[74] It is also of great concern that the incidence of abruptio placentae is increasing.[75] Naeye was one of the first researchers to demonstrate the association between cigarette smoking and abruptio placentae.[68] In mothers who had smoked more than 10 cigarettes per day and for more than 6 years, the prevalence of abruptio placentae was 32 per 1000 births, significantly more than the 10 per 1000 for those who never smoked. Several later studies confirmed the association between abruptio placentae and cigarette smoking.[76-79]

All these findings were confirmed by a meta-analysis of 8 studies. These studies, published between 1975 and 1994, addressing 42,207 sample cases. The odds ratios ranged between 1.39 and 3.99. The lowest 95 % CI was 1. Pooled data gave an odds ratio of 1.62 (95 % CI 1.46-1.77). Sub-analyses, adjusting for confounders, did not change the odds ratio much except for the studies where the placentas were examined histologically, where the OR increased to 2.42 (95 % CI 1.53-3.31.)

Another large meta-analysis on cigarette smoking and abruptio placentae was published in 1999.[80] A total of 1,358,083 pregnancies was examined from seven case-control studies and six cohort studies. The overall incidence of abruptio placentae was 0,64 %. Smoking was associated with a 90 % increased risk as the odds ratio was 1.9 (95 % CI 1.8-2.0). It was estimated that 15 –25 % of episodes of abruptio placentae were caused by smoking. The study also found that hypertensive disorders increased the risk of abruptio placentae.

A more recent and large population-based cohort study confirmed the association between smoking and abruptio placentae.[81] A total of 46,313 singleton births were analysed. Smoking increased the risk of abruptio placentae by almost 100 % (OR 1.99; 95 % CI 1.72-2.30)

In a study at Tygerberg Hospital, where abruptio placentae is the most common cause of intrauterine death, the risk of abruptio placentae from cigarette smoking was higher than in the previously mentioned studies (OR 4.01; 95 % CI 1.15-15.31). However, the fact that this study was hospital based could have increased the risks of abruptio placentae. [72]

Results of these three large studies therefore demonstrated a clear association between cigarette smoking and abruptio placentae (Table V).

Table V. Association between smoking and abruptio placentae

Authors	Years of study	Deliveries	Risk of abruption
Castle et al. 1999	1975-1994	42,207	OR 2.42 (95 % CI 1.53-3.31)
Mortensen et al. 2001	1991-1998	46,313	1.99 (95 % CI 1.72.2.30)
Ananth et al. 1999	1966-1997	1,358,083	1.9 (95 % CI 1.8-2.0)

There are several reasons why cigarette smoking can lead to abruptio placentae. Naeye[68] observed necrosis in the decidua basalis at the margin of the placenta in women who continued to smoke during pregnancy. He attributed the necrosis to possible placental ischaemia caused by reduced blood flow. The area of necrosis then probably provided the nidus from where the premature separation of the placenta started. Another possibility is placental inflammation from amniotic fluid infection associated with cigarette smoking.[82] Lower levels of ascorbic acid which leads to defective collagen synthesis and decreased levels of folic acid which affects the placentation, may also play a role.[70]

The association between abruptio placentae and fetal growth restriction may refer to a pathological process that affects both fetal and placental growth.[83] The most likely reason is poor placentation as there is a strong association between severe pre-eclampsia and abruptio placentae.[84 85] These findings are also supported by Ananth et al. who found that mothers with singleton pregnancies and various forms of hypertensive diseases, have increased risks of abruptio placentae, particularly when they smoke.[86] These findings are supported by a previous study which found a strong association between hypertensive disorders and abruptio placentae and an interaction between hypertension and cigarette smoking.[87]

Premature Rupture of Membranes

In 1980 Evaldson et al. described the association between premature rupture of membranes and heavy smoking.[88] Several later studies confirmed the association.[89-92]

However, one study, in a small number of patients, showed no association between smoking and the outcome of preterm premature rupture of membranes (PROM).[93] In their meta-analysis, Castles et al.[14] identified 6 studies on PROM of which 5 were case controlled and one cohort. Odds ratios varied between 1.6 and 4.93. Lower 95 % CIs were less than 1 in only one study. The pooled OR was 1.70 (95 % CI 1.18-2.25). Four studies were adjusted for confounders, giving an OR of 1.81 (95 % CI 1.36-2.26). A large Swedish study, which included 2,377 women with PROM, found a rate of 6.5 /1000 among non-smokers compared to 11.5/1000 in heavy smokers. For women who smoked 1-9 cigarettes per day, the rate was 9.3/1000.[94]

Several primary causes have been suggested for the higher prevalence of PROM among smokers. The most common of these are vitamin C deficiency, zinc deficiency, and a decrease in the functional capacity of protease inhibitors.[67]

Preterm Delivery

Preterm delivery is of great concern as it is a major cause of neonatal mortality and morbidity. In industrialized countries about 5-10 % of births are premature.[95] However, in developing countries the prevalence may double. The increased frequency of preterm delivery in mothers who smoke during pregnancy has been highlighted in many recent review articles.[12 67 95]

The association was also confirmed by a large recent meta-analysis.[96] Using modern electronic ways, 104 citations and 64 published articles in English were identified but after applying strict selective criteria (prospective design, reported rates on preterm delivery, defined gestational age) only 20 studies remained. Data on 22,566 smokers during pregnancy were available for analysis. Although the first study analyzed was published in 1964, most were published between 1966 and 1997. Odds ratios for the different studies varied between 0.08 and 2.97. However, only 2 studies showed a protective effect, but not statistically significant. Lower 95 % CIs were less than one in only 8 studies. The combined odds ratio was 1.27(95 % CI 1.21-1.33). They also addressed the effect of number of cigarettes smoked per day. This was difficult as the studies used different ways to categorize the severity of smoking. However, it was shown that light to moderate and severe smoking during pregnancy had odds ratios of 1.22 (95 % CI 1.13-1.32) and 1.31 (95 % CI 1.20-1.42) respectively. The effect of the duration of smoking could not be established.

Another recently published study addressed several previously unresolved aspects of smoking and preterm labour.[97] This study addressed the effects of smoking on the very small baby (27-32 completed weeks of gestation) as well as the effects of parity, hypertension and the causes of preterm delivery. Mothers were recruited from the French Epipage cohort study.[98] The data of 956 singletons, born alive between 27 and 32 completed weeks of gestation, in five of the nine regions included in the Epipage study, were analyzed. Information on smoking and social characteristics was available for 90 % of cases. The control group consisted of 959 term singleton neonates born in the nine regions of the Epipage study. Their findings were that mothers of very preterm infants were significantly younger, lighter, more likely to live alone, had lower educational levels, were less often employed, had had more previous spontaneous or induced abortions and a lower parity.

The main causes for the preterm delivery were gestational hypertension, maternal bleeding without hypertension, preterm premature rupture of membranes without hypertension or bleeding, spontaneous labor without hypertension and bleeding or preterm premature rupture of membranes. Low to moderate smoking was defined as one to nine cigarettes a day and heavy smoking as 10 or more. Social factors, known to influence the duration of pregnancy, were also considered. A significant association was found between very preterm deliveries and maternal smoking (crude OR 2.0; 95 % CI 1.6-2.6). The association remained significant after they have adjusted for potential confounding variables (OR 1.7; 95 % CI 1.3-2.2). A significant dose-effect was observed. Mothers with gestational hypertension who smoked, had a lower risk for very preterm delivery. However, all the other mechanisms of preterm delivery were associated with more very premature deliveries in smokers. The fact that pre-eclampsia occurs more frequently in primigravidae, most likely explains why smoking is less often associated with preterm labor in this group of patients.

These large and precisely done studies therefore confirm the association between preterm birth and the smoking of cigarettes (Table VI).

Table VI. Association between smoking and preterm labour

Authors	Years of study	Deliveries	Risk of preterm delivery
Shah et al. 2000	1966-1997	22,566	OR 1.27 (95 % CI 1.21-1.33)
Burguet et al. 2004	1997	959 very premature	2.0 (95 % CI 1.6-.2.6)

There are several possible reasons for the high prevalence of preterm labour in smokers.

The partial or complete abruption of the placenta may lead to preterm labor. Additionally, the associated lack of ascorbic acid[99] may lead to decreased amounts of collagen III and elastin, leading to premature rupture of membranes.[100] Higher levels of platelet activating factor, a strong stimulant of smooth muscle activity, may also play a contributing role.[101] Smoking may also have a direct effect on the endometrium, increasing it's sensitivity to oxytocin.[102]

Low Birth Weight

Maternal cigarette smoking carries the greatest risk for restricted fetal growth than any of the commonly used substances.[103] It has been shown that smoking is responsible for 15 % of all preterm births but for 20 – 30 % of all infants with low birth weights.[67] A similar observation was made in a local study at Tygerberg Hospital. The mean gestational age of mothers who smoked was 37 weeks, in contrast to the 37.7 weeks of non-smokers. Twenty per cent of infants weighed below the 10th centile for gestational age.[53] Many low birth weight babies are premature, but some of them are born after 37 weeks gestation and weigh less than 2500 g. There are also babies of smokers born at term and who have birth weights above 2500 g, but have birth weights below the 10th centile for the specific gestational age. This indicates that cigarette smoking affects both gestational age and fetal growth.

As the effects of smoking on the duration of pregnancy have been discussed, and as a later section will deal with fetal growth, the effects on low birth weight as such will not be discussed further.

More Perinatal Complications in Preeclampsia

According to the meta-analysis of Castles et al.[14], five studies addressed the association between pre-eclampsia and smoking. All showed a reduction in the number of cases of pre-eclampsia, with ORs ranging from 0.45 to 0.71. Upper 95 % CIs were above one in two studies.[104] Pooled data of the five studies have an OR of 0.51 (95 % CI 0.37-0.63). All studies used strict diagnostic criteria and adjusted for confounders. These findings were also supported by another study, not included in the meta-analysis.[105] This study addressed singleton births in Sweden, from 1987-1993, born to nulliparous women of 15 to 34 years. There were 1931 perinatal deaths in the 317,652 births. Compared to non-smokers the relative risk of mild pre-eclampsia was 0.6 (95 % CI 0.5-0.6) and of severe pre-eclampsia 0.5 (95 % CI 05-0.6). A clear dose-response relationship was found.

Mild pre-eclampsia was associated with increased rates of abruptio placentae (1 %) and SGA (11 %) but not of perinatal death. Severe pre-eclampsia substantially increased the rates of abruptio placentae (2.6 %), SGA (25 %) and perinatal deaths. Smoking was also associated with adverse perinatal outcome in women without hypertension. In addition, smoking increased the rates of perinatal mortality, abruptio placentae and SGA associated with severe pre-eclampsia substantially when compared to non-hypertensive pregnancies. Heavy smoking further increased these complications. For example, when the mother with severe pre-eclampsia or eclampsia smoked 10 or more cigarettes per day, the perinatal mortality rate increased by 12/1000, the rate of abruptio placentae by 3.6 % and the SGA rate by 40 %. Another recent large study, in 47,932 singleton births, confirmed the inverse association between smoking and pre-eclampsia (OR 0.55; 95 % CI 0.48-0.62).[81] Only one study failed to find an association between maternal smoking and a reduced frequency of pre-eclampsia.[106] Of the 493 pregnant women studied, only 360 completed all the questionnaires. In this group, the prevalence of smoking during pregnancy decreased from 20.3 % to 3.4 %. Inclusion bias or the high quitting rate could have reduced the effects of smoking on the prevalence of pre-eclampsia.

According to all these studies, the risk of pre-eclampsia is reduced by cigarette smoking, but continuation of smoking, once the mother has developed pre-eclampsia, increases the complications of pre-eclampsia.

No specific reasons for the reduction of pre-eclampsia could be found. It is postulated that hypotensive effects of thiocyanate and carbonmonoxide and the inhibitory effect of nicotine on thromboxane may be involved. The vasoconstrictive effects of cotinine could play a role in increasing the complications of pre-eclampsia.

Effects on the Fetus

Smoking of cigarettes by the pregnant mother may affect the fetus in several ways (Table VII).

Table VII. Effects of cigarette smoking on the fetus

Intrauterine growth restriction
Fewer accelerations of the fetal heart rate
Reduction in number of fetal breathing movements
Intrapartum asphyxia
Unexplained intrauterine death

Intrauterine Growth Restriction

The effects of cigarette smoking on fetal growth cannot be discussed without firstly looking at the effects of caffeine on fetal growth as some pregnant women may use both substances. In a study on 111 mothers who had delivered of small-for-gestational-age (SGA) babies, comparing them with 747 appropriately grown infants, it was found that the risk of SGA birth almost doubled when the mother had a high rather than low caffeine intake in the third trimester of pregnancy.[107] The effects of a high caffeine intake was also confirmed in another detailed study.[51] Pregnant non-smokers, consuming more than 300 mg caffeine per day, had statistically significant lower weights of newborns. However, the lengths and head circumferences of newborns were not affected significantly. Cigarette smoking had similar effects. However, findings of a large study were different. In this case, the study was done prospectively and was population based. Caffeine exposure was accurately determined at 6-12 and 32-34 completed weeks of gestation in 953 women. Plasma cotinine levels were also obtained at these periods. In the analysis, the effects of many covariates, that could have affected the birth weight, were excluded. No association between birth weight and caffeine exposure could be found. It is therefore likely that the reduction of birth weight, as found in many studies, is rather due to the simultaneous smoking of cigarettes than the consumption of caffeine alone.

In addition, cigarette smoking not only affects birth weight but also the length and head circumference of the infant.[108] The lowering effect of smoking on the birth weight was most significant in mothers who were underweight and increased their cigarette consumption during pregnancy.[109] The fact that smoking in the third trimester can reduce body length and birth weight was also confirmed in another study [110] as well as its more severe effects on fetal growth among older mothers.[111] It has been found that cigarette smoking accounts for a 2.7-5.2 % variation in infant birth weight and that most of the increase in birth weight after quitting is attributed to the independent effect of smoking on fetal growth restriction.[112]

It is important to note that infants of smokers are symmetrically small at birth.[113] This finding most likely indicates that the effects of smoking are present during the whole pregnancy and not only during the last part. It also means that there is most likely a direct effect on the placenta as found in a study where Doppler flow velocity waveforms were determined in 183 pregnancies complicated by growth restriction and 549 appropriately grown fetuses.[114] In logistic models, smoking during pregnancy, among other findings, was significantly associated with an increased risk of growth restriction complicated by abnormal umbilical artery flow velocity waveforms (OR 2.56; 95 % CI 1.56-4.22). Smoking also correlated significantly with the occurrence of absent and reversed end diastolic velocity. One can therefore conclude that smoking has a direct effect on the vascular system on the fetal side of the placenta, which can be interpreted as a reduction of placental function.

Environmental tobacco smoke exposure also has an effect on birth weight. In this study, 183 pregnant women were monitored during pregnancy by doing serial ultrasound fetal measurements and cotinine levels. In a multiple regression analysis, a statistically significant negative correlation was found between the biparietal diameter of the fetus and cotinine levels.[115] In cases where the serum cotinine levels were below 10 ng/ml, indicating passive smoking, the cotinine level at 20-24 weeks gestation was inversely associated with the birth weight.

Intrapartum Asphyxia

Although no direct effect on intrapartum asphyxia could be found, there is a great indirect effect as cigarette smoking increases the risk of abruptio placentae, placenta praevia and placental insufficiency, some of the main causes of intrapartum asphyxia. In addition, cigarette smoking causes a reduction in accelerations of the fetal heart [116] and a reduction in fetal breathing movements in normal and abnormal pregnancies.[117] The effects are most likely caused by nicotine rather than carbon monoxide, as nicotine containing chewing gum produced similar effects on breathing movements. The smoking of herbal cigarettes, which increased the carboxyhaemoglobin concentrations similar to those found after smoking tobacco cigarettes, didn't have the same effect.

Unexplained Intrauterine Deaths

In developing countries, unexplained antepartum fetal death and sudden infant death syndrome (SIDS) are major causes of perinatal and infant mortality. The association between cigarette smoking and increased perinatal mortality rates is well accepted.[67] The main causes of perinatal deaths are low birth weight, SGA, and placenta praevia and abruptio placentae. According to the data on 360,000 births, the relative risk of fetal mortality among primigravidas, smoking less than one packet of cigarettes per day was 1.36 (95 % CI 1.16-1.59). When they smoked more than one packet per day, the fetal mortality increased by nearly 40 %; RR 1.62 (95 % CI 1.34-1.97).[118] Excluding known causes of intrauterine death, there is also an association between smoking and unexplained intrauterine deaths. Froen et al.[119] studied all cases of sudden intrauterine unexplained death (SIUD) and SIDS in Oslo and the surrounding county of Akershus from 1986-1995. There were 76 cases of SIUD and 78 of SIDS. Although smoking was associated with SUID, heavy smoking was found more often in SIDS cases and mothers were older. This association of higher maternal age and smoking with intrauterine death was also confirmed by a study on singleton live births in the United States between 1995 and 1997.[120]

In a hospital based cohort study on 34,394 births from 1995 to 2002, 27.2 % of the 360 antepartum deaths were unexplained. Cigarette smoking was not associated with unexplained fetal deaths but there could have been underreporting as cigarette smoking was not acceptable in the community where the study was done.[121] In addition, a large population-based individually matched case-control study in 702 cases of stillbirths and controls in Sweden found more stillbirths among blue-collar workers. The risk of stillbirth among smokers was higher than in the controls; OR1.4 (95 % CI 1.1-1.9) for smoking 1-9 cigarettes per day and 1.7 (95 % CI 1.2-2.4) for smoking 10 and more cigarettes per day.[122] These findings are supported by a large study in Norway, addressing 291 stillbirths. It is therefore certain that cigarette smoking increases the risks of sudden unexplained stillbirths.[123]

Infant Deaths and Sudden Infant Death Syndrome

The association between cigarette smoking and SIDS is well-known.[67 124] In a survey of live births in 1997, Salihu et al. found that 13.2% of pregnant women smoked. Their infant mortality, when compared to non-smokers, was 40 % higher.[125] SGA rather than preterm birth was the main mechanism for the excess infant mortality. They estimated that about 5 % of infant deaths in the United States is caused by maternal smoking during pregnancy.

In another large case-control study, in 239 SIDS cases and 239 controls, a strong correlation with abruptio placentae was found (OR 7.94, 95 % CI 1.34-47.12). This finding is very important in the light of the strong association between abruptio placentae and smoking during pregnancy.[126] The association between abruptio placentae and SIDS was also confirmed in a recent nested case-control study addressing 12,404 SIDS deaths and 49,616 controls (OR 1.57; 95 % CI 1.24-1.98).[127] In a most recent case-control study, the problem of SIDS was addressed in 20 regions in Europe. Data for more than 60 variables were obtained from the records of 745 SIDS cases. Logistic regression was used to calculate odds ratios for every factor in isolation and to construct multivariate models. There were 2,411 live controls. If the mother smoked, significant risks were associated with bed-sharing (at 2 weeks OR 27; 95 % CI 13.3-54.9). It was found that this increase in OR was partly attributable to the mother's use of alcohol.[128]

Nutritional Status

In a study in 118 smokers and 172 non-smoking controls, it was found that zinc is unable to reach the smoker's fetus. In contrast, infants of non-smokers appear to be able to maintain an adequate zinc status due to depletion of maternal zinc.[129] Another study confirmed the decrease in the red blood cell zinc levels in the umbilical cord in infants of mothers who smoke.[130]

Cleft Lip and Palate

A meta-analysis of the association between maternal smoking during pregnancy and syndromic orofacial clefts was done on 24 case-control studies.[131] Statistically significant associations were found between maternal smoking and cleft lip, with or without cleft palate

(RR 1.34; 95 % CI 1.25-1.44) and between smoking and cleft palate(RR 1.22; 95 % CI 1.10-1.35)

Effects on Breast Milk

Cigarette smoking has a wide range of effects on lactation and breast milk. It causes a reduction in milk production.[132 133] Nicotine is found in breast-milk of all smoking mothers and there is a direct correlation between the amount of nicotine in the milk and number of cigarettes smoked.[134] In addition, maternal cigarette smoking in early pregnancy is associated with higher plasma lipid levels and lower total lipid and docosahexaenoic acid content in the first months of lactation.[135]

Effects on Children

Maternal cigarette smoking leads to an increase of several complications in children.[136-139] The most common effects are listed in Table VIII.

Table VIII. Health effects of tobacco exposure on children

Acute and chronic middle ear disease
Reduction of lung function
Length retardation
Childhood asthma
Adult asthma and chronic obstructive pulmonary disease
Antisocial behaviour
Attention deficit hyperactivity disorder

Effects on Offspring

The delayed consequences of cigarette smoking are only now becoming apparent. The offspring of mothers who smoked more than 10 cigarettes per day have lower sperm counts.[140] There are also indications that maternal smoking is related to testicular cancer in their sons.[141]

Passive Smoking

It has been shown that environmental tobacco smoke (ETS), which includes both prenatal and postnatal exposure, has major effects on children's health. The greatest effect is on the respiratory system during the first years of life.[142] Exposure to ETS during pregnancy is also associated with a higher risk of SGA babies.[143] Newborns of mothers who have been exposed to ETS weighed 138 g less at birth than babies of unexposed groups (p=0.014). Paternal smoking is also associated with an increased risk of early pregnancy loss.[145]

Smoking and Alcohol

There is a strong association between the use of alcohol and cigarette smoking during pregnancy. Users of alcohol very often smoke cigarettes but most of the cigarette smoking does not drink. It is difficult to separate the effects as few studies looked prospectively at the simultaneous effect of both substances during pregnancy.

Prevention of Adverse Effects on the Fetus

Although it is best for mothers to quit smoking before they try to conceive, some women are not motivated to stop or find it impossible to break the addictive habit. Under these circumstances micronutrient supplementation may correct some of the low levels of vitamin C, beta-carotene, vitamin B 6 and 12 and folic acid levels found in pregnancy. [145]

References

[1] Garrett BE, Rose CA, Henningfield JR. Tobacco addiction and pharmacologic interventions. *Expert Opin Pharmacother* 2001;2:1548-1555.

[2] American College of Obstetricians and Gynecologists. *Smoking and Women's Health.* ACOG Educational Bulletin 240. Washington, DC: ACOG, 1997.

[3] Parran TV. The physician's role in smoking cessation. *J Respir Dis* 1998;19:S6-S12.

[4] PHS. Treating tobacco use and dependence: a systems approach. *A guide for health care administrators, insurers, managed care organizations, and purchasers.* US Health Service November 2000; Internet citation: http://www.cis.nci.nih.gov.

[5] Women and Smoking: *A report of the Surgeon General – 2001.* www.cdc.gov/tobacco.

[6] Surgeon General's Report on Women and Smoking: *Marketing Cigarettes to Women.* http://www.cdc.gov/tobacco.

[7] Women and Smoking: *A report of the Surgeon General – 2001.* ttp://www.cdc.gov/tobacco.

[8] Steyn K, Yacht D, Stander I, Fourie JM. Smoking in urban pregnant women in South Africa. *S Afr Med J* 1997;87:460-463.

[9] Baris E, Brigdan LW, Prindiville J, Da Costa e Silva VL, Chitanondh H, Chandiwana S. Research priorities for tobacco control in developing countries: a regional approach to a global consultative process. *Tobacco Control* 2000; 9:217-223.

[10] Surgeon General's Report on Women and Smoking: *What is needed to reduce smoking among women.* http://www.cdc.gov/tobacco.

[11] US Department of Health and Human Services. National Centre for Chronic Disease Prevention and Health Promotion. Office on Smoking and Health. *Women and Smoking. A Report of the US Surgeon General, 2001.* Tobaccco Use and Reproductive Outcomes Fact Sheet http://www.cdc.gov/tobacco.

[12] Ashmead GG. Smoking and pregnancy. *J Mat Fet Neonat Med* 2003;14:297-304.

[13] Women and Smoking: *A report of the Surgeon General – 2001.* Tobacco Use and Reproductive Outcome. http://www.cdc.gov/tobacco.

[14] Castles A, Adams EK, Melvin CL, Kelsch C, Boulton ML. Effects of smoking during pregnancy. Five meta-analyses. *Am J Prev Med* 1999;16:208-215.

[15] Johnstone FD. Smoke screen around the fetus. *Lancet* 1990;335:361.

[16] Baker RR, Pereira Da Silva JR, Smith G. The effect of tobacco ingredients on smoke chemistry. Part I: Flavourings and additives. *Food Chem Toxicol* 2004;42(Suppl):3-37.

[17] Baker RR, Pereira Da Silva JR, Smith G. The effect of tobacco ingredients on smoke chemistry. Part II: Casing ingredients. *Food Chem Toxicol* 2004;42(Suppl):39-52.

[18] Baker RR, Massey ED, Smith G. An overview of the effects of tobacco ingredients on smoke chemistry and toxicity. *Food Chem Toxicol* 2004;42(Suppl):53-83.

[19] Shields PG. Epidemiology of tobacco carcinogenesis. *Curr Oncol Rep* 2000;2:257-262.

[20] Brigham J. The addiction model. In: Samet JM, Yoon S-Y eds. *Women and the Tobacco Epidemic.* World Health Organization, 2001: 99-118.

[21] Morse D, Sethi J. Carbon monoxide and human disease. *Antioxid Redox Signal* 2002;4:331-338.

[22] Zevin S, Saunders S, Gourlay SG, Jacob P, Benowitz NL. Cardiovascular effects of carbon monoxide in cigarette smoke. *J Am Coll Cardiol* 2001;38:1633-1638.

[23] Ritz B, Yu F. The effect of ambient carbon monoxide on low birth weight among children born in southern California between 1989 and 1993. *Environ Health Perspect.* 1999;1071:17-25.

[24] Haustein KO. Cigarette smoking, nicotine and pregnancy. *Int J Pharmacol Ther* 1999;37:417-427.

[25] Bush PG, Mayhew TM, Abramovich DR, Aggett PJ, Burke MD, Page KR. Maternal cigarette smoking and oxygen diffusion across the placenta. *Placenta* 2000;21:824-833.

[26] Van Gilder TJ, Remington PL, Fiore MC. The direct effect of nicotine use on human health. *Wis Med J* 1997;96:43-48.

[27] Lambers DS, Clark KE. The maternal and fetal physiological effects of nicotine. *Semin Perinatol* 1996;20:115-126.

[28] Hellstrom-Lindahl E, Nordberg A. Smoking during pregnancy: a way to transfer addiction to the next generation? *Respiration* 2002:69:289-293.

[29] Pittilo MR. Cigarette smoking, endothelial injury and cardiovascular disease. *Int J Exp Pathol* 2000;81:219-230.

[30] Puranik R, Celermajer DS. Smoking and endothelial function. *Prog Cardiovasc Dis* 2003;45:443-458.

[31] Lain KY, Wilson JW, Crombleholme WR, Ness RB, Roberts JM, Smoking during pregnancy is associated with alterations in markers of endothelial function. *Am J Obstet Gynecol* 2003;189:1196-1201.

[32] Salafia C, Shiverick K. Cigarette smoking and pregnancy II: vascular effects. *Placenta* 1999;20:273-279.

[33] Zhang J, Ying X, Lo Q, Kallner A, Xui RJ, Henriksson P, Bjorkhen I. A single high dose of vitamin C counteracts the acute negative effect on microcirculation induced by cigarette smoking. *Microvasc Res* 1999;58:305-311.

[34] Lehr HA, Weyrich AS, Saetzler RK, Jurek A, Arfors KE, Zemmerman GA et al. Vitamin C blocks inflammatory platelet-activating mimetics created by cigarette smoking. *J Clin Invest* 1997;99:2300-2301.

[35] Fenech M. the role of folic acid and vitamin B12 in genomic stability of cells. *Mutar Res* 2001;475:57-67.

[36] Fowler B. The folate cycle and disease in humans. *Kidney Int Suppl* 2001; 78: S221-S229.

[37] McDonald SD, Perkins SL, Jodouin CA, Walker MC. Folate levels in pregnant women who smoke: an important gene/environment interaction. *Am J Obstet Gynecol* 2002;187:620-625.

[38] Pincock S. BMA says smoking harms reproductive capacity. *Lancet* 2004;363:628.

[39] Stillman RJ, Rosenberg MJ, Sachs BP. Smoking and reproduction. *Fertil Steril* 1986;46:545-566.

[40] Hughes EG, Yeo J, Claman P, YoungLai EV, Sagle MA, Daya S, Collins JA. Cigarette smoking and the outcomes of in vitro fertilization: measurement of effect size and levels of action. *Fertil Steril* 1994;62:807-814.

[41] Künzie R, Mueller MD, Hänggi W, Birkhäuser MH, Drescher H, Bersinger NA. Semen quality of male smokers and nonsmokers in infertile couples. *Fertil Steril* 2003; 79:297-291.

[42] Feichtinger W, Papalambrou K, Poehl M, Krischker U, Neumann K. Smoking and in vitro fertilization: a meta-analysis. *J Ass Reprod Gen*et 1997;14:596-599.

[43] Zenzes MT, Reed TE, Wang P, Klein J. Cotinine, a major metabolite of nicotine, is detectable in follicular fluids of passive smokers in *in vitro* fertilization therapy. *Fertil Steril* 1996;66:614-619.

[44] Kmietowicz Z. Smoking is causing impotence, miscarriages, and infertility. *BMJ* 2004; 328:364; The impact of smoking on sexual, reproductive and child health www.bma.org.uk.

[45] Zenzes MT. Smoking and reproduction: gene damage to human gametes and embryos. *Hum Reprod Update* 2000;6:122-131.

[46] VanVoorhis BJ, Dawson JD, Stovall DW, Sparks AE, Syrop CH. The effects of smoking on ovarian function and fertility during assisted reproduction cycles. *Obstet Gynecol* 1996;88:785-791.

[47] Salafia C, Shiverick K. Cigarette smoking and pregnancy I: ovarian, uterine and placental effects. *Placenta* 1999;20:265-272.

[48] Ashfaq M, Janjua MZ, Nawaz,M. Effects of maternal smoking on placental morphology. *J Ayub Med Coll Abbottabad* 2003;15:12-15.

[49] Genbacev O, McMaster MT, Zdravkovic T, Fisher SJ. Disruption of oxygen-regulated responses underlies pathological changes in the placentas of women who smoke or who are passively exposed to smoke during pregnancy. *Reprod Toxicol* 2003;17:501-518.

[50] Larsen LG, Clausen HV, Jonsson L. Stereologic examination of placentas from mothers who smoke during pregnancy. *Am J Obstet Gynecol* 2002;186:531-537.

[51] Balat O, Ugur MG, Pence S. The effect of smoking on the fetus and placenta in pregnancy. *Clin Exp Obstet Gynecol 2003*;30;57-59.

[52] Floyd R, Rimer B, Giovino G, Mullen P, Sullivan S. A review of smoking in pregnancy: effect on pregnancy outcomes and cessation efforts. *Annu Rev Pub Health* 1993;14:379-411.

[53] Odendaal HJ, Van Schie DL, De Jeu RM. Adverse effects of cigarette smoking on preterm labour and abruptio placentae. *Int J Gynecol Obstet* 2001;74:287-288.

[54] Haworth JC, Ellestad-Sayed JJ, King J, et al. Fetal growth retardation in cigarette-smoking mothers is not due to decreased maternal food intake. *Am J Obstet Gynec* 1980;137:719-723.

[55] King JC, Fabro S. Alcohol consumption and cigarette smoking: effect on pregnancy. *Clin Obstet Gynecol* 1983;26:437-448.

[56] Mishra GD, Dobson AJ, Schofield MJ. Cigarette smoking, menstrual symptoms and miscarriage among young women. *Aust N Z J Public Health* 2000;24:413-420.

[57] Ness RB, Grisso JA, Hirschinger N, Markovic N, Shaw LM, Day NL, Kline J. Cocaine and tobacco use and the risk of spontaneous abortion. *N Engl J Med* 1999;340:333-339.

[58] Chatenoud L, Parazzini F, di Cintio E, Zanconato G, Benzi G, Bortolus R, La Vecchia C. Paternal and maternal smoking habits before conception and during the first trimester: relation to spontaneous abortion. *Ann Epidemiol* 1998;8:520-526.

[59] Makrydimas G, Sebire NJ, Vlassis N, Nicolaides KH. Fetal losses following ultrasound diagnosis of a live fetus at 6-10 weeks of gestation. *Ultrasound Obstet Gynecol* 2003:22:368-372.

[60] Windham GC, Swan SH, Fenster L. Parental cigarette smoking and the risk of spontaneous abortion. *Am J Epidemiol* 1992;135:1394-1403.

[61] Pattinson HA, Taylor PJ, Pattinson, MH. The effect of cigarette smoking on ovarian function and early pregnancy outcome of in vitro fertilization treatment. *Fertil Steril* 1991;55:780-783.

[62] Wisborg K, Kesmodel U, Henriksen TB, Hedegaard M, Secher NJ. A prospective study of maternal smoking and spontaneous abortion. *Acta Obstet Gynecol Scand* 2003;82:936-941.

[63] Rasch V. Cigarette, alcohol, and caffeine consumption: risk factors for spontaneous abortion. *Acta Obstet Gynecol Scand* 2003;82:182-188.

[64] Leviton A, Cowan L. A review of the literature relating caffeine consumption by women to their risk of reproductive hazards. *Food Chem Toxicol* 2002;40:1271-1310.

[65] Bouyer J, Coste J, Shojaei T, Pouly J-L, Fernandez H, Gerbaud L, Job-Spira N. Risk factors for ectopic pregnancy: a comprehensive analysis based on a large case-control, population-based study in France. *Am J Epidemiol* 2003;157:185-194.

[66] Bunyavejchevin S, Havanond P, Wisawasukmongchol W. Risk factors for ectopic pregnancy. *J Med Assoc Thai* 2003;86:S417-S421.

[67] Andres RL, Day M-C. Perinatal complications associated with maternal tobacco use. *Semin Perinatol* 2000;5:231-241.

[68] Naeye R. Abruptio placentae and placenta previa: frequency, perinatal mortality, and cigarette smoking. *Obstet Gynecol* 1980;55:701-704.

[69] Fiaz AS, Ananth CV. Etiology and risk factors for placenta previa: an overview and meta-analysis of observational studies. *J Matern Fetal Neonatal Med* 2003;13:175-190.

[70] Cnattingius S. The epidemiology of smoking during pregnancy: Smoking prevalence, maternal characteristics, and pregnancy outcomes. *Nicotine Tobacco Res* 2004;6: S125-S140.

[71] Handler AS, Mason ED, Rosenburg DL, Davis EG. The relationship between exposure during pregnancy to cigarette smoking and cocaine use and placenta praevia. *Am J Obstet Gynecol* 1994;170:884-889.

[72] Williams M, Mittendorf R, Lieberman E, Monson R, Schoenbaum S, Genest D. Cigarette smoking during pregnancy in relation to placenta praevia. *Am J Obstet Gynecol* 1991;165:28-32.

[73] Christianson RF. Gross differences between the placentas of smokers and nonsmokers. *Am J Epidemiol* 1979;110:178-187.

[74] Prins CA, Theron GB, Steyn DW, Geerts LTGM, De Jong G. Total perinatally related wastage at Tygerberg Hospital – a comparison between 1986 and 1993. *S Afr Med J* 1997; 87:808-814.

[75] Saftlas AF, Olson DR, Atrash HK, Rochat R, Rowley D. National trends in the incidence of abruptio placentae, 1979-1987. *Obstet Gynecol* 1991;78:1081-1086.

[76] Voigt L, Hollenbach KA, Krohn MA, Daling JR, Hickok D. The relationshop of abruptio placentae with maternal smoking and small for gestational age infants. *Obstet Gynecol* 1990;75:771-774.

[77] Raymond EG, Mills J. Placental abruption: maternal risk factors and associated fetal conditions. *Acta Obstet Gynecol Scand* 1993:72:633-639.

[78] Kramer MS, Usher RH, Pollack R, Boyd M, Usher S. Etiologic determinants of abruptio placentae. *Obstet Gynecol* 1997;89:221-226.

[79] Hladky K, Yankowitz J, Hansen WF. Placental abruption. *Obstet Gynecol Surv* 2002;57:299-305.

[80] Anath CV, Smulian JC, Vintzileos AM. Incidence of placental abruption in relation to cigarette smoking and hypertensive disorders during pregnancy: a meta-analysis of observational studies. *Obstets Gynecol* 1999;93:622-628.

[81] Mortensen, JT, Thulstrup AM, Larsen H, Moller M, Sorensen HT. Smoking, sex of the offspring, and risks of placental abruption, placenta previa, and preeclampsia: a population-based cohort study. *Acta Obstet Gynecol Scand* 2001;80:894-898.

[82] Naeye RL. Effects of maternal cigarette smoke on the fetus and placenta. *Br J Obster Gynaecol* 1978;85:732-737.

[83] Kramer MS, Usher RH, Pollack R, Boyd M, Usher S. Etiologic determinants of abruptio placentae. *Obstet Gynecol* 1997;89:221-226.

[84] Hall DR, Odendaal HJ, Steyn DW, Grové D. Expectant management of early onset, severe pre-eclampsia: maternal outcome. *Br J Obstet Gynaecol* 2000;107:1252-1257.

[85] Odendaal HJ, Hall DR, Grové D. Risk factors for and perinatal mortality of abruptio placentae in patients hospitalised for early onset severe pre-eclampsia – a case controlled study. *J Obstet Gynaecol* 2000;20:358-364.

[86] Ananth CV, Smulian JC, Demissie K, Vintzeleos AM, Knuppel RA. Placental abruption among singleton and twin pregnancies in the United States: risk factor profiles. *Am J Epidemiol* 2001;153:771-778.

[87] Ananth CV, Savitz DA, Bowes WA, Luther ER. Influence of hypertensive disorders and cigarette smoking on placental abruption and uterine bleeding during pregnancy. *Br J Obstet Gynecol* 1997;104:572-578.

[88] Evaldson G, Lagrelius A, Winiarski J. Premature rupture of the membranes. *Acta Obstet Gynecol Scand* 1980;57:385-393.

[89] Miller HC, Jekel JF. Epidemiology of spontaneous premature rupture of membranes: factors in pre-term births.*Yale J Biol Med* 1989;62:241-251.

[90] Williams MA, Mittendorf R, Stublefield PG, Lieberman E, Schoenbaum SC, Monson RR. Cigarettes, coffee, and preterm premature rupture of membranes. *Am J Epidemiol* 1992;135:895-903.

[91] Spinillo A, Nicola S, Piazzi G, Ghazal K, Colonna L, Baltaro F. Epidemiological correlates of preterm premature rupture of membranes. *Int J Gynecol Obstet* 1994; 47:7-15.

[92] Harlow BL, Frigoletto FD, Cramer DW, Evans JK, LeFevre ML. Bain RP, et al. Determinants of preterm delivery in low-risk pregnancies. The RADIUS Study Group. *J Clin Epidemiol* 1996;49:441-448.

[93] Myles TD, Espinoza R, Meyer W, Bieniarz A, Nguyen T. Effects of smoking, alcohol, and drugs of abuse on the outcome of "expectantly" managed cases of preterm premature rupture of membranes. *J Mat Fet Med* 1998;7:157-161.

[94] Kyrklund-Blomberg NB, Cnattingius S. Preterm birth and maternal smoking: Risks related to gestational age and onset of delivery. *Am J Obstet Gynecol* 1998;179: 1051-1055.

[95] Haram K, Mortensen JH, Wollen AL. Preterm delivery: an overview. *Acta Obstet Gynecol Scand*; 2003:82:687-704.

[96] Shah NR, Bracken MB. A systematic review and meta-analysis of prospective studies on the association between maternal cigarette smoking and preterm delivery. *Am J Obstet Gynecol* 2000; 182:465-472.

[97] Burguet A, Kaminski M, Abraham-Lerat L, Schaal JP. Cambonie G, Fresson J, et al. The complex relationship between smoking in pregnancy and preterm delivery. Results of the Epipage study. *BJOG* 2004;111:258-265.

[98] Larroque B, Brèart G, Kaminski M, et al. Survival of very preterm infants: Epipage, a population-based cohort study. *Arch Dis Child* In Press.

[99] Woods Jr JR, Plessiinger MA, Miller RK. Vitamins C and E: missing links in preventing preterm premature rupture of membranes? *Am J Obstet Gynecol;* 2001:185:5-10.

[100] Hadley CB, Main DM, Gabbe SG. Risk factore for preterm premature rupture of membranes. *Am J Perinatol* 1990;7:374-379.

[101] Hoffman DR, Romero R, Johnson JM. Detecting platelet-activating factor in the amniotic fluid of complicating pregnancies. *Am J Obstet Gynecol;*1990:162:525-528.

[102] Egawa M, Yasuda K, Nakajima T, Okada H, Yoshimura T, Yuri T et al. Smoking enhances oxytocin-induced rhythmic myometrial contraction. *Biol Reprod* 2003;68:2272-2280.

[103] Chiriboga CA. Fetal alcohol and drug effects. *The Neurologist* 2003;9:267-279.

[104] Klonoff-Cohen H, Edelstein S, Savitz D. Cigarette smoking and preeclampsia. *Obstet Gynecol* 1993;81:541-544.

[105] Cnattingius S, Mills JL, Yuen J, Erikson O, Ros HS. The paradoxical effect of smoking in preeclamptic pregnancies: Smoking reduces the incidence but increases the rates of perinatal mortality, abruptio placentae, and intrauterine growth restriction. *Am J Obstet Gynecol* 1997;177:156-161.

[106] Ioka A, Tsukuma H, Nakamuro K. Lifestyles and pre-eclampsia with special attention to cigarette smoking. *J Epidemiol* 2003;**13**:90-95.

[107] Vik T, Bakketeig LS, Trygg KU, Lund-Larsen K, Jacobsen G. High caffeine consumption in the third trimester of pregnancy: gender-specific effects on fetal growth. *Pediatr Perinat Epidemiol* 2003;17:324-331.

[108] Johnson AA, Knight EM, Edwards CH, Oyemade UJ, Cole OJ, Westney OE, et al. Selected lifestyle practices in urban African American women-relationships to pregnancy outcome, dietary intakes and anthropometric measurements. *J Nutr* 1994;124:S963-S972.

[109] Laml T, Hartmann BE, Kirchengast S, Preyer O, Albrecht AE, Husslein PW. Impact of maternal anthropometry and smoking on neonatal birth weight. *Gynecol Obstet Invest* 2000;50:231-236.

[110] Omhi H, Hirooka K, Mochizuki Y. Fetal growth and the timing of exposure to maternal smoking. *Pediatr Int* 2002;44:55-59.

[111] Cnattingius S. Maternal age modifies the effect of maternal smoking on intrauterine growth retardation but not on late fetal death and placental abruption. *Am J Epidemiol* 1007;145:319-323.

[112] Secker-Walker RH, Vacek PM. Relationships between cigarette smoking during pregnancy, gestational age, maternal weight gain, and infant birth weight. *Addict Behav* 2003;28:55-66.

[113] Ong KK, Preece MA, Emmett PM, Ahmed ML, Dunger DB. Size at birth and early childhood growth in relation to maternal smoking, parity, and infant breast-feeding: longitudinal birth cohort study and analysis. *Pediatr Res* 2002;52:863-867.

[114] Spinillo A, Bergante C, Gardella M, Mainini R, Montanari L. Interaction between risk factors for fetal growth retardation associated with abnormal umbilical artery Doppler studies. *Acta Obstet Gynecol Scand* 2004;83:431-435.

[115] Hanke W, Sobala W, Halinka J. Environmental tobacco smoke exposure among pregnant women: impact on fetal biometry at 20-24 weeks of gestation and newborn child's birth weight. *Int Arch Occup Environ Health* 2003;77:47-52.

[116] Phelan JP. Diminished fetal reactivity with smoking. *Am J Obstet Gynecol* 1980;136:230-233.

[117] Manning FA, Feyerabend C. Cigarette smoking and fetal breathing movements. *Br J Obstet Gynaecol* 1976;83:262-270.

[118] Kleinman J, Pierre MJ, Madans J, Land G, Schramm W. The effect of maternal smoking on fetal and infant mortality. *Am J Epidemiol* 1088;127:274-282.

[119] Froen JF, Arnestad M, Vege A, Irgens LM, Rognum TO, Saugstad OD, et al. Comparative epidemiology of sudden infant death syndrome and sudden intrauterine unexplained death. *Arch Dis Chils Fetal Neonatal Ed* 2002;87:F118-F121.

[120] Salihu HM, Shumpert MN, Aliyu MH, Alexander MR, Kirby RS, Alexander GR. Stillbirths and infant deaths associated with maternal smoking among mothers aged >/=40years: a population study. *Am J Perinatol* 2004;21:121-129.

[121] Chibber R. Unexplained antepartum fetal deaths: what are the determinants? *Arch Gynecol Obstet* 2004.

[122] Stephansson O, Dickman PW, Johansson AL, Cnattingius S. The influence of socioeconomic status on stillbirth risk in Sweden. *Int J Epidemiol* 2001;30:1296-1301.

[123] . Froen JF, Arnestad M, Frey K, Vege A, Saugstad OD, Stray-Pedersen B. Risk factors for sudden intrauterine unexplained death: epidemiologic characteristics of singleton sases in Oslo, Norway, 1986-1995. *Am J Obstet Gynecol* 2001;184:694-702.

[124] Froen JF, Arnestad M, Vege A, Irgens LM, Rognum TO, Saugstad OD, et al. Comparative epidemiology of sudden infant death syndrome and sudden intrauterine unexplained death. *Arch Dis Chils Fetal Neonatal Ed* 2002;87:F118-F121.

[125] Salihu HM, Aliyu MH, Pierre-Louis BJ, Alexander GR. Levels of excess infant deaths attributable to maternal smoking during pregnancy in the United States. *Matern Child Health J* 2003;7:219-227.

[126] Klonoff-Cohen HS, Srinivasan IP, Edelstein SL. Prenatal and intrapartum events and sudden infant death syndrome. *Pediatr Perinat Epidemiol* 2002;16:82-89.

[127] Getahun D, Amre D, Rhoads GG, Demissie K. Maternal and obstetric risk factors for sudden infant death syndrome in the United States. *Obstet Gynecol* 2004;103:646-652.

[128] Carpenter RG, Irgens LM, Blair PS, England PD, Flemming P, Huber JG, et al. Sudden unexplained infant deaths in 20 regions in Europe: case-control study. *Lancet* 2004;363: 185-191.

[129] Kuhnert BR, Kuhnert PM, Lazebnik N, Erhard P. The effect of maternal smoking on the relationship between maternal and fetal zinc status and infant birth weight. *J Am Coll Nutr* 1988;7:309-316.

[130] Kuhnert PM, Kuhnert BR, Erhard P, Brashear WT, Groh-Wargo SL, Webster S. The effect of smoking on placental and fetal zinc status. *Am J Obstet Gynecol* 1987;157:1241-1246.

[131] Little J, Cardy A, Munger RG. Tobacco smoking and oral clefts: a meta-analysis. *Bull World Health Organ* 2004;82:213-218.

[132] Vio F, Salazar G, Infante C. Smoking during pregnancy and lactation and its effect on breast-milk volume. *Am J Clin Nutr* 1991;54:1011-1026.

[133] Hopkinson JM, Schanler RJ, Fraley JK, Garza C. Milk production by mothers of premature infants: influence of cigarette smoking. *Pediatrics* 1992;90:934-938.

[134] Perlman HH, Dannenberg AM, Sokoloff N. The excretion of nicotine in breast milk and urine from cigarette smoking: its effect on lactation and the nursing. *J Am Med Assoc* 1942;28:1003-1009.

[135] Agostoni C, Marangoni T, Grandi F, Lammardo AM, Giovannini M, Riva E, Galli C. Earlier smoking habits are associated with higher serum lipids and lower milk fat and polyunsaturated fatty acid content in the first 6 months of pregnancy. *Eur J Clin Nutr* 2003;57:1466-1472.

[136] Hofhuis W, de Jongste JC, Merkus PJFM. Adverse health effects of prenatal and postnatal tobacco smoke exposure on children. *Arch Dis Child* 2003;88:1086-1090.

[137] Jaakkola JJ, Grissler M. Maternal smoking in pregnancy, fetal development, and childhood asthma. *Am J Public Health* 2004;94:136-140.

[138] Thapar A, Fowler T, Rice F, Scourfield J, van den Bree M, Thomas I, et al. Maternal smoking during pregnancy and attention deficit hyperactivity disorder symptome in offspring. *Am J Psychiatry* 2003;160:1985-1989.

[139] Karatza AA, Varvargou A, Beratis NG. Growth up to 2 years in relationship to maternal smoking during pregnancy. *Clin Pediatr (Phila)* 2003;42:533-541.

[140] Storgaard L, Bonde JP, Ernst E, Spano M, Anderson CY, Frydenberg M, Olsen J. Does smoking during pregnancy affect sons'sperm counts? *Epidemiology* 2003;14:261-262.

[141] Pettersson A, Kaijser M, Richiardi L, Askling J, Ekbom A, Akre O. Women smoking and testicular cancer: one epidemic causing another? *Int J Cancer* 2004;109:941-944.

[142] DiFranza JR, Aligne CA, Witzman M. Prenatal and postnatal environmental tobacco smoke exposure and children's health. *Pediatrics* 2004; 113: 1007-1015.

[143] Goel P, Singh I, Aggarwal A, Dua D. Effects of passive smoking on outcome in pregnancy. *J Postgrad Med* 2004;50:12-16.

[144] Venners SA, Wang X, Chen C, Wang L, Guang W, Huang A, et al. Paternal smoking and pregnancy loss: a prospective study using a biomarker of pregnancy. *Am J Epidemiol* 2004;159:993-1001.

[145] Cogswell ME, Weisberg P, Spong C. Cigarette smoking, alcohol use and adverse pregnancy outcomes: implications for micronutrient supplementation. *J Nutr* 2003:133:1722S-1731S.

In: Trends in Smoking and Health Research
Editors: J. H. Owing, pp. 105-125

ISBN: 1-59454-391-7
© 2005 Nova Science Publishers, Inc.

Chapter VI

Intrauterine Exposure to Tobacco Inhaled Products and Subsequent Obesity

*André Michael Toschke**

Ludwig-Maximilians-University of Munich

Abstract

Objective

The association between maternal smoking in pregnancy and offspring's overweight and obesity was observed by chance at first. Overweight and obesity tend to increase in their prevalences. Childhood obesity often persists throughout adulthood. Therapeutic interventions are far from satisfactory results. Therefore, prevention of overweight and obesity is a major public health issue. For effective prevention strategies exact identification of modifiable risk factors is required. In order to assess the impact of intrauterine tobacco exposure on overweight and obesity, 3 cross sectional studies were performed.

Setting

Southern Germany

Participants

n=8,765 (survey I), n= 6,483 (survey II) and n=4,974 (survey III) German children aged 5.0 to 6.9 years

---

* Phone/Fax: +49 – 89 – 71009-307/-315; E-mail address: michael.toschke@LRZ.uni-muenchen.de; url: http://www.epiresearch.info/

Main Outcome Measures

Overweight and obesity at school entry was defined as body mass index (weight in kilograms divided by squared height in meters) >90th percentile and >97th percentile (survey I and II) or according to sex- and age-specific body mass index cutpoints proposed by the International Obesity Task Force (survey III). Questions on maternal smoking differentiated between smoking in pregnancy vs. non-smoking in pregnancy (survey I and II) and additionally smoking in early pregnancy or smoking throughout pregnancy (survey III).

Results

Offspring of mothers who smoked in pregnancy had higher prevalences of overweight and obesity in all 3 surveys. These associations could not be explained by confounding due to a number of constitutional, sociodemographic and lifestyle factors. The adjusted odds ratios for smoking in pregnancy and offspring's obesity indicated a risk for offspring of smoking mothers twice as much compared to offspring of non-smoking mothers. Smoking in early pregnancy yielded similar odds ratios for childhood overweight and obesity compared to smoking throughout pregnancy.

Conclusions

The association between maternal smoking in pregnancy and offspring's overweight and obesity could be reproducibly observed in 3 surveys. Since adjustment for a wide range of potential confounders could not explain this association and smoking after pregnancy was not associated with childhood obesity, intrauterine exposure rather than family lifestyle factors associated with smoking appears to be instrumental. The first trimester has been identified as the critical period. Women of reproductive age should be advised to quit smoking prior to pregnancy.

Abbreviations

BMI   body mass index
CI   confidence interval
OR   odds ratio

Introduction

The long-known association between active cigarette smoking and increased mortality due to several subsequent diseases such as cardiovascular disease [1] or bronchial carcinoma [2] is well documented and there is no doubt about the evidence of smoking as a multiple risk factor for human health nowadays. Nevertheless, a high prevalence of active smoking with approximately 46.5 million U.S. smoking residents in 1999 [3] reflects its unbroken popularity. Smoking remains the leading cause of death in the US with a total of 442,398 persons who died prematurely each year as a result of smoking from 1995—1999 [3] and approximately 435,000 deaths (18.1% of total US deaths) in 2000 [4]. While active smoking remains a personal decision, passive smoking does not. Although some associations between passive smoking and diseases such as childhood asthma could be observed [5, 6], the majority of multiple possible risks of passive smoking could not yet. This might be due to the difficulty of measuring the exposure of passive smoking. A particular form of passive smoking is intrauterine exposure to tobacco inhaled products.

Simpson already described an association between maternal smoking during pregnancy and low infant birth weight in 1957 [7], which was confirmed by Yerushalmy et al. and Butler et al. in 1971/1972 [8, 9]. The reduction in birth weight was about 100 to 300g in different studies. Simultaneously the risks for perinatal mortality and for sudden unexpected death were increased among offspring of smoking mothers [10, 11].

In an epidemiological study on risk factors for childhood obesity, von Kries et al. reported a surprising finding with respect to the long-known association between maternal smoking and low infant birth weight: *"..., whereas maternal smoking during pregnancy was positively correlated with being overweight or obese"* [12]. This study enrolling 9,357 German children obtained data on anthropometric measures at school entry and a wide number of potential risk factors such as formula feeding or smoking during pregnancy. Although the primary focus of this study was a risk factor analysis for childhood asthma, additional analysis pointed to an association between breastfeeding and obesity which the World Health Organization (WHO) exclaimed as global epidemic of the 21st century [13].

After smoking induced deaths, deaths due to poor diet and physical inactivity (obesity) which account for approximately 400,000 US deaths (16.6% of total US deaths), are following as death cause no. 2 in the U.S. [4].

The association between intrauterine tobacco exposure and obesity might be wondering at first impression because of the long known association between maternal smoking during pregnancy and low birth weight. There might be 4 possibilities to explain this association with respect to low birth weight: 1) smoking in pregnancy has no real impact on offspring's obesity but is confounded through social class or other risk factors, 2) low birth weight is only a transition state to later obesity, 3) the effect of intrauterine tobacco exposure on low birth weight is independent of the effect of intrauterine exposure to tobacco on obesity, or 4) the effect of intrauterine tobacco exposure on obesity is due to a mixture of effects 2) and 3). To disentangle these possibilities, we performed a number of studies on school entry children.

Material and Methods

Structure of Surveys Associated with the Obligatory School Entry Health Examinations in Bavaria, Germany

Most results of our studies were based on surveys associated with the school entry health examinations [12, 14-16]. The structure of the surveys contains 5 steps, starting with the development of study design and preparing the parental questionnaire at our institute, the Bavarian State Ministry of Environment, Health and Consumer Protection and collaborating institutes (Fig. 1). The first data collection on individual level (children/parents) is performed by local public health offices participating in the study, followed by the second data collection at our institute where the data of local public health offices were collected. After that all questionnaires and additional data are administered by an external data entry. Finally additional plausibility checks and analysis are performed at our institute (Fig. 1).

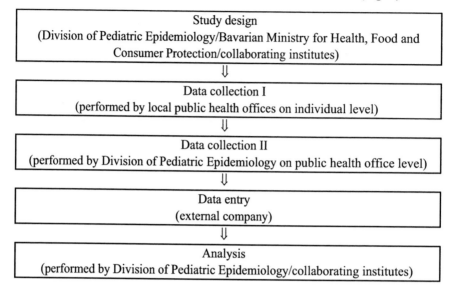

Figure 1. Structure of surveys associated with the obligatory school entry health examinations in Bavaria, Germany

The Obligatory School Entry Examination in Bavaria, Germany, as a Data Source

In Bavaria, all children in the year before school entry had to pass a medical investigation by physicians of respective local public health offices until 2001. Routine measurements included examination of stature and weight in a standardized manner (measurements in underwear only; usage of calibrated stadiometers and balances). Since 2001 only children not participating in the well-baby-check up U9 (60-64 months) are seen by doctors of public health offices, but all children still have to pass audiometry and visual tests carried out by nurses (SMAs –,Sozial-Medizinische Assisstentinnen'). The nurses of the public health offices, which participate in our surveys, still obtain data on height and weight in a standardized manner.

Meanwhile, we performed five surveys associated with the school entry examinations: two focused on risk factors for asthma (1997 and 1998), two on risk factors for overweight (1999/2000 and 2001) and the recent study focused on environmental risks and children's health such as motor development, faculty of speech, sunburns etc.. While both asthma surveys were carried out in rural regions the following surveys were carried out in a mixture of rural, suburban and urban areas. Since 1999 nurses (SMAs) of six out of 72 Bavarian public health offices have regularly collaborated and obtained additional data on school entry children and their parents. A possible selection bias by participating public health offices seems to be unlikely since in these communities the distributions of body mass index (BMI), gender and the number of siblings in the compulsory health examinations were similar to those in all regions in Bavaria suggesting that the study region is representative for Bavarian children [16]. The study region of the obesity focused surveys consists of one densely populated area (847 inhabitants/km^2; the city of Ingolstadt), a population in the outskirts of the city of Augsburg (214 inhabitants/km^2), and four rural areas (Miesbach, Günzburg, Kitzingen, and areas surrounding Regensburg), each with less than 200 inhabitants/km^2 [16].

While school entry health examinations were obligatory, participation in additional associated studies was voluntary. Parents received questionnaires and invitations to participate in the study together with invitations for the school entry examinations of their child. The self-administered questionnaires were collected at the date of child's school entry examination and linked to data of routine and additional measurements carried out by the nurses (SMAs). The questionnaires contain a routine part including questions on e.g. parental education as surrogate for social class and parts on lifestyle, sociodemographic and constitutional questions possibly associated with the main focus of the respective survey. Social class is estimated by parental education because unfortunately other questions to assess social class such as current occupancy or family income in particular, are not answered satisfactorily in Germany [17].

Prior to study initiation nurses got a schooling for additional measurements. The training consisted of one complete day learning the investigations by general instruction followed by practicing in small groups.

Response rates of >75% for each survey (>80% in the recent one) reflect good acceptance compared to other population-based studies. Foreign families were underrepresented which might be due to incapacity in the German language or lack of questionnaires in the respective mother tongue (Tab. 1). Therefore the analysis was confined to German children.

Thus, the school entry health examinations still provide a suitable access to complete cohorts of German children in the year before school entry and studies linked to the school entry health examination stand a chance to be representative.

Table 1. Underrepresentation of Non-German families in surveys associated with the school entry health examinations

Area	non German nationality (% of study population)	non German nationality (% - Stat. yearbook 1997)
Ingolstadt	12.9	18.4
Miesbach	6.2	6.1
Schwandorf	1.9	2.6
Augsburg Land	5.1	7.7
Günzburg	10.9	13.1
Ostallgäu	7.4	6.9

Data Entry and Quality Control

The data entry was performed by an external professional data entry company (Fig. 1). The same data were entered by two persons (double entry) and both entries were matched in order to detect data entry errors. Additionally, basic plausibility checks were undertaken by the data entry company. Implausible data was revised according to information of parental answers in the original questionnaires.

The quality of the external data entry company was always controlled at our institute. A 1% random sample of collected questionnaires were compared to the electronic dataset delivered by the data entry company. Entry errors were clearly below 1%/variable and 0.0023%/variable for the recent surveys reflecting a valid data entry.

Statistical Analysis and Possible Confounding

Odds ratios are a useful statistical tool to describe, to measure and to interpret effects of explaining variables on dichotomous outcomes (overweight/obesity – yes/no). Since overweight and obesity are the most common nutritional diseases, the rare disease assumption cannot be assumed and the odds ratio as an approximation for the relative risk is probably possible. An odds ratio of 1.0 describes no effect (unity), while an odds ratio above 1 describes a risk factor and an odds ratio below 1 describes a protective factor. To adjust for possible confounding factors in an analysis with a dichotomous outcome variable a multiple logistic regression model is a suitable tool [18].

A confounder is a factor that is associated to both the exposure variable and the outcome variable [19]. A confounder is able to explain the discrepancy between the desired (but unobservable) counterfactual risk (which the exposed would have had, had they been unexposed) and the unexposed risk that was its substitute. In order for a factor to explain this discrepancy and thus confound, it must be capable of affecting or at least predicting the risk in the unexposed (reference) group, and not be affected by the exposure or the disease [19].

In associations between smoking and health outcomes, consideration of confounding plays a major role. One could imagine that for instance a effect of smoking on a specific health outcome is strongly confounded by the pathway: 1) smoking is related to low social class, 2) low social class might be related to other unhealthy behaviors associated with the health outcome such as unhealthy nutrient intake, 3) by not taking into account low social class in the analysis, the real impact of smoking on the health outcome might be overestimated. In our topic, maternal smoking in pregnancy and offspring's obesity, it is obvious that low maternal social class is associated with both smoking in pregnancy and offspring's obesity. Thus a risky behavior associated with low social class might confound the association between smoking and offspring's obesity and adjustment for e.g. social class by multiple regression analysis is important.

In a multiple regression analysis the explaining variable of interest (exposure) is included as well as possible confounding variables (covariates) and interaction terms. Analogously to multiple linear regression analysis, the effect of the exposure is adjusted for all other covariates included in the model. Thus in absence of sources of residual confounding such as e.g. imprecise measures of covariates the effect estimator may reflect an unbiased result at least with respect to the considered covariates.

Results

The 1997 Obligatory School Entry Health Examination in Bavaria (Seheb) Revisited

A more detailed analysis of the data obtained during the obligatory school entry health examination on smoking and obesity yielded surprising results. For 8,765 parents-children pairs full information on maternal smoking before, during and after pregnancy was available.

Overweight and obesity were defined according to the proposal of the European Childhood Obesity Group with a body mass index of greater than the age- and sex specific 90th percentile for overweight and greater than the 97th percentile for obesity [20]. The reference values for the BMI were based on the age and sex specific distributions of all 115,530 German children who were investigated during the 1997 obligatory school entry health examination in Bavaria, Germany.

Offspring of mothers who smoked during pregnancy had an adjusted odds ratio of 1.92 (95%CI 1.29-1.73) for obesity at school entry. Interestingly offspring of mothers who smoked before pregnancy, but not throughout pregnancy had a similar increased risk for obesity at school entry; the analysis yielded an adjusted odds ratio of 1.74 (95%CI 1.29-2.34) [15]. Therefore, we concluded that mothers who smoked before pregnancy and not throughout pregnancy stopped smoking during pregnancy and the effect of smoking in pregnancy on offspring's obesity may be related to the early course of pregnancy [15]. Starting smoking after pregnancy was not associated with offspring's overweight or obesity.

Typical methodological considerations associated with cross sectional surveys such as reverse causality have to be carefully addressed. However, reverse causality regarding the temporal sequence can be ruled out, because intrauterine tobacco exposure always precedes later obesity.

Unfortunately, we could not adjust for important possible confounding factors for obesity such as e.g. parental obesity since this survey was conducted to identify risk factors for childhood asthma and special potential obesity related confounders such as maternal and paternal height and weight were not obtained. The effect of maternal smoking in pregnancy on offspring's obesity could only be adjusted for breast-feeding, parental education, low birth weight and prematurity [15]. Therefore, we performed another study to further investigate the role of potential confounding.

The 1999-2000 Obligatory School Entry Health Examination in Bavaria (SEHEB) – Controlling for Confounding

The additional survey associated with the 1999-2000 school entry health examination was focused on risk factors for childhood obesity. A wide range of potential obesity related risk factors, protective factors or confounders, respectively had been obtained.

Potential confounders for the association between smoking in pregnancy and offspring's obesity included parental education, parental obesity at school entry, single parenthood at school entry, population density, time of introduction of complementary foods, giving a caloric bottle to sleep in the first year of life, birth weight, high weight gain during the first year of life, amount of television watching or playing videogames at school entry, regular sport activities in a club at school entry, eating snacks in front of television at school entry, having main meals alone at school entry, present total caloric intake, breastfeeding and having a warm meal for supper at school entry [16]. The question on maternal smoking differentiated between the periods of smoking before pregnancy, during pregnancy, in the child's first year of life and smoking at school entry. The question was supposed to be answered with yes or no. If yes, the number of cigarettes smoked daily was asked for by categories of less than 10, 10-20, and more than 20 for each period separately. Overweight and obesity were defined as a body mass index (BMI) >90th and >97th percentile, respectively [20].

Most questionnaires had been answered by the mother only (81.1 percent) followed by both parents (16.1 percent), or by the father only (2.4 percent). Some 6,483 children could be analyzed after excluding children-parents pairs with missing information on maternal smoking status, weight or height. A total of 3,847 mothers said that they had ever smoked of whom 638 mothers stated that they had smoked throughout pregnancy.

The prevalence of offspring's overweight for maternal smoking during pregnancy increased with the amount of cigarettes from 8.1 percent (95%CI 7.2%-9.0%) for offspring of never smoking mothers to 14.1 percent (95%CI 11.1%-17.7%) for offspring of mothers who smoked less than 10 cigarettes daily during pregnancy up to 17.0 percent (95%CI 10.1%-26.2%) for offspring of mothers who smoked 10 or more than 10 daily cigarettes in pregnancy. Accordingly the prevalence of offspring's obesity increased with the amount of maternal daily cigarettes in pregnancy from 2.2 percent (95%CI 1.7%-2.7%)] for offspring of never smoking mothers to 5.7 percent (95%CI 3.7%-8.2%) for offspring of mothers who smoked less than 10 cigarettes daily during pregnancy up to 8.5 percent (95%CI 3.7%-16.1%) for offspring of mothers who smoked 10 or more daily cigarettes in pregnancy. A significant Cochran-Armitage trend test (p<0.001) confirmed a clear dose response relationship.

After adjustment the odds ratio for maternal smoking and overweight was 1.43 (95%CI 1.07-1.90) and for obesity 2.06 (95%CI 1.31-3.23). The size of the effect was in the range of long-known risk factors such as frequent television watching or use of videogames [16]. The most marked reduction of the odds ratio was observed after introduction of parental education as a surrogate for social class.

The 2001-2002 Obligatory School Entry Health Examination in Bavaria (SEHEB) – Identifiying the Critical Period

Since we could observe a similar effect among offspring of smoking mothers who smoked before but not throughout pregnancy in the 1997 school entry health examination [21], the main purpose of this survey was to further disentangle the critical time period. Therefore, the questions on maternal smoking in categories of none, 1-9, 10-20 and >20 cigarettes daily differentiated between a) smoking 3 months before pregnancy, b) smoking until pregnancy diagnosis, c) smoking until, but not beyond the 12th gestational week, d) persistent smoking from the 12th gestational week (after last menstrual period) until birth, e) smoking in the child's first year of life and smoking at the time of the child's school entry health examination [14]. With additional information on time of pregnancy diagnosis (after last menstrual period) b) could be assessed.

Overweight and obesity were defined according to sex- and age-specific cutpoints for body mass index (weight in kilograms divided by height in meters squared) proposed by the International Obesity Task Force that are equivalent to the widely used cutpoints of 25 and 30 for adult overweight and obesity, respectively [22]. Information on potential confounding factors included parental education, parental obesity, single parenthood, population density at region of residence, birth weight, high infant weight gain, watching television at school entry, playing electronic games at school entry, physical activity at school entry and breastfeeding.

Some 3,564 mothers reported never smoking and 1,028 smoked prior to pregnancy, of whom smoked 406 throughout pregnancy. There were 513 mothers who had smoked during the first trimester only (at least when pregnancy was diagnosed (mean 7.5 weeks) or at maximum until the 12th week), but not throughout pregnancy.

The highest quitting rate regarding maternal smoking in pregnancy could be observed between gestational week 4 and 8 (Fig. 2). Mothers with high educational level stopped smoking slightly more often than mothers with a low educational level (Fig. 2).

The prevalence of offspring's overweight or obesity increased for both maternal smoking in the first trimester only and maternal smoking throughout pregnancy. Maternal smoking throughout pregnancy was associated with a low educational level, a lower prevalence of breastfeeding, and an increased prevalence of parental obesity, low birth weight, prematurity, single parenthood, high infant weight gain, and watching television/playing electronic games [14]. On the other hand, smoking during the first trimester only was only associated with a lower educational level, less breastfeeding and single parenthood.

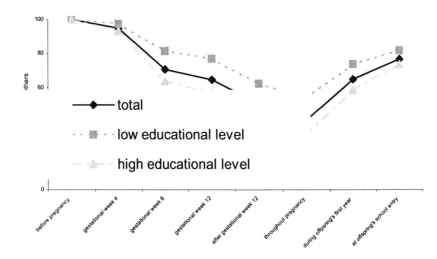

Figure 2. Portion of mothers who smoked in pregnancy compared to mothers who smoked 3 months before pregnancy. Mothers with high educational level stopped smoking slightly more often than mothers poor education.

Unadjusted odds ratios for offspring's overweight/obesity were higher for smoking throughout pregnancy compared to smoking in the first trimester only: 1.85 (95%CI 1.38-2.47) for overweight and 3.23 (95%CI 2.00- 5.21) for obesity and smoking throughout pregnancy compared to 1.66 (95%CI 1.27-2.18) for overweight at school entry and 2.41 (95%CI 1.49-2.91) for obesity at school entry and maternal smoking in the first trimester only. However, after adjusting the odds ratios for overweight and obesity and maternal smoking throughout pregnancy and for maternal smoking in the first trimester only became similar with 1.23 (95%CI 0.89-1.70) and 1.70 (95%CI 1.02- 2.87) for maternal smoking throughout pregnancy and 1.52 (95%CI 1.14-2.01) and 2.22 (95%CI 1.33- 3.69) for smoking in early pregnancy only. A comparison between offspring of mothers who smoked in the early course of pregnancy only and offspring of mothers who smoked throughout pregnancy showed a slightly but not significant greater odds ratio for smoking in the first trimester only with 1.03 (95%CI 0.56-1.91) [14]. Breastfeeding was the most marked confounder for smoking throughout pregnancy.

Discussion

Main Findings of Surveys Associated with the School Entry Health Examinations (SEHE)

The main finding of the surveys associated to the school entry health examination is a higher prevalence of overweight and obesity among children of mothers who smoked in pregnancy. This association could not be explained by a wide range of potential confounding factors. The critical period for this effect seems to be the early course of pregnancy. Our analysis also suggest that after adjustment for breastfeeding and other potential confounding factors continuing to smoke beyond the first trimester may not independently further increase the risk of offspring's obesity.

The absent effect of starting smoking after pregnancy on offspring's overweight or obesity and the unchanged odds ratio for overweight/ obesity and intrauterine tobacco exposure in early pregnancy only supports the hypothesis of a direct metabolic effect.

Methodological Considerations

Although the results of our studies are in accordance with those from other studies regarding the strength of observed effects for obesity risks such as low educational level [23, 24], high weight gain [25, 26], high birth weight [24], parental obesity [27, 28], watching television and playing electronic games [29, 30], physical activity [31, 32] and breastfeeding [12, 33-35], some methodological constraints have to be considered.

The reliability and validity of an outcome and an exposure measure has to be carefully considered referring to estimating associations. While the outcome measure overweight or obesity can be determined unbiased and reliable, underreporting of smoking due to socially accepted answers could be an issue. Results from other studies suggest that self-reported smoking is accurate in general [36], although the number of cigarettes per day may be biased toward round numbers (particularly 1 box or 20 cigarettes, respectively, per day) [37]. Since we compared non-smoking mothers with smoking mothers, digit preference was unlikely a factor in our analysis.

In the 2001-2002 survey for instance 20.7% of mothers said that they had smoked at the beginning of pregnancy compared to 18.6% in Sweden in 1999 [38]. Nondifferential denial of smoking during any period would result in classification of smokers as never smokers (reference group) and thus in bias towards unity. Since low educational level was associated with obesity [24], denial of any smoking during pregnancy by highly educated mothers could result in spurious increased risk estimates for maternal smoking, and stratification by educational level would result in different odds ratios by strata. This difference could not be observed [14]. If mothers who claimed to have stopped smoking in pregnancy continued to smoke, this difference should be reflected in lower birth weights, because the risk of low birth weight and prematurity is mainly determined by smoking during the last trimester [39, 40]. The observed rates of low birth weight among offspring of mothers who smoked in the first trimester only (9.0 percent) were almost identical to those for nonsmokers (7.0 percent) but were higher for those who smoked throughout pregnancy (15.0 percent). This finding indicated that the self-reported smoking data were broadly accurate [14].

Multiple regression models require complete information for the outcome, the exposure and covariates. Restriction to children for whom there was complete information could result in selection bias. However, additional analysis in which multiple imputation [41] was used and unadjusted analysis for all children resulted in similar odds ratios assuming no selection bias by restriction to complete cases.

To reduce residual confounding by categorizing or dichotomizing metric variables [42], all covariates were modeled in their ordinal or continuous forms in additional analyses [14]. Similar odds ratios could be observed for both analyses, including categorized and ordinal or continuous covariates assuming no residual confounding by categorization of covariates.

Although we could observe a dose response relationship for smoking throughout pregnancy [16] which provides additional support for associations, a dose response is not a required finding in studies on maternal smoking in pregnancy and offspring's obesity due to difficulties in obtaining. First of all the exact beginning and end of the critical period remains unknown, although we could delimit the period to the first trimester. Second, the amount of daily smoked cigarettes have to stay constant and may not vary too much between the different times of ascertainment.

Overweight and obesity at school entry might only be a transitional state and obese school entry children of smoking mothers might turn into normal adults later in life comparable to infants with a high early weight gain [43]. Since a longitudinal cohort study up to the age of 33 years of age could observe the same association (see below) [44], a transitional state seems to be unlikely.

Other Studies on Intrauterine Tobacco Exposure and Obesity

The National Child Development Study

The National Child Development study started in 1958 as perinatal mortality survey. It included all births in Great Britain born in the first week of March 1958. Information was obtained on 98% of births totaling 17,414 with follow up of survivors at ages 7, 11, 16, 23 and 33 years (11,405 subjects were included in the 33- year survey) [45]. Biases associated with sample attrition have tended to be small, although in the direction of under representing more deprived social groups over time [45]. Montgomery and Ekbom reported an association between maternal smoking in pregnancy and offspring's obesity at age 33 years [44] which afterwards was confirmed by an independent analysis of another group resulting in the same result [46]. The association found in the National Child Development Study could not be explained by confounding [44, 46] (Tab. 2). The prospective design taking smoking history from medical files and the fact that reporting biases in smoking behavior in 1958 seem to be unlikely due to the limited knowledge of adverse effects of maternal smoking on offspring's health at that time further support our hypothesis that our observed association is not a consequence of confounding by socially accepted answers in our studies.

Birth Cohort Study from Norway

Vik et al. reported an association between maternal smoking in pregnancy and offpsring's overweight at the age of 5 years [40]. A re-analysis focusing on maternal smoking and overweight was later performed by Wideroe et al. [47]. In this Norwegian population based birth cohort study 336 children were included. The outcome measures at age 5 were overweight as a body mass index greater the 85th percentile or skinfold thickness greater than the 85th percentile, respectively (Tab. 2). The additional measure of skinfold thickness indicates that the association between maternal smoking in pregnancy and overweight is not due to a simple deficit in length growth and thus independent of the outcome measure body mass index.

Comparison of Study Results

A comparison of effect estimates for the association of maternal smoking in pregnancy and offspring's obesity between different studies is difficult, because different exposure variables (period of maternal smoking in pregnancy), outcome variables (definition of overweight/obesity, age at outcome) and different covariates (adjustment) were used within studies. Table 2 gives an overview on human studies on intrauterine tobacco exposure and overweight or obesity, respectively.

Possible Biological Mechanisms

The long known association between smoking and low birth weight seems to contradict the observed effect of intrauterine tobacco exposure and obesity at first sight. At second sight one might recognize that low birth weight and obesity are independent consequences of maternal smoking in pregnancy. First, adjusting for birthweight could not explain the effect of maternal smoking in pregnancy on offspring's obesity, which supports the hypothesis of independent effects. Second, the effect of maternal smoking in pregnancy on offspring's obesity is likely to be determined in early pregnancy [14], while the effect of maternal smoking in pregnancy on low birth weight seems to be due to late pregnancy [39, 40]. Therefore low birthweight due to maternal smoking in pregnancy cannot be interpreted as a transition state for later obesity.

Table 2. Studies on the association between intrauterine tobacco exposure and subsequent obesity

Authors (publication year)	Type of study	Definition of maternal smoking	Definition of outcome	no. subjects (age of outcome measure)	adjusted odds ratio (95%CI)
Montgomery & Ekbom (2002) [44] (Power et al.; 2002) [46]	National birth cohort study (NCDS)	after 4th pregnancy month (30%)	OB* (BMI>30 kg/m²)	4,917 (33 years)	1.34 (1.07-1.69) for medium smokers 1.38 (1.06-1.79) for heavy smokers
Vik et al. (1996) [40] (Wideroe et al.; 2003) [47]	birth cohort study	in gestational week 17 (31%)	OW* (BMI>85th percentile/ skinfold thickness>85th percentile)	336 (5 years)	2.9 (1.3-6.6) for BMI measure 2.4 (1.0-5.5) for skinfold thickness
Toschke et al. (2002) [15]	cross sectional study	during pregnancy	OW* (BMI>90th percentile) OB* (BMI>97th percentile)	8,765 (5-6 years)	1.58 (1.23-2.04) OW* 1.92 (1.29-2.86) OB*
von Kries et al. (2002) [16]	cross sectional study	during pregnancy	OW* (BMI>90th percentile) OB* (BMI>97th percentile)	6,483 (5-6 years)	1.43 (1.07-1.90) OW* 2.06 (1.31-3.23) OB*
Toschke et al. (2003) [14]	cross sectional study	in the 1st trimester/ throughout pregnancy	OB*/OW* (according to the proposed cutpoints by the International Obesity Task Force [22]	4,974 (5-6 years)	1.52 (1.14-2.01) OW* SM 1st trimester 2.22 (1.33-3.69) OB* SM 1st trimester 1.23 (0.89-1.70) OW* SM throughout pregnancy 1.70 (1.02-2.87) OB* SM throughout pregnancy

* OB = obesity; OW = overweight; SM = smoking

A potential source of bias includes confounding by parental obesity. We observed that obese mothers were more likely to smoke in pregnancy. It is also known that obese mothers often have obese partners [48] which could result in selection of genetic mechanisms increasing obesity risk among their children. Since adjustment for parental obesity could not explain the association between intrauterine tobacco exposure and obesity a genetic explanation is unlikely the cause for an increased obesity prevalence among offspring.

Breastfeeding is the most important confounding factor in our study and was responsible for the most marked reduction of risk estimates for maternal smoking throughout pregnancy and offspring's obesity. This might be due to insufficient milk production among smokers [49-51] although other studies suggest psychological rather than physiological reasons for lower breastfeeding rates in smoking mothers [52]. Since the interaction of breastfeeding with maternal smoking was not significantly associated with obesity in offspring ($p > 0.6$ for both outcomes (overweight/obesity) and two different exposures (smoking in the first trimester only/smoking throughout pregnancy)), breastfeeding appears to be a confounder rather than an effect modifier. Therefore some of the association of maternal smoking in *later* pregnancy might be due to a deficit in breastfeeding, as well as other associated characteristics.

Other Potential Biological Mechanisms Assume Metabolic Imprinting as Important Condition

Metabolic Imprinting

Humans and animals are sensitive to external conditions that modulate ontogenic pathways and thereby exert persistent influences on diverse functional outcomes. The term metabolic imprinting is intended to encompass adaptive responses to specific nutritional conditions early in life that are characterized by a) susceptibility limited to a critical ontogenic window early in development, b) a persistent effect lasting through adulthood, c) a specific and measurable outcome (that may differ quantitatively among individuals), and d) a dose-response or threshold relation between a specific exposure and outcome [53].

Konrad Lorenz [54] chose the term imprinting instead of programming to refer to the setting of certain animal behavior (geese) that resulted from early experience. Central to his definition was the fact that the imprinting may only occur during a narrowly-defined period in the individuals life (critical period), and moreover, that the imprinted behavior cannot be 'forgotten'! These criteria coincide with the first two parts of metabolic imprinting. The last two parts of the definition narrow the biological phenomena under consideration to specific relations appropriate for mechanistic characterization [53]. Waterland and Garza propose the following mechanisms: a) induced variations in organ structure, b) alterations in cell number, c) clonal selection, d) metabolic differentiation, and d) hepatocyte polyploidization [53]. The most complex and probably most developmentally relevant potential mechanism of metabolic imprinting is through an effect on metabolic differentiation. Metabolic imprinting is also known as Barker Hypothesis due to his large and profound work on this topic [55-65].

Dutch Famine Study

The Dutch Famine Study is a classic epidemiologic study among survivors of the Dutch Famine during World War II, from 1944-45 [66]. It was observed that offspring of mothers who were exposed to famine in the first trimester were more likely to be obese while offspring of mothers who were exposed to famine in the last trimester were less likely to be obese strongly supporting the hypothesis of metabolic imprinting as an important cause for obesity.

Thiocyanat and Thyroid Gland

It is known that smoking causes a reduced competitive iodine uptake through thiocyanat (SCN-), a degradation product of cyanide (CN-) which is an ingredient of tobacco smoke. This leads to a higher prevalence of struma among smokers. Levels of 8 to 12 mg/l thiocyanat (SCN-) can be observed among smokers. Particularly women with a subclinical hypothyreodism are affected. It is also known that thiocyanat is able to pass the placenta and thus thiocyanat might be able to affect the foetal thyroid gland [67-72]. The function of the thyroid gland mainly influences resting energy expenditure and thus development of overweight or obesity.

Appetite Control and Neuroendocrine Dysregulation

Smoking in the 1st trimester could mimic fetal malnutrition by reduced food intake of the mother or reduced blood supply by vasoconstrictive effects on maternal and uteroplacental vasculature [73]. Thus smoking would reflect a surrogate for hunger in the 1st trimester which accounted for higher proportions of obese offspring in the Dutch Famine Study (Fig. 3) [74, 75]. Nutritional deprivation may affect the differentiation of hypothalamic centers regulating food intake, growth and number of filled adipocytes [76]. Additionally, agents of inhaled tobacco might have a potentiating effect on hypothalamic structures resulting in impaired insulin signaling and metabolism. Some animal and human studies indicate an effect of intrauterine nicotine exposure on neurobehavioral impulse control [77-81]. However, in an analysis of the NCDS birth cohort study we could not observe altered appetite control among offspring of smoking mothers [82]. Since Montgomery and Ekbom could observe an association between maternal smoking in pregnancy and glucose intolerance/ diabetes [44], we favor the hypothesis of a neuroendocrine mechanism by impaired insulin signaling.

Figure 3. Metabolic imprinting during pregnancy. An exposure during a critical period might change the metabolism irreversibly.

Smoking in the First Trimester vs. Throughout Pregnancy

We hypothesize that maternal smoking in the first trimester of pregnancy has a more profound influence on the risk of obesity in offspring due to neuroendocrine or other metabolic dysregulation than maternal smoking in later pregnancy. We suggest that the apparently greater influence of smoking in later pregnancy is largely due to confounding, such that children of mothers who smoke throughout pregnancy are more likely to accumulate further risks for obesity that are not caused directly by maternal smoking during pregnancy. We could demonstrate this by a comparison of smoking in the 1st trimester only with smoking throughout pregnancy for risk of overweight or obesity in the same logistic regression model in which no difference could be observed between the to exposures and obesity. The statistically significantly raised odds ratios for obesity and overweight in offspring associated with maternal smoking in the first trimester of pregnancy are only marginally affected by multiple adjustments for other risks associated with obesity. In contrast with this, the odds ratios associated with smoking throughout pregnancy are notably reduced by adjustment for the other obesity risks. This is consistent with the hypothesis that smoking in the first trimester of pregnancy has a direct metabolic effect on offspring, while smoking in later pregnancy is a marker of familial, cultural and material circumstances that influence obesity risk through other mechanisms.

Smoking throughout pregnancy might even dilute the effect of smoking in the first trimester, as smoking-related fetal malnutrition may have a similar influence to nutritional deprivation in the last trimester of pregnancy observed in the Dutch famine study, which was associated with a *decreased* risk of obesity [66].

The effects of confounding (that may vary with time of exposure) and potentially contradictory influences of smoking in early and late pregnancy are likely to result in inconsistent associations of smoking during pregnancy and offspring's obesity. To disentangle these various influences, research into this subject should identify the period during pregnancy when the mother smoked, as well as quantifying the potential confounding influences of breastfeeding and other exposures that occur after birth.

Prevalences of Obesity vs. Prevalences of Smoking

To assess a possible coincidence between an increased prevalence of maternal smoking in pregnancy and increased prevalences of obesity, one has to consider a time lag of about 20 to 40 years. This is due to delayed obesity prevalences which are usually reported among adults.

Although prevalences of overall smoking tend to decrease in industrialized Western countries, prevalences of smoking among fertile women 20 to 40 years ago do not [83]. The fact that teenage smoking is still popular should be a central warning.

It also should be noticed that smoking is associated with poor education and income and childhood obesity in western societies is mainly a problem of children from families with poor education and income. Therefore assessing an increase in smoking of poorly educated mothers in childbearing age is a major challenge. It also might be possible that at least a part of the adiposity epidemic in children mainly affects children from poorly educated families.

Advice to Fertile Women

The observed association of early fetal tobacco-related exposure and subsequent obesity underlines the importance of advising women on smoking cessation in contexts such as gynecology and obstetric outpatient clinics. Like folic acid supplementation, smoking cessation is another challenge where for a successful outcome it must occur prior to conception. Women of reproductive age should be advised that they should stop smoking before attempting to become pregnant, as cessation after they find out that they are pregnant may be too late to protect their baby from potential obesity and the associated risks.

Future Studies

Randomized human studies of maternal smoking in pregnancy are not possible for ethical reasons. But some possible observational human studies to be performed might enlighten biological mechanisms. A study among offspring of mothers who took nicotine patches during pregnancy and mothers without nicotine exposure during pregnancy could assess the influence of the ingredient nicotine. Unfortunately in Germany nicotine patch therapy during pregnancy is not common so that a basis for this kind of study is missing.

Other human studies could assess the function of the thyroid gland among obese offspring of smoking mothers. This could give a more insightful look at the thiocyanat hypothesis.

Experimental teratologic studies are in the best position for detecting biological mechanisms or ingredients of tobacco smoke that are responsible for the effect of intrauterine tobacco exposure on obesity.

References

[1] Doll R, Hill AB. The mortality of doctors in relation to their smoking habits; a preliminary report. *Br Med J* 1954;4877:1451-5.

[2] Doll R, Hill AB. Smoking and carcinoma of the lung; preliminary report. *Br Med J* 1950;2(4682):739-48.

[3] Annual smoking-attributable mortality, years of potential life lost, and economic costs--United States, 1995-1999. *MMWR Morb Mortal Wkly Rep* 2002;51(14):300-3.

[4] Mokdad AH, Marks JS, Stroup DF, Gerberding JL. Actual causes of death in the United States, 2000. *Jama* 2004;291(10):1238-45.

[5] Hu FB, Persky V, Flay BR, Zelli A, Cooksey J, Richardson J. Prevalence of asthma and wheezing in public schoolchildren: association with maternal smoking during pregnancy. *Ann Allergy Asthma Immunol* 1997;79(1):80-4.

[6] DiFranza JR, Aligne CA, Weitzman M. Prenatal and postnatal environmental tobacco smoke exposure and children's health. *Pediatrics* 2004;113(4 Suppl):1007-15.

[7] Simpson WJ. A preliminary report on cigarette smoking and the incidence of prematurity. *Am J Obstet Gynecol* 1957;73(4):807-15.

[8] Yerushalmy J. The relationship of parents' cigarette smoking to outcome of pregnancy -- implications as to the problem of inferring causation from observed associations. *Am J Epidemiol* 1971;93(6):443-56.

[9] Butler NR, Goldstein H, Ross EM. Cigarette smoking in pregnancy: Its influence on birth weight and perinatal mortality. *Br Med J* 1972;1972 ii:127-30.

[10] Schellscheidt J, Jorch G, Menke J. Effects of heavy maternal smoking on intrauterine growth patterns in sudden infant death victims and surviving infants. *Eur J Pediatr* 1998;157(3):246-51.

[11] Schellscheidt J, Oyen N, Jorch G. Interactions between maternal smoking and other prenatal risk factors for sudden infant death syndrome (SIDS). *Acta Paediatr* 1997;86(8):857-63.

[12] von Kries R, Koletzko B, Sauerwald T, von Mutius E, Barnert D, Grunert V, et al. Breast feeding and obesity: cross sectional study. *BMJ* 1999;319:147-50.

[13] WHO. Diet, physical activity and health. www.who.int/hpr/physactiv/economic.benefits.shtml 2003.

[14] Toschke AM, Montgomery SM, Pfeiffer U, von Kries R. Early intrauterine exposure to tobacco-inhaled products and obesity. *Am J Epidemiol* 2003;158(11):1068-74.

[15] Toschke M, Koletzko B, Jr Slikker W, Hermann M, Von Kries R. Childhood obesity is associated with maternal smoking in pregnancy. *Eur J Pediatr* 2002;161(8):445-8.

[16] von Kries R, Toschke AM, Koletzko B, Slikker W, Jr. Maternal smoking during pregnancy and childhood obesity. *Am J Epidemiol* 2002;156(10):954-61.

[17] Heller G, Müller U. Die Standarddemographie nach dem ADM-ASI-Statistisches Bundesamt. In: Ahrens W, Bellach BM, Jöckel KH, editors. *Messung soziodemographischer Merkmale in der Epidemiologie*. München: RKI-Schriften 1/98, MMV Medizin Verlag; 1998. p. 54-65.

[18] Kleinbaum DG. *Logistic Regression - A Self-Learning Text*. New York, Berlin, Heidelberg: Springer; 1994.

[19] Rothman KJ, Greenland S. Measures of Effect and Association. In: Rothman KJ, Greenland S, editors. *Modern Epidemiology*. 2nd ed. Philadelphia: Lippincott Williams & Wilkins; 1998. p. 47-66.

[20] Poskitt EM. Defining childhood obesity: the relative body mass index (BMI). European Childhood Obesity group. *Acta Paediatr* 1995;84(8):961-3.

[21] Toschke AM, Koletzko B, Slikker W, Jr., Hermann M, von Kries R. Childhood obesity is associated with maternal smoking in pregnancy. *Eur J Pediatr* 2002;161(8):445-8.

[22] Cole TJ, Bellizzi MC, Flegal KM, Dietz WH. Establishing a standard definition for child overweight and obesity worldwide: international survey. *Bmj* 2000;320(7244):1240-3.

[23] Troiano RP, Flegal KM. Overweight children and adolescents: description, epidemiology, and demographics. *Pediatrics* 1998;101(3):497-504.

[24] Rasmussen F, Johansson M. The relation of weight, length and ponderal index at birth to body mass index and overweight among 18-year-old males in Sweden. *Eur J Epidemiol* 1998;14(4):373-80.

[25] Ong KK, Ahmed ML, Emmett PM, Preece MA, Dunger DB. Association between postnatal catch-up growth and obesity in childhood: prospective cohort study. *Bmj* 2000;320(7240):967-71.

[26] Stettler N, Zemel BS, Kumanyika S, Stallings VA. Infant weight gain and childhood overweight status in a multicenter, cohort study. *Pediatrics* 2002;109(2):194-9.

[27] Locard E, Mamelle N, Billette A, Miginiac M, Munoz F, Rey S. Risk factors of obesity in a five year old population. Parental versus environmental factors. *Int J Obes Relat Metab Disord* 1992;16(10):721-9.

[28] Stunkard AJ, Sorensen TI, Hanis C, Teasdale TW, Chakraborty R, Schull WJ, et al. An adoption study of human obesity. *N Engl J Med* 1986;314(4):193-8.

[29] Dietz WH, Jr., Gortmaker SL. Do we fatten our children at the television set? Obesity and television viewing in children and adolescents. *Pediatrics* 1985;75(5):807-12.

[30] Robinson TN. Reducing children's television viewing to prevent obesity: a randomized controlled trial. *Jama* 1999;282(16):1561-7.

[31] Pate RR, Dowda M, Ross JG. Associations between physical activity and physical fitness in American children. *Am J Dis Child* 1990;144(10):1123-9.

[32] Moore LL, Nguyen US, Rothman KJ, Cupples LA, Ellison RC. Preschool physical activity level and change in body fatness in young children. The Framingham Children's Study. *Am J Epidemiol* 1995;142(9):982-8.

[33] Armstrong J, Reilly JJ. Breastfeeding and lowering the risk of childhood obesity. *Lancet* 2002;359(9322):2003-4.

[34] Gillman MW, Rifas-Shiman SL, Camargo CA, Jr., Berkey CS, Frazier AL, Rockett HR, et al. Risk of overweight among adolescents who were breastfed as infants. *Jama* 2001;285(19):2461-7.

[35] Toschke AM, Vignerova J, Lhotska L, Osancova K, Koletzko B, Von Kries R. Overweight and obesity in 6- to 14-year-old Czech children in 1991: protective effect of breast-feeding. *J Pediatr* 2002;141(6):764-9.

[36] Patrick DL, Cheadle A, Thompson DC, Diehr P, Koepsell T, Kinne S. The validity of self-reported smoking: a review and meta-analysis. *Am J Public Health* 1994;84(7): 1086-93.

[37] Klesges RC, Debon M, Ray JW. Are self-reports of smoking rate biased? Evidence from the Second National Health and Nutrition Examination Survey. *J Clin Epidemiol* 1995;48(10):1225-33.

[38] Wallskar H. *Smoke-free cildren - a report. The first ten years.* Stockholm: The Swedish Cancer Society, the Swedish Heart-Lung Foundation, the Swedish National Institute of Public Health; 2003.

[39] Cliver SP, Goldenberg RL, Cutter GR, Hoffman HJ, Davis RO, Nelson KG. The effect of cigarette smoking on neonatal anthropometric measurements. *Obstet Gynecol* 1995;85(4):625-30.

[40] Vik T, Jacobsen G, Vatten L, Bakketeig LS. Pre- and post-natal growth in children of women who smoked in pregnancy. *Early Hum Dev* 1996;45(3):245-55.

[41] Rubin DB, Schenker N. Multiple imputation in health-care databases: an overview and some applications. *Stat Med* 1991;10(4):585-98.

[42] Brenner H, Blettner M. Controlling for continuous confounders in epidemiologic research. *Epidemiology* 1997;8(4):429-34.

[43] Toschke AM, Grote V, Koletzko B, von Kries R. Identifying children at high risk for overweight at school entry by weight gain during the first 2 years. *Arch Pediatr Adolesc Med* 2004;158(5):449-52.

[44] Montgomery SM, Ekbom A. Smoking during pregnancy and diabetes mellitus in a British longitudinal birth cohort. *Bmj* 2002;324(7328):26-7.

[45] Ferri E, editor. Life at 33. The fifth follow up of the National Child Development Study. London: *National Children's Bureau*; 1993.

[46] Power C, Jefferis BJ. Fetal environment and subsequent obesity: a study of maternal smoking. *Int J Epidemiol* 2002;31(2):413-9.

[47] Wideroe M, Vik T, Jacobsen G, Bakketeig LS. Does maternal smoking during pregnancy cause childhood overweight? *Paediatr Perinat Epidemiol* 2003;17(2):171-9.

[48] Hebebrand J, Wulftange H, Goerg T, Ziegler A, Hinney A, Barth N, et al. Epidemic obesity: are genetic factors involved via increased rates of assortative mating? *Int J Obes Relat Metab Disord* 2000;24(3):345-53.

[49] Haug K, Irgens LM, Baste V, Markestad T, Skjaerven R, Schreuder P. Secular trends in breastfeeding and parental smoking. *Acta Paediatr* 1998;87(10):1023-7.

[50] Vogel A, Hutchison BL, Mitchell EA. Mastitis in the first year postpartum. *Birth* 1999;26(4):218-25.

[51] Hill PD, Aldag JC. Smoking and breastfeeding status. *Res Nurs Health* 1996;19(2):125-32.

[52] Amir LH, Donath SM. Does maternal smoking have a negative physiological effect on breastfeeding? The epidemiological evidence. *Birth* 2002;29(2):112-23.

[53] Waterland RA, Garza C. Potential mechanisms of metabolic imprinting that lead to chronic disease. *Am J Clin Nutr* 1999;69(2):179-97.

[54] Lorenz K. *Studies in animal and human behavior*. Cambridge, MA: Harvard University Press; 1970.

[55] Barker DJ. Fetal and infant origins of adult disease. London: *BMJ* Publishing Group; 1992.

[56] Barker DJ, Osmond C. Low birth weight and hypertension. Bmj 1988;297(6641):134-5.

[57] Barker DJ, Osmond C, Golding J, Kuh D, Wadsworth ME. Growth in utero, blood pressure in childhood and adult life, and mortality from cardiovascular disease. *Bmj* 1989;298(6673):564-7.

[58] Barker DJP, Winter PD, Osmonds C, Margetts B, Simmonds SJ. Weight in Infancy and Death from Ischaemic Heart Disease. *Lancet* 1989;ii: 1989:577-80.

[59] Barker DJ. The fetal and infant origins of adult disease. *Bmj* 1990;301(6761):1111.

[60] Barker DJ, Bull AR, Osmond C, Simmonds SJ. Fetal and placental size and risk of hypertension in adult life. *Bmj* 1990;301(6746):259-62.

[61] Barker DJ, Osmond C, Meade TW. Early growth and clotting factors in adult life. *Bmj* 1992;304(6833):1052.

[62] Barker DJ, Meade TW, Fall CH, Lee A, Osmond C, Phipps K, et al. Relation of fetal and infant growth to plasma fibrinogen and factor VII concentrations in adult life. *Bmj* 1992;304(6820):148-52.

[63] Barker DJ. Fetal origins of coronary heart disease. *Bmj* 1995;311(6998):171-4.

[64] Barker DJ, Osmond C, Simmonds SJ, Wield GA. The relation of small head circumference and thinness at birth to death from cardiovascular disease in adult life. *Bmj* 1993;306(6875):422-6.

[65] Barker DJ, Martyn CN, Osmond C, Hales CN, Fall CH. Growth in utero and serum cholesterol concentrations in adult life. *Bmj* 1993;307(6918):1524-7.

[66] Ravelli GP, Stein ZA, Susser MW. Obesity in young men after famine exposure in utero and early infancy. *N Engl J Med* 1976;295(7):349-53.

[67] Knudsen N, Laurberg P, Perrild H, Bulow I, Ovesen L, Jorgensen T. Risk factors for goiter and thyroid nodules. *Thyroid* 2002;12(10):879-88.

[68] Bartalena L, Bogazzi F, Tanda ML, Manetti L, Dell'Unto E, Martino E. Cigarette smoking and the thyroid. *Eur J Endocrinol* 1995;133(5):507-12.

[69] Chanoine JP, Toppet V, Bourdoux P, Spehl M, Delange F. Smoking during pregnancy: a significant cause of neonatal thyroid enlargement. *Br J Obstet Gynaecol* 1991;98(1):65-8.

[70] Christensen SB, Ericsson UB, Janzon L, Tibblin S, Melander A. Influence of cigarette smoking on goiter formation, thyroglobulin, and thyroid hormone levels in women. *J Clin Endocrinol Metab* 1984;58(4):615-8.

[71] Muller B, Zulewski H, Huber P, Ratcliffe JG, Staub JJ. Impaired action of thyroid hormone associated with smoking in women with hypothyroidism. *N Engl J Med* 1995;333(15):964-9.

[72] Utiger RD. Cigarette smoking and the thyroid. *N Engl J Med* 1995;333(15):1001-2.

[73] Horta BL, Victora CG, Menezes AM, Halpern R, Barros CF. Low birthweight, preterm births and intrauterine growth retardation in relation to maternal smoking. *Paediatr Perinat Epidemiol* 1997;11:140-51.

[74] Ravelli GP, Belmont L. Obesity in nineteen-year-old men: family size and birth order associations. *Am J Epidemiol* 1979;109(1):66-70.

[75] Ravelli AC, van Der Meulen JH, Osmond C, Barker DJ, Bleker OP. Obesity at the age of 50 y in men and women exposed to famine prenatally. *Am J Clin Nutr* 1999;70(5):811-6.

[76] Keesey RE. Physiological regulation of body weight and the issue of obesity. *Med Clin North Am* 1989;73(1):15-27.

[77] Levin BE, Routh VH. Role of the brain in energy balance and obesity. *Am J Physiol* 1996;271(3 Pt 2):R491-500.

[78] Peters MA, Ngan LL. The effects of totigestational exposure to nicotine on pre- and postnatal development in the rat. *Arch Int Pharmacodyn Ther* 1982;257(1):155-67.

[79] Yanai J, Pick CG, Rogel-Fuchs Y, Zahalka EA. Alterations in hippocampal cholinergic receptors and hippocampal behaviors after early exposure to nicotine. *Brain Res Bull* 1992;29(3-4):363-8.

[80] Levin ED, Slotkin TA. Developmental Neurotoxicity of Nicotine. In: Slikker W, Chang L, editors. *Handbook of Developmental Neurotoxicology*: Academic Press; 1998.p. 587-615.

[81] Kandel DB, Wu P, Davies M. Maternal smoking during pregnancy and smoking by adolescent daughters. *Am J Public Health* 1994;84(9):1407-13.

[82] Toschke AM, Ehlin AG, von Kries R, Ekbom A, Montgomery SM. Maternal smoking during pregnancy and appetite control in offspring. *J Perinat Med* 2003;31(3):251-6.

[83] Rohrmann S, Becker N, Kroke A, Boeing H. Trends in cigarette smoking in the German centers of the European Prospective Investigation into Cancer and Nutrition (EPIC): the influence of the educational level. *Prev Med* 2003;36(4):448-54.

In: Trends in Smoking and Health Research
Editors: J. H. Owing, pp. 127-144

ISBN: 1-59454-391-7
© 2005 Nova Science Publishers, Inc.

Chapter VII

Review: Environmental Tobacco Smoke and the Health of Children

Vanita Economou[1][1], Yue Chen[1] and Nancy Edwards[1,2]
[1]Department of Epidemiology and Community Medicine, University of Ottawa
[2]School of Nursing, University of Ottawa

Abstract

Environmental tobacco smoke (ETS) exposure continues to be a major health concern for children. During pregnancy, ETS exposure is linked with obstetric complications, premature deliveries and fetal growth retardation. In children, ETS exposure results in negative respiratory health effects including an increase in lower respiratory tract infections, asthma exacerbation, reduced lung function, and an increased risk of sudden infant death syndrome (SIDS). ETS exposure in children is also considered to be an important risk factor for neurodevelopmental and behavioral problems and is associated with some childhood cancers. The major source of ETS for young children is from their smoking parents or other household members. Children are particularly vulnerable to the effects of ETS and suffer involuntarily as they usually have no control over their exposure. From a population level perspective, large numbers of children experience these risks because of the high prevalence of ETS exposure both in the home and in public places. Future studies employing longitudinal study designs and changes in exposure classifications will further explain the negative health effects. In addition, research in countries where maternal smoking is rare will help distinguish between the effects of ETS exposure among young children who have experienced in utero exposure versus postnatal exposure versus in utero and postnatal exposure. Reducing ETS exposure provides a number of policy challenges: regulating ETS exposure in the home and in public places. A research agenda that would guide the choice of policy options will be considered.

---

[1]   E-mail address: v_econ@yahoo.com

Introduction

The health burden of environmental tobacco smoke (ETS) exposure remains high. ETS exposure can cause a number of negative health outcomes in women and children, yet these health consequences are preventable. There have been extensive studies examining the relationship between ETS and health over the past two to three decades. Some of the major scientific agencies and committees including the U.S. Environmental Protection Agency [1], the U.K. Department of Health [2], and the World Health Organization (WHO) Division of Noncommunicable Diseases Tobacco Free Initiative [3] have reviewed the scientific literature and concluded that ETS is causally linked to respiratory health effects in both children and adults who are non-smokers, and middle ear diseases and sudden infant death syndrome (SIDS) in children. The WHO [3] estimates that almost half of the world's children breathe air polluted by tobacco smoke, particularly at home from their smoking parents or other household members. ETS exposed children suffer involuntarily as they usually have no control over their exposure. Infants and children are also particularly vulnerable to the effects of ETS as they have smaller airway passages, faster respiratory rates, and less mature immune response systems. The large body of scientific evidence of the adverse effects of ETS on child health, and the high prevalence of child ETS exposure, constitute a substantial public health threat.

With definitive scientific evidence, an increasing number of countries have supported policies to reduce tobacco consumption. Most recently a historic tobacco control pact was adopted by the World Health Assembly. On May 21, 2003, the 192 members of the WHO unanimously adopted the Framework Convention on Tobacco Control that aims to decrease tobacco-related deaths and diseases [4]. The adverse health effects associated with ETS exposure are specifically noted in the convention and form part of the guiding principles that include the need to take measures to protect all persons from exposure to tobacco smoke [5]. Translating research into policy options will help advance the efforts towards reducing the health effects of ETS exposure.

The purpose of this review is to provide an update on the health effects of ETS exposure in children and pregnant women and to discuss the areas of research that will help guide ETS-related policy development. This chapter summarizes key findings from previous reviews on ETS and fetal and children's health, and adds findings from some recent studies published between January 1997 to December 2003. The review begins with a general discussion of ETS exposure and measurement followed by a summary of ETS exposure and pregnancy, and ETS exposure and children's health. Subsequently, discussions on the issues of the level of ETS exposure children receive from maternal versus paternal ETS exposure, and economic consequences related to ETS are presented. To conclude, some suggestions for areas of future research that will aid ETS-related policy development are described.

Description of ETS Exposure

ETS exposure occurs when someone shares the same air space as a smoker and is exposed to harmful smoke fumes. It is often referred to as "passive" or "involuntary" smoking because of its indirect nature. Cigarette smoking produces both mainstream smoke, directly inhaled through a burning cigarette, and sidestream smoke, which drifts from the burning end. ETS is a mixture of sidestream smoke and exhaled mainstream smoke by the smoker. Among these types of smoke, there are over 4000 components of which 42 are known carcinogens [1]. Sidestream smoke is the main component of ETS and contains as much as 30 times the concentrations as mainstream smoke [1, 6]. The U.S. EPA concluded that ETS is a group A carcinogen, a known human cancer causing compound. ETS exposure can occur anywhere where there is an active smoker present, in the house, at work, and even outdoors. For young children in particular, the primary source of exposure to ETS occurs in the home because that is where they spend most of their time [7]. Household ETS exposure is related to the amount of cigarette consumption, the volume of enclosed space, the time spent indoors, and the indoor ventilation.

Measurement of ETS Exposure

The extent of exposure to ETS is difficult to estimate accurately. Factors such as the hours of exposure, room size, ventilation, and distance from the smoker all have an impact. There are two main methods for the measurement of ETS exposure. First, there is the method that relies on self-reports. Self-reported ETS exposure is usually obtained through self-administered questionnaires, but is also obtained from telephone or face-to-face interviews. The second method for the measurement of ETS exposure is the use of ETS biomarkers such as nicotine and its metabolites from biological samples. The majority of ETS studies have relied on self-reports for their assessment of ETS exposure. Self-reports are a useful and easy method for obtaining estimates of ETS exposure. However, when diary entries are compared to self-reports, it is clear that self-reports tend to underestimate the amount smoked per day resulting in an underestimate of ETS exposure of the child or pregnant woman [8]. Therefore, ETS studies relying on self-reports, are subject to misclassification bias. There is also misclassification that arises when only parents are asked about their smoking in the home but there are other household members that also smoke in the home. Similarly, ETS exposure involves more than exposure at home. ETS exposure can occur in childcare settings and in public places. It is virtually impossible to get an accurate measure of total ETS exposure. Some of the differences may be controlled by examining socio-economic differences that would be linked to differential levels of exposure in the workplace. The misclassification error probably worsens with increasing age of children. As infants, they are most likely to be exposed within their home, with much less exposure in other settings. As toddlers and preschoolers however, they will be in play groups, day care settings etc. At these ages, attempting to get a more thorough description of ETS exposure in different settings where the child spends time becomes increasingly important. However, even with this measurement limitation, ETS studies still consistently show significant negative children's health effects from ETS. The use of objective measures such as ETS biomarkers, has increased in recent years to deal with some of the misclassification issues and to explore the dose-response effect associated with ETS exposure. At present, the biomarker cotinine, obtained through either samples of the urine, blood, saliva, or hair of individuals is accepted as the most specific and sensitive method for ETS exposure assessment [9]. This measure of ETS works satisfactorily for pregnant women and the ETS exposure of their fetus, and for assessing smoking among parents. It does not however account for other sources of ETS exposure among children such as day care settings. Perhaps for these settings, the presence or absence of ETS policies and their enforcement can be used as proxy measures of ETS exposure.

ETS Exposure and Pregnancy

ETS exposure and maternal smoking during pregnancy are linked to a number of negative pregnancy outcomes. The health consequences of ETS can begin even before birth, while the fetus is still developing in the mother's womb. Maternal smoking exposes the fetus to components of tobacco smoke that cross the placental barrier, as does ETS exposure of non-smoking pregnant women [10]. Maternal smoking during pregnancy has been implicated with various health consequences including extrauterine pregnancy, placenta previa, abruptio placentae, premature labor, intrauterine growth retardation, a low Agpar score at 5 minutes, stillbirths, neonatal deaths, and spontaneous abortion [11-14]. Active smoking of the mother is also associated with a reduced risk of gestational hypertension and preeclampsia [15-18]. Some of these negative health effects have also been observed in non-smoking pregnant women exposed to ETS. Based on existing evidence, both the California EPA [7] and the WHO [3] have declared that ETS exposure of the non-smoking mother is causally related to reduced fetal growth in birth weight and small-for-gestational-age (SGA). In Windham et al.'s [19] meta-analysis of the literature, a pooled odds ratio (OR) of 1.2 [95% confidence interval (CI): 1.1-1.3] is reported for all studies examining low birth weight at term or SGA. The pooled estimate of mean birth weight indicated a decrement of 28 grams (95% CI: -41 to -16) for non-smoking women exposed to ETS. In Lindbohm et al.'s [20] review, they report a 25-40 gram reduction in the mean birth weight. While the mean estimate of birth weight reduction is small in magnitude, a potential shift of the birth weight distribution would put infants whose health is already compromised, into even higher risk categories. From a population health perspective, a small change in the average birth weight or an increase in risk for SGA of 20 percent could affect large numbers of infants because of the high prevalence of ETS exposure [3, 19, 21]. Of relevance to the question of policy is the observation that in more recent studies of low birth weight and SGA, the positive association with ETS is reflected, but to a lesser degree [22-29]. Mitchell et al. [29] explain that with increased public awareness of the effects of ETS on fetal health, more non-smoking pregnant women may be requesting that their partners or other household members smoke outside, reducing their ETS exposure levels. Coupled with the increasing number of workplaces with non-smoking policies, pregnant women may be exposed to less ETS alleviating some of the fetal health effects.

ETS exposure is also implicated with other adverse pregnancy outcomes. Some studies have found associations between ETS exposure of non-smoking mothers and preterm delivery [25, 26, 30]. Jaakkola et al. [26] found that the adjusted OR's for high and medium exposure categories were associated with an increased risk for preterm delivery, with ORs of 6.12 (95% CI: 1.31-28.7) and 1.30 (95% CI: 0.30-5.58), respectively. Ahluwalia et al. [30] also found that women aged 30 years or older had a significantly increased risk for preterm birth. Additionally, Windham et al. [25] reported a strong association between very preterm birth and ETS exposure in non-smoking women. Further, recent studies have been carried out on the effects of ETS exposure on birth length, head circumference, and spontaneous abortion

[23, 24, 31-33]. Some results are suggestive of a positive association, but most studies find inconclusive results or no evidence of a positive association.

A better understanding of the biological pathways of ETS exposure would help explain the differential effects of ETS exposure on fetal outcomes. Studies have been conducted on the effects of ETS exposure on biological changes occurring in neonates and the placenta [34-36]. In a recent study by Colak et al. [34] active smoking and passive smoking by the mother were found to have a negative effect on blood bone formation markers in newborns. This could potentially disturb normal bone formation and development during childhood. Subtle negative consequences on fetal oxygenation from observed increases in circulating absolute nucleated red blood cell counts have also been found in infants whose mothers were exposed to ETS during pregnancy [35]. In addition, Lackmann et al. [36] found that passive maternal smoking during pregnancy increases neonatal serum levels with polychlorinated biphenyls (PCB's) and hexachlorobenzenes (HCB's). The former and the latter compounds possess tumor-promoting properties and have been identified as probably and possibly carcinogenic to humans, respectively [37, 38]. Thus, ETS exposure of non-smoking pregnant women can play an important role in hindering the growth and healthy development of the fetus. ETS exposure during pregnancy has some immediate effects on fetal development and may produce some biological changes that have longer term consequences, not evident at birth. For this reason, longitudinal studies of ETS exposure would be helpful in determining some of the long-term effects.

ETS Exposure and Children's Health

Sudden Infant Death Syndrome

Both maternal smoking during pregnancy and ETS exposure in infants, have been linked to sudden infant death syndrome [2, 3, 7, 39]. In a systematic review by Anderson and Cook [40], the adjusted pooled OR for SIDS from prenatal maternal smoking was 2.08 (95% CI: 1.83-2.38). This indicates that there is a twofold increase in the risk of SIDS for infants whose mothers smoke during pregnancy. In a recent review by Mitchell and Milerad [41] for the WHO International Consultation on ETS and Child Health, similar conclusions were reached. Recent studies from England by Leach et al. [42] and from Denmark by Wisborg et al. [43], also confirm that maternal smoking during pregnancy is associated with a significantly increased risk for SIDS. The reviews by Anderson and Cook [40] and Mitchell and Milerad [41] also found strong evidence for a postnatal ETS effect. However, because there was a strong correlation between ETS exposures for the prenatal and postnatal time periods, it was difficult to assess their comparative contributions. To obtain clear evidence for an ETS effect, Mitchell and Milerad [41] reviewed 6 studies examining SIDS and paternal smoking where the mother was a nonsmoker. They found some evidence that ETS exposure increases the risk of SIDS with a pooled relative risk of 1.39 (95% CI: 1.11-1.74). Yet, the authors suspected that after confounding adjustments, this estimate would be reduced and thus made no conclusive statements. Future studies in this exposure group would help clarify to what extent household tobacco smoke exposure alone contributes to the risk of SIDS. Future studies also need to ascertain a more accurate indication of ETS dose including the extent to which non-smoking pregnant women have been exposed to ETS in their homes or at work.

Respiratory Health and Middle Ear Diseases

Conclusions of a causal linkage have been made for a number of respiratory health effects and ETS. ETS exposure causes lower respiratory tract infections such as pneumonia and bronchitis, chronic respiratory symptoms such as coughing and wheezing, worsening of asthma, and middle ear disease [1, 3, 7]. The evidence surrounding ETS and decreased lung function also suggests a causal relationship. Chen [44] demonstrated that adult cigarette smoking affects respiratory outcomes in children not only through the direct effects of the toxic components of tobacco smoke, but also as a result of the increased exposure to adult smokers' respiratory symptoms. A more recent series of review articles summarizing the epidemiological evidence for the effects of ETS on respiratory illness in children yielded consistent findings [14, 45-47]. During the first three years of life, children who live in a household where either parent smokes are 1.57 (95% CI: 1.42-1.74) times more likely to develop lower respiratory illness than children living in homes with non-smoking parents [48]. Paternal smoking alone causes a 1.3 fold increase in risk. In an additional meta-analysis by Li et al. [49], the combined OR for hospitalization for lower respiratory tract infections among ETS exposed children was found to be 1.93 (95% CI: 1.66-2.25). Even after adjustment for confounding factors, the associations with parental smoking remain, and show evidence of a dose-response relationship. Recent studies also show that ETS exposed children are at an increased risk for lower respiratory illnesses compared to non-ETS exposed children [50-52]. In the study by Ribeiro et al. [53] the absence of a positive association was explained by the fact that both exposure groups included a small number of mostly older children with high socioeconomic status, satisfactory housing, and who spent the majority of their time at school contributing to a protective effect because of their generally better health status . In addition, the incidence of respiratory infections was investigated over only a three month period that could have limited the opportunity to observe different effects between exposure groups. Moreover, the authors noted that the children lived in very polluted atmospheric conditions that could have contributed to respiratory infections in both exposure groups.

Furthermore lung function in children is also compromised by ETS exposure. Children have been found to experience deficits in their respiratory flow rates, and expiratory volumes. In a review by Cook et al. [54], the combination of study results yielded a 1.4 (95% CI: 1.0-1.9) percent reduction in forced expiratory volume in one second (FEV_1), in children exposed to parental smoking compared with those not exposed. Greater effects were found for mid expiratory flow rates, 5 (95% CI: 3.3-6.6) percent reduction, and end expiratory flow rates, 4.3 (95% CI: 3.1-5.5) percent reduction. Where ETS exposure was explicitly identified it was usually postpartum maternal smoking. In a recent systematic review by Stocks and Dezateux [55], they noted that there was also consistent evidence from the literature demonstrating significant changes in tidal flow patterns in infants whose mothers smoked during pregnancy prior to any postnatal exposure. From their preliminary meta-analysis, they reported that forced expiratory flows could be reduced on average by 20 percent in infants whose mothers smoke. However, Bek et al. [56] found no significant evidence of a negative health effect from maternal smoking only from paternal smoking. They attributed this to the fact that their study population consisted of relatively few smoking women. Thus, it is important that anti-smoking campaigns and/or reduced household smoking be directed at both women and men.

Asthma is the most common chronic disease in childhood and environmental factors have been found to play an important role in determining both onset and severity [3, 57]. As previously mentioned asthma exacerbation has been causally linked to ETS and there is also suggestive evidence that ETS can cause childhood asthma [1, 7, 39]. It is possible that ETS exposed children are increasingly susceptible to respiratory symptoms and disease due to decreased lung capacity. In a systematic review by Cook and Strachan [47], the pooled OR for asthma prevalence from either parent smoking is 1.21 (95% CI: 1.10-1.34). Some of the recent studies, have found similar positive associations for ETS exposed children [51, 52, 58-62]. Clear dose-response relationships are also observed when asthmatic symptoms are reduced as parents stop smoking and as the children grow older, thus spending less time at home with their parents [61, 62]. In an ecological study of parental smoking and asthmatic symptoms in children by Mitchell and Stewart [63], high male smoking rates were associated with a lower risk of asthmatic symptoms in children. Because of the ecological nature of the study, the findings should not be directly compared to the well-established individual-level association. Rather, the authors suggest that there are other important risk factors for asthma that explain the international differences.

Strong and consistent evidence also exists to support that ETS exposure in children can cause other chronic respiratory symptoms. The pooled OR's from any ETS household exposure are 1.24 (95% CI: 1.17-1.31) for wheeze, 1.40 (95% CI: 1.27-1.53) for cough, 1.35 (95% CI: 1.13-1.62) for phlegm, and 1.31 (95% CI: 1.08-1.59) for breathlessness [47]. While maternal smoking is associated with a greater effect, the effect of only paternal smoking is still significant. Overall consistent findings are observed in recent studies [51, 52, 60, 64-67]. In the two studies by Lam et al. [64, 65] of Chinese children in China and Hong Kong, significant positive associations were found for respiratory symptoms and ETS even with only paternal smoking in the household.

Infants and children of smoking parents are also found to experience significantly more acute and chronic middle ear diseases. Over 40 studies were investigated by Strachan and Cook [68] across a range of different middle ear diseases. A pooled OR of the order of 1.2-1.5 summarizes the effect of any parental ETS exposure on the incidence and recurrence of acute otitis media and the prevalence of middle ear effusion [68]. Several recent studies and an additional systematic review support the conclusion that ETS exposure is associated with recurrent ear infections [69-73]. Frequent bouts of middle ear effusion can lead to delays in language development and deafness [74]. These adverse health effects represent common ailments experienced by many children. Thus, the small increases in average individual risk translate into large population risks and constitute a substantial public health burden.

Neurodevelopmental and Behavioural Effects

ETS is an important risk factor for neurodevelopmental and behavioural problems in children [3]. Both ETS exposure of non-smoking women during pregnancy, and children's postnatal ETS exposure, can contribute to small adverse effects. Children of smokers tend to perform more poorly in school [75]. They are found to have lower scores in cognitive functioning tests with particular deficits in language and auditory processing, and tend to have more behavioural problems, including conduct disorders, hyperactivity and decreased attention spans [75]. Further, in a recent study by Chang et al. [76] infants who were exposed to in utero smoke were found to have decreased arousal responses compared to those of non-smoking mothers. Eskenazi [75] has summarized the commonly accepted mechanism for these effects as altered brain development, that results from fetal hypoxia due to either nicotine in cigarette smoke that acts to reduce blood flow to the fetus or possibly from carbon monoxide which produces higher levels of carboxyhemoglobin. The results are suggestive of a causal effect, yet these types of studies are difficult to interpret because of the complex number of genetic and socioenvironmental factors influencing neurodevelopment and behaviour.

Childhood Cancers

Some studies have also linked ETS exposure to childhood cancers. In the WHO International Consultation on ETS and Child Health Report [3], it was concluded that there is suggestive evidence that parental smoking may increase the risk of some childhood cancers. The tumours most often associated with ETS exposure during pregnancy or childhood are childhood brain tumours and leukaemia-lymphoma. In a meta-analysis by Boffetta et al. [77], the pooled OR estimates from maternal smoking during pregnancy were equivocal, 1.11 (95% CI: 1.0-1.23) for overall cancer risk and 1.14 (95% CI: 0.90-1.44) for leukemia. However, paternal smoking was associated with increased risks for brain tumours [relative risk (RR): 1.22; 95% CI: 1.05-1.40], and lymphomas (RR: 2.08; 95% CI: 1.08-3.98). Upon examination of several recent studies [78-84] no conclusive statements can be made. Some estimates suggest an overall increase in tumour and cancer risk but fail to reach statistical significance. However, in one large case-control study conducted in Shanghai [78], there was a moderate increased risk for all cancers (OR: 1.7; 95% CI: 1.2-2.5) and strong risks for lymphomas (OR: 4.5; 95% CI: 1.2-16.8) and acute lymphocytic leukemia (OR: 3.8; 95% CI: 1.3-12.3) among children under the age of 5 whose fathers smoked for more than 5 pack years prior to conception.

Cardiovascular Effects

So far, the evidence of an ETS effect on the cardiovascular health of children and adults is only suggestive. Currently, there are no good non-invasive measures of early atherosclerosis to test the hypothesis that ETS causes premature atherogenesis in children [85]. Hence, conclusions must rely on evidence from adult and animal studies, and pediatric studies with intermediate endpoints to cardiovascular diseases. In adults, both active and passive smoking have been concluded to cause cardiovascular disease (CVD), stroke and atherosclerosis. These disorders have lengthy natural histories that can be influenced by a suite of childhood risk factors [10]. There is also some evidence from intermediate endpoints which suggests that ETS exposure in children may accelerate the development of CVD. Some of the potential adverse effects in children are noted in a review by Gidding [85] for the WHO, and include harmful changes in oxygen transport, high density lipoprotein (HDL) cholesterol, and endothelial function. Studies in this area are limited, and thus future research into this area would be valuable.

Other Health Effects

Many other health effects in children have been associated with ETS exposure. Aligne et al. [86] and Williams et al. [87] found evidence for some association between ETS exposure and the risk of dental caries. ETS has been associated with invasive meningococcal disease and legg-calve-perthes disease, which can both lead to serious health consequences [88-90]. In addition, even minimal parental smoking is associated with reductions in plasma ascorbate concentrations (Vitamin C) in children [91]. This could be meaningful to populations of children who only ingest marginal amounts of vitamin C. Additionally, a strong positive association was found in a longitudinal study of maternal smoking during pregnancy and diabetes in adulthood [92]. Restricted activity, bed confinement and school absence have also been associated with ETS exposure [93]. Furthermore, children of mothers who smoked during their pregnancy are at a greater risk of obesity during early childhood [94]. Finally, recent evidence suggests that children exposed to ETS also have increased blood lead level concentrations [95]. Lead exposure and poisoning are associated with a variety of harmful health effects including, anemia, growth problems, decreased intelligence and behavioural problems[96].

Maternal vs. Paternal ETS Exposure

One of the main concerns in children's ETS research is how to differentiate between maternal and paternal ETS exposure. Some studies have attempted to examine whether exposure from maternal or paternal smoking is more important. Most studies have tended to focus on the effects of maternal smoking on children since the mother most often plays the dominant role in child development. When maternal smoking is rare it is possible to confirm the role of paternal smoking and help distinguish between the effects of in utero exposure to tobacco smoke and postnatal exposure. Chen et al. [97, 98] conducted two birth cohort studies in Shanghai, China where there were no known mothers who were smokers. The results identify father's smoking behaviour as well as those of other household members as significant risk factors in inpatient hospital admissions for respiratory disease and in the cumulative incidence of bronchitis/pneumonia in early life. In a study by Bek et al. [56] in Turkey, the important role of paternal smoking in populations where maternal smoking is rare was also confirmed. Further research in areas where maternal smoking is rare will help confirm the influence of paternal smoking on children's health.

Economic Burden of Children's ETS Exposure

The health effects of ETS exposure for pregnant women and children have serious economic consequences. In a paper by Peters et al. [99] on the economic burden of ETS on Hong Kong families, it was concluded that exposure to ETS was associated with an annual total cost for doctors visits between US$338 042 to US$991 591. Aligne and Stoddard [100] also performed an economic evaluation of the medical effects of parental smoking on children in the U.S. They estimated that ETS exposure resulted in an annual medical expenditure burden of $4.6 billion and loss of life costs amounting to $8.2 billion. More recently, in a meta-analysis by Peat et al. [101] it was reported that between 500 to 2500 excess hospitalizations and between 1000 to 5000 excess diagnoses per 100 000 children worldwide for respiratory infections could be attributed to ETS exposure from parental smoking. Thus, ETS exposure places a large burden on a family's financial resources and excess demands on the health care system. It is important to note that these costs are avoidable. While parents can play a large role in protecting their children from the ill effects of ETS, government policies are also essential to support the efforts of families and care-providers to reduce ETS exposure during pregnancy and childhood.

Future Research

ETS exposure is a major children's health challenge and a pervasive problem. The WHO estimates that at least 700 million children worldwide are exposed to ETS [3]. The overwhelming amount of scientific evidence supports the fact that children exposed to ETS experience a number of different ETS-related health problems. There are three spheres of research evidence required to address the problem. First, etiological research continues to uncover casual links between ETS and health risks. A refined understanding of the biological pathways whereby ETS exposure produces health effects is foundational for this research. Additional studies employing longitudinal study designs will help strengthen and explain the conclusions of causality by eliminating problems relating to selection and information bias. This study design could be particularly helpful in the research effort of ETS exposure and asthma incidence, where there are inconsistencies relating to causation. The complexity of smoking and ETS also requires a research approach that addresses the suite of influential factors. Different factors need to be considered as confounders or effect modifiers in the relationship between ETS and specific health outcomes. For example, the protective effect of breastfeeding may influence the relationship between ETS exposure and associated health outcomes. The WHO [3] recommends that where longitudinal studies are underway, analyses to investigate how changes in exposure are related to changes in outcome would help elucidate the role of ETS in certain health problems. In particular, common health ailments such as ear infections or lower respiratory illnesses could be used as clinical outcome measures in ETS intervention studies. Since these health effects are highly prevalent, and have short clinical histories, changes in the frequency of these effects can be measured quickly and easily. In addition, research in countries where maternal smoking is rare will help distinguish between parental effects and effects of in utero exposure to tobacco smoke and postnatal exposure. This research effort will also allow for cross-cultural comparisons of ETS health effects. ETS exposure and tobacco use are greatly influenced by cultural values and different community level factors. Cross-cultural comparisons can help identify attributes that are either protective or risk inducing for ETS exposure and ETS-related health effects. This will help with understanding the mechanisms responsible for causing ETS-related health problems and will help identify potential intervention strategies for reducing ETS exposure. This research area would benefit from the use of multi-level studies that recognize the importance of the interactions between individual and community level factors.

Second, more thorough and more accurate ETS prevalence estimates are required in order to provide direction for interventions including ETS reduction policies [3]. ETS exposure needs to be assessed in various settings including the workplace, the home, day care settings and other public places. The emerging evidence showing a dose-response relationship between ETS exposure and health outcomes, highlights the need to document the cumulative impact of ETS exposure on children across different settings. Future studies of ETS exposure must try to avoid the problem of underestimating ETS exposure, a difficulty that arises when only the proximal ETS environment (i.e. parent's smoking patterns) is considered. The use of ETS biomarkers would also allow for a better characterization of exposure rates especially for the short term effects of ETS.

Third, research is required to examine the impact of ETS reduction and enforcement policies on children's ETS exposure rates. A wide range of ETS reduction policies have been implemented in many settings. Understanding the key elements of effective ETS policies and how these policies are supported by other initiatives such as public education on ETS exposure are important areas of study. Comparisons across jurisdictions and across international settings would provide important evidence of the contextual factors that may lead to a differential impact of particular policies. Further, it is proposed that additional emphasis be placed on ecological studies that compare communities that have established ETS by-laws in public places and workplaces with those that have none. This may generate evidence that is needed to inform public policy decisions. Determining how ETS and other tobacco-related policies may be harmonized across jurisdictions would support worldwide efforts to achieve a sustained commitment towards ETS reduction efforts.

Finally, future research needs to focus on reducing and eliminating tobacco-related health disparities. This research area explores the links between health status and economic, social and political inequities. Recently Fagan et al. [102] summarized recommendations for future research directions towards eliminating tobacco-related health disparities that were made at the National Conference on Tobacco and Health Disparities in 2002. The recommendations called for an increased understanding of tobacco use, addiction and health effects in disadvantaged and special populations. Similarly, the inequitable impact of ETS-reduction policies on different socioeconomic groups needs to be better understood.

There has been substantial progress made in the field of ETS research, most notably in the area of causal health effects. This provides a very solid base for work that needs to be undertaken so that comprehensive interventions can be put in place to address this pervasive problem.

Acknowledgment

This work is partly supported by the Canadian Institutes of Health Research. Dr. Yue Chen holds an Investigator Award from the Canadian Institutes of Health Research. Dr. Nancy Edwards holds a Nursing Chair funded by the Canadian Health Services Research Foundation, the Canadian Institutes of Health Research, and the Ontario Ministry of Health and Long-term Care.

References

[1]   U.S. Environmental Protection Agency (1992). Respiratory health effects of passive smoking: *Lung cancer and other disorders*, Office of Health and Environmental Assessment: Washington, D.C.

[2]   U.K. Department of Health (1998). *Report of the scientific committee on tobacco and health*, The Stationery Office.

[3]   World Health Organization Division of Noncommunicable Diseases Tobacco Free Initiative (1999). *International consultation on environmental tobacco smoke (ETS) and child health*, World Health Organization: Geneva.

[4]   World Health Organization Press Releases. (2003 05 21) World Health Assembly adopts historic tobacco control pact. Available from: URL: http://www.who.int/media centre/releases/2003/prwha1/en/

[5]   World Health Organization (2003 05 21). WHO Framework Convention on Tobacco Control. Available from: URL:
         http://www.who.int/tobacco/areas/framework/final_text/en/index.html

[6]   Kurtz, M.E., Johnson, S.M., and Rosslee, B. (1992). Passive Smoking - Directions for Health-Education among Malaysian College-Students. *International Journal of Health Services* **22**, 555-565.

[7]   California Environmental Protection Agency (1997). *Health effects of exposure to environmental tobacco smoke*, Office of Environmental Health Hazard Assessment: California.

[8]   Eliopoulos, C., Klein, J., Chitayat, D., Greenwald, M., and Koren, G. (1996). Nicotine and cotinine in maternal and neonatal hair as markers of gestational smoking. *Clin Invest Med* **19**, 231-242.

[9]   Tutka, P., Wielosz, M., and Zatonski, W. (2002). Exposure to environmental tobacco smoke and children health. *Int J Occup Med Environ Health* **15**, 325-335.

[10]   Samet, J.M. (1998). Synthesis: *The health effects of tobacco smoke exposure on children*, World Health Organization Division of Noncommunicable Diseases Tobacco Free Initiative.

[11]   Savitz, D.A., Dole, N., Terry, J.W., Jr., Zhou, H., and Thorp, J.M., Jr. (2001). Smoking and pregnancy outcome among African-American and white women in central North Carolina. *Epidemiology* **12**, 636-642.

[12]   Kallen, K. (2001). The impact of maternal smoking during pregnancy on delivery outcome. *Eur J Public Health* **11**, 329-333.

[13]   Billaud, N., and Lemarie, P. (2001). Negative effects of maternal smoking during the course of pregnancy. *Arch Pediatr* **8**, 875-881.

[14]   Hofhuis, W., de Jongste, J.C., and Merkus, P.J. (2003). Adverse health effects of prenatal and postnatal tobacco smoke exposure on children. *Arch Dis Child* **88**, 1086-1090.

[15]   Mortensen, J.T., Thulstrup, A.M., Larsen, H., Moller, M., and Sorensen, H.T. (2001). Smoking, sex of the offspring, and risk of placental abruption, placenta previa, and preeclampsia: a population-based cohort study. *Acta Obstet Gynecol Scand* **80**, 894-898.

[16] Xiong, X., Wang, F.L., Davidge, S.T., Demianczuk, N.N., Mayes, D.C., Olson, D.M., and Saunders, L.D. (2000). Maternal smoking and preeclampsia. *J Reprod Med* **45**, 727-732.

[17] North, R.A., Taylor, R., Li Zhou, R., and Schellenberg, J.C. (2000). The relationship of smoking, preeclampsia, and secretory component. *Am J Obstet Gynecol* **183**, 136-139.

[18] Conde-Agudelo, A., Althabe, F., Belizan, J.M., and Kafury-Goeta, A.C. (1999). Cigarette smoking during pregnancy and risk of preeclampsia: a systematic review. *Am J Obstet Gynecol* **181**, 1026-1035.

[19] Windham, G.C., Eaton, A., and Hopkins, B. (1999). Evidence for an association between environmental tobacco smoke exposure and birthweight: a meta-analysis and new data. *Paediatr Perinat Epidemiol* **13**, 35-57.

[20] Lindbohm, M.L., Sallmen, M., and Taskinen, H. (2002). Effects of exposure to environmental tobacco smoke on reproductive health. *Scand J Work Environ Health* **28** Suppl 2, 84-96.

[21] Loke, A.Y., Lam, T.H., Pan, S.C., Li, S.Y., Gao, X.J., and Song, Y.Y. (2000). Exposure to and actions against passive smoking in non-smoking pregnant women in Guangzhou, China. *Acta Obstet Gynecol Scand* **79**, 947-952.

[22] Dejin-Karlsson, E., Hanson, B.S., Ostergren, P.O., Sjoberg, N.O., and Marsal, K. (1998). Does passive smoking in early pregnancy increase the risk of small-for-gestational-age infants? *Am J Public Health* **88**, 1523-1527.

[23] Fried, P.A., Watkinson, B., and Gray, R. (1999). Growth from birth to early adolescence in offspring prenatally exposed to cigarettes and marijuana. *Neurotoxicol Teratol* **21**, 513-525.

[24] Perera, F.P., Jedrychowski, W., Rauh, V., and Whyatt, R.M. (1999). Molecular epidemiologic research on the effects of environmental pollutants on the fetus. *Environ Health Perspect* **107** *Suppl* 3, 451-460.

[25] Windham, G.C., Hopkins, B., Fenster, L., and Swan, S.H. (2000). Prenatal active or passive tobacco smoke exposure and the risk of preterm delivery or low birth weight. *Epidemiology* **11**, 427-433.

[26] Jaakkola, J.J., Jaakkola, N., and Zahlsen, K. (2001). Fetal growth and length of gestation in relation to prenatal exposure to environmental tobacco smoke assessed by hair nicotine concentration. *Environ Health Perspect* **109**, 557-561.

[27] Nafstad, P., Fugelseth, D., Qvigstad, E., Zahlen, K., Magnus, P., and Lindemann, R. (1998). Nicotine concentration in the hair of nonsmoking mothers and size of offspring. *Am J Public Health* **88**, 120-124.

[28] Sadler, L., Belanger, K., Saftlas, A., Leaderer, B., Hellenbrand, K., McSharry, J.E., and Bracken, M.B. (1999). Environmental tobacco smoke exposure and small-for-gestational-age birth. *Am J Epidemiol* **150**, 695-705.

[29] Mitchell, E.A., Thompson, J.M., Robinson, E., Wild, C.J., Becroft, D.M., Clark, P.M., Glavish, N., Pattison, N.S., and Pryor, J.E. (2002). Smoking, nicotine and tar and risk of small for gestational age babies. *Acta Paediatr* **91**, 323-328.

[30] Ahluwalia, I.B., Grummer-Strawn, L., and Scanlon, K.S. (1997). Exposure to environmental tobacco smoke and birth outcome: increased effects on pregnant women aged 30 years or older. *Am J Epidemiol* **146**, 42-47.

[31] Wang, X., Tager, I.B., Van Vunakis, H., Speizer, F.E., and Hanrahan, J.P. (1997). Maternal smoking during pregnancy, urine cotinine concentrations, and birth outcomes. A prospective cohort study. *Int J Epidemiol* **26**, 978-988.

[32] Chatenoud, L., Parazzini, F., di Cintio, E., Zanconato, G., Benzi, G., Bortolus, R., and La Vecchia, C. (1998). Paternal and maternal smoking habits before conception and during the first trimester: relation to spontaneous abortion. *Ann Epidemiol* **8**, 520-526.

[33] Windham, G.C., Von Behren, J., Waller, K., and Fenster, L. (1999). Exposure to environmental and mainstream tobacco smoke and risk of spontaneous abortion. *Am J Epidemiol* **149**, 243-247.

[34] Colak, O., Alatas, O., Aydogdu, S., and Uslu, S. (2002). The effect of smoking on bone metabolism: maternal and cord blood bone marker levels. *Clin Biochem* **35**, 247-250.

[35] Dollberg, S., Fainaru, O., Mimouni, F.B., Shenhav, M., Lessing, J.B., and Kupferminc, M. (2000). Effect of passive smoking in pregnancy on neonatal nucleated red blood cells. *Pediatrics* **106**, E34.

[36] Lackmann, G.M., Angerer, J., and Tollner, U. (2000). Parental smoking and neonatal serum levels of polychlorinated biphenyls and hexachlorobenzene. *Pediatr Res* **47**, 598-601.

[37] International Agency for Research on Cancer (1998). Hexachlorobenzene. Available from: URL: http://www-cie.iarc.fr/htdocs/monographs/suppl7/hexachlorobenzene.html

[38] International Agency for Research on Cancer (1998). Polychlorinated Biphenyls. Available from: URL: http://www-cie.iarc.fr/htdocs/monographs/suppl7/polychlorinatedbiphenyls.html

[39] Australian National Health and Medical Research Council (1997). *The health effects of passive smoking.*

[40] Anderson, H.R., and Cook, D.G. (1997). Passive smoking and sudden infant death syndrome: review of the epidemiological evidence. *Thorax* **52**, 1003-1009.

[41] Mitchell, E.A., and Milerad, J. (1998). *Smoking and sudden infant death syndrome*, World Health Organization Division of Noncommunicable Diseases Tobacco Free Initiative.

[42] Leach, C.E., Blair, P.S., Fleming, P.J., Smith, I.J., Platt, M.W., Berry, P.J., and Golding, J. (1999). Epidemiology of SIDS and explained sudden infant deaths. CESDI SUDI Research Group. *Pediatrics* **104**, e43.

[43] Wisborg, K., Kesmodel, U., Henriksen, T.B., Olsen, S.F., and Secher, N.J. (2000). A prospective study of smoking during pregnancy and SIDS. *Arch Dis Child* **83**, 203-206.

[44] Chen, Y. (1991). Adult respiratory disease mediates the effect of smoking on cumulative incidence of bronchitis/pneumonia in infants. *Int J Epidemiol* **20**, 822-823.

[45] Chan-Yeung, M., and Dimich-Ward, H. (2003). Respiratory health effects of exposure to environmental tobacco smoke. *Respirology* **8**, 131-139.

[46] Landau, L.I. (2001). Parental smoking: asthma and wheezing illnesses in infants and children. *Paediatr Respir Rev* **2**, 202-206.

[47] Cook, D.G., and Strachan, D.P. (1999). Health effects of passive smoking-10: Summary of effects of parental smoking on the respiratory health of children and implications for research. *Thorax* **54**, 357-366.

[48] Strachan, D.P., and Cook, D.G. (1997). Health effects of passive smoking .1. Parental smoking and lower respiratory illness in infancy and early childhood. *Thorax* **52**, 905-914.

[49] Li, J.S., Peat, J.K., Xuan, W., and Berry, G. (1999). Meta-analysis on the association between environmental tobacco smoke (ETS) exposure and the prevalence of lower respiratory tract infection in early childhood. *Pediatr Pulmonol* **27**, 5-13.

[50] Blizzard, L., Ponsonby, A.L., Dwyer, T., Venn, A., and Cochrane, J.A. (2003). Parental smoking and infant respiratory infection: how important is not smoking in the same room with the baby? *Am J Public Health* **93**, 482-488.

[51] Hajnal, B.L., Braun-Fahrlander, C., Grize, L., Gassner, M., Varonier, H.S., Vuille, J.C., Wuthrich, B., and Sennhauser, F.H. (1999). Effect of environmental tobacco smoke exposure on respiratory symptoms in children. SCARPOL Team. Swiss Study on Childhood Allergy and Respiratory Symptoms with Respect to Air Pollution, Climate and Pollen. *Schweiz Med Wochenschr* **129**, 723-730.

[52] Gergen, P.J., Fowler, J.A., Maurer, K.R., Davis, W.W., and Overpeck, M.D. (1998). The burden of environmental tobacco smoke exposure on the respiratory health of children 2 months through 5 years of age in the United States: Third National Health and Nutrition Examination Survey, 1988 to 1994. *Pediatrics* **101**, E8.

[53] Ribeiro, S.A., Furuyama, T., Schenkman, S., and Jardim, J.R. (2002). Atopy, passive smoking, respiratory infections and asthma among children from kindergarten and elementary school. *Sao Paulo Med J* **120**, 109-112.

[54] Cook, D.G., Strachan, D.P., and Carey, I.M. (1998). Health effects of passive smoking. 9. Parental smoking and spirometric indices in children. *Thorax* **53**, 884-893.

[55] Stocks, J., and Dezateux, C. (2003). The effect of parental smoking on lung function and development during infancy. *Respirology* **8**, 266-285.

[56] Bek, K., Tomac, N., Delibas, A., Tuna, F., Tezic, H.T., and Sungur, M. (1999). The effect of passive smoking on pulmonary function during childhood. *Postgrad Med J* **75**, 339-341.

[57] Gold, D.R. (2000). Environmental tobacco smoke, indoor allergens, and childhood asthma. *Environ Health Perspect* **108** Suppl 4, 643-651.

[58] Ponsonby, A.L., Couper, D., Dwyer, T., Carmichael, A., Kemp, A., and Cochrane, J. (2000). The relation between infant indoor environment and subsequent asthma. *Epidemiology* **11**, 128-135.

[59] Tariq, S.M., Hakim, E.A., Matthews, S.M., and Arshad, S.H. (2000). Influence of smoking on asthmatic symptoms and allergen sensitisation in early childhood. *Postgrad Med J* **76**, 694-699.

[60] Mannino, D.M., Moorman, J.E., Kingsley, B., Rose, D., and Repace, J. (2001). Health effects related to environmental tobacco smoke exposure in children in the United States: data from the Third National Health and Nutrition Examination Survey. *Arch Pediatr Adolesc Med* **155**, 36-41.

[61] Mannino, D.M., Homa, D.M., and Redd, S.C. (2002). Involuntary smoking and asthma severity in children: data from the Third National Health and Nutrition Examination Survey. *Chest* **122**, 409-415.

[62] Zheng, T., Niu, S., Lu, B., Fan, X., Sun, F., Wang, J., Zhang, Y., Zhang, B., Owens, P., Hao, L., Li, Y., and Leaderer, B. (2002). Childhood asthma in Beijing, China: a population-based case-control study. *Am J Epidemiol* **156**, 977-983.

[63] Mitchell, E.A., and Stewart, A.W. (2001). The ecological relationship of tobacco smoking to the prevalence of symptoms of asthma and other atopic diseases in children:

the International Study of Asthma and Allergies in Childhood (ISAAC). *Eur J Epidemiol* **17**, 667-673.

[64] Lam, T.H., Chung, S.F., Betson, C.L., Wong, C.M., and Hedley, A.J. (1998). Respiratory symptoms due to active and passive smoking in junior secondary school students in Hong Kong. *Int J Epidemiol* **27**, 41-48.

[65] Lam, T.H., Hedley, A.J., Chung, S.F., and Macfarlane, D.J. (1999). Passive smoking and respiratory symptoms in primary school children in Hong Kong. Child Health and Activity Research Group (CHARG). *Hum Exp Toxicol* **18**, 218-223.

[66] Lux, A.L., Henderson, A.J., and Pocock, S.J. (2000). Wheeze associated with prenatal tobacco smoke exposure: a prospective, longitudinal study. ALSPAC Study Team. *Arch Dis Child* **83**, 307-312.

[67] Henderson, A.J., Sherriff, A., Northstone, K., Kukla, L., and Hruba, D. (2001). Pre- and postnatal parental smoking and wheeze in infancy: cross cultural differences. Avon Study of Parents and Children (ALSPAC) Study Team, European Longitudinal Study of Pregnancy and Childhood (ELSPAC) Co-ordinating Centre. *Eur Respir J* **18**, 323-329.

[68] Strachan, D.P., and Cook, D.G. (1998). Health effects of passive smoking. 4. Parental smoking, middle ear disease and adenotonsillectomy in children. *Thorax* **53**, 50-56.

[69] Adair-Bischoff, C.E., and Sauve, R.S. (1998). Environmental tobacco smoke and middle ear disease in preschool-age children. *Arch Pediatr Adolesc Med* **152**, 127-133.

[70] Ilicali, O.C., Keles, N., Deger, K., and Savas, I. (1999). Relationship of passive cigarette smoking to otitis media. *Arch Otolaryngol Head Neck Surg* **125**, 758-762.

[71] Ilicali, O.C., Keles, N., Deger, K., Sagun, O.F., and Guldiken, Y. (2001). Evaluation of the effect of passive smoking on otitis media in children by an objective method: urinary cotinine analysis. *Laryngoscope* **111**, 163-167.

[72] Lieu, J.E., and Feinstein, A.R. (2002). Effect of gestational and passive smoke exposure on ear infections in children. *Arch Pediatr Adolesc Med* **156**, 147-154.

[73] Gaffney, K.F. (2000). Tobacco smoke exposure and pediatric otitis media: an empirical basis for practice. *Lippincotts Prim Care Pract* **4**, 508-514.

[74] Kraemer, M.J., Marshall, S.G., and Richardson, M.A. (1984). Etiologic factors in the development of chronic middle ear effusions. *Clin Rev Allergy* **2**, 319-328.

[75] Eskenazi, B. (1998). Association of in utero or postnatal environmental tobacco smoke exposure and neurodevelopmental and behavioural problems in children, World Health Organization Division of Noncommunicable Diseases Tobacco Free Initiative.

[76] Chang, A.B., Wilson, S.J., Masters, I.B., Yuill, M., Williams, J., Williams, G., and Hubbard, M. (2003). Altered arousal response in infants exposed to cigarette smoke. *Arch Dis Child* **88**, 30-33.

[77] Boffetta, P., Tredaniel, J., and Greco, A. (1998). *Parental tobacco smoke and childhood cancer*, World Health Organization Division of Noncommunicable Diseases Tobacco Free Initiative.

[78] Ji, B.T., Shu, X.O., Linet, M.S., Zheng, W., Wacholder, S., Gao, Y.T., Ying, D.M., and Jin, F. (1997). Paternal cigarette smoking and the risk of childhood cancer among offspring of nonsmoking mothers. *J Natl Cancer Inst* **89**, 238-244.

[79] Brondum, J., Shu, X.O., Steinbuch, M., Severson, R.K., Potter, J.D., and Robison, L.L. (1999). Parental cigarette smoking and the risk of acute leukemia in children. *Cancer* **85**, 1380-1388.

[80]   Schuz, J., Kaatsch, P., Kaletsch, U., Meinert, R., and Michaelis, J. (1999). Association of childhood cancer with factors related to pregnancy and birth. *Int J Epidemiol* **28**, 631-639.

[81]   Infante-Rivard, C., Krajinovic, M., Labuda, D., and Sinnett, D. (2000). Parental smoking, CYP1A1 genetic polymorphisms and childhood leukemia (Quebec, Canada). *Cancer Causes Control* **11**, 547-553.

[82]   Hu, J., Mao, Y., and Ugnat, A.M. (2000). Parental cigarette smoking, hard liquor consumption and the risk of childhood brain tumors--a case-control study in northeast China. *Acta Oncol* **39**, 979-984.

[83]   Sorahan, T., McKinney, P.A., Mann, J.R., Lancashire, R.J., Stiller, C.A., Birch, J.M., Dodd, H.E., and Cartwright, R.A. (2001). Childhood cancer and parental use of tobacco: findings from the inter-regional epidemiological study of childhood cancer (IRESCC). *Br J Cancer* **84**, 141-146.

[84]   Filippini, G., Maisonneuve, P., McCredie, M., Peris-Bonet, R., Modan, B., Preston-Martin, S., Mueller, B.A., Holly, E.A., Cordier, S., Choi, N.W., Little, J., Arslan, A., and Boyle, P. (2002). Relation of childhood brain tumors to exposure of parents and children to tobacco smoke: the SEARCH international case-control study. Surveillance of Environmental Aspects Related to Cancer in Humans. *Int J Cancer* **100**, 206-213.

[85]   Gidding, S.S. (1998). *Effects of passive smoking on the cardiovascular system in children and adolescents*, World Health Organization Division of Noncommunicable Diseases Tobacco Free Initiative.

[86]   Aligne, C.A., Moss, M.E., Auinger, P., and Weitzman, M. (2003). Association of pediatric dental caries with passive smoking. *Jama* **289**, 1258-1264.

[87]   Williams, S.A., Kwan, S.Y., and Parsons, S. (2000). Parental smoking practices and caries experience in pre-school children. *Caries Res* **34**, 117-122.

[88]   Kriz, P., Bobak, M., and Kriz, B. (2000). Parental smoking, socioeconomic factors, and risk of invasive meningococcal disease in children: a population based case-control study. *Arch Dis Child* **83**, 117-121.

[89]   Fischer, M., Hedberg, K., Cardosi, P., Plikaytis, B.D., Hoesly, F.C., Steingart, K.R., Bell, T.A., Fleming, D.W., Wenger, J.D., and Perkins, B.A. (1997). Tobacco smoke as a risk factor for meningococcal disease. *Pediatr Infect Dis J* **16**, 979-983.

[90]   Mata, S.G., Aicua, E.A., Ovejero, A.H., and Grande, M.M. (2000). Legg-Calve-Perthes disease and passive smoking. *J Pediatr Orthop* **20**, 326-330.

[91]   Preston, A.M., Rodriguez, C., Rivera, C.E., and Sahai, H. (2003). Influence of environmental tobacco smoke on vitamin C status in children. *Am J Clin Nutr* **77**, 167-172.

[92]   Montgomery, S.M., and Ekbom, A. (2002). Smoking during pregnancy and diabetes mellitus in a British longitudinal birth cohort. *Bmj* **324**, 26-27.

[93]   Mannino, D.M., Siegel, M., Husten, C., Rose, D., and Etzel, R. (1996). Environmental tobacco smoke exposure and health effects in children: results from the 1991 National Health Interview Survey. *Tob Control* **5**, 13-18.

[94]   von Kries, R., Toschke, A.M., Koletzko, B., and Slikker, W., Jr. (2002). Maternal smoking during pregnancy and childhood obesity. *Am J Epidemiol* **156**, 954-961.

[95]   Mannino, D.M., Albalak, R., Grosse, S., and Repace, J. (2003). Second-hand smoke exposure and blood lead levels in U.S. children. *Epidemiology* **14**, 719-727.

[96] National Research Council (1993). *Measuring lead exposure in infants, children, and other sensitive populations* (Washington, DC: National Academy Press).

[97] Chen, Y., and Li, W.X. (1986). The effect of passive smoking on children's pulmonary function in Shanghai. *Am J Public Health* **76**, 515-518.

[98] Chen, Y., Li, W.X., Yu, S.Z., and Qian, W.H. (1988). Chang-Ning Epidemiological-Study of Childrens Health .1. Passive Smoking and Childrens Respiratory-Diseases. *International Journal of Epidemiology* **17**, 348-355.

[99] Peters, J., McCabe, C.J., Hedley, A.J., Lam, T.H., and Wong, C.M. (1998). Economic burden of environmental tobacco smoke on Hong Kong families: scale and impact. *J Epidemiol Community Health* **52**, 53-58.

[100] Aligne, C.A., and Stoddard, J.J. (1997). Tobacco and children. An economic evaluation of the medical effects of parental smoking. *Arch Pediatr Adolesc Med* **151**, 648-653.

[101] Peat, J.K., Keena, V., Harakeh, Z., and Marks, G. (2001). Parental smoking and respiratory tract infections in children. *Paediatr Respir Rev* **2**, 207-213.

[102] Fagan, P., King, G., Lawrence, D., Petrucci, S.A., Robinson, R.G., Banks, D., Marable, S., and Grana, R. (2004). Eliminating tobacco-related health disparities: directions for future research. *Am J Public Health* **94**, 211-217.

In: Trends in Smoking and Health Research
Editors: J. H. Owing, pp. 145-184

ISBN: 1-59454-391-7
© 2005 Nova Science Publishers, Inc.

Chapter VIII

Adolescent Tobacco Use

Brenda M. Elliott and Neil E. Grunberg

Medical & Clinical Psychology
Uniformed Services University
Bethesda, Maryland, USA

Abstract

Despite wide-spread publicity and knowledge that tobacco use poses serious health risks, adolescent tobacco use is increasing in the United States and worldwide. Every day more than 4000 children under the age of 18 begin smoking in the United States alone (CDC, 2003; SMA, 2002). Of these children, one third eventually will die from smoking-related causes. In addition, the fact that 90% of adult smokers began smoking before age 20 indicates that adolescence is a critical target period for tobacco prevention. Susceptibility to tobacco use in adolescents includes social, psychological, environmental, and biobehavioral factors that influence tobacco initiation and maintenance.

This chapter provides an overview of adolescent tobacco use. It begins with a summary of the magnitude of this situation and the relevant epidemiology. It then discusses reasons why adolescence is a vulnerable phase in life for tobacco initiation and reviews the psychosocial, psychobiological, and environmental factors that influence tobacco initiation and maintenance. Next, this chapter discusses the physical and mental health effects of adolescent smoking. The chapter ends by reviewing intervention and cessation strategies to reduce adolescent smoking and how current findings may be used to develop prevention programs to deter adolescent smoking or treatment strategies to decrease adolescent smoking.

Introduction

Despite the well-publicized deleterious effects of tobacco smoking and the addictive liability of nicotine, over 4000 adolescents start smoking every day in the United States (Gilpin et al., 1999; CDC, 2003). In addition, another 2000 adolescents become established smokers (i.e., lifetime level of 100 cigarettes) every day. Further, over six million of today's

American children will die prematurely from smoking-related diseases (CDC, 1996). Although not all of the children who try tobacco smoking become life-long smokers, more than one-third of high-school students smoke at least once a month and another 17% of high-school students report smoking almost every day (USDHHS, 1988; ALF, 2001). Further, more than 90% of adult smokers report first trying a tobacco product before age 18 (Gilpin et al., 1999; USDHHS, 1994). These reports suggest that: (1) smoking in adolescence is a major health problem; (2) adolescence is a critical vulnerable period for the initiation of tobacco use; (3) adolescence should be a target age group for tobacco prevention.

This chapter focuses on adolescent tobacco use including its prevalence, effects, reasons why adolescents smoke, and suggestions for how to prevent tobacco use and how to encourage cessation in adolescents. The first section presents the epidemiology of adolescent tobacco. The second section reviews the psychosocial, psychobiological, and environmental factors that influence adolescent tobacco initiation and maintenance. The third section reviews the physical and mental health effects of adolescent smoking. The fourth section discusses the treatments available for adolescent smoking. The fifth and final section discusses directions for future research intended to prevent tobacco use initiation.

Epidemiology of Adolescent Smoking

Overview

Adolescence is a particularly vulnerable time for the initiation of tobacco use. Individuals who delay smoking initiation until after age 18 are less likely to become established smokers (Pierce et al., 1996; USDHHS, 1994). The majority of what is known about current trends in adolescent smoking has been collected using nationally-based school (e.g., Monitoring the Future; Johnston et al., 2002) and household surveys (e.g., National Household Survey on Drug Abuse; Kopstein, 2001). According to the National Household Survey on Drug Abuse (Kopstein, 2001), the most common age for trying a first cigarette is between 14 and 15 years old and the most frequent age at which one progresses to regular smoking is between 16 and 17 years old. After the mid-twenties, declines in smoking initiation occur (Chassin et al., 2000), suggesting that early intervention is important to circumvent the trajectory of cigarette smoking.

Fortunately, not all adolescents who experiment with cigarette smoking go on to become daily smokers. However, initiation of smoking in adolescence does increase the likelihood of becoming a daily smoker. Overall, the number of adolescents who experiment with smoking (but do not progress to daily smoking) rapidly decreases with age, whereas the number of adolescents who progress to daily smoking increases with age (ALF, 2001).

Smoking Experimentation

According to the National Youth Tobacco Survey (NTYS) conducted by the American Legacy Foundation (ALF) and the Center for Disease Control (CDC), nearly two-thirds of high school students and one-third of middle school students have tried a puff or more of a cigarette (ALF, 2001). Among adolescents, rates of smoking initiation vary depending on age and ethnicity and to a lesser extent on gender. The majority of national surveys report that African-American youth are less likely to initiate smoking than are Whites or Latinos (Nelson et al., 1995; Alexander et al., 2001; Griesler et al., 2002). Recent findings from the NYTS (ALF, 2001) and Ellickson (2004), however, suggest that African- Americans exhibit higher smoking initiation rates than do Whites. These recent reports are at odds with data gathered over the past decade. Whether the new data indicate a dramatic shift in ethnic differences or a sampling error is unclear at this time. Regardless of such discrepancies, African-American youth are consistently less likely to transition to daily regular smoking and are more likely to quit smoking than are Whites and Latinos. The specific factors that account for ethnic differences in smoking patterns have been the topic of speculation but are unclear (Kandel et al., 2004).

Lifetime Use

"Lifetime use" refers to having ever smoked daily (ALF, 2001). This measure, therefore, includes past tobacco users and current users, but excludes those individuals who only have experimented with tobacco smoking. Rates of lifetime smoking differ from rates of initiation and are believed to provide a better indicator of progression to daily or "regular" smoking. According to the NTYS (ALF 2001), only 4% of middle-school students report smoking daily. By high school, 20% of students report daily smoking. Most national surveys reveal that Whites and Latinos are more likely than African-Americans to progress to daily smoking (CDC, 1997; Epstein et al., 1998; Johnston et al., 2002; Kopstein, 2001; Kandel et al., 2004). For example, Kandel et al. (2004) recently reported that the transition to daily smoking is generally higher among White (18.8%) and Latino (15.9 %) than among Black (9.6%) youths. Currently, there are no significant gender differences in rates of lifetime use among middle or high-school youth (Simons-Morton et al., 1999; ALF, 2001).

Frequent Use

"Frequent use" is another method of classifying smoking behavior and refers to smoking on 20 or more days during the past 30 days (ALF, 2002). According to results from the National Youth Tobacco Survey (ALF, 2001), only 2% of middle-school smokers could be classified as frequent smokers with no marked differences based on race or ethnicity. Among high-school students, the rates of frequent smoking are substantially higher (13.2 %) and ethnic differences exist. Specifically, African-Americans (5.3 %) and Latinos (9.9 %) are less likely than are Whites (16.5 %) to become frequent smokers. There currently are no gender differences in frequent smoking among middle-school or high-school students surveyed. This lack of a gender difference is markedly different from the extreme male dominance of smoking that existed for decades in the early and mid 20th Century.

Factors Influencing Adolescent Tobacco Use

Overview

Adolescence is a sensitive time of life for the initiation of smoking. By the age of 18, more than two-thirds of teenagers have experimented with cigarette smoking with peak experimentation occurring between 13 and 16 years of age (USDHHS, 1994; Duncan et al., 1995). Initiation and maintenance of tobacco during adolescence is influenced by an interplay of psychosocial, biological, and environmental factors (USDHHS, 1994). A summary of these factors is presented in Table 1.

Table 1. Factors influencing adolescent tobacco initiation and maintenance

Psychosocial	Sociodemographic Factors
	Interpersonal factors
	Attitudes/expectation/perceptions
	Co-morbidity with mental health problems
	Personal factors
Psychobiological	Appetite control
	Affective regulation
	Cognitive regulation
	Addiction
Environmental	Socioeconomic status
	Exposure to tobacco advertisements and products

Psychosocial Factors

Overview

Psychosocial factors are the most widely studied variables that directly and indirectly affect an individual's choice to use tobacco. Given that young people are particularly vulnerable to psychosocial influences, prevention efforts to reduce adolescent smoking must seriously take these factors into consideration. The following section reviews those psychosocial factors that appear to have the greatest influence on smoking initiation and maintenance. A list of these factors is presented in Table 2.

Sociodemographic Factors

Age

The specific developmental stage of adolescence predicts smoking initiation (Alexander et al., 1983; Coombs et al., 1986). According to the results from the National Youth Tobacco Survey conducted by the American Legacy Foundation and the Center for Disease Control (ALF, 2001), nearly two-thirds of high school students and one-third of middle school students have tried a puff or more of a cigarette. First experimentation with smoking generally begins in the early part of adolescence, during the transition from elementary school to middle school. During the high-school years, rates of smoking onset level off. Smoking rates among high school students (i.e., 15- to 17-year-old adolescents) declined from 34.5 % in 2000 to 28.4 % in 2003 (CDC, 2003). In contrast, rates of smoking among middle-school groups have remained steady over the past seven years at approximately 13.3 % (CDC, 2003).

Table 2. Psychosocial factors relevant to initiation of tobacco smoking during adolescence

Sociodemographic	Developmental stage (age)
	Gender
	Ethnicity
Interpersonal	Role models
	Peers
	Parents Other
Attitudes/Expectation/Perceptions	Perceived benefits of smoking
	Perceived risks of smoking
	Commitment against use
Co-morbidity	Co-abuse of other substances
	Depression
	Anxiety
Personal Factors	Risk-taking
	Self-esteem
	Self-efficacy

Gender

Over the last century, gender differences in use patterns among youth have changed dramatically. Currently, rates of smoking among American boys and girls are comparable. Historically, however, gender differences have been the norm rather than the exception (Grunberg et al., 1991; CDC, 2000). In the early 1900s, adolescent boys were significantly more likely to smoke than were adolescent girls. This gender gap persisted for several decades. Then, in the 1940s adolescent smoking rates reached a peak for boys, gradually declined, and finally reached an asymptote in the 1980s. Smoking rates for adolescent boys have remained relatively stable since that time (CDC, 2000). For adolescent females, smoking prevalence peaked in the early 1970s partially as a result of intensive advertising of cigarettes to women, and then gradually declined. Because the decline for females was less dramatic than that of males, the once wide gender gap narrowed and smoking rates among males and females became more similar (CDC, 2000). During the 1990s, prevalence rates increased for both groups, but rates between males and females remained almost indistinguishable. Rates of cigarette smoking among boys and girls have remained roughly equivalent for the past decade (CDC, 2000).

Ethnicity

Rates of smoking among adolescents also vary by ethnicity. These ethnic differences, however, are most pronounced in children among the higher age groups (i.e., older teenagers). Over the past decade, roughly 25 % White, 20% Latino, but only 14% African-American adolescents smoke daily (Griesler & Kandel, 1998; Headen et al., 1991). Ellickson and colleagues (2004) compared 10-year smoking trends in four racial groups (White, Hispanic, African American, and Asian) and found that while Hispanic and African-Americans initi smoking earlier than Whites and Asians, African-Americans and Asians are less likely t

Whites and Hispanics to become regular/daily smokers. These investigators proposed that differences in social pressures and parental disapproval of smoking behavior contribute to these observed effects. Specifically, African-American adolescents are less likely to progress to regular smoking because their social environment becomes less conducive to smoking (i.e., less parental approval and peer support) and because they do not develop strong smoking intentions or pro-smoking attitudes. Whites, in contrast, were more likely to have friends who smoked and were less likely to experience parental disapproval of smoking behavior. Ellickson et al.'s (2004) finding that African-Americans are more likely to initiate smoking, contrasts with earlier reports of low smoking initiation and maintenance rates among this ethnic group.

Interpersonal Factors

Children learn how to smoke (Sargent & DiFranza, 2003). Social environment has a powerful influence on early smoking initiation. Children learn how to smoke and they may learn about the perceived benefits of smoking from their parents, their friends, and from the media (Sargent & DiFranza, 2003). These role models can portray the message that smoking is acceptable and even desirable.

Parental Smoking

Parental smoking has been identified as an important predictor of adolescent smoking. In fact, of adolescents who smoke, 75% have at least one parent who smokes (Bauman et al., 1990; Green et al., 1991; Morris et al., 1993; Moolchan et al., 2000). Compared with adolescents whose parents had never smoked, adolescents whose parents smoked currently or had ever smoked were two to three times more likely to smoke themselves (Bewley, 1978; Alexandar et al., 1983; Bauman et al., 1990). In addition, parental smoking predicted smoking onset of adolescent girls aged 12-18 (Chassin, 1986; Hunter et al., 1987; Sussman et al., 1987). Parents who smoke may influence adolescent smoking by modeling the behavior or by providing ready access to cigarettes. It also is possible that the association between parental and peer smoking may be explained by heritable effects (Baker et al., 2004). Further studies are needed to understand the factors that contribute to this relationship and the extent to which strengthening parental bonds or family communication might reduce the risk of smoking among adolescents.

Peer Smoking

Peer smoking may be the single most important factor in determining tobacco initiation and use in adolescence (Friedman et al., 1985; Conrad et al., 1992; Flay et al., 1998; O'Loughlin et al., 1998; Kobus, 2003). Young people who never smoked are twice as likely to begin smoking in the next year if their peers smoke (Pederson, 1986; Santi et al., 1991; Conrad et al., 1992). Bauman et al. (1990) reported that adolescents who smoked frequently did so in the presence of their peers. Further, having a close friend who smoked was predictive of smoking initiation whereas having a majority of friends who smoked was predictive of tobacco maintenance (Leventhal et al., 1988). Hahn and colleagues (1990) reported that more than 60% of 11-17 year olds reported trying their first cigarette in the presence of a close friend. Non-smoking adolescents who affiliated with smokers were more likely to transition to cigarette smoking than were adolescents without friends who smoke (Urberg, et al., 1997; Flay et al., 1998). In addition, adolescents were more likely to initiate smoking if their friends approved of smoking or encouraged them to smoke (Duncan et al., 1995; Flay et al., 1998). In contrast, when adolescents' primary contacts were with non-smoking peers or anti-smoking peers, they were less likely to initiate smoking (Kobus et al., 2003).

Explanations for why peers exert such a powerful influence on adolescent smoking vary. Peers normalize behavior and help adolescents to determine what behaviors are prevalent and socially-acceptable (Conrad et al., 1992). Engaging in shared behaviors provides a means of bonding and allows adolescents to feel better connected to their social network (Baker et al., 2004). Interestingly, several studies have suggested that peer influences are greater for girls than for boys (Chassin et al., 1992; Waldron et al., 1991). Further, Hu and colleagues (1995) and Flay and colleagues (1998) reported adolescent girls frequently had more smoking friends than did adolescent boys. Together, these reports suggest that girls may be more susceptible to social influences than boys.

Attitudes Expectations and Perceptions

Perceived Benefits of Smoking

Many adolescents who initiate smoking do so for its perceived benefits. Beliefs about the perceived benefits of smoking range from weight control to peer acceptance. Adolescents who smoke are likely to view smoking as a way to cope with stressful situations, gain acceptance from peers, overcome boredom, or regulate weight and appetite (Perry et al., 1987; Simons-Morton et al., 1999). Chassin et al. (1984) suggested that positive attitudes about smoking are a reliable predictor of the transition to regular smoking. Botvin et al. (1983) found that older students (i.e., 13-14 year olds) were more likely than were younger students (i.e., 11-12 year olds) to identify positive aspects of smoking, which may explain the high rates of smoking initiation among this age group. Dalton et al. (1999) suggested that such positive outcome expectations may better predict smoking initiation than knowledge about negative smoking outcomes. If so, then prevention efforts should include information that challenges these positive expectations or provide alternative means of achieving these outcomes (i.e., stress management, anxiety reduction).

Knowledge about the Health Consequences of Smoking

Knowledge about the long-term health consequences of smoking is generally not a good predictor of smoking initiation in adolescence (Collins et al., 1987; Conrad et al., 1992). Most adolescents are aware of the health risks associated with smoking but this knowledge does not seem to deter them from starting to smoke. This apparent indifference has been attributed, in part, to the adolescent's sense of immortality (Gerber & Newman, 1989). Further, adolescents are even more likely than are adults to discount the long-term consequences of a given behavior and generally do not believe that any deleterious health effects will develop in the short run (Green et al., 1994; Slovic, 2000). A lack of concern for smoking related consequences has been associated with greater smoking initiation (Botvin et al., 1992). In addition, adolescents who dismiss the adverse health effects of smoking are more like to initiate smoking and maintain smoking behavior into adulthood (Mittelmark et al., 1987; Swan et al., 1990).

Commitment against Use

The commitment to not smoke is inversely related to smoking initiation. Specifically, adolescents who hold negative beliefs about smoking and make a commitment to never smoke are less likely to start smoking. In contrast, adolescents who hold neutral or positive beliefs about smoking are more susceptible to smoking (Pierce et al., 1996). Altman et al. (1996) found that the odds of susceptibility to tobacco use were greater among adolescents who had been exposed to or participated in a tobacco-promotion campaign. Further, this cognitive susceptibility remained even after controlling for peer and parental smoking behavior. Jackson (1998) reported similar findings with children ages 8-10. Together, these findings suggest that children who lack a firm commitment to not smoke are more susceptible to smoking initiation and that identifying early attitudes about smoking may help to prevent efforts to curb early smoking onset.

Co-abuse of Other Substances

Adolescents who use other drugs may be more likely to smoke cigarettes. Generally it is assumed that substance use and abuse among adolescents begins with nicotine and progresses to harder drugs, a phenomenon frequently referred to as the "Gateway Hypothesis" (Kandel, 2002). A study by Lai et al. (2000), for example, found that individuals who had smoked cigarettes were far more likely to use cocaine, heroin, and marijuana, findings that are consistent across race, age, and gender. More recent findings, however, suggest that drugs such as alcohol and marijuana may precede tobacco onset. Amos et al. (2004), for example, reported that while tobacco use preceded marijuana use in most cases, a proportion of adolescents started smoking tobacco after experimenting with marijuana. Flay et al. (1998) reported that alcohol use and marijuana use predicted levels of tobacco smoking among boys and girls. Several other studies have reported that, among adolescents, alcohol use and tobacco use frequently co-occur or that alcohol use precedes tobacco use (Kandel & Faust, 1975; Johnson et al., 2000; Ritchey et al., 2001).

Psychological Factors

Psychological factors also contribute to smoking initiation and maintenance. Adolescents who initiate and maintain smoking often report that smoking has calming and pleasurable effects (Leventhal & Avis, 1976; Klitzke et al., 1990). Smoking also can be a coping strategy for students who have low self-image or who experience frequent dysphoric states (Semmer et al., 1987). Other psychological factors identified as contributing to smoking behavior in youth include: neuroticism, depression, hopelessness, and anxiety (Breslau et al., 1993a). Several investigators have reported that depressive symptoms predict adolescent smoking behavior (Kandel & Davies, 1986; Anda et al., 1990; Zhu et al., 1999). Vogel et al. (2003) reported that adolescents who received higher scores on the Instrumental Helplessness and Social Introversion scores of the Major Depression Inventory were more likley to initiate smoking and smoke for more years. Killen et al. (1997) studied 1900 adolescents over a 4-year period and found that higher levels of depression at baseline prospectively predicted smoking onset. Similar findings were reported by Kandel and Davies (1986); adolescent depressive symtoms were prospecively related to current and lifetime cigarette use in young adulthood. Among adolescents, personality factors such as low self-esteem, impulsivity, conduct disorder, and rebelliousness also have been associated with drug use, including cigarette smoking (Adger, 1991; Teichman et al., 1989; Shedler & Block, 1990). These findings suggest that adolescents with emotional and behavioral problems may be at greater risk for cigarette smoking. Clinicians who work with youth and investigators intersted in developing tobacco control programs should consider these risks and incorporate measures of assessing personality and mood in tobacco treatment programs.

Personal Factors

Risk-Taking

In adolescence, deviant behaviors such as risk-taking and rebelliousness have been associated with drug abuse, including cigarette smoking (Jessor & Jessor, 1977; Dinn et al., 2004; Burt et al., 2000). Adolescent tobacco users generally are described as being more rebellious, risk-taking, impulsive, and novelty-seeking than are their non-smoking counterparts (Dinn et al., 2004; Barefoot et al., 1989; Lipkus et al., 1994; Simons-Morton et al., 1999; Burt et al., 2000). In addition, Chassin et al. (1989) found that deviance was a significant predictor of cigarette smoking in high school students. Similarly, Turbin and colleagues (2000) found that deviant-prone adolescents were more likely to engage in risky behaviors, including smoking. Explanations for this relationship are less clear and may include peer affiliations, sensation seeking, or less concern about negative consequences. Jessor and Jessor (1977) speculated that rebellious teens may be less likely to consider the long-term negative consequences of smoking and may smoke as a way to attain adult status. Alternatively, rebellious teens may smoke to obtain reinforcement and attention from others, perhaps as a way to increase self-esteem.

Self-Esteem

The process of identity-formation is central part of adolescent development. An adolescent's sense of self worth develops during the adolescent period and is influenced largely by interactions with peers, parents, and teachers. Therefore, behaviors that bring approval from others are likely to enhance self-esteem and are more likely to be repeated, even if these behaviors are accompanied by some cost to the individual. Several studies, for example, have reported that individuals with low self-esteem are more likely than individuals with high self-esteem to initiate smoking (Young & Werch, 1990; Botvin et al., 1992; Stacy et al., 1992; Conrad et al., 1992). Adolescents with low self-esteem may be more likely to initiate smoking if their role models who smoke are perceived as socially desirable, attractive, and tough. Adolescents may believe that smoking will bestow upon them these same qualities, increasing the likelihood that others will perceive them more favorably (Chassin et al., 1990; Mitchell, 1997; Mitchell & Amos, 1997).

Self-Efficacy

Self–efficacy is defined as an individual's belief in their ability to reach a desired goal (Bandura, 1986; Ellickson and Hayes, 1990; DeVries et al., 1990). For adolescents, self-efficacy is an important predictor of smoking initiation (Bandura, 1986). Specifically, the less an adolescent feels s/he can resist the pressure to smoke, the more likely s/he will be likely to initiate smoking (Ellickson and Hays, 1990; DeVries et al., 1990). In contrast, higher self-efficacy appears to protect against peer influences to smoke (Conrad et al., 1992). Tobacco-control programs should devise ways to empower young people to resist the pressure to start smoking and strengthen motivation to quit.

Psychobiological Factors

Overview

In addition to psychosocial reasons for smoking, adolescents report smoking to obtain its psychobiological effects (see Table 3). Specifically, adolescents report smoking to reduce anxiety, to control appetite and body weight, to regulate mood states, to improve attention, and for nicotine's reinforcing or stimulating actions (Baker et al., 2004). Identification of how these factors contribute to smoking is important because the more an adolescent views smoking as beneficial, the more likely s/he is likely to initiate smoking. The following sections review the available research examining the biological effects of nicotine that may influence tobacco-smoking initiation. Although cigarettes contain roughly 400 chemicals and cigarette smoke delivers 4000 chemicals, nicotine is particularly important with regard to nicotine's biobehavioral effects because nicotine crosses the blood-brain-barrier, acts at specific receptors in the brain, and has many behavioral effects including addiction, attention regulation, weight reduction, and various psychological effects (USDHHS, 1988; Corrigall, 1999). The effects of nicotine, therefore, are emphasized in this section. Results from animal studies are included in this section because animal models of nicotine exposure provide an excellent way to isolate and study these specific psychobiological effects of adolescent smoking.

Table 3. Overview of Psychobiological Factors Relevant to Adolescent Smoking

Positive reinforcement	Stimulating actions
Body weight control	General appetite control Specific food consumption
Affective control	Stress control Anxiolysis
Cognitive enhancement	Increase attention
Addiction	Dependence Tolerance Withdrawal

Positive Reinforcement

Nicotine is a psychomotor stimulant that produces positive subjective sensations of reward and these effects are likely to contribute to smoking initiation and maintenance (Ikard et al., 1969; Garrett & Griffiths, 2001). Adult smokers reliably cite the positive stimulating effects of nicotine as reasons for smoking (USDDHS, 1988; Copeland et al., 1995). Further, many adolescents who smoke report that smoking brings pleasurable effects (USDDHS, 1988).

Animal models of nicotine exposure have provided additional information for the reinforcing effects of nicotine. Adolescent rats are more sensitive than adult rats to the activity-stimulating effects of nicotine – actions that may reflect dopaminergic stimulation. Further, for adolescent males these activity-stimulating effects persisted even in the absence of nicotine (Faraday et al., 2001, 2003). Anticipated positive effects of nicotine also include expectations about nicotine's effect to control weight and appetite, increase attention, and reduce negative mood states. These specific effects of smoking are discussed separately below.

Body Weight Control

Adolescents, especially adolescent girls, may be influenced to smoke by their beliefs that smoking affects appetite and body weight. The belief that smoking cigarettes curbs weight gain and reduces appetite has been prospectively associated with smoking initiation, particularly among adolescent girls (Austin & Gortmaker, 2001). This expectation is likely based on reports that adult smokers weigh less than non-smokers (Grunberg, 1982; Wack & Rodin, 1982; Fisher & Gordon, 1985; USDHHS, 1988) and that smoking cessation results in weight gain (Grunberg 1982; USDHHS, 1988; Faraday et al., 2003). Given these reports, it is not surprising that many young girls report initiating smoking in an effort to control their weight (Camp et al., 1993; Charlton, 1984; French et al., 1994). Camp (1993), for example, reported that 40-50% of girls who initiate smoking do so to control appetite and weight. French et al. (1994) reported that adolescent girls who reported weight concerns and who engaged in weigh-regulating behaviors were twice as likely to initiate smoking than were girls without such concerns.

Given the support for the nicotine-body weight relationship in adult human smokers, it is not surprising that people generalize these findings to adolescents and that many people view this effect as positive. Recent animal studies, however, question whether the body weight effects in adult generalize to adolescents. Specifically, Faraday et al. (2001) examined the effects of nicotine on feeding and body weight in adolescent and adult rats and found that nicotine reduces feeding and body weight in adult males and females and in adolescent males, but had no effects in adolescent females. These results are striking because many adolescent girls report that they smoke to reduce appetite and body weight, yet nicotine's appetite-and body weight-reducing effects may not occur until adulthood. Smoking initiation and maintenance by adolescent girls, therefore, may be based on inaccurate perceptions of how nicotine will affect them. If the results from such studies extend to humans, then challenging these inaccurate perceptions may be the key to early intervention and prevention, particularly for adolescent girls.

Psychological Factors

Stress and Anxiety Reduction

Psychosocial stress has been associated with smoking in adolescence. Adolescents frequently report that they smoke to cope with stress or to manage negative affect (Mates & Allison, 1992). Whether stress predicts smoking onset is less clear. Byrne and Maznov (2003) examined this question using a prospective investigation and reported that for female adolescents, but not for male adolescents, self-reports of stress predicted smoking onset a year later. Pederson et al. (1997) reported that sixth grade student who endorsed problem solving as an effecting coping mechanism were less likely to smoke, whereas students who endorsed substance abuse and ventilation of feelings as preferred coping methods were more likely to smoke. More recently, Koval et al. (2002) evaluated the relationship between stress and smoking among sixth graders and eighth graders and found that for both males and females, increasing levels of stress were associated with increasing levels of smoking.

The effects of nicotine to reduce anxiety in adolescent rats have only recently been investigated. The findings from these studies yield conflicting results with some studies reporting that nicotine is anxiolytic (i.e., anxiety reducing) and other studies reporting that nicotine is anxiogenic (i.e., anxiety inducing). Cheeta et al. (2001) evaluated nicotine's effects in the social interaction test-a measure of generalized anxiety, and reported that nicotine was anxiolytic at low dosages for adolescent females and at higher dosages for adolescent males. Elliott et al. (2004) examined nicotine's effects on the elevated plus maze (a measure of specific anxiety) and found that nicotine was anxiolytic for adolescent males, but anxiogenic for adolescent females. Together, these findings suggest that nicotine's actions to reduce anxiety in adolescence might differ based on gender and the context in which anxiety occurs.

Cognitive Enhancement

Attentional Regulation

Smokers frequently report smoking to enhance attention. Research with human smokers suggests that smoking does increase attention (Conners et al., 1996). Further, recent research suggests that individuals with attention-deficit/hyperactivity disorder (ADHD) use nicotine to enhance attention and/or cognitive performance (Levin et al., 1996). Whereas most adolescents do not report smoking to increase attention, the preponderance of smoking among attention-disordered youth suggests that attentional regulation may play a role in why adolescents maintain cigarette smoking (Whalen et al., 2003; Flory & Lynam, 2003). Molina and Pelham (2003) offered further support for this relationship with their finding that the inattention symptoms of ADHD are better predictors of cigarette use than are hyperactivity symptoms.

Addiction

Dependence

Nicotine dependence is characterized by tolerance, withdrawal, unsuccessful efforts to cut down use, cravings, and continued used despite knowledge of harmful effects (USDHHS, 1988; DSM-IV, 1994). Like adults, adolescents who smoke are likely to experience symptoms of dependence, making cessation difficult (FDA, 1995; Kessler et al., 1996; Gallup, 1992; USDHHS, 1994). Many adolescents progress to dependence much quicker than do adults, exhibiting signs of nicotine dependence in a few days to weeks after initiation, even before they become regular smokers (Chen & Miller, 1998; Breslau et al., 2001). For adults, the typical development of dependence involves several stages starting with first cigarette and progressing eventually to sustained use. For adolescents, daily nicotine use is not necessary for dependence to develop (Shiffman, 1991; Lamkin & Houston, 1998). In fact, dependence develops for some adolescents before the onset of daily smoking (McNeill et al., 1987; Barker, 1994; Dappen et al., 1996). McNeill et al. (1987) reported that 46% of occasional smokers aged 11-17 reported symptoms of withdrawal. DiFranza and colleagues (2000; 2002) reported that 22% of subjects who reported occasional smoking endorsed symptoms of nicotine dependence after four weeks of initiation. O' Loughlin et al. (2003) reported that even those adolescents who had smoked only once or twice reported symptoms of nicotine dependence (e.g., cravings, withdrawal, and self-medication symptoms). Girls reported more symptoms than did boys even though they smoked at the same rate. Other studies report that individuals who begin smoking in adolescence are likely to smoke for a greater number of years and to smoke more heavily as adults (Ershler et al., 1989; Breslau et al., 1993b; Chen & Millar, 1998). Together, these findings suggest that symptoms of nicotine dependence play an important role in the early stages of smoking and that tobacco-control programs should offer ways to attenuate these symptoms.

Withdrawal

Although adolescents report interest in quitting, many report little success (USDHHS, 1994). Adding to the difficulty quitting is the finding that many adolescents who try to quit experience withdrawal effects (McNeill et al., 1986; Smith et al., 1996; Stanton, 1995). Symptoms of nicotine withdrawal include: dysphoria, depressed mood, frustration, anger, irritability, difficulty concentrating, restlessness, increased appetite, and cravings (USDHHS, 1988; DSM-IV, 1994). Ehrsler et al. (1989) reported that more than half of adolescents who try to quit smoking experience such withdrawal symptoms. Other studies have yielded similar findings with reports of withdrawal symptoms occurring in greater than 50% of adolescent smokers (Colby et al., 2000). Adolescents report that the experience of these symptoms is one of the primary reasons why quitting smoking is so difficult (Johnson et al., 1982). In 2000, the National Youth Tobacco Survey revealed that among adolescents who smoke, more than half want to stop smoking and have tried to quit smoking at least once during the past 12 months (Johnston et al., 1998; CDC, 2001). Of the more than 60% of adolescent smokers who report wanting to quit, less than 5% are successful (Burt and Peterson, 1998). Findings from animal models provide additional information about the mechanisms underling these effects and why quitting smoking may be so difficult.

In adult rats, nicotine cessation results in a characteristic behavioral profile. While the effect of nicotine cessation in adolescent rats has not been as extensively studied, some information on the behavioral effects of nicotine withdrawal exists and is available for comparison. For example, nicotine cessation in adolescent rats appears to result in a persistent anxiogentic profile — a finding that might be consistent with withdrawal symptoms commonly reported in humans (Slawecki et al; 2002; 2003; Trauth et al., 2000). Further, intracerbroventricular administration of corticotropin releasing factor (CRF), a peptide associated with behavioral indices of stress and anxiety, results in a neurophysiological profile comparable to the effects of adolescent nicotine cessation. Nicotine cessation also is associated with weight gain -- an undesirable effect for most smokers (Grunberg, 1991; 1992; Faraday et al., 2001). Together, these findings suggest that adolescent exposure induces neural alterations resembling anxiety that are long-lasting and likely to contribute to difficulties with smoking cessation.

Environmental Risk Factors

Socioeconomic Status

Socioeconomic status (SES) is inversely related to smoking behavior such that low SES is associated with increased smoking behavior (Conrad et al., 1992). Conrad and his colleagues reviewed twenty-one prospective studies on the relationship between parental SES and adolescent smoking. Of these studies, 76% supported the inverse relationship (i.e., low SES and greater smoking rates). Tyas and Pederson (1998) conducted a similar review and found that more than half of the studies conducted in the United States reported an inverse relationship between parental SES and adolescent smoking. More recently, Soteriades and DiFranza (2003) examined the association between parental SES and adolescent smoking using a multiple-variable-adjusted logistic regression model in a sample of Massachusetts youth These investigators found a significant inverse relationship between parental SES and adolescent smoking. Further, while parental smoking mediated this relationship, it could not fully explain the association. The exact mechanism underling this inverse relationship between SES and smoking is less clear. While it is possible that differences in exposure to health-promoting resources explain this relationship, another intriguing explanation exists. That is, it is possible that exposure to different environments alters the brain in ways that makes an individual more or less sensitive to nicotine's actions.

Enriched vs. Non-enriched Environments

Exposure to different environments may influence tobacco smoking by altering nicotine's actions. Findings from animal studies suggest that the environment in which an animal is reared can alter drug actions. Specifically, it has been reported that animals reared in enriched environments, characterized by the presence of objects and other animals, exhibit greater response to the behavioral actions of morphine, cocaine, and amphetamines (Boyle et al., 1991; Bowling et al., 1993; Bowling & Bardo, 1994; Bardo et al., 1995; Bardo et al, 1997; Phillips et al., 1994). In addition, Green et al. (2003) reported that enrichment-reared rats exhibited less sensitivity than isolation rats and less sensitivity than socially-reared rats to the activity-stimulating effects of acute and repeated nicotine administration (0.2 mg/kg and 0.8 mg/kg). Grunberg et al. (under review) recently replicated and extended Green et al.'s (2003) findings by using a wider dose-response range of nicotine (0.1 mg/kg, 0.5 mg/kg, or 1.0 mg/kg) and a different enrichment paradigm (smaller cages and fewer animals). It is well-established that exposure to different environments alters the morphology of the brain, including changes in cortical thickness and dendritic branching (Hebb, 1947; Rosenzweig, 1962; 1966; Altman & Das, 1964; Diamond, 1967; Rosenzweig et al., 1972; Greenough, 1975; Greenough et al., 1987). The studies of environmental exposure and drug actions suggest that the brain also may be altered in ways that makes it more responsive to the actions of specific drugs and changes vulnerability to drug abuse. More research in this areas is needed to understand the underlying mechanisms for these observed effects and whether they might explain the observed difference in susceptibility to drug abuse across different socioeconomic and social conditions.

Media

Children and adolescents develop their intentions to smoke and their expectations about smoking prior to ever starting. Expectations about the effects of smoking are based largely on observations of other people who smoke. These observations help to shape perceptions about the consequences of smoking behavior and influence the observer's intent to smoke or not to smoke. For children and adolescents, role models include professional athletes, musicians, and actors. When these people glamorize smoking, portray smoking as an effective way to reduce stress, associate tobacco use with sexual activities, or look attractive when they smoke, adolescents' attitudes towards smoking are greatly affected. Unfortunately, tobacco use in the media does not accurately reflect rates of smoking in the general population and generally does not reveal the health hazards that result from tobacco use. Tobacco use in television and movies occurs at much higher rates than do smoking rates among the general population (Hazan et al., 1997; Glantz, 2003; 2004; Stockwell & Glantz, 1994). In fact, smoking in movies increased from a minimum of five incidences per hour in 1980 to 11 incidents per hours in 2002, a level comparable to that observed in the 1950s when smoking was twice as prevalent in reality as it is currently (Glantz, 2004). The media, therefore, creates an unrealistic representation of smoking behavior for impressionable youth and presents only positive impressions of this deadly behavior.

The media exerts a powerful influence on adolescent smoking initiation and maintenance such that adolescents exposed to media images of smoking are more likely to smoke (Distefan et al., 1999; Tickle et al., 2001; Sargent et al., 2001; Sargent et al., 2002; Dalton et al., 2003). Sargent et al. (2002) conducted a cross-sectional school-based survey to examine the relationship between exposure to tobacco smoking in movies and subsequent smoking behavior. These investigators reported that those adolescents who were exposed to more smoking images in the movies and on television were more likely to endorse positive expectations about smoking. Exposure to smoking in movies also has been linked with smoking initiation in cross-sectional studies (Dalton et al., 2003). After controlling for baseline characteristics, adolescents who have the highest exposure to movie smoking were three times more likely to initiate smoking compared with adolescents who had lower exposures to movie smoking (Dalton et al., 2003). Similar findings have been reported by other investigators (Distefan et al., 1999; Tickle et al., 2001; Sargent et al., 2001). These findings suggest that exposure to smoking in the media may shape attitudes about smoking and make the initiation of smoking more likely. Adolescent smoking also is associated with tobacco advertising (Romer & Jamison, 2002) such that greater trends in cigarette smoking track cigarette advertising campaigns (Pierce & Gilpin, 1995).

Health Effects of Smoking

Overview

The deleterious health effects of cigarette smoking are well-documented and widely-publicized (USDHHS, 1986; 1989; 1994). Cigarette smoking has been causally linked to a number of serious health problems, including cancers, cardiovascular diseases, and chronic obstructive lung diseases (USDHHS, 1986; 1988; 1994). Substantial evidence exists that the health problems associated with smoking are directly correlated with the duration and intensity of use (USDHHS, 1994). Given that earlier onset is associated with heavier and more long-term use, the earlier one starts smoking, the greater is the risk for more serious and adverse health consequences. For children, tobacco smoking poses a particular risk for respiratory diseases.

Table 4. Health Consequences of Adolescent Smoking

Physical Consequences	Cardiovascular effects
	Reduced physical fitness
	Other
Mental Health Consequences	Depression
	Anxiety
Drub Abuse liability	Nicotine addiction
	Other drug addiction

Physical Health Consequences

Respiratory Disease

Cigarette smoking (directly and passively) is a cause of respiratory problems in children and adolescents. Specifically, children and adolescents who smoke are more likely to experience a greater frequency of coughing, wheezing, dyspnea, and phlegm (USDHS, 1984; 1994; Holland & Elliott, 1968; Bates, 1989). Further, these effects occur with as little as one cigarette per week (Bewley et al., 1973). In adults, cigarette smoking has been identified as a risk factor for asthma (Gwynn, 2004). Although no studies have associated cigarette smoking with onset of asthma in adolescents, cigarette smoking does adversely affects lung function in children and adolescents as evidenced by reduced lung capacity and reduced lung growth among smokers (Arday et al., 1995; USDHHS, 1994), potentially putting children who smoke at risk for developing asthma later in life. In addition, smoking impairs the efficacy of short-term oral corticosteroid treatments for those adolescents who already suffer from asthma (Chaudhuri et al., 2003). Further, high school seniors who are regular smokers are twice as likely to report poorer overall health and three times as likely to report shortness of breath, coughing, and wheezing (Arday et al., 1995). In addition to these short-term adverse effects, adolescent smoking is associated with poor adult health (USDHHS, 1994). In some studies, these effects were reduced following several weeks of abstinence (USDHHS, 1994).

In addition to the more immediate respiratory effects associated with adolescent smoking, smoking during childhood and adolescence may increase the risk of developing respiratory problems in adulthood (CDC, 1994). Specifically, reduced lung growth and inflammatory processes that result from early smoking compromises the function of the adult lung. In fact, there is some evidence to suggest that lung damage acquired from smoking during childhood exceeds the damage associated with adult-onset smoking (Tager et al., 1985).

Cardiovascular Diseases

Cardiovascular diseases are relatively uncommon in children and adolescents. However, several studies have reported that the atherosclerois that precedes cardiovascular disease frequently begins in childhood and may become clinically significant in young adulthood (McNamara, et al., 1971; Strong, 1986). Children who smoke are more likely to develop atherosclerois compared with children who do not smoke (Strong & Richards, 1976; McGill & McMahan, 1998).

Reduced Physical Fitness

Smoking reduces physical performance and endurance in adolescence, even among the most physically fit individuals. These effects are the result of reduced oxygen-carrying capacity of the blood and increased heart rate, associated with smoking. Marti et al. (1988) found that adolescent smokers took longer to sprint and run long distances than did their non-smoking peers. Further, smokers had higher resting heart rates and blunted heart rate responses to exercise compared to non-smoking peers (Gidding et al., 1992; Sidney et al., 1993).

Other Physical Health Consequences

In addition to the increased risks of respiratory and cardiovascular diseases, adolescents who smoke cigarettes have a higher risk of cancers, stroke, and obstructive lung disease, compared to non-smoking peers (USDHHS, 1994). Further, if current tobacco use patterns persist, then one third of adolescents who start smoking eventually will die from smoking-related diseases (CDC, 1996). In addition to the physical health consequences of smoking, adolescents who smoke also are at greater risk of becoming addicted to nicotine and other illicit substances and possibly may increase their risk of developing mental health disorders, including anxiety and depression (Pbert, 2003).

Mental Health Consequences

Depression and Anxiety

Individuals who are depressed or anxious smoke at higher rates than do individuals who do not experience these symptoms (Anda et al., 1990; Breslau et al., 1991, 2004). This relationship between smoking and mood disorders is well established and is based on clinical and epidemiological studies (Anda et al., 1990; Breslau et al., 1991, 2004). The direction of this relationship, however, is less clear. Generally, it is assumed that smoking follows depressive and anxiety symptoms. That is, the smoker smokes to alleviate unpleasant or negative affect. Recent evidence from human and animal studies, however, suggests that smoking in adolescence may increase symptoms of anxiety and depression by predisposing smokers to develop these mood symptoms as adults. In other words, people who smoke are more likely to get depressed (Goodman & Capitman, 2000; Windle & Windle, 2001; Vogel et al., 2003)

A few studies have provided compelling evidence that smoking cigarettes may put an individual at greater risk for developing anxiety and depression. Goodman and Capitman (2000), for example, conducted a prospective study to determine the direction of the relationship between cigarette smoking and depressive symptoms in teen-agers and found that for non-depressed teen-agers, cigarette smoking was the strongest predictor of developing high depressive symptoms. In contrast, high depressive symptoms did not predict the development of heavy smoking among non-smoking individuals. The authors concluded from these results that cigarette smoking might contribute to the development of depressive symptoms in teen-agers. Other studies have reported similar results. Brown et al. (1996) examined a sample of 1700 adolescents and found that smoking prospectively predicted major depressive disorders, even when other psychiatric disorders were controlled for. Similarly, Choi et al. (1997) reported similar findings in a sample of 6800 adolescents. More recently, Windle & Windle (2001) found that, even after controlling for alcohol use and delinquent behavior, heavy and persistent levels of smoking predicted increases in depressive symptoms across a 1.5 year interval. Other investigators have found a similar relationship between smoking and anxiety disorders. Johnson et al. (2000) reported that heavy smoking during adolescence was correlated with the development of anxiety disorders in adulthood. In the Johnson et al. (2000) study, the opposite was not true in that the existence of anxiety disorders in adolescence did not predict smoking in adulthood. Because in humans the trajectory of this relationship can be affected by a number of intervening variables (i.e., genetics, social support, stress), animal models provide an additional way of examining the proposed relationship between smoking and onset of depressive or anxiety symptoms.

Animal studies have provided additional support for this intriguing and unexpected relationship between smoking and mood disorders. Slawecki et al. (2003), for example, reported that rats exposed to nicotine during adolescence exhibit increased anxiety-like behavior when tested as adults. Faraday et al. (2003) reported that rats exposed to nicotine during adolescence exhibited persistent hyperactivity in adulthood in the absence of nicotine. These effects did not occur for animals first exposed to nicotine as adults. Therefore, while it may be more natural to assume that depression and anxiety precede smoking, perhaps as a means of self-medication, it also is possible that smoking leads to depressive and anxiety. Such a relationship is plausible when one considers that persistent smoking may alter brain biochemistry in ways that may make the brain more vulnerable to such symptoms. More data from animal models are needed to examine the direction and strength of this relationship and perhaps offer explanations for how this effect occurs. Further, regardless of the direction of the relationship between smoking and mood disorders, it is clear that smoking and mood disorders are related. Therefore, interventions designed to treat cigarette use should consider this relationship and when appropriate include assessments of underlying internalizing problems such as depression, anxiety, and low self esteem (Windle & Windle, 2001) when providing treatment to adolescent smokers.

Drug Abuse Potential

Nicotine

Individuals who start smoking at an earlier age are more likely to smoke as adults. There is some evidence that adolescents become dependent and experience more severe withdrawal symptoms compared to adults. The experience of such symptoms makes quitting more difficult and is likely to lead to more prolonged and heavy use (Ershler et al., 1989; Breslau et al., 1993; 1996).

Other Drug Use

While not all adolescents who smoke go on to use or abuse other drugs, tobacco smoking is a reliable predictor of subsequent drug use. In fact, few drug users go on to use illicit drugs before experimenting with nicotine (Kandel, 1975, 2002). Adolescent users of tobacco are more likely than non-users to progress to other drugs of abuse (Fleming et al., 1989; Welte & Barnes, 1987). Lewinsohn et al. (1999) used a longitudinal data base to assess the impact of adolescent cigarette smoking on the occurrence of other drugs (e.g., alcohol, cannabis etc) during young adulthood. These investigators reported that cigarette smoking in adolescence was associated with higher risk for drug use disorders by young adulthood. Further, of adolescent smokers, those who were classified as daily smokers were at significantly increased risk for future cannabis use and hard-drug use disorders. Torabi et al. (1993) found that the relative risk ratio for illicit drug users was 10 - 30 times higher for adolescents who smoked a pack or more a day compared to their non-smoking peers. This relationship may be biologically based. Fowler et al. (1996), for example, reported that smokers had less monoamine oxidase (MAO-B) in their brains, an enzyme that breaks down dopamine, than did non-smokers or former smokers. These investigators proposed that smoking's effects to enhance dopamine levels in the brain might augment the pleasure obtained from using other drugs of abuse (i.e., heroin, cocaine, and alcohol), making the abuse of other drugs more likely.

Animal studies have provided evidence that complements and extends these human findings. Klein (2001), for example, reported that early nicotine exposure alters later consumption of opiates in male, but not female rats. Adriani et al. (2003) reported that rats first exposed to nicotine during the adolescent period are more likely to self-administer nicotine than are saline-exposed controls or animals first exposed to nicotine during adulthood. Faraday et al. (2003) reported that male rats exposed to nicotine in adolescence exhibited greater sensitivity to nicotine when it was re-administered during adulthood. Specifically, these investigators found that rats that were first administered nicotine, as adults did not exhibit this enhanced sensitivity. Together with reports from humans, these findings support the notion that smoking in adolescence may enhance susceptibility to nicotine's effects or potentially predispose individuals to use other drugs of abuse.

In summary, smoking negatively impacts health, alters the brain, and may even cause later problems with anxiety and depression. These adverse health effects and the particular vulnerability of the adolescent period point to the need for effective tobacco cessation and prevention programs to curb adolescent smoking. As discussed, the reasons for initiation of smoking during adolescence are complex and likely influenced by a number of social, psychological, environmental, and biobehavioral factors. Adding to that complexity is the fact that nicotine dependence occurs more quickly in adolescence — a fact that may make it more difficult for adolescents to quit. Prevention and treatment interventions must be developed with these factors in mind. This next section reviews the current treatment approaches used to help adolescents quit smoking and the relative effectiveness of these available approaches. This section is followed by a discussion of prevention programs that are available to deter smoking, before it starts and what is currently known about the effectiveness of these prevention efforts. The chapter ends by discussing opportunities for future research and proposed strategies for reducing adolescent smoking.

Treating Tobacco Use in Adolescence

Overview

Many adolescents are motivated to quit smoking, but quitting may be difficult and unsuccessful. Burt and Pederson (1998) conducted a longitudinal study in Washington State and found that among high school seniors who had reported trying to quit, only 21% achieved abstinence. Symptoms of withdrawal and absence of support for smoking have been identified by adolescents as factors that make quitting smoking difficult. According to a report by the CDC (1994), 93% of smokers aged 10-22 reported symptoms of withdrawal following quit attempts. Despite evidence that quitting smoking is so difficult for adolescents, few smoking cessation programs have been evaluated (Sussman et al., 1999). Instead, efforts have focused on intervention programs to deter adolescent smoking before it starts. While valuable, such efforts do little for the adolescent who already has started smoking and who has become addicted to nicotine. Identifying methods of helping adolescents quit smoking is important at every stage of smoking. Early intervention efforts may reduce the likelihood of becoming addicted while later intervention efforts may help to reduce the long-term adverse consequences of continued smoking.

Nicotine Replacement

The high levels of nicotine dependence observed among adolescent smokers suggest that adolescents may be good candidates for nicotine replacement therapy (NTR)(Prokhorov et al., 1996). Existing data on the efficacy of NTR products in adolescents indicate only modest success (Henningfield, 1995). Only a few studies have evaluated the efficacy of NTR and these studies have provided only minimal support for the effectiveness of such treatments to maintain abstinence long- term. Smith and colleagues (1996) conducted a pilot nicotine patch study of twenty-two adolescent smokers and found minimal support for the effectiveness of the patch. Specifically, adolescents who received the patch experienced withdrawal symptom relief and a significant reduction in the number of cigarettes smoked per day. However, only one adolescent maintained abstinence after one year. Hurt et al. (2000) evaluated the effectiveness of six weeks of nicotine patch therapy in 100 adolescents (ages 13 -17). These investigators found that nicotine patch therapy plus minimal behavioral intervention was not effective for treatment of adolescent smoking with an estimated 6-month abstinence rate of only 5%.

In addition to the limited information regarding the efficacy of NTR products for adolescents, few data exist on the safety, pharmacokinetics, and abuse liability of these products for adolescents. The lack of such data precludes the ability to accurately adequately assess the cost/benefit ratio of their use in adolescents. Additional information on the specific effects and side effects of NTR products in adolescence is necessary before such medications can be prescribed as the main line of treatment for adolescent smokers.

Education

Currently, the most effective interventions for adolescent smokers are school and community-based programs that target teenagers and teach social, behavioral, and coping skills (Sussmann, 2002; McDonald et al., 2003). The effectiveness of these tobacco cessation programs, however, may be further increased by understanding why adolescents smoke (Vuckovic et al., 2003). Adolescents frequently repot smoking to reduce negative affect or increase feelings of relaxation. Programs that encourage adolescents to quit smoking without providing alternative means of obtaining these desirable consequences are likely to be ineffective. In addition to providing information to teens about alternatives for smoking, cessation programs should provide adolescent with information about what to expect following cessation. Vuckovic et al. (2003) conducted a focus group to examine the challenges adolescents face when quitting smoking. Several adolescents acknowledged that they wanted information about what to expect physically and emotionally during withdrawal, how long such effect would last, and how to combat urges associated with smoking triggers. The adolescent who is equipped with such information may be better able to tolerate the adverse withdrawal effects and experience more success with cessation.

Preventing Tobacco Use in Adolescence

Overview

As reviewed in this chapter, smoking behavior in adolescents is influenced by a complex interplay of psychosocial, environmental, and behavioral factors. A multifactorial prevention approach that targets these different areas is needed to maximize the effectiveness of prevention efforts (CDC, 2002; Backinger et al., 2003). As reviewed in this chapter, research suggests that intentions, attitudes, and beliefs about smoking precede actual smoking experimentation. Therefore, prevention programs should include strategies aimed at changing perceptions about the benefits of smoking, providing youth with alternatives for obtaining these perceived benefits, and increasing the commitment not to smoke. Efforts to prevent tobacco smoking in youth include state mandated educational programs designed to increase children's awareness about health consequences of smoking, state laws restricting cigarette sales to minors, large scale counter-advertising programs, and global initiatives (e.g., American Legacy Foundation, Youth Tobacco Initiative, Campaign for Tobacco Free Kids) designed to disseminate information about the negative effects of smoking and to increase anti-smoking attitudes.

Education in School

In the 1989 report on the *Health Effects of Smoking*, the Surgeon General emphasized the importance of directing efforts to decrease tobacco use at children and adolescents (USDHHS, 1989). As part of this report, the Surgeon General advocated for nation-wide comprehensive school health education programs that include tobacco prevention. Today, several states have adopted laws mandating that education about smoking and the associated health risks be included in the schools (ALF, 2001). When designing educational programs targeted at preventing tobacco youth, it is particularly important to consider what types of messages adolescents are most responsive to (Vuckovic, 2003). Several studies have suggested that teaching adolescents about the long-term, negative health consequences of smoking has little effect (ALF, 2002; Tobler, 1986; Tobler & Stratton, 1997). As reviewed in this chapter, positive outcome expectations, however, do predict smoking onset. Specifically, adolescents who perceive that smoking has positive consequences are more likely to smoke (Unger & Chen, 1999; Huang et al., 2000). Given this knowledge, it would seem beneficial to gain a better understanding of what expectations adolescents have regarding smoking effects (i.e., weight reduction, stress reduction) and provide them with alternative means of achieving these desired outcomes. It might also be valuable to emphasize more immediate, negative effects of smoking that are relevant to adolescents and teenagers (e.g., that smoking can lead to difficulties in sexual performance of males).

Understanding the types of messages adolescents respond to also is important when considering ways to maximize the effectiveness of school-based and community-based programs. Huang et al. (2000) evaluated youth's response to school-based prevention programs and found that perceived usefulness of the information presented at school and the perceived availability of social resources to cope with smoking-related issues was inversely related to smoking susceptibility. Specifically, students who perceived the information presented at school as less helpful were less likely to benefit from the school-based programs. Further, those adolescents who perceived that they had less supportive resources (i.e., peer, counselor) available to them also were less likely to benefit from the programs. These findings suggest that the attitudes and opinions of adolescents should be taken into account when developing prevention programs. Specifically, understanding what type of messages adolescents respond to (i.e., negative vs. positive) and how to increase their perceived access to supportive resources may increase the effectiveness of school-based programs.

Restricting Sale of Tobacco Products to Minors

In 1996, the FDA issued a regulation that prohibited the sale of tobacco products to minors (i.e., persons under age 18) and required that persons under 27 provide picture identification before purchasing tobacco products (FDA, 1996). The effectiveness of this nation-wide regulation in reducing access to cigarettes for youth has been hampered by the fact that compliance with these regulations varies widely. Recently, Levinson et al. (2002) conducted a study to evaluate the effect of this regulation on youth access to cigarettes. These investigators found that cigarette sales actually increased when the minors showed identification, suggesting that salespersons paid little attention to whether these minors were actually legal. It appears that requiring that adolescents provide ID does not guarantee that underage access to cigarettes will not occur. Instead, minors who show picture identification ironically may be more likely to gain access to cigarettes. Similar findings were obtained from the Youth Risk Tobacco Surveillance (YRBS) (CDC, 1999). According to the 1999 YRBS survey, about two-thirds of students (69.6%) who purchased or tried to purchase cigarettes during the past month in a store or gas station were not asked to show proof of age. Ethnic differences in these rates also existed such that African American male students (19.8%) were significantly less likely to be asked to show proof of age than were white (36.6%) and Hispanic (53.5%) male students.

Counter Advertising

Because of the strong influence of the media on tobacco initiation and maintenance, counter-marketing strategies have been developed to reduce cigarette smoking prevalence. The effectiveness of these campaigns has only recently been investigated. Siegel and Biener (2000) interviewed 12-15 year olds who had been exposed to the Massachusetts Antismoking Media Campaign and found that those who recalled an anti-smoking message were less likely to progress to regular smoking. Sly et al. (2002) interviewed a sample of 12-17 year olds exposed to the Florida Truth campaign and found a significant inverse association between smoking initiation and ad exposure. These findings suggest that counter-advertising may, in fact, reduce smoking initiation. More research in this area is needed to determine the strength of this relationship and the types of ads that have had the greatest effect to reduce or delay smoking initiation among adolescents.

Changing the Social Environment

The social environment has a powerful influence on smoking behavior in adolescents. Both peer and parental smoking behavior are associated with the initiation and maintenance of smoking in adolescents. Specifically, those adolescents who perceive that their parents approve of smoking are more likely to initiate smoking. Adolescents who perceive the opposite are less likely to initiate smoking. These differences in social acceptance of smoking behavior have been used to explain ethnic disparities in the transition to regular smoking such that African-Americans who experience greater parental disapproval and less peer support for smoking are less likely than Whites to transition to regular smoking (Mermelstein, 1999). These reports also suggest that changing the social environment, particularly by advocating for pro-smoking messages by parents and peers may decrease the transition to regular smoking. Providing information to families about how to establish this goal should be included in tobacco-control efforts.

Globally-Based Initiatives   √

Youth Tobacco Prevention (YPTI)

The YPTI, sponsored by the Robert Wood Johnson Foundation (RWF), was a project designed to increase the quantity, quality, and effectiveness of youth tobacco prevention research using interdisciplinary, multidisciplinary, and trandisciplinary strategies (YPTI,

1998). The YPTI included working groups of scientists, scholars, educators, practitioners, and policy-makers who identified critical research questions, identified training needs to conduct transdisciplinary research, identified barriers to youth tobacco prevention research (e.g., funding), and encouraged communication among funding organizations and people interested in youth tobacco research. The YPTI successfully encouraged many scientists to address issues relevant to tobacco use and prevention. In addition, the report of the YTPI played a meaningful role to convince federal and private funding organizations to identify youth tobacco use and prevention as a priority research topic.

American Legacy Foundation

The American Legacy Foundation (ALF) was established in March, 1999, as part of the Master Settlement Agreement (MSA) and is funded primarily by payments designated by the settlement. The MSA was a global legal settlement between most of the states of the United States and the tobacco industry that included restrictions on advertising tobacco products, funding for tobacco treatment and research programs, and limits on lawsuits against the tobacco industry. The ALF is a national independent public health foundation that develops national programs addressing the health effects of tobacco use, particularly in youth. The primary goals of this foundation are youth tobacco prevention and youth tobacco cessation. One of ALF's public education campaigns that targets adolescent smokers is the Truth® campaign. This campaign uses advertising and promotional events to provide teens with evidence-based information about the negative health consequences of tobacco smoking (ALF, 2002). Studies examining the effectiveness of this campaign have found that exposure to Truth advertisements are consistently associated with an increase in anti-tobacco attitudes and beliefs (Healton, 2001; Farrelly et al., 2002).

Campaign for Tobacco-Free Kids

The Campaign for Tobacco-Free Kids is a national, non-governmental initiative developed to protect children from tobacco addiction. The stated goals of the initiative are to: (1) deglamorize tobacco use through counter-advertising; (2) change public policies at federal, state, and local levels to protect adolescents from tobacco use; (3) involve organizations (medical, civic, educational, religious) in fighting the war against youth tobacco use. The initiative works to raise awareness about the deleterious effects of tobacco smoking to decrease smoking initiation. Data collection assessing the effectiveness of this initiative is ongoing. What is known is that community and policy initiatives that use a multi-pronged approach to prevention are more effective than any single approach.

Future studies should examine how to empower youth to quit smoking and to encourage them to become involved in prevention efforts (NCI, 2001l; Backinger et al. 2003). Success in these areas will likely maximize the effectiveness of prevention programs.

Summary and Conclusions

Despite the widely publicized health hazards of tobacco use and societal changes to restrict tobacco use in the United States (e.g., in public places, on airplanes, in restaurants), many adolescents continue to begin using tobacco products and then become hooked. The psychosocial, psychobiological, and environmental reasons for these phenomena have received an increased amount of research attention over the past 10 years. Unfortunately, this accumulation of knowledge has had a modest impact on youth tobacco initiation. Health-care practitioners and scientists, foundations, and governments are working to decrease adolescent tobacco use, but it is a remarkable difficult struggle. Educating health-care practitioners, the general public, and kids themselves about the health risks of tobacco and the great addiction liability certainly are reasonable steps, but innovative approaches to this situation are needed. Pessimists (or realists) may argue that adolescents, by their nature (psychologically and biologically), will ignore any adult sources of information and will purposely take risks. If so, then the only way to reduce youth tobacco use would be to restrict access and to increase prices. Optimists (who also might be realists) may argue that there is some way to convey to kids the dangers of smoking tobacco and that the effective means to convey this information may offer insight into better ways to avoid other health risks and to promote other healthy behaviors. We remain optimists.

References

[1]   Adger, H. (1991). Problems of alcohol and other drug use and abuse in adolescents. *Journal of Adolescent Health*, **12**, 606-613.

[2]   Adriani, W., Spijker, S., Deroche-Gamonet, V., Laviola, G., Le Moal, M., Smit, A.B., & Piazza, P.V. (2003). Evidence for enhanced neurobehavioral vulnerability to nicotine during periadolescence in rats. *Journal of Neuroscience*, **1**, 4712-4716.

[3]   Alexander, H.M., Callcott, R., Dobson, A.J., Hardes, G.R., Lloyd, D.M., O'Connell, D.L., & Leeder, S.R. (1983). Cigarette smoking and drug use in school children: IV— factors associated with changes in smoking behavior. *International Journal of Epidemiology*, **12**, 59-66.

[4]   Alexander, C., Piazza, M., Mekos, D., & Valente, T. (2001). Peers, schools, and adolescent cigarette smoking. *Journal of Adolescent Health*, **29**, 22-30.

[5]   Altman, J. & Das, G.D. (1964). Autoradiographic examination of the effects of enriched environment on the rate of glial multiplication in the adult rat brain. *Nature*, **204**, 1161-1163.

[6]   Altman, D.G., Foster, V., Rasernick-Douss, L., & Tye, J.B. (1989). Reducing the illegal sale of cigarettes to minors. *Journal of the American Medical Association*, **261**, 221-224.

[7]   Altman, D.G., Levine, D.W., Coeytauk, R, Slade, J., & Jaffe, R. (1996). Tobacco promotion and susceptibility to tobacco use among adolescents 12 through 17 years in a nationally representative sample. *American Journal of Public Health*, **86**, 1590-1593.

[8]   American Legacy Foundation (2001). Cigarette smoking among youth: Results from the 2000 National Youth Tobacco Survey. Washington D.C.: American Legacy Foundation. *Legacy First Look Report* **7**.

[9]   American Psychiatric Association (1994). *Diagnostic Statistical Manual of Mental Disorders*. Washington, D.C.: American Psychiatric Assoc. 4th edition.

[10]   Amos, A., Wiltshire, S., Bostock, Y., Haw, S., & McNeill, A. (2004). You can't go without a fag—you need it for your hash—a qualitative exploration of smoking and young people. *Addiction*, **99**, 77-81.

[11] Anda, R.F., Williamson, D.F., Escobedo, L.G., Mast, E.E., Giovino, G.A., & Remington, P.L. (1990). Depression and the dynamics of smoking. A national perspective. *Journal of the American Medical Association,* **264**, 1541-1545.

[12] Arday, D.R., Giovino, G.A., Schulman, J., Nelson, D.E., Mowrey, P., & Samet, J.M. (1995). Cigarette smoking and self-reported health problems among U.S. high school seniors, 1982-1989. *American Journal of Health Promotion,* **10**, 111-6.

[13] Austin, S. & Gortmaker, S. (2001). Dieting and smoking initiation in early adolescent girls and boys: a prospective study. *American Journal of Public Health,* **91**, 46-450.

[14] Backinger, C.L., Fagan, P., Matthews, E., & Grana, R. (2003). *Tobacco contr*ol, 12, 46-53.

[15] Barker, D. (1994). Reasons for tobacco use and symptoms of nicotine withdrawal among adolescent and young adult tobacco users. United States, 1993. *Mortality and Morbidity Weekly Report,* **43***,* 745-750.

[16] Baker, T.B., Brandon, T.H., & Chassin, L. (2004). Motivational influences on cigarette smoking. *Annual Review of Psychology,* **55**, 463-491.

[17] Bandura, A. (1986). *Social foundations of thought and action. A social cognitive theory.* Englewood Cliffs (NJ): Prentice Hall.

[18] Barefoot, J.C., Smith, R.H., Dahlstrom, W.G., & Williams, R.B. (1989). Personality predictors of smoking behavior in a sample of physicians. *Psychology and Health,* **3**, 37-43.

[19] Bates, D.V. (1989). *Respiratory Function in Disease.* 3rd ed. Philadelphia: W.B. Saunders Company.

[20] Bauman, K.E., Brown, J.D., Bryan, E.S., Fisher, L.A., Padgett, C.A., & Sweeney, J.M. (1988). Three mass media campaigns to prevent adolescent cigarette smoking. *Preventive Medicine,* **17**, 510-530.

[21] Bauman, K.E., Foshee, V.A., Linzer, M.A., & Koch, G.G. (1990). Effect of parental smoking classification on the association between parental and adolescent smoking. *Addictive Behavior,* **15**, 413-422.

[22] Bewley, B.R., Hallil, T., & Snaith, A.H. (1973). Smoking by primary schoolchildren prevalence and associated respiratory symptoms. *British Journal of Preventive and Social Medicine,* 27, 150-153.

[23] Bewley, B.R. (1978). Smoking in childhood. *Postgraduate Medicine,* **54**, 197-199.

[24] Botvin, E.M., Botvin, G.J., & Baker, E. (1983). Developmental changes in attitudes toward cigarette smokers during early adolescence. *Psychological Reports,* **53**, 547-553.

[25] Botvin, G.J., Baker, E., Goldberg, C.J., Dunesbury, L., & Botvin, E.M. (1992). Correlates and predictors of smoking among black adolescents. *Addictive Behaviors,* **17**, 97-103.

[26] Bardo M.T., Bowling, S.L., Rowlett, J.K., Manderscheis, P., Buxton, S.T., & Dwoskin, L.P. (1995). Environmental enrichment attenuates locomotor sensitization, but not *in-vitro* dopamine release induced by amphetamine. *Pharmacology Biochemistry and Behavior,* **51**: 397-405.

[27] Bardo, M.T., Robinet, P.M., Hammer, R.F. (1997). Effect of differential rearing environments on morphine-induced behaviors opioid receptors and dopamine synthesis. *Neuropharmacology* **36**, 251-259.

[28] Bowling, S., Rowlett, J.K., & Bardo, M.T. (1993). The effect of environmental enrichment on amphetamine-stimulated locomotor activity dopamine synthesis and dopamine release. *Neuropharmacology* **32**: 885-893.

[29] Bowling, S.L. & Bardo, M.T. (1994). Locomotor and rewarding effects of amphetamine in enriched, social and isolate reared rats. *Pharmacology Biochemistry and Behavior,* **48**, 259-264

[30] Boyle, A.E., Gill, K., Smith, B.R., & Amit, Z. (1991). Differential effects of an early housing manipulation on cocaine-induced activity and self-administration in laboratory rats. *Pharmacology Biochemistry and Behavior,* **39**, 269-274.

[31] Breslau, N., Kibley, M.M., & Andreski, P. (1991). Nicotine dependence, major depression, and anxiety in young adults. *Archives of General Psychiatry,* **48**, 1069-1074.

[32] Breslau, N., Kibley, M.M., & Andreski, P. (1993a). Vulnerability to psycopathology in nicotine-dependent smokers: An epidemiologic study of young adults. *American Journal of Psychiatry,* **150**, 941-946.

[33] Breslau, N., Fenn, N., & Peterson, E. L. (1993b). Early smoking initiation and nicotine dependence in a cohort of young adults. *Drug Alcohol Dependence* **33**, 129-37.

[34] Breslau, N., Kibley, M.M., & Andreski, P. (1994). DSM-III-R nicotine dependence in young adults: prevalence, correlates and associated psychiatric disorder. *Addiction,* **89**, 743-754.

[35] Breslau, N. & Peterson, E. L. (1996). Smoking cessation in young adults: age a initiation of cigarette smoking and other suspected influences. *American Journal of Public Health,* **86**, 214-220.

[36] Breslau, N., Johnson, E.O., Hiripi, E., & Kessler, R. (2001). Nicotine dependence in the United States: Prevalence, trends, and smoking persistence. *Archives of General Psychiatry,* **58**, 817-818.

[37] Breslau, N., Novak, S.P., & Kessler, R.C. (2004). Daily smoking and the subsequent onset of psychiatric disorders. *Psychological Medicine,* **34**, 323-333.

[38] Brown, R.A., Lewinsohn, P.M., Seeley, J.R., & Wagner, E.F. (1996). Cigarette smoking, major depression, and other psychiatric disorders among adolescents. *Journal of the American Academy of Child and Adolescent Psychiatry,* **35**, 1602-1610.

[39] Burns, D.M. & Johnston, L.D. (2001). Overview of recent changes in adolescent smoking behavior. *Smoking and Tobacco Control Monograph,* **14**, 1-8.

[40] Burt, R. D., & Peterson, A.V. (1998). Smoking cessation among high school seniors. *Preventive Medicine,* **27**, 319-27.

[41] Burt, R.D., Dinh, K.T., Peterson, A.V., & Sarason, I.G. (2000). Predicting adolescent smoking: A prospective study of personality variables. *Preventive Medicine,* **30**, 115-125.

[42] Byrne, D.G., Byrne, A.E., & Reinhart, M.I. (1995). Personality, stress, and the decision to commence cigarette smoking in adolescence. *Journal of Psychosomatic Research,* **39**, 59-62.

[43] Byrne D.G, & Mazanov, J. (2003). Adolescent stress and future smoking behavior: a prospective investigation. *Journal of Psychosomatic Research,* **54**, 313-21.

[44] Camp, D.E., Klesges, R.C., & Relyea, G. (1993). The relationship between body weight concerns and adolescent smoking. *Health Psychology,* **12**, 24-32.

[45]   Centers for Disease Control and Prevention (1996). Projected smoking-related deaths among youth. *Morbidity and Mortality Weekly report (MMWR)*, **45**, 971-974.

[46]   Centers for Disease Control and Prevention. (1997). Tobacco use among high school students-United States. *Journal of School Health*, **68**, 202-204.

[47]   Centers for Disease Control and Prevention (2000). Youth tobacco surveillance-United States, 1998-1999. CDC Surveillance Summaries (October 13). *Morbidity and Mortality Weekly reports*, **49**, 1-94.

[48]   Center for Disease Control and Prevention (2003). Tobacco use among middle and high school students-United States, 2002. *Morbidity and Mortality Weekly Report (MMWR)*, **52**, 1096-1098.

[49]   Charlton, A. (1984). Smoking and weight control in teenagers. *Public Health*, **98**, 277-281.

[50]   Charlton, A. (1986). Children who smoke. *Health at School*, **1**, 125-127.

[51]   Chassin, L., Presson, C.C., Sherman, S.J., Corty, E., & Olshavsky, R.W. (1984). Predicting the onset of cigarette smoking in adolescents: A longitudinal study. *Journal of Applied Social Psychology*, **14**, 224-243.

[52]   Chassin, L., Presson, C.C., Sherman, S.J., Montello, D., & McGrew, J. (1986). Changes in peer and parent influence during adolescence: longitudinal versus cross-sectional perspectives on smoking initiation. *Developmental Psychology*, **22**, 327-334.

[53]   Chassin, L., Presson, C.C., & Sherman, S.J. (1989). Constructive vs. destructive deviance in adolescent-health related behaviors. *Journal of Youth and Adolescence*, **18**, 245-262.

[54]   Chassin, L., Presson, C.C., & Sherman, S.J. (1990). Social psychological contributions to the understanding and prevention of adolescent cigarette smoking. *Personality and Social Psychology*, **16**, 133-151.

[55]   Chassin, L., Presson, C., Sherman, S.J., & Edwards, D.A. (1992). The natural history of cigarette smoking and young adult social roles. *Journal of Health and Social Behavior*, **33**, 328-347.

[56]   Chassin, L., Presson, C.C., Pitts, S.C., & Sherman, S.J. (2000). Smoking cigarettes may put an individual at greater risk for developing anxiety and depression. *Health Psychology*, **9**, 223-31.

[57]   Chaudhuri, R. Livingston, E., McMahon, A.D., Thomson, L., Borland, W., & Thomson, N.C. (2003). Cigarette smoking impairs the therapeutic response to oral corticosteriolds in chronic asthma. *American Journal of Respiratory and Critical Care Medicine*, **168**, 1265-66.

[58]   Cheeta, S., Irvine, E.E., Tucci, S., Sandhu, J., & File, S.E. (2001). In adolescence, female rats are more sensitive to the anxiolytic effect of nicotine than are male rats. *Neuropsychopharmacolgy*, **25**, 601-607.

[59]   Chen, J. & Millar, W.J. (1998). Age of smoking initiation: Implications for quitting. *Health Report*, **8**, 39-46.

[60]   Choi, W.S., Patten, C.A., Gillin, J.C., Kaplan, R.M., & Pierce, J. P. (1997). Cigarette smoking predicts development of depressive symptoms among U.S. adolescents. *Annals of Behavioral Medicine*, **19**, 42-50.

[61]   Colby, S.M., Tiffany, S.T., Shiffman, S., & Niaura, R. S. (2000). Are adolescent smokers dependent on nicotine? A review of the evidence. *Drug and Alcohol Dependence*, **59**, S83-95. Collins, L.M., Sussman, S., Rauch, J.M., Dent, C.W., Johnson,

C.A., Hansen, W.B., & Flay, B.R. (1987). Psychosocial predictors of young adolescent cigarette smoking: A sixteen-month, three-wave longitudinal study. *Journal of Applied Social Psychology,* **17**: 554-573.

[62] Conners, C.K., Levin, E.D., Sparrow, E., Hinton, S.C., Erhardt, D., Meck, W.H., Rose, J.E., & March, J. (1996). Nicotine and attention in adult attention deficit hyperactivity disorder (ADHD). *Psychopharmacology Bulletin,* **32**, 67-73.

[63] Conrad, K. M., Flay, B. R. & Hill, D. (1992). Why children start smoking cigarettes: predictors of onset. *British Journal of Addiction,* **87**, 1711–1724.

[64] Coombs, R.H., Fawzy, F.I., & Gerber, B.E. (1986). Patterns of cigarette, alcohol, and other drug use among children and adolescents. A longitudinal study. *International Journal of Addiction,* **21**, 897-913.

[65] Copeland, A.L., Brandon, T.H., & Quinn, E.P. (1995). The smoking consequences questionnaire-Adult: measurement of smoking outcome expectancies of experienced smokers. *Psychological Assessment,* **7**, 484-494.

[66] Corrigall, W.A. (1999). Nicotine self-administration in animals as a dependence model. *Nicotine Tobacco Research,* **1**, 11-20.

[67] Dalton, M.A., Sargent, J.D., Beach, M.L., Bernhardt, A.M., & Stevens, M. (1999). Positive and negative outcome expectations of smoking: implications for prevention. *Preventive Medicine,* **29**, 460-465.

[68] Dalton, M.A., Sargent, J.D., Beach, M.L., Titus-Ernstoff, L., Gibson, J.J, Ahrens,

[69] M.B, Tickle, J.J, & Heatherton, T.F. (2003). Effect of viewing smoking in movies on adolescent smoking initiation: a cohort study. *Lancet,* **362**, 281-5.

[70] Dappen, A., Schwartz, R.H., & O'Donnell, R. (1996). A survey of adolescent smoking patterns. *Journal of the American Board of Family Practice,* **9**, 7-13.

[71] De Vries, H., Kok, G., & Dijkstra, M. (1990). Self-efficacy as a determinant of the onset of smoking and interventions to prevent smoking in adolescents. In: Drenth, P.J., Sergeant, J.A., Takens, R.J. (eds). *European perspectives in psychology, clinical health, stress and anxiety, neuropsychology, psychophysiology.* New York: John Wiley and Sons, Inc.

[72] Diamond, M.C. (1967). Extensive cortical depth measurements and neuron size increases in the cortex of environmentally enriched rats. *Journal of Comparative Neurology,* **131**, 357-364.

[73] DiFranza, J.R., Rigotti, N.A., McNeill, A.D., Ockene, J.K, Savageau, J.A., Cyr, D.S, & Coleman, M. (2000). Initial symptoms of nicotine dependence in adolescents. *Tobacco Control,* **9**, 313-319.

[74] DiFranza, J., Savageau, N.A., Rigotti, K., Fletcher, J.K., Ockene, A.D., McCeill, M., Coleman, C., & Wood, C. (2002). Development of symptoms of nicotine dependence in youths: 30-month follow-up data from the DANDY study. *Tobacco Control,* **11**, 228-235.

[75] Dinn, W.M., Aycicegi, A., & Harris, C.L. (2004). Cigarette smoking in a student sample: Neurocognitive and clinical correlates. *Addictive Behavior,* **29**, 107-126.

[76] Distefan, J.M., Gilpin, E.A., Sargent, J.D., & Pierce, J.P. (1999). Do movie stars encourage adolescents to start smoking? Evidence from California. *Preventive Medicine,* **28**, 1-11.

[77] Duncan, T.E., Tidlesley, E., Duncan, S.C., & Hops, H. (1995). The consistency of family and peer influences on the development of substance use in adolescence. *Addiction, 90,* 1647-1660.

[78] Elders, M.J., Perry, C.L., Eriksen, M.P., & Giovino, G.A. (1994). The report of the Surgeon General: Preventing tobacco use among young people. *American Journal of Public Health, 84,* 543-547.

[79] Ellickson, P.L. & Hays, R.D. (1990). Beliefs about resistance self-efficacy and drug prevalence. Do they really affect drug use? *International Journal of the Addictions, 25,* 1353-1378.

[80] Ellickson, P., Orlando, M., Tucker, J.S., & Klein, D. (2004). From adolescence to young adulthood: Racial/ethnic disparities in smoking. *American Journal of Public Health, 9,* 28-35.

[81] Elliott, B.M., Faraday, M.M., Phillips, J.M., & Grunberg, N.E. (2004). Effects of nicotine on elevated plus maze and locomotor activity in male and female adolescent and adult rats. *Pharmacology Biochemistry and Behavior, 77,* 21-28.

[82] Epstein, J., Botvin, G., & Diaz, T. (1998). Ethnic and gender differences in smoking prevalence among a longitudinal sample of inner-city adolescents. *Journal of Adolescent Health, 23,* 160-166.

[83] Ershler, J., Leventhal, H., Fleming, R., & Glynn, K. (1989). The quitting experience for smokers in sixth through twelfth grades. *Addictive Behavior, 14,* 365-378.

[84] Faraday, M.M., Elliott, B.M., & Grunberg, N.E. (2001). Adult vs. adolescent rats differ in biobehavioral responses to chronic nicotine administration. *Pharmacology Biochemistry and Behavior, 70,* 475-489.

[85] Faraday, M.M., Elliott, B.M., Phillips, J.M., & Grunberg, N.E. (2003). Adolescent and adult male rats differ in sensitivity to nicotine's activity effects. *Pharmacology Biochemistry and Behavior, 74,* 917-931.

[86] Farrelly, M.C., Healton, C.G., Davis, K.C., Messeri, P., Hersey, J.C., & Haviland, M.L. (2003). Getting to the truth: evaluating national tobacco countermarketing campaigns. *American Journal of Public Health, 93,* 703.

[87] Fisher, M. & Gordon, T. (1985). The relation of drinking and smoking habits to diet: The lipid research clinics prevalence study. *American Journal of Clinical Nutrition, 41,* 623-630.

[88] Fisher, L.A. & Bauman, K.E. (1988). Influence and selection in the friend-adolescent relationship: Findings from studies of adolescent smoking and drinking. *Journal of Applied Social Psychology, 18,* 283-294.

[89] Flay, B. R., Hu, F. B. & Richardson, J. (1998) Psychosocial predictors of different stages of cigarette smoking among high school students. *Preventive Medicine, 27,* A9–A18.

[90] Fleming, R., Leventhal, H., Glynn, K., & Ershler, J. (1989). The role of cigarettes in the initiation and progression of early substance use. *Addictive Behaviors, 14,* 261-272.

[91] Flory, K & Lynam, D. (2003). The relation between attention deficit hyperactivity disorder and substance abuse: What role does conduct disorder play? *Clinical Child and Family Psychology Review, 6,* 1-16.

[92] Food and Drug Administration (1995). *Regulations restricting the sale and distribution of cigarettes and smokeless tobacco products to protect children and adolescents.* Proposed rule. Federal Register, 21 CFR Part 801 et al., pp 41314-41787.

[93] Fowler, J.S., Volkow, N.D., Wang, G.J., Pappas, N., Logan, J., Macgregor, R., Alexoff, D., Shea, C., Schyler, D., Wolf, A.P., Warner, D., Zezulkova, I., & Cilento, R. (1996). Inhibition of monoamine oxidase B in the brains of smokers. *Nature, 379*, 733-736.

[94] French, S.A. & Perry, C.L. (1996). Smoking among adolescent girls: Prevalence and etiology. *Journal of the American Medical Women's Association, 51*, 25-28.

[95] French, S.A., Perry, C.L., Leon, G.R., & Fulkerson, J.A. (1994). Weight concerns, dieting behavior, and smoking initiation among adolescents: A prospective study. *American Journal of Public Health, 84*, 1818-1820.

[96] Friedman, L. S., Lichtenstein, E. & Biglan, A. (1985) Smoking onset among teens: an empirical analysis of initial situations. *Addictive Behaviors, 10*, 1–13.

[97] Gallup, G.G. (1992). *Teen-age attitudes and behavior concerning tobacco. Report of the Findings.* Princeton, NJ.

[98] Garrett, B.E. & Griffiths, R.R. (2001). Intravenous nicotine and caffeine: subjective and physiological effects in cocaine abusers. *The Journal of Pharmacology and Experimental Therapueutics, 296*, 486-494.

[99] Gerber, R.W. & Newman, I.M. (1989). Predicting future smoking of adolescent experimental smokers. *Journal of Youth and Adolescence, 18*, 191-201.

[100] Gidding, S.S., Xie, I., Liu, K., Manokio,T., Flack, J., Perkins, L., et al. (1992). Smoking has race/gender specific effects on resting cardiac function: The CARDIA study. *Circulation, 85*, 877.

[101] Gilpin, E.A, Choi, W.S., Berry, C., & Pierce, J. (1999). How many adolescents start smoking each day in the United States? *Journal of Adolescent Health, 25*, 248-255.

[102] Glantz, S.A. (2003). Smoking in movies: A major problem and a real solution. *Lancet, 362*, 258-260.

[103] Glantz, S.A. , Kacirk, K.W., & McCulloh, C. (2004). Back to the future: Smoking in the movies in 2002 compared with 1950 levels. *American Journal of Public Health, 94*, 261-263.

[104] Goodman, E. & Capitman, J. (2000). Depressive symptoms and cigarette smoking among teens. *Pediatrics, 106*, 748-55.

[105] Green, G., Macintyre, S., West, P., & Ecob, R. (1991). Like parent like child? Associations between drinking and smoking behavior of parents and their children. *British Journal of Addiction, 86*, 745-758.

[106] Green, L., Fry, A., & Myerson, J. (1994). Discounting of delayed rewards: a life-span comparison. *Psychological Science, 5*, 33-36.

[107] Green, T.A., Cain, M.E., Thompson, M., & Bardo, M.T. (2003). Environmental enrichment decreases nicotine-inducted hyperactivity in rats. *Psychopharmacology, 170*, 235-241.

[108] Greenough, W.T. (1975). Experimental modification of the developing brain. *American Scientist, 63*, 37-46.

[109] Greenough, W.T., Black, J.E., & Wallace, C.S. (1987). Experience and brain development. *Child Development, 58*, 539-559.

[110] Griesler, P.C., & Kandel, D.B. (1998). Ethnic differences in correlates of adolescent cigarette smoking. *Journal of Adolescent Health, 23*, 167-180.

[111] Griesler, P.C., Kandel, D.B., & Davies, M. (2002). Ethnic differences in predictors of initiation and persistence of adolescent cigarette smoking in the National Longitudinal Survey of Youth. *Nicotine and Tobacco Research, 4*, 72-93.

[112] Grunberg, N.E. (1982). The effects of nicotine and cigarette smoking on food consumption and taste preferences. *Addictive Behaviors, 7,* 317-331.

[113] Grunberg, N.E., Winders, S.E., & Wewers, M.E. (1991). Gender differences in tobacco use. *Health Psychology, 10,* 143-153.

[114] Grunberg, N. E. (1991). Smoking cessation and weight gain. *The New England Journal of Medicine, 324,* 78-769.

[115] Grunberg, N. E. (1992). Cigarette smoking and body weight: A personal journey through a complex field. *Health Psychology, 11,* 26-31.

[116] Gwynn, R.C. (2004). Risk factors for asthma in U.S. adults: results from the 2000 Behavioral Risk Factor Surveillance System. *Asthma, 41,* 91-98.

[117] Hahn, G., Charlin, V.L., Sussman, S., Dent, C.W., Manzi, J., & Stacy, A.W. et al. (1990). Adolescents' first and most recent use situations of smokeless tobacco and cigarettes: Similarities and differences. *Addictive Behaviors, 15,* 439-448.

[118] Hazan, A.R., Lipton, H.L., & Glantz, S.A. (1994). Popular films do not reflect current tobacco use. *American Journal of Public Health, 84,* 998-1000.

[119] Headen, S.W., Bauman, K.E., Deane, G.D., & Koch, G.G. (1991). Are the correlates of cigarette smoking initiation different for black and white adolescents. *American Journal of Public Health, 81,* 854-858.

[120] Healton, C. (2001). Who's afraid of the truth? *American Journal of Public Health, 91,* 554-558.

[121] Hebb, D.O. (1947). The effects of early experience on problem solving at maturity. *American Psychologist, 2,* 307-308.

[122] Henningfield, J.E., Clayton, R., & Pollin, W. (1990). Involvement of tobacco in alcoholism and illicit drug use. *British Journal of Addiction, 85,* 279-292.

[123] Henningfield, J.E. (1995). Nicotine medications for smoking cessation. *New England Journal of Medicine, 333,* 1196-203.

[124] Holland, W.W. & Elliott, A. (1968). Cigarette smoking, respiratory symptoms, and anti-smoking propaganda. An experiment. *Lancet, 1,* 41-43.

[125] Hu, F.B., Flay, B.R., Hedeker, D., Siddiqui, O., & Day, L.E. (1995). The influences of friends' and parental smoking on adolescent smoking behavior: The effects of time and prior smoking. *Journal of Applied Social Psychology, 25,* 2018-204.

[126] Huang, T.T., Unger, J.B., & Rohrbach, L.A. (2000). Exposure to and perceived usefulness of school-based tobacco prevention programs: associations with susceptibility to smoking among adolescents. *Journal of Adolescent Health, 27,* 248-254.

[127] Hunter, S.M., Croft, J.B., Vizelberg, I.A., & Berenson, G.S. (1987). Psychosocial influences on cigarette smoking among youth in a southern community: The Bogalusa heart study. *Morbidity and Mortality Weekly Report, 36,* 17S-25S.

[128] Hurt, R.D., Croghan, G.A., Beede, S.D., Wolter, T.D., Croghan, I.T., & Patten, C.A. (2000). Nicotine patch therapy in 101 adolescent smokers: Efficacy withdrawal symptom relief, and carbon monoxide and plasma cotinine levels. *Archives of Pediatric and Adolescent Medicine, 154,* 31-37.

[129] Ikard, F.F., Green, D., & Horn, D. (1969). A scale to differentiate between types of smoking as related to management of affect. *International Journal of Addictions, 4,* 649-59.

[130] Jackson, C., Henricksen, L., Dickinson, D., Messer, L., & Robertson, S.B. (1998). A longitudinal study predicting patterns of cigarette smoking in late childhood. *Health Education and Behavior, 25*, 436-437.

[131] Jackson, C. (1998). Cognitive susceptibility to smoking and initiation of smoking during childhood: A longitudinal study. *Preventive Medicine, 27*, 129-134.

[132] Jessor, R. & Jessor, S.L. (1977). *Problem behavior and psychosocial development: A longitudinal study of youth.* New York: Academic Press.

[133] Johnson P.B., Boles, S.M., Vaughan, R., & Kleber, H.D. (2000). The co-occurrence of smoking and binge drinking in adolescence. *Addictive Behavior, 25*, 779-83.

[134] Johnston, L.D., O'Malley, P.M., Bachman, J.G. (2002). Monitoring the Future: National Survey Results on Drug use, 1975-2001, Volume 1: Secondary School Students. Bethesda, Md: National Institute on Drug Abuse: NIH publication 02-5106.

[135] Kandel, D.B. (1975). Stages in adolescent involvement in drug use. *Science, 190*, 912-914.

[136] Kandel, D.B., Davies, M., Karus, D., & Yamaguchi, K. (1986). The consequences in young adulthood of adolescent drug involvement. An overview. *Archives of General Psychiatry, 43*, 746-754.

[137] Kandel, D.B., & Davies, M. (1986). Adult sequelae of adolescent depressive symptoms. *Archives of General Psychiatry, 43* 255-62.

[138] Kandel, D., & Faust, R. (1975). Sequence and stages in patterns of adolescent drug use. *Archives of General Psychiatry, 32*, 923-932.

[139] Kandel, D.B. (2002). Stages and pathways of drug involvement. *Examining the Gateway Hypothesis.* NY: Cambridge University Press.

[140] Kandel, D.B., Kiros, G.E., Schaffran, C., & Hu, M.C. (2004). Racial/ethnic differences in cigarette smoking initiation and progression to daily smoking: A multilevel analysis. *American Journal of Public Health, 94*, 128-135.

[141] Kendler, K, S., Neale, M.C., Maclean, C.J., Heath, A.C., Eaves, L.J., & Kessler, R.C. (1993). Smoking and major depression: A causal analysis. *Archives of General Psychiatry, 50*, 36-43.

[142] Kobus, K. (2003). Peers and adolescent smoking. *Addiction, 1*, 37-55.

[143] Kopstein, A. (2001). Tobacco use in America: Findings from the 1999 National Household Survey on Drug Abuse. Rockville. Md: *Substance Abuse and Mental Health Services Administation.* DHHS publication SMA02-3622.

[144] Koval, J.J., Pederson, L.L., Mills, C.A., McGrady, G.A., & Carvajal, S.C. (2002). Models of the relationship of stress, depression, and other psychosocial factors to smoking behavior: A comparison of a cohort of students in grades 6 and 8. *Preventive Medicine, 30*, 463-477.

[145] Kessler, D.A., Nantanblut, S.L., Wilkenfeld, J.P., Corraine, C.C., Mayl, S.L., Bernstein, I.B.G., & Thompson, L. (1996). Nicotine addiction: A pediatric disease. *New England Journal of Medicine, 335*, 931-937.

[146] Killen, J.D., Robinson, T.N., Haydel, K.F., Hayward, C., Wilson, D.M., Hammer, L.D., Litt, I.F., & Taylor, C.B. (1997). Prospective study of risk factors for the initiation of cigarette smoking. *Journal of Consulting and Clinical Psychology, 64*, 1011-1016.

[147] Klein, L.C. (2001). Effects of adolescent nicotine exposure on opioid consumption and neuroendocrine responses in adult male and female rats. *Experimental and Clinical Psychopharmacology, 9*, 251-261.

[148] Klitzke, M., Irwin, R., Lombardo, T.W., & Christoff, K.A. (1990). Self-monitored smoking motives. *Journal of Substance Abuse,* **2**, 121-27.

[149] Kobus, K. (2003). Peers and adolescent smoking. *Addiction,* **98**, 37-55.

[150] Kopstein, A. (2001). Tobacco use in America findings from the 1999 National Household Survey on Drug Abuse. Rockville, MD: Substance Abuse and Mental Health Services Administration. *Office of Applied Studies.*

[151] Koval, J.J., Pederson, L.L., Mills, C.A., McGrady, G.A., & Carvajal, S.C. (2000). Models of the relationship of stress, depression, and other psychosocial factors to smoking behavior: a comparison of a cohort of students in grades 6 and 8. *Preventive Medicine,* **30**, 463-77.

[152] Lai, S., Lai, H., Page, J.B., & McCoy, C.B. (2000). The association between cigarette smoking and drug abuse in the United States. *Journal of Addictive Disorders,* **19**, 11-24.

[153] Lamkin, L., & Houston, T.P. (1998). Nicotine dependency and adolescence; preventing and treating. *Adolescent Medicine,* **25**, 125-135.

[154] Leventhal, H. & Avis, N. (1976). Pleasure, addiction, and habit: Factors in verbal report of factors in smoking behavior? *Journal of Abnormal Psychology,* **85**, 478-488.

[155] Leventhal, H., Fleming, R., & Glynn, K. (1988). A cognitive developmental approach to smoking interention. In: Maes S, Spielberger, C.D., Defares, P.B., Sarason, I.G., (eds). Topics in health psychology: *Proceedings of the first annual expert conference in health psychology.* New York: John Wiley and Sons.

[156] Leventhal, H., Keeshan, P., Baker, T., & Wetter, D. (1991). Smoking prevention: towards a process approach. *British Journal of Addiction,* **86**, 583-587.

[157] Levin, E.D., Conners, C.K., Sparrow, E., Hinton, S.C., Erhardt, D., Meck, W.H., Rose, J.E., & March, J. (1996). Nicotine effects on adults with attention-deficit/hyperactivity disorder. *Psychopharamacology,* **123**, 55-63.

[158] Levinson, A.H., Hendershott, S., & Byers, T.E. (2002). The ID effect on youth access to cigarettes, *Tobacco Control,* **11**, 296-299.

[159] Lewinsohn, P.M., Rhode, P., & Brown, R. A. (1999). Level of current an past smoking as predictors of future substance use disorders in young adulthood. *Addiction,* **94**, 913-921.

[160] Lipkus, I.M., Barefoot, J.C., Williams, R.B., & Siegler, I.C. (1994). Personality measures as predictors of smoking initiation and cessation in the UNC Alumni Heart Study. *Health Psychology,* **13**, 149-55.

[161] Lucas, K. & Lloyd, B. (1999). Starting smoking: girls' explanations of the influence of peers. *Journal of Adolescence,* **22**, 647–655.

[162] Marti, B., Albelin, T., Minder, C.E., & Vader, J.P. (1988). Smoking, alcohol consumption, and endurance capacity: an analysis of 6,500 19-year-old conscripts and 4,100 joggers. *Preventive Medicine,* **17**, 79-92.

[163] Mates D. & Allison K.R. (1992). Sources of stress and coping responses of high school students. *Adolescence,* **27**, 461-74.

[164] McDonald, P., Colwell, B., & Backinger, C.L. (2003). Better practices for youth tobacco cessation: Evidence of a review panel. *American Journal of Health Behavior,* **27**, 144-157.

[165] McGill, H.C. & McMahan, C.A. (1998). Determinants of atherosclerosis in the young. Pathobiological determinants of atherosclerosis in youth (PDAY) Research Group. *American Journal of Cardiology, 82*, 30T-36T.

[166] McNamara, J.J., Molot, M.A., Stremple, J.F., & Cutting, R.T. (1971). Coronary artery disease in combat casualties in Vietnam. *Journal of the American Medical Association, 216*, 1185-1187.

[167] McNeill, A.D., West, R., Jarvis, M., Jackson, P., & Bryant, A. (1986). Cigarette withdrawal symptoms in adolescent smokers. *Psychopharmacology, 90*, 533-536.

[168] McNeill, A.D., Jarvis, M.J., & West, R.J. (1987). Subjective effects of cigarettes smoking in adolescents. *Psychopharmacology, 92*, 115-117.

[169] Mermelstein, R. (1999). Ethnicity, gender, and risk factors for smoking initiation: an overview. *Nicotine Tobacco Research, 1* Supp 2, S39-43.

[170] Mitchell, L. (1997). Loud, sad, or bad: young people's perceptions of peer groups and smoking. *Health Education Research, 12*, 1-14.

[171] Mitchell, L. & Amos, A. (1997). Girls, pecking order, and smoking. *Social Sciences and Medicine, 44*, 1861-1869.

[172] Mittlemark, M.B., Murray, D.M., Luepker, R.V., Pechacek, T.F., Pechacek, T.F., Pirie, P.L., & Pallonen, U.E. (1987). Predicting experimentation with cigarettes: The childhood antecedents of smoking study (CASS). *American Journal of Public Health, 77*, 206-208.

[173] Molina, B.S. & Pelham, W.E. (2003). Childhood predictors of adolescent substance use in a longitudinal study of children with ADHD. *Journal of Abnormal Psychology, 112*, 497-507.

[174] Moolchan, E.T., Ernst, M., & Henningfield, J.E. (2000). A review of tobacco smoking in adolescents: treatment implications. *Journal of the American Academy of Child and Adolescent Psychiatry, 39*, 682-693.

[175] Morris, G.S., Vo, A.N., Bassin, S., Savaglio, D., & Wong, N.D. (1993). Prevalence and sociobehavioral correlates of tobacco use among Hispanic children: The tobacco resistance activity program. *Journal of School Health, 63*, 391-396.

[176] National Cancer Institute (2001). Changing adolescent smoking prevalence. *Smoking and Tobacco Control Monograph*, 14, Bethesda, Maryland, US Department of Health National Cancer Institute (NIH Publication No. 02-5086).

[177] Nelson D.E., Giovino G.A., Shopland D.R., Mowery P.D., Mills S.L., & Eriksen M.P. (1995). Trends in cigarette smoking among US adolescents, 1974 through 1991. *American Journal of Public Health, 85*, 34-40.

[178] O'Loughlin, J., Paradis, G., Renaud, L., & Sanchez-Gomez, L. (1998). One-year predictors of smoking initiation and of continued smoking among elementary schoolchildren in multiethnic, low-income, inner-city neighborhoods. *Tobacco Control, 7*, 268-275.

[179] O'Loughlin, J., DiFranza, J., Tyndale, R., Meshefedjian, G., McMillan-Davey, & Clark, P., et al. (2003). Nicotine-dependence symptoms are associated with smoking frequency in adolescents. *American Journal of Preventive Medicine, 25* (3), 219-226.

[180] Pbert, L., Moolchan, E., Muramoto, M., Winickoff, J., Curry, S., Lando H., Ossip-Klein, D., Prokhorov, A.V., DiFranza, J., & Klein, J.D. (2003*). Pediatrics, 111*, E650-E660

[181] Pederson, L.L. (1986). Change in variables related to smoking from childhood to late adolescence: an eight year longitudinal study of a cohort of elementary school students. *Canadian Journal of Public Health, 77*, 33-39.

[182] Pederson L.L., Koval, J.J, & O'Connor, K. (1997). Are psychosocial factors related to smoking in grade-6 students? *Addictive Behaviors, 22*, 169-81.

[183] Perry, C.L., Murray, D.M., & Klepp, K.I. (1987). Predictors of adolescent smoking and implications for prevention. *Morbidity and Mortality Weekly Report (MMWR), 36*, 41S-45S.

[184] Petraitis, J., Flay, B.R., Miller, T.Q., Torpy, E.J., & Griener, B. (1998). Illicit substance use among adolescents: a matrix of prospective predictors. *Substance Use and Misuse, 33*, 2561-2604.

[185] Phillips G.D., Howes, S.R., Whitelaw, R.B., Wilkinson, L.S., Robbins, T.W., & Everitt B.J. (1994) Isolation rearing enhances the locomotor response to cocaine and a novel environment, but impairs the intravenous self-administration of cocaine. *Psychopharmacology* 115: 407-418

[186] Pierce, J. & Gilpin, E. (1995). A historical analysis of tobacco marketing and the uptake of smoking by youth in the United States: 1890-1977. *Health Psychology, 14*, 500-508.

[187] Pierce, J.P. & Gilpin, E.A. (1996). How long will today's new adolescent smoke be addicted to cigarettes. *American Journal of Public Health, 86*, 253-256.

[188] Prokhorov, A.V., Pallonen, U.E., Fava, J.L., Ding, L., & Niaura, R. (1996). Measuring nicotine dependence among high-risk adolescent smokers. *Addictive Behaviors, 21*, 117-127.

[189] Popham, W., Potter, L., Hetrick, M., Muthen, L., Duerr, J., & Johnson, M. (1994). Effectiveness of the California 1990-1991 tobacco education media campaign. *American Journal of Preventive Medicine, 10*, 319-326.

[190] Ritchey, P.N., Reid, G.S., & Hasse, L.A. (2001). The relative influence of smoking on drinking and drinking on smoking among high school students in a rural tobacco-growing county. *Journal of Adolescent Health, 29*, 386-94.

[191] Romer, D. & Jamieson, P. (2001). Do adolescents appreciate the risks of smoking? Evidence from a national survey. *Journal of Adolescent Health, 29*, 12-21.

[192] Rosenzweig, M.R., Krech, D., Bennett, E.L., & Diamond, M. (1962). Effects of environmental complexity and training on brain chemistry and anatomy. A replication and extension. *Journal of Comparative and Physiological Psychology, 55*, 429-437.

[193] Rosenzweig, M.R. (1966). Environmental complexity, cerebral change, and behavior. *American Psychologist, 21*, 321-332.

[194] Rosenzweig, M.R., Bennett, E.L., & Diamond, M.C. (1972). Brain changes in response to experience. *Scientific American, 226*, 22-29.

[195] Santi, S., Best, J.A., Brown, K.S., & Cargo, M. (1991). Social environment and smoking initiation. *International Journal of the Addictions, 25*, 881-903.

[196] Sargent, J.D., Beach, M.I., Dalton, M.A, Mott, L.A., Tickle, J.J., Ahrens, M.B., & Heatherton, T.F. (2001). Effect of seeing tobacco use in films on trying smoking among adolescents: cross-sectional study. *British Medical Journal, 323*, 1394-1397.

[197] Sargent, J.D., Dalton, M.A.., Beach, M.I., Mott, M.S. Tickle, J.J., Ahrens, B., & Heatheron, T. (2002). Viewing tobacco use in movies: Does it shape attitudes that mediate adolescent smoking? *American Journal of Preventive Medicine, 22*, 137-145.

[198] Sargent, J.D. & DiFranza, J.R. (2003). Tobacco control for clinicians who treat adolescents. CA *Cancer Journal for Clinicians, 53*, 102-123.

[199] Schiffman, S. (1991). Refining models of dependence: Variations across persons and situations. *British Journal of Addiction, 86*, 811-815.

[200] Semmer, N.K., Cleary, P.D., Dwyer, J.H., Fuchs, R., & Lippert, P. (1987). Psychosocial predictors of adolescent smoking in two German cities: The Berlin-Bremen Study. *Morbidity and Mortality Weekly Report, 4*, 3S-10S.

[201] Shedler, J. & Block, J. (1990). Adolescent drug use and psychological health. A longitudinal inquiry. *American Psychologist, 45*, 612-630.

[202] Sidney, S., Sternfeld, B., Gidding, S.S., Jacobs, D.R., Bild, D.E., Oberman, A., Haskell, W.L., Crow, R.S., & Gordon , J.M. (1993). Cigarette smoking and submaximal exercise test duration in a biracial population of young adults: The CARDIA study. *Medicine and Science in Sports and Exercise, 25*, 911-916.

[203] Siegel, M. & Biener, L. (2000). The impact of antismoking media campaign on progress to established smoking: results of a longitudinal youth study. *American Journal of Public Health, 90*, 380-386.

[204] Simons-Morton B, Crump A.D., Haynie D.L., Saylor K.E., Eitel P., & Yu, K. (1999). Psychosocial, school, and parent factors associated with recent smoking among early-adolescent boys and girls. *Preventive Medicine, 28*, 138-48.

[205] Slawecki, C.J. & Ehlers, C.L. (2002). Lasting effects of adolescent nicotine exposure on the electroencephalogram, event related potentials, and locomotor activity in the rat. Brain Research *Developmental Brain Research, 138*, 15-25.

[206] Slawecki C.J., Gilder, A., Roth, J., & Ehlers, C.L. (2003). Increased anxiety-like behavior in adult rats exposed to nicotine as adolescents. *Pharmacology Biochemistry and Behavior, 75*, 355-61.

[207] Slovic, P. (2000). What does it mean to know a cumulative risk? Adolescent's perceptions of short-term and long-term consequences of smoking. *Journal of Behavioral Decision Making, 13*, 259-66.

[208] Sly, D.F., Trapido, E., & Ray, S. (2002). Evidence of the dose effects of an antitobacco counteradvertising campaign. *Preventive Medicine, 35*, 511-518.

[209] Smith, T.A., House, R.J., and Croghan, I.T., Gauvin, T.R., Colligan, R.C., Offord, K.P., Gomez-Dahl, L.C., & Hurt, R.D. (1996). Nicotine patch therapy in adolescent smokers. *Pediatrics, 98*, 659-667.

[210] Smith, J.K., Neill, J.C., & Costall, B. (1997) Post weaning housing conditions influence the behavioral effects of d-amphetamine and cocaine. *Psychopharmacology (Berlin)* **131**: 23-33

[211] Soteriades E.S, & DiFranza J. (2003). Parent's socioeconomic status, adolescents' disposable income, and adolescents' smoking status in Massachusetts. *Brain Research,* **880**, 167-72.

[212] Stacy, A.W., Sussman, S., Dent, C.W., Burton, D., & Glay, B.R. (1992). Moderators of peer social influence in adolescent smoking. *Personality and Social Psychology Bulletin,* **18**, 163-172.

[213] Stanton, W.R. (1995). DSM-III-R tobacco dependence and quitting during late adolescence. *Addictive Behaviors, 20*, 595-603.

[214] Stockwell, T.F. & Glantz, S.A. (1997). Tobacco use is increasing in popular films. *Tobacco Control, 6*, 269-271.

[215] Strong, J.P. & Richards, M.L. (1976). Cigarette smoking and atherosclerosis in autopsied men. *Atherosclerosis,* **23**, 451-476.

[216] Strong, J.P. (1986). Coronary atherosclerosis in soldiers. A clue to the natural history of atherosclerosis in the young. *Journal of the American Medical Association,* **256**, 2863-2866.

[217] Substance Abuse and Mental Health Services Administration (2002). Summary of findings from the 200 National Household Survey on Drug Abuse: Volume II. Technical appendices and selected data tables. Rockville, Maryland: U.S. Department of Health and Human Services, NHSDA; DHHS publication no. (SMA) 02-3759.

[218] Sussman, S., Dent, C.W., Flay, B.R., Hansen, W.B., & Johnson, C. A. (1987). Psychosocial predictors of cigarette onset by white, black, hispanic, and asian adolescents in Southern California. *Morbidity and Mortality Weekly Report,* **36**, 11S-17S.

[219] Sussman, S., Dent, C.W., Nezami, E., Stacy, A.W., Burton, D., & Flay, B.R. (1998). Reasons for quitting and smoking temptation among adolescent smokers: gender differences. *Substance Use Misuse,* **33**, 2703-2720.

[220] Sussman, S., Dent, C.W., Severson, H., Burton, D., & Flay, B.R. (1998). Self-initiated quitting among adolescent smokers. *Preventive Medicine,* **27**, A19-28.

[221] Sussman, S., Lichtman, K., Ritt, A., & Pallonen, U.E. (1999). Effects of thirty-four adolescent tobacco use cessation and prevention trials on regular users of tobacco products. *Substance Use Misuse,* **34**, 1469-1503.

[222] Sussman, S., Dent, C.W., & Lichtman, K. (2001). Outcomes of teen smoking cessation program. *Addictive Behaviors,* **26**, 425-438.

[223] Sussman, S. (2002). Effects of sixty six adolescent tobacco use cessation trials and seventeen prospective studies of self-initiated quitting. *Tobacco Induced Diseases,* **1**, 35-81.

[224] Swan, A.V., Creeser, R., & Murray, M. (1990). When and why children first start to smoke. *International Journal of Epidemiology,* **19**, 323-330.

[225] Tager, I.B., Munoz, A., Rosner, B., Weiss, S.T., Carey, V., & Speizer, F.E. (1985). Effect of cigarette smoking on the pulmonary function of children and adolescents. *American Review of Respiratory disease,* **131**, 752-759.

[226] Teichman, M., Barnea, Z., & Rahav, G. (1989). Personality and substance use among adolescents: A longitudinal study. *British Journal of Addiction,* **84**, 181-190.

[227] Terry, T.K., Huang, B.A., Unger, J.B., & Rohrbach, L.A. (2000). Exposure to, and perceived usefulness of school-based tobacco prevention programs: Associations with susceptibility to smoking among adolescents. *Journal of Adolescent Health,* **27**, 248-254.

[228] Tickle, J.J., Sargent, J.D., Dalton, M.A., Beach, M.L., & Heatherton, T.F. (2001). Favorite movie start, their tobacco use in contemporary movies, and its association with adolescent smoking. *Tobacco Control,* **10**, 16-22.

[229] Tobler, N.S. (1986). Meta-analysis of 143 adolescent drug prevention education programs: Quantitative outcome results of program participation compared to a control or comparison group. *Journal of Drug Issues,* **16**, 537-567.

[230] Tobler, N.S., & Stratton, H.H. (1997). Effectiveness of school-based drug prevention programs: A meta-analysis of the research. *The Journal of Primary Prevention,* **18**, 71-128.

[231] Torabi, M.R., Bailey, W.J., & Majd-Jabbari, M. (1993). Cigarette smoking as a predictor of alcohol and other drug use by children and adolescents: Evidence of the "gateway drug effect." *Journal of School Health, 63*, 302.306.

[232] Trauth, J.A., Seidler, F.J., & Slotkin, T. A. (2000). Persistent and delayed behavioral changes after nicotine treatment in adolescent rats. *Brain Research, 880*, 167-172.

[233] Turbin, M.S., Jessor, R., & Costa, F.M. (2000). Adolescent cigarette smoking: health-related behavior or normative transgression? *Prevention Science, 1*,115-24.

[234] Tyas, S.L, & Pederson, L.L. (1998). Psychosocial factors related to adolescent smoking: A critical review of the literature. *Tobacco Control,7*, 409–420.

[235] USDHHS (1986). The health consequences of using smokeless tobacco. *A report of the advisory committee to the Surgeon General.* U.S. Department of Health and Human Services, Public health Service, National Institute of Health. NIH Publication O. 86-2874.

[236] USDHHS (1988). The health consequences of smoking: Nicotine addiction. *A report of the Surgeon General. US Department of Health and Human Services*, Public Health Service, Centers for Disease Control, Center for Health Promotion and Education, Office on Smoking and Health. DHHS Publication NO. (CDC) 88-8406.

[237] USDHHS (1989). Reducing the health consequences of smoking: 25 years of progress: *A report of the Surgeon General*, 1988. US Department of Heath and Human Services, Public Health Service, Centers for Disease Control, Center for Health Promotion an Education, Office on Smoking and Health. DHHS Publication No. (CDC) 89-8411.

[238] USDHHS. (1994). Preventing tobacco use among young people: *A report of the Surgeon General* (Rep. No. 23). Atlanta, GA: USDHHS

[239] Unger, J.B. & Chen, X. (1999). The role of social networks and media receptivity in predicting age of smoking initiation. *Addictive Behaviors, 24*, 371-381.

[240] Urberg, K.A., Degirmencioglu, S.M., & Pilgrim, C. (1997). Close friend and group influence on adolescent cigarette smoking on adolescent initiation and escalation of smoking. *Journal of Health and Social Behavior, 35*, 248-265.

[241] Virgili, M., Owen, N., & Sverson, H.H., (1991). Adolescent's smoking behavior and risk perceptions. *Journal of Substance Abuse, 3*, 315-324.

[242] Vogel, J.S., Hurford, D.P., Smith, J.V., & Cole, A. (2003). The relationship between and smoking in adolescents. *Adolescence, 149*, 57-74.

[243] Vuckovic, N., Polen, M.R., & Hollis, J.F. (2003). The problem is getting us to stop. What teens say about smoking cessation. *Preventive Medicine, 37*, 209-218.

[244] Wack, J.T. & Rodin, J. (1982). Smoking and its effects on body weight and the systems of caloric regulation. *American Journal of Clinical Nutrition, 35*, 366-380.

[245] Waldron, I., Lyle, D., & Brandon, A. (1991). Gender differences in teenage smoking. *Women and Health, 17*, 65-90.

[246] Welte, J.W. & Barnes, G.M. (1987). Youthful smoking: patterns and relationships to alcohol and other drug use. *Journal of Adolescence, 10*, 327-340.

[247] Whalen, C.K., Jamner, L.D., Henker, B., Gehricke, J.G., & King, P.S. (2003). Is there a link between adolescent cigarette smoking and pharmacotherapy for ADHD. *Psychology of Addictive Behaviors, 17*, 332-335.

[248] Windle, M. & Windle, R.C. (2001). Depressive symptoms and cigarette smoking among middle adolescents: prospective associations and intrapersonal and interpersonal influences. *Journal of Consulting and Clinical Psychology, 69*, 215-226.

[249] Young, M. & Werch, C.E. (1990). Relationship between self-esteem and substance use among students in fourth through twelfth grade. Wellness Perspectives: *Research Theory and Practice, 7*, 31-44.

[250] Youth Tobacco Prevention Initiative (1998). *Report from the working groups of the youth tobacco prevention initiative.* Washingtion, D.C.: Center for the Advancement of Health.

[251] Zhu, S., Sun, J., Billings, S.C., Choi, W.S., & Marlarcher, A. (1999). Predictors of smoking cessation in U.S. adolescents. *American Journal of Preventive Medicine, 16*, 202-207.

In: Trends in Smoking and Health Research
Editors: J. H. Owing, pp. 185-201

ISBN: 1-59454-391-7
© 2005 Nova Science Publishers, Inc.

Chapter IX

Cigarette Smoking and Aneurysmal Subarachnoid Hemorrhage

Susan C. Williams

Department of Neurosurgery; Columbia University, and the New York Presbyterian Hospital, New York, NY

Anthony L. D'Ambrosio

Department of Neurosurgery; Columbia University, and the New York Presbyterian Hospital, New York, NY

E. Sander Connolly Jr.*

Department of Neurosurgery; Columbia University, and the New York Presbyterian Hospital, New York, NY

Abstract

This review briefly discusses the incidence, presentation, and associated complications of an aneurysmal subarachnoid hemorrhage (aSAH). Subsequently, the effects of cigarette smoking on aneurysm formation, growth, and eventual rupture as well as the influence of cigarette smoking on the delayed development of cerebral vasospasm following aSAH will be examined.

Introduction

The involvement of cigarette smoking in the pathogenesis of a variety of diseases such as lung cancer, myocardial infarction, and erectile dysfunction is well known.[1] There is no organ system in the body that is not adversely affected by the toxic effects of combusted tobacco. The adverse role of cigarette smoking in cerebrovascular disease is well documented

---

*   E. Sander Connolly Jr., M.D.; Department of Neurological Surgery; Columbia University, College of Physicians & Surgeons; 710 West 168th Street; New York, NY 10032; Fax: (212) 305-2026; Office: (212) 305-0376; Email address: esc5@columbia.edu

and the harmful effects of smoking are most evident in patients who develop an aneurysmal subarachnoid hemorrhage (aSAH).[2-5]

The association between cigarette smoking and aSAH is strong. Only statistically significant correlations between cigarette smoking and an increased risk of aSAH have been documented.[6] In multiple case-control and cohort studies, active smoking increases the odds of developing an aSAH two to eleven times.[2,4,5,7,8-11] Forty to seventy-five percent of aSAH patients have a past history of smoking or currently smoke, which is a much higher percentage than the general adult population.[5,12,13] Patients who smoke greater than twenty cigarettes per day are most at risk, and a definite dose-response relationship between the number of cigarettes smoked and risk of aSAH has been shown.[2,14,15] Furthermore, the age of aneurysm rupture is significantly different between smokers and nonsmokers with female smokers developing aSAH 7-10 years earlier than nonsmokers and male smokers developing aSAH 2-6 years earlier.[5]

This review briefly discusses the incidence, presentation, and associated complications of an aSAH. Subsequently, the effects of cigarette smoking on aneurysm formation, growth, and eventual rupture as well as the influence of cigarette smoking on the delayed development of cerebral vasospasm following aSAH will be examined.

Aneurysmal Subarachnoid Hemorrhage

Incidence

Aneurysmal SAH is a severe disease that affects patients early in life and at an earlier age than other types of stroke, such as ischemic stroke or intracerebral hemorrhage.[16,18] Approximately one million to twelve million people harbor intracranial aneurysms in the United States leading to the rupture of over 28,000 aneurysms annually.[16] Although they only represent 6-8% of all strokes, aSAH accounts for 25% of all cerebrovascular deaths. Mortality rates in the first month following aSAH have been reported to be as high as 50%[17]; among the remaining survivors, 50% are left severely disabled. The peak age for aSAH is 55-60 years with approximately 20% of cases occurring between the ages of 15-45.[19]

Clinical Presentation

Rupture of an intracranial aneurysm and the subsequent development of acute aSAH occurs suddenly, often without warning and requires immediate medical attention. The most common presentation of aSAH is an unusually severe headache, classically described as "the worst headache of my life". It can be accompanied by nausea and vomiting, syncope, neck pain (meningismus), photophobia, and focal neurological deficits such as a third nerve palsy causing diplopia and ptosis.[20]

Typically, the aneurysm is located on a major artery at the base of the brain and ruptures into the subarachnoid space, situated between the arachnoid and pia matter of the meninges covering the brain and spinal cord (Figure 1).

Patients are evaluated clinically using a grading scale; the most commonly used grading scale is the Hunt and Hess (H&H) classification system[21]. The H&H system grades patients on a scale of 1 to 5 with a grade 1 patient having the least deficit (i.e. mild headache and/or nuchal rigidity) to a grade 5 patient having the most deficit (i.e. deep coma, decerebrate rigidity, moribund appearance). Mortality correlates well with Hunt and Hess grade. "Good-grade" patients (H&H Grade 1 and 2) have a reduced mortality rate of 20%[20] compared to that of "poor-grade" patients (H&H Grade 4 and 5) who have a mortality rate of approximately 70%.[22]

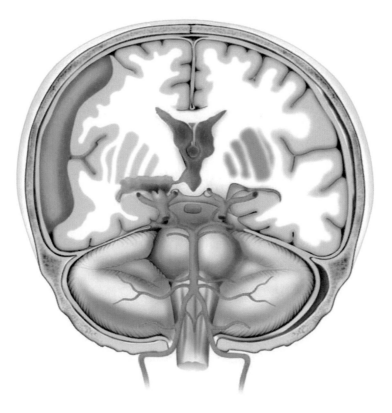

Figure 1. The rupture of an aneurysm at the base of the brain leading to a subarachnoid hemorrhage. Aneuysms commonly occur at vessel bifurcations.

Post-hemorrhage Complications

In patients surviving the initial hemorrhage, major secondary complications include aneurysm rebleeding[23] and cerebral vasospasm.[24] Cerebral vasospasm is a delayed, sustained contractile response of intracranial arteries causing decreased blood flow.[24] The reduction in cerebral blood flow from vessel narrowing can lead to cerebral ischemia and neurological deficit. These neurological deficits appear as alterations in consciousness, disorientation, or as focal neurological deficits such as new-onset weakness or speech difficulty. Approximately one in three patients with a ruptured aneurysm[25] will develop symptomatic cerebral vasospasm following aSAH and its occurrence is increased in patients who smoke cigarettes.[5,13]

Aneurysm Formation

Aneurysms are acquired degenerative lesions that develop as a result of hemodynamic stress and a variety of contributing factors. The development of multiple intracranial aneurysms is often due in part to a congenital or familial susceptibility.[26] Hypertension, atherosclerosis, female gender, age, cigarette smoking, alcohol consumption, asymmetry of the circle of Willis, and cerebral arteriovenous malformations have all been shown to increase the risk of aneurysm formation or SAH.[2,5,7,10] Although age, female gender, and vascular malformations may be risk factors for the formation of an aneurysm, the only seemingly indisputable modifiable risk factors for aneurysm formation and rupture are cigarette smoking, alcohol consumption, and to a lesser extent hypertension.[2,5,7,10]

There is significant evidence for the role of cigarette smoking in aneurysm formation[27], multiplicity[15], growth[27], and rupture.[7] While the mechanism by which smoking leads to intracranial aneurysm formation is not entirely understood, one hypothesis is that smoking promotes degradation of elastin in the walls of blood vessels. In addition, cigarette smoking has antiestrogenic properties and can hasten aneurysm formation in post-menopausal women. In a study by Juvela et al.[12], smoking status and female sex were highly correlated with the risk of formation of new aneurysms and the growth of known aneurysms. Female gender and smoking independently were associated with aneurysm growth of $\geq$1mm a year; however, growth of $\geq$3mm a year was associated only with smoking.[12,26] Furthermore, in patients predisposed to intracranial aneurysm formation, cigarette smoking and female gender cooperatively increase the risk of having multiple aneurysms.[26]

Role of Inflammation in Aneurysm Formation

There is evidence to suggest that the development and eventual rupture of cerebral aneurysms is the result of chronic inflammation. The pathophysiology of unruptured and ruptured aneurysms is different. The wall of ruptured aneurysms has been found to be more fragile with greater macrophage infiltration when compared to unruptured aneurysms.[28] Macrophages are phagocytic cells responsible for numerous homeostatic, immunological, and inflammatory processes. This macrophage infiltration results in loss of smooth muscle cells and in degradation of vessel wall matrix proteins. The immature macrophage is a monocyte. After migration into tissue, monocytes undergo further differentiation to become multifunctional tissue macrophages. Up-regulated expression of monocyte chemotactic protein-1 (MCP-1) in the aneurysm wall and presence of monocyte-like cells has been demonstrated.[29] Cigarette smoking increases the adherence and transendothelial migration of monocytes into the arterial wall.[30,31] Typically this interaction is studied in atherosclerosis where subendothelial monocytes are the likely precursors to foam cells found in atheromatous plaques.

Role of Alpha-1-Antitrypsin and Elastase in Aneurysm Formation

Elastase is secreted by macrophages in response to inflammation[32], and acts by cleaving elastin, type III collagen, and other connective tissue proteins found in the vessel wall. Cigarette smoking induces an inflammatory response and it is possible that there is an increased level of elastase due to this increased level of inflammation. In other areas of aneurysm pathogenesis, such as abdominal aortic aneurysm (AAA) formation, increased elastase activity has been linked to aneurysm formation and rupture.[33] In an experimental *in vivo* model of abdominal aortic aneurysm, when elastase was applied to an abdominal aorta vessel wall, the wall dilated and formed an aneurysm.[34] These results suggest that the presence of elastase within the aortic media leads to aneurysm formation.

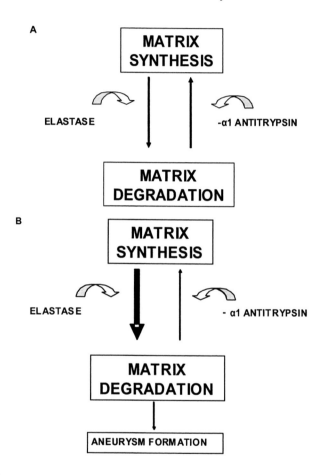

Figure 2 (A). The normal balance between Elastase and α-1 Antitrypsin in vessel wall (matrix) synthesis and matrix degradation. (B) α-1 Antitrypsin has decreased activity with cigarette smoking leading to increased activity of Elastase and vessel wall degradation. Aneurysm formation is theorized to develop, in part, due to this increase in elastase activity.

In patients with ruptured or unruptured intracranial aneurysms, the ratio of serum elastase to alpha-1-antitrypsin is significantly higher compared to controls.[35] Increased urinary excretion of elastin degradation products[36] and reduced activity of alpha-1-antitrypsin[37] are found in smokers. Alpha-1-antitrypsin (α-1 AT) inactivates the proteolytic enzyme elastase by binding to it and forming an inactive complex. Cigarette smoking decreases the affinity of α-1 AT for elastase 2000-fold.[38-41] Furthermore, patients who actively smoke at the time of aneurysm rupture have reduced alpha-1- antitrypsin levels whereas control subjects and patients with unruptured aneurysms do not.[37] Thus, decreased activity of α-1 AT allows elastase to go unchecked and elastin degradation in the vessel wall is increased (Figure 2). Smoking promotes the degradation of elastin in the wall of the vessel making the wall susceptible to dilation in areas of high blood pressure or turbulence, such as at vessel bifurcations.

Role of Hormonal Factors in Aneurysm Formation

As previously mentioned, smoking status and female gender are highly correlated with the risk of formation of new aneurysms and to the growth of known aneurysms.[12,26] The pathogenesis of aneurysm formation in women is due in part to hormonal factors.[42] It has been postulated that estrogen has an inhibitory effect on aneurysm formation and a female preponderance for SAH is evident after the fourth decade. The collagen content of cerebral arteries is thought to diminish after menopause and thus, the vessel is predisposed to the formation of an aneurysm.[43] Cigarette smoking has antiestrogenic properties and can hasten aneurysm formation in post-menopausal women. A weakened arterial wall, whether due to elastin degradation or decreased estrogen, is capable of forming an aneurysm under certain conditions such as elevated blood pressure or in areas of maximal turbulence.[26]

Outcome after Aneurysm Rupture

Although smoking has been associated with the increased formation, growth, multiplicity, and rupture of aneurysms it has not been correlated with higher mortality rates following aSAH.[12,44,45,46] Longstreth et al.[45] conducted a study looking at 30-day survival following aSAH and found that active smoking status before SAH had no significant effect on mortality. Other studies have also shown a nonsignificant association between active smoking status or the number of cigarettes smoked per day and mortality or poor outcome.[44,46] Juvela et al.[12] showed a significant association between the rupture of an aneurysm and cigarette smoking, but smoking did not affect mortality after the aneurysm had ruptured (45% compared with 43%). This study consisted of 141 patients and had an average follow-up period of 18.1 years. The apparent lack of an association between SAH-related mortality and cigarette smoking is perplexing as cigarette smoking before SAH has been shown to increase the risk for symptomatic vasospasm[5], a major contributor to morbidity and mortality following SAH. The pathophysiology of vasospasm is discussed below.

Cerebral Vasospasm after Subarachnoid Hemorrhage

The presence of subarachnoid blood following an aSAH is sufficient to produce severe constriction of the cerebral arteries. This process is known as delayed cerebral vasospasm (CVS) and classically occurs 4 to 10 days after aneurysm rupture. Vasospasm following aSAH is a major cause of morbidity and mortality.[47] In the first two weeks following aSAH, CVS can increase the mortality 1.5 to 3-fold.[48]

The reduction in cerebral blood flow from vessel narrowing in CVS leads to delayed ischemic neurological deficits. These neurological deficits can appear as alterations in consciousness, disorientation, or as focal neurological deficits such as new onset weakness or speech difficulty. However, only 30% of patients with CVS becomes clinically symptomatic.[47] In one series, of the approximately 67%[49] of patients who developed angiographic vasospasm, only half developed a delayed neurological deficit. Predicting the neurological decline of a patient with CVS can be difficult and early detection is essential to ensure rapid treatment before ischemic damage occurs.

The treatment for vasospasm aims to prevent or reverse this pathological arterial narrowing and thus, prevent cerebral ischemia. Nimodipine and intra-arterial verapamil, both calcium channel blockers, and hypertensive hypervolemic hemodilutional therapy (Triple H therapy) are used for this purpose. For those patients refractory to medical therapy, mechanical dilation of narrowed intracranial vessels is accomplished by transluminal angioplasty.[25]

Smoking and Cerebral Vasospasm

In a study conducted by Weir et al. of nearly 3500 patients from North America and Europe, smokers had increased odds of developing angiographic vasospasm compared to non smokers.[5] A smaller study by Lasner et al.[13] also demonstrated an increased risk between symptomatic vasospasm and cigarette smoking. Thus, the arteriopathy that leads to the increased formation and rupture of intracranial aneurysms in cigarette smokers also extends to impaired vascular reactivity.

Further, smoking has been associated with vasospasm in a variety of other organ systems. In the development of coronary arterial vasospasm, cigarette smoking has been identified as the most important risk factor.[50-52] Epidemiological studies have indicated that the risk in developing cigarette smoking-related cardiovascular disease was related to the nicotine content of the cigarette.[53,54,55] Therefore, the deleterious effect of nicotine on the vasculature has been the primary focus of research related to pathological role of cigarette smoking and cardiovascular disease. Experimental evidence has shown the ability of nicotine to either cause direct injury to the blood vessel wall [56-58] or modulate the synthesis of vasoactive agents capable of promoting vasospasm.[59,60]

Pathophysiology of Cerebral Vasospasm

Several factors are likely to be involved in the pathophysiology of CVS, although the primary pathogenic mechanisms have yet to be completely elucidated (*Figure 3*). The presence of blood in the subarachnoid space creates an environment conducive to vasospasm. The amount of subarachnoid blood within the basal cisterns detected on an early post-hemorrhage head computerized tomography (CT) scan (i.e within 48 hours) is the main predictor for the occurrence of CVS following aneurysmal rupture.[61]

Oxyhemoglobin (OxyHb), a breakdown product of the blood, most likely serves as the initiating factor for arterial wall contraction. OxyHb acts by either a direct effect on the vascular smooth muscle, or indirectly by causing the release of vasoactive substances such as endothelin-1 (ET-1) and by the production of free radicals.[62] Erythrocyte hemolysis begins immediately after SAH and continues until all the erythrocytes are phagocytosed or lysed, releasing a large amount of hemoglobin into the cerebral spinal fluid in the first couple of days following the bleed. OxyHb is released as erythrocytes in the blood clot lyse and release their contents into the subarachnoid space.

Cerebral arteries slowly develop a long-lasting contraction after exposure to hemoglobin *in vitro*[63] and cerebral arteries have been found to be more responsive to the OxyHb form of hemoglobin than systemic arteries.[64] Further, OxyHb stimulates the release of a potent vasoconstrictor, ET-1, from vascular endothelial cells and also stimulates the release of vasoconstricting prostaglandins such as prostaglandin F2-α.[65] An imbalance between vasoconstrictors like endothelin-1 (ET-1) and certain prostaglandins, and vasodilators such as nitric oxide and prostacyclin leads to the development of vasospasm.

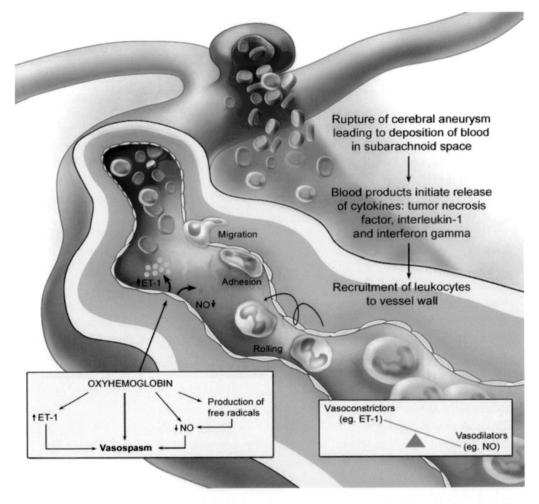

Figure 3. The role of inflammation, decreased nitric oxide (NO), and increased levels of endothelin-1 (ET-1) in the development of delayed vasospasm following aneurysmal subarachnoid hemorrhage. Inflammation is considered to play a role in the development of vasospasm in part due to the increased transmigration of inflammatory cells into the vessel wall. Nitric oxide, a vasodilatory agent, is decreased following aneurysmal subarachnoid hemorrhage (aSAH) due to scavenging by blood breakdown products that arise from the SAH blood clot. Levels of ET-1 are elevated following aSAH.

Endothelin-1

Role of Endothelin-1 in Subarachnoid Hemorrhage

ET-1 is one of three distinct isoforms (ET-1, ET-2, and ET-3) of endothelin and has a more marked constrictive effect on cerebral arteries than do the other two isoforms.[66] The isoforms of endothelin are synthesized by endothelium and other tissues. Endothelin-1 and -3 are found in brain and endothelial cells and they act on at least two receptor types, ET_A and ET_B. ET_A receptors are found mainly on vascular smooth muscle cells and help mediate vasoconstriction.[65] ET_B receptors are found on both vascular smooth muscle cells and on endothelial cells. ET_B receptors on vascular smooth muscle cells mediate vasoconstriction. ET_B receptors on endothelial cells stimulate the release of nitric oxide and mediate vasodilitation. Increased concentrations of ET-1 found in the cerebral spinal fluid after SAH[67,68] has been shown to correlate with delayed cerebral ischemia and vasospasm after SAH.[69] Furthermore, studies have demonstrated that ET receptor antagonists prevent or decrease experimental vasospasm.[70,71]

However, not all studies have demonstrated elevated endothelin levels in the CSF or plasma after SAH, and the effect of ET receptor antagonists on post-SAH cerebral vasospasm is not entirely clear.[69] Although endothelin may not be the main mediator of vasospasm, the imbalance that occurs between vasodilatory and vasoconstricting substances after SAH allows endothelin-induced vasoconstriction to act unopposed. ET-1 production is normally inhibited by nitric oxide[72]; after SAH, nitric oxide is decreased and the effects of endothelin are no longer opposed.

Endothelin-1 and Cigarette Smoking

ET-1 concentrations are acutely elevated after smoking a cigarette.[73,74] In a study conducted by Haak et al.[73], ET-1, corticotropin, cortisol levels, heart rate, and blood pressure were determined before and 1, 3, 5, 10, 20, and 30 minutes after smoking. Smoking a high-tar cigarette resulted in a significant increase in ET-1 levels within 10 minutes, followed by an increase in corticotropin levels within 20 minutes after smoking. Increases in heart rate and systolic blood pressure were likewise higher. Acute cigarette exposure has been shown to increase the expression of ET-1 messenger RNA (mRNA) in heart and lung tissues, but with chronic cigarette exposure, the effect of smoking on ET-1 mRNA in cardiovascular tissues became insignificant.[75]

Basal levels of ET-1 are elevated in smokers compared to non-smokers.[76] Studies have found that plasma ET-1 levels are elevated in both light (1 to 10 cigarettes/day) and heavy (10 to 40 cigarettes/day) smokers in a dose-dependent fashion.[73,77] Thus, whether the increase in ET-1 production in response to active smoking is a transient phenomenon and restricted only to the acute phase of smoking or whether it increases the basal levels of ET-1 in chronic smokers remains unclear. However, it is an interesting question to consider as ET-1 has been implicated as a mediator of both coronary artery spasm and CVS after SAH.[78-80]

Nitric Oxide

Role of Nitric Oxide in Vasospasm

Whereas ET-1 is vasoconstrictive and mitogenic in its effects on the underlying vascular smooth muscle, nitric oxide (NO) is vasodilatory and antiproliferative. Nitric oxide acts by binding to soluble guanylate cyclase in vascular smooth muscle which catalyzes the conversion of guanosine triphosphate to cyclic guanosine monophosphate (cGMP). Relaxation of vascular smooth muscle and thus vasodilation occurs when cGMP levels increase. Further, increased cGMP levels inhibit vascular smooth muscle cell proliferation and adhesion of platelets and leukocytes to the vessel wall.[81] Therefore, NO plays an important role in the interaction between the endothelium and blood. Decreased NO activity may predispose patients to hypertension, thrombosis, and vasospasm.[82]

Nitric oxide is produced normally by the endothelium from L-arginine by nitric oxide synthase (NOS). Endothelium-dependent impairment of vasodilatation has been shown to be due to a decrease in NO production by endothelial NO synthase (eNOS).[83,84] The eNOS protein is confined primarily to the endothelium and platelets. Decreased immunoreactivity of NOS in the adventitia of vasospastic blood vessels in a primate model of SAH has been shown.[85] This decreased activity of NOS leads to the decreased production of NO. Inflammatory cells infiltrating the periarterial space after SAH release free radicals capable of consuming NO.[86] Therefore, reduction in NO levels after SAH could be due to scavenging of NO by hemoglobin or consumption of NO by free radicals formed from hemoglobin oxidation.

Nitric Oxide and Cigarette Smoking

Smoking interferes in the synthesis of NO by decreasing the supply of L-arginine[87] and by producing superoxides that are capable of reacting with NO to form peroxynitrite. Peroxynitrite is a strong oxidant that is capable of causing significant damage to cell membranes. Also, cigarette smoking can directly suppress eNOS thereby further decreasing NO levels.[88,89] The mechanisms by which cigarette smoke may reduce the expression of eNOS are uncertain. Tobacco smoke contains a high concentration of NO and NO itself exerts a negative feedback on its synthesis.[90,91] Downregulation of NOS in cells of the respiratory tract by this mechanism has been suggested to explain the reduced concentration of exhaled NO in smokers.[92]

Endothelial Dysfunction

Endothelial dysfunction, manifested as impaired, endothelium-dependent, NO-mediated vasodilation, is associated with both passive[93] and active[94] cigarette smoking. Studies have shown that smoking produces endothelial dysfunction,[95, 96] but the substance of cigarette smoke responsible for the pathogenesis of vascular disease is not clear. Nicotine may play a role in the cardiovascular effects of smoking because it impairs endothelium-dependent vasodilatation[97] and regulates the production of growth factors by endothelial cells.[98]

A study by Murohara et al.[99] demonstrated that cigarette smoke extract impairs endothelium-dependent dilation of porcine coronary arteries by superoxide anion–mediated degradation of endothelium derived relaxing factor (EDRF) (i.e. nitric oxide).[99] Increased production of superoxide anions, which rapidly inactivates EDRF,[100] is a characteristic feature of experimental models of atherosclerosis[101,102] and importantly contributes to the impairment of endothelium-dependent vascular relaxation.[103] Smokers appear to be particularly susceptible to the activity of oxygen free radicals, and plasma indexes of lipid peroxidation are increased in smokers.[104] Thus, free radicals generated by long-term smoking may deleteriously affect coronary endothelial vasodilator function in addition to the atherosclerotic plaque load itself and may be responsible for the decreased flow-dependent dilation observed in smokers.

Conclusion

Active smoking status has been clearly shown to increase the formation and rupture of cerebral aneurysms with 40% of aSAH being attributed to current smoking.[3,12] Structural damage to the arterial wall leads to the development of aneurysms and their rupture and there is evidence for the role of smoking in aneurysm formation[27], growth[27], multiplicity[15], and rupture.[7] Although the mechanisms of aneurysm formation are not known, an increase in elastin degradation and suppression of estrogen by cigarette smoking likely contribute to the formation and growth of aneurysms. As cigarette smoking is a significant risk factor for the development of aneurysmal subarachnoid hemorrhage, it is important to counsel patients towards smoking cessation. Even with the advancement in surgical and medical care for aneurysms, prevention of aneurysmal subarachnoid hemorrhage is clearly favorable to treatment after an aneurysm has ruptured.

An association between cigarette smoking and cerebral vasospasm as well as vasospasm in other systems has been demonstrated. Following aSAH, vasospasm is one of the leading causes of morbidity and mortality as it causes delayed cerebral ischemia. An imbalance between vasoconstrictive agents and vasodilatory agents leads to the development of vasospasm and there is evidence that cigarette smoking may contribute to this imbalance. This is evidenced by both the acute and chronic elevations in the vasoconstrictor endothelin-1 and in the decline of the vasodilator nitric oxide seen in cigarette smokers. As cigarette smoking is one of the few modifiable risk factors for the development of a cerebral aneurysm and contributes to the morbidity associated with aneurysm rupture, clinicians should aggressively counsel patients towards smoking cessation.

References

[1]   Thun MJ AL, Henley SJ. . Smoking vs. other risk factors as the cause of smoking-attributable deaths: Confounding in the courtroom. *JAMA* 2000;284:706-712.

[2]   Juvela S. Prevalence of risk factors in spontaneous intracerebral hemorrhage and aneurysmal subarachnoid hemorrhage. *Archives of Neurology* 1996;53(8):734-40.

[3]   Ruigrok YM BE, Rinkel GJ. Attributable risk of common and rare determinants of subarachnoid hemorrhage. *Stroke* 2001;32(5):1173-1175.

[4]   Teunissen LL RG, Algra A, van Gijn J. Risk factors for subarachnoid hemorrhage: a systematic review. *Stroke* 1996;27(3):544-9.

[5]   Weir BK KG, Kassell NR, Schultz JR, Truskowski LL, Sigrest A. Cigarette smoking as a cause of aneurysmal subarachnoid hemorrhage and risk for vasospasm: a report of the *Cooperative Aneurysm Study. Journal of Neurosurgery* 1998;89(3):405-11.

[6]   Juvela S. Cigarette Smoking and Death Following Subarachnoid Hemorrhage. *Journal of Neurosurgery* 2001;95:551-554.

[7]   Juvela S HM, Numminen H, Koskinen P. Cigarette smoking and alcohol consumption as risk factors for aneurysmal subarachnoid hemorrhage. *Stroke* 1993;24(5):639-46.

[8]   Anderson CS FV, Bennett D, Lin R-B, Hankey G, Jamrozik K, for the Australasian Cooperative Research on Subarachnoid, Group HSA. Active and Passive Smoking and the Risk of Subarachnoid Hemorrhage. An International Population-Based Case-Control Study. *Stroke* 2004;35:633-637.

[9]   Bonita R. Cigarette smoking, hypertension and the risk of subarachnoid hemorrhage: A population-based case-control study. *Stroke* 1986;17:831-835.

[10]   Longstreth WT NL, Koepsell TD, van Belle G. Cigarette smoking, alcohol use, and subarachnoid hemorrhage. *Stroke* 1992;23:1242-1249.

[11]   Kissela BM SL, Woo D, Khoury J, Carrozzella J, Pancioli A, Jauch E, Moomaw CJ, Shukla R, Gebel J, Fontaine R, Broderick J. Subarachnoid hemorrhage: a preventable disease with a heritable component. *Stroke* 2002;33:1321-1326.

[12]   Juvela S PM, Poussa K. Natural history of unruptured intracranial aneurysms: probability of and risk factors for aneurysm rupture. *Journal of Neurosurgery* 2000;93(3):379-87.

[13]   Lasner TM WR, Riina HA, King JT Jr, Zager EL, Raps EC, Flamm ES. Cigarette smoking-induced increase in the risk of symptomatic vasospasm after aneurysmal subarachnoid hemorrhage. *Journal of Neurosurgery* 1997;87(3):381-4.

[14]   Broderick JP VC, Brott TG, Kernan WN, Brass LM, Feldmann E, Morgenstern LB, Wilterdink JL, Horwitz RI for the Hemorrhagic Stroke Project Investigators. Major Risk Factors for Aneurysmal Subarachnoid Hemorrhage in the Young are Modifiable. *Stroke* 2003;34:1375-1381.

[15]   Juvela S. Risk factors for multiple intracranial aneurysms. Stroke 2000;31:392-397.

[16]   Broderick JP BT, Tomsick T, Miller R, Huster G. Intracerebral Hemorrhage more than twice as common as Subarachnoid Hemorrhage. *Journal of Neurosurgery* 1993;78(2):188-91.

[17]   Hop JW RG, Algra A, van Gijn J. Case-fatality rates and functional outcome after subarachnoid hemorrhage: a systematic review. *Stroke* 1997;28(3):660-664.

[18]   Adams HP BM, Biller J, et al. Nonhemorrhagic Cerebral Infarction in *Young Adults. Archives of Neurology* 1986;43:793-6.

[19]   Biller J TG, Kassell NF, Adams HP Jr., Beck DW, Boarini DJ. Spontaneous Subarachnoid Hemorrhage in Young Adults. *Neurosurgery* 1987;21(664-7).

[20]   Greenberg MS. Handbook of Neurosurgery. Fifth ed. New York, NY: Thieme Medical Publishers, 2001.

[21]   Hunt WE HR. Surgical Risk as Related to Time of Intervention in the Repair of Intracranial Aneurysms. *Journal of Neurosurgery* 1968;28:14-20.

[22]   Wilby MJ SM, Whitfield PC, Hutchinson PJ, Menon DK, Kirkpatrick PJ. Cost-Effective Outcome for Treating Poor-Grade Subarachnoid Hemorrhage. *Stroke* 2003;34:2508-2511.

[23]   Broderick JP BT, Duldner JE, Tomsick T, Leach A. Initial and recurrent bleeding are the major causes of death following subarachnoid hemorrhage. *Stroke* 1994;25(7): 1342-1347.

[24]   Findlay JM MR, Weir BK. Current concepts of pathophysiology and management of cerebral vasospasm following aneurysmal subarachnoid hemorrhage. *Cerebrovascular & Brain Metabolism Reviews* 1991;3(4):336-61.

[25]   Weir B ML. Cerebral Vasospasm. Clin. *Neurosurg.* 1993;40:40-55.

[26]   Qureshi AI SJ, Parekh PD, Sung G, Geocadin R, Bhardwaj A, Tamargo RJ, Ulatowski JA. Risk factors for multiple intracranial aneurysms. *Neurosurgery* 1998;43(1):22-26.

[27]   Juvela S PK, Porras M. Factors affecting formation and growth of intracranial aneurysms: a long-term follow-up study. *Stroke* 2001;32(2):485-91.

[28]   Kataoka K TM, Asai T, Kinoshita A, Ito M, Kuroda R. Structural Fragility and Inflammatory Response of Rupture Cerebral Aneurysms. A Comparative Study Between Rupture and Unruptured Cerebral Aneurysms. *Stroke* 1999;30:1396-1401.

[29]   Cao Y ZJ, Wang S, Zhong H, Wu B. Monocyte chemoattractant protein-1 mRNA in human intracranial aneurysm walls. Chung-Hua Yu Fang i Hsueh Tsa Chih *[Chinese Journal of Preventive Medicine]*. 2002;36(7):519-21.

[30]   Kalra VK YY, Deemer K, et al. Mechanism of cigarette smoke condensate induced adhesion of human monocytes to cultured endothelial cells. *Journal of Cell Physiology* 1994;160:154-162.

[31]   Shen Y RV, Sultana C, et al. Cigarette smoke condensate induced adhesion molecule expression and transendothelial migration of monocytes. *American Journal of Physiology* 1996;270:H1624-H1633.

[32]   Hubbard RC FG, Gadek J, Pacholok S, Humes J, Crystal RG. Neutrophil accumulation in the lung in alpha 1-antitrypsin deficiency. Spontaneous release of leukotriene B4 by alveolar macrophages. *Journal of Clinical Investigation* 1991;88(3):891-7.

[33]   Cohen JR MC, Margolis I, Chang J, Wise L. Altered aortic protease and antiprotease activity in patients with ruptured abdominal aortic aneurysms. *Surgery, Gynecology & Obstetrics* 1987;164(4):355-8.

[34]   Anidjar S SJ, Gentric D, Lagneau P, Camilleri JP, Michel JB. Elastase-induced experimental aneurysms in rats. *Circulation* 1990;82(3):973-81.

[35]   Baker CJ FA, Connolly ES Jr., Baker KZ, Solomon RA. Serum elastase and alpha-1-antitrypsin levels in patients with ruptured and unruptured cerebral aneurysms. *Neurosurgery* 1995;37(1):56-62.

[36]   Stone PJ GD, O'Connor GT, Ciccolella DE, Breuer R, Bryan-Rhadfi J, Shaw HA, Franzblau C, Snider GL. Elastin and collagen degradation products in urine of smokers with and without chronic obstructive pulmonary disease. *American Journal of Respiratory & Critical Care Medicine* 1995;151(4):952-9.

[37]   Gaetani P TF, Tancioni F, Klersy C, Forlino A, Baena RR. Activity of alpha 1-antitrypsin and cigarette smoking in subarachnoid haemorrhage from ruptured aneurysm. *Journal of the Neurological Sciences* 1996;141(1-2):33-8.

[38]   Carp H MF, Hoidal JR, Janoff A. Potential mechanism of emphysema: alpha 1-proteinase inhibitor recovered from lungs of cigarette smokers contains oxidized methionine and has decreased elastase inhibitory capacity. *Proceedings of the National Academy of Sciences of the United States of America* 1982;79(6):2041-5.

[39]   Beatty K BJ, Travis J. Kinetics of association of serine proteinases with native and oxidized alpha-1-proteinase inhibitor and alpha-1-antichymotrypsin. *Journal of Biological Chemistry* 1980;255(9):3931-4.

[40]   Nowak D RU. Nicotine inhibits alpha-1-proteinase inhibitor inactivation by oxidants derived from human polymorphonuclear leukocytes. *Experimental Pathology* 1990;38(4):249-55.

[41]   Evans M PW. Damage to human alpha-1-antiprotease inhibitor by aqueous cigarette tar extracts and the formation of methionine sulfoxide. *Chem Res Toxicol* 1992;5:654-660.

[42]   Mhurchu CN AC, Jamrozik K, Hankey G, Dunbabin D; Australasian Cooperative Research on Subarachnoid Hemorrhage Study (ACROSS) Group. Hormonal factors and risk of aneurysmal subarachnoid hemorrhage: an international population-based, case-control study. *Stroke* 2001;32(606-12):606-12.

[43]   Longstreth WT NL, Koepsell TD, van Belle G. Subarachnoid Hemorrhage and Hormonal Factors in Women. A Population-based Case-Control Study. *Annals of Internal Medicine* 1994;121(3):168-173.

[44]   Juvela S. Alcohol consumption as a risk factor for poor outcome after aneurysmal subarachnoid haemorrhage. *BMJ* 1992;304:1663-1667.

[45]   Longstreth WT Jr NL, Koepsell TD, et al. Clinical course of spontaneous subarachnoid hemorrhage: a population-based study in King County, Washington. *Neurology* 1993;43:712-718.

[46]   Morris KM SM, Foy PM. Smoking and subarachnoid haemorrhage: a case control study. *British Journal of Neurosurgery* 1992;6:429-432.

[47]   Kassell NF TJ, Haley EC Jr, Jane JA, Adams HP, Kongable GL. The International Cooperative Study on the Timing of Aneurysm Surgery. Part 1: Overall management results. *Journal of Neurosurgery* 1990;73(1):18-36.

[48]   Treggiari-Venzi M SP, Romand JA. Review of Medical Prevention of Vasospasm after Aneurysmal Subarachnoid Hemorrhage: A Problem of Neurointensive Care. *Neurosurgery* 2001;48:249-262.

[49]   Weir B GM, Hansen J, et al. Time course of vasospasm in man. *Journal of Neurosurgery* 1978;48:173-178.

[50]   Caralis DG DU, Kern MJ, Cohen JD. Smoking is a risk factor for coronary spasm in young women. *Circulation* 1992;85:905-909.

[51]   Nobuyoshi M AM, Nosaka H, Kimura T, Yokoi H, Hamasaki N, Shindo T, Kimura K, Nakamura T, Nakagawa Y. Statistical analysis of clinical risk factors for coronary artery spasm: identification of the most important determinant. *American Heart Journal* 1992;124(1):32-8.

[52]   Sugiishi M TF. Cigarette smoking is a major risk factor for coronary spasm. 1993 1993;87(1):76-9.

[53]   Aronow WS aSA. The effect of low-nicotine cigarettes on angina pectoris. *Annals of Internal Medicine* 1969;71:599-601.

[54]   Auerback O CH, Garfinkle L, and Hammond EC. Cigarette Smoking and coronary artery disease. *Chest* 1976;70:697-705.

[55]   Hill P aWE. Smoking and cardiovascular disease: effect of nicotine on the serum epinephrine and corticoids. *American Heart Journal* 1974;87:491-496.

[56]   Booyse FM OG, and Quarfoot AJ. Effects of Chronic Oral Consumption of Nicotine on the Rabbit Aortic Endothelium. *American Journal of Pathology* 1981;102:229-238.

[57] Hladove CJ. Endothelial injury by nicotine and its prevention. *Experientia* 1978;35:1585-1586.

[58] Zimmerman M aMJ. The effect of nicotine on aortic endothelium: a quantitative ultrastructure study. *Atherosclerosis* 1987;63:33-41.

[59] Armitage AK. Effects of nicotine and tobacco smoke on blood pressure and release of catecholamines from the adrenal glands. *British Journal of Pharmacology* 1965;25: 512-526.

[60] Seidler FJ aST. Effects of chronic nicotine administration on the denervated rat adrenal medulla. *British Journal of Pharmacology* 1976;56:201-208.

[61] Fisher CM KJ, Davis JM. Relation of cerebral vasospasm to subarachnoid hemorrhage visualized by computerized tomographic scanning. *Neurosurgery* 1980;6(1):1-9.

[62] Macdonald RL WB. A review of hemoglobin and the pathogenesis of cerebral vasospasm. *Stroke* 1991;22:971-982.

[63] Ohta T KH, Yoshikawa Y, Shimizu K, Funatsu N, Yamamoto M, and Toda N. *Cerebral vasospasm and hemoglobins: Clinical and experimental studies*. Baltimore: Williams & Wilkins, 1980.

[64] Toda N SK, and Ohta, T. Mechanism of cerebral arterial contraction induces by blood constituents. *Journal of Neurosurgery* 1980;53:312-322.

[65] Weir B SM, and Macdonald R. Etiology of cerebral vasospasm. *Acta Neurochirgica* 1999;72:27-42.

[66] Zimmermann M SV. Endothelin and Subarachnoid Hemorrhage: *An Overview*. *Neurosurgery* 1998;43(4):863-875.

[67] Seifert V LB, Zimmermann M, Roux S, Stolke D. Endothelin concentration in patients with aneurysmal subarachnoid hemorrhage. Correlation with cerebral vasospasm, delayed ischemic neurological deficits, and volume of hematoma. *Journal of Neurosurgery* 1995;82:55-62.

[68] Suzuki R MH, Hirata Y, Marumo F, Isotani E, Hirakawa K. The role of endothelin-1 in the origin of cerebral vasospasm in patients with aneurysmal subarachnoid hemorrhage. *Journal of Neurosurgery* 1992;77:96-100.

[69] Juvela S. Plasma endothelin concentrations after aneurysmal subarachnoid hemorrhage. *Journal of Neurosurgery* 2000;92:390-400.

[70] Macdonald RL JL, Lin G, Marton LS, Hallak H, Marcoux F, Kowalczuk A. Prevention of vasospasm after subarachnoid hemorrhage in dogs by continuous intravenous infusion of PD 156707. *Neurol Med Chir* [Suppl] 1998;38:138-145.

[71] Roux S LB, Gray GA, Sprecher U, Clozel M, Clozel JP. The role of endothelin in experimental cerebral vasospasm. *Neurosurgery* 1995;37:78-86.

[72] Pluta RM BR, Afshar JK, Clouse K, Bacic M, Ehrenreich H, Oldfield EH. Source and cause of endothelin-1 release into cerebrospinal fluid after subarachnoid hemorrhage. *Journal of Neurosurgery* 1997;87:287-294.

[73] Haak T JE, Raab C, et al. Elevated endothelin-1 levels after cigarette smoking. *Metabolism* 1994;43:267-269.

[74] Lee W.O. WSM. Production of endothelin by cultured human endothelial cells following exposure to nicotine or caffeine. *Metabolism* 1999;48:845-848.

[75] Adachi C NM, Ishihara Y, et al. Effects of acute and chronic cigarette smoking on the expression of endothelin-1 mRNA of the cardiovascular tissues in rats. *Journal of Cardiovascular Pharmacology* 2000;36:S198-200.

[76] Hirai Y AH, Fujiura Y, Hiratsuka A, Enomoto M, Imaizumi T,. Plasma endothelin-1 level is related to renal function and smoking status but not to blood pressure: an epidemiological study. *Journal of Hypertension* 2004;22(4):713-718.

[77] Yildiz L AF, Kaynar H, Bakan N. Increased plasma endothelin-1 in heavy and light smokers. *Clinical Chemistry* 1996;42:483-484.

[78] Artigou JY SJ, Carayon A, et al. Variations in plasma endothelin concentration during coronary spasm. *European Heart Journal* 1993;14:780-784.

[79] Caner HH KA, Arthur A, et. al. Systemic administration of an inhibitor of endothelin-converting enzyme for attenuation of cerebral vasospasm following experimental subarachnoid hemorrhage. *Journal of Neurosurgery* 1996;85:917-922.

[80] Onoda K OS, Ogihara K, et al. Inhibition of vascular contraction by intracisternal administration of preproendothelin-1 mRNA antisense oligoDNA in a rat experimental vasospasm model. *Journal of Neurosurgery* 1996;85:846-852.

[81] Vanhoutte PM BC, and Mobouli JV. Endothelium-derived relaxing factors and converting enzyme inhibition. *American Journal of Cardiology* 1005;76:3E-12E.

[82] Oemar BS TM, Godoy N, Brovkovich V, Malinski T, Luscher TF. Reduced endothelial nitric oxide synthase expression and production in human atherosclerosis. *Circulation* 1998;97(25):2494-8.

[83] Yamamoto S NS, Yokoyama T, Tyu H, Uemura K,. Subarachnoid hemorrhage impairs cerebral blood flow response to nitric oxide but not to cyclic GMP in large cerebral arteries. *Brain Research* 1997;757:1-9.

[84] Hino A TY, Weir B, Takeda J, Yano H, Bell GI, Macdonald RL. Changes in endothelial nitric oxide synthase mRNA during vasospasm after subarachnoid hemorrhage in monkeys. *Neurosurgery* 1996;39:562-568.

[85] Pluta RM TB, Dawson TM, Snyder SH, Boock RJ, Oldfield EH. Loss of nitric oxide synthase immunoreactivity in cerebral vasospasm. *Journal of Neurosurgery* 1996;84:648-654.

[86] Hatake K WI, Kakishita E, Hishida S. Impairment of endothelium-dependent relaxation in human basilar artery after subarachnoid hemorrhage. *Stroke* 1992;23:1111-1117.

[87] Hutchison SJ RM, Sudhir K, Sievers RE, Zhu BQ, Sun YP, Chou TM, Deedwania PC, Chatterjee K, Glantz SA, Parmley WW. Chronic dietary L-arginine prevents endothelial dysfunction secondary to environmental tobacco smoke in normocholesterolemic rabbits. *Hypertension* 1997;29(5):1186-91.

[88] Higman DJ SA, Buttery L, Hicks RC, Springall DR, Greenhalgh RM, Powell JT. Smoking impairs the activity of endothelial nitric oxide synthase in saphenous vein. Arteriosclerosis, *Thrombosis & Vascular Biology* 1996;16(4):546-52.

[89] Barua RS AJ, Reynolds LJ, DeVoe MC, Zervas JG, Dhanonjoy CS. Heavy and Light Cigarette Smokers Have Similar Dysfunction of Endothelial Vasoregulatory Activity An In Vivo and In Vitro Correlation. *Journal of the American College of Cardiology* 2002;39(11):1758-1763.

[90] Buga GM GJ, Rogers NE, Ignarro LJ. Negative feedback regulation of endothelial cell function by nitric oxide. *Circulation Research* 1993;73:808-812.

[91] Assreuy J CF, Liew FY, Moncada S. Feedback inhibition of nitric oxide synthase activity by nitric oxide. *British Journal of Pharmacology* 1993;108:833-837.

[92] Kharitonov SA RR, Yates D, Keatings V, Barnes PJ. Acute and chronic effects of cigarette smoking on exhaled nitric oxide. *American Journal of Respiratory & Critical Care Medicine* 1995;152:609-612.

[93] Celermajer DS AM, Clarkson P, Robinson J, McCredie R, Donald A, Deanfield JE. Passive smoking and impaired endothelium dependent arterial dilatation in healthy young adults. *New England Journal of Medicine* 1996;334:150-154.

[94] Celermajer DS SK, Georgakopoulos D, Bull C, Thomas O, et al. Cigarette smoking is associated with dose-related and potentially reversible impairment of endothelium-dependent dilation in healthy young adults. *Circulation* 1993;88:2149-55.

[95] Moreno H. Jr. CS, Urae A., Tangphao O., Abiose A.K., Hoffman B.B., Blaschke T.F.,. Endothelial dysfunction in human hand veins is rapidly reversible after smoking cessation. *American Journal of Physiology* 1998;275:H1040-H1045.

[96] Chalon S. MHJ, Hoffman B.B., Blaschke T.F.,. Angiotensin-converting enzyme inhibition improves venous endothelial dysfunction in chronic smokers. *Clin. Pharmacol. Ther.* 1999;65:295-303.

[97] Mayhan W.G. PKP. Effect of nicotine on endothelium-dependent arteriolar dilatation in vivo. *American Journal of Physiology* 1997;272:H2337-H2342.

[98] Cucina A. CV, Sapienza P., Borrelli V., Lucarelli M., Scarpa S., Strom R., Santoro-D'Angelo L., Cavallaro A.,. Nicotine regulates basic fibroblast growth factor and transforming growth factor beta-1 production in endothelial cells. Biochem. *Biophys. Research Commun.* 1999;257:306-312.

[99] Murohara T KK, Ohgushi M, Sugiyama S, Yasue H,. Cigarette smoke extract contracts isolated porcine coronary arteries by superoxide anion-mediated degradation of EDRF. *American Journal of Physiology* 1994;266:H874-H880.

[100] Gryglewski RJ PR, Moncada S. Superoxide anion is involved in the breakdown of endothelium-derived vascular relaxing factor. *Nature* 1986;320:454-455.

[101] Minor RL MP, Guerra R, Bates JN, Harrison DG. Diet-induced atherosclerosis increases the release of nitrogen oxides from rabbit aorta. *Journal of Clinical Investigation* 1990;86:2109-2116.

[102] Ohara Y PT, Harrison DG. Hypercholesterolemia increases endothelial superoxide anion production. *Journal of Clinical Investigation* 1993;91:2546-2551.

[103] Mügge A EJ, Peterson TE, Hofmeyer TG, Heistad DD, Harrison DG. Chronic treatment with polyethylene-glycolated superoxide dismutase partially restores endothelium-dependent vascular relaxations in cholesterol-fed rabbits. *Circulation Research* 1991;69:1293-1300.

[104] Duthie GG WK. Smoking, antioxidants, essential fatty acids and coronary heart disease. *Biochem Soc Trans* 1990;18:1051-1054.

In: Trends in Smoking and Health Research
Editors: J. H. Owing, pp. 203-215

ISBN: 1-59454-391-7
© 2005 Nova Science Publishers, Inc.

Chapter X

Cigarette Smoking, Second-Hand-Smoke, and Adolescent Skeletal Health

Afrooz Afghani[1]* and C. Anderson Johnson[2]
[1]College of Health Sciences, Touro University International, Cypress, CA; [2]Department
of Preventive Medicine, Keck School of Medicine, University of Southern California,
Los Angeles, CA

Abstract

Introduction/Purpose

Although the relationship between cigarette smoking and bone loss during adulthood is well established, the effect of smoking and second-hand-smoke on bone mass in adolescents is unknown. Because of the high prevalence of smoking among the adults living in China and the adolescent period being a critical time for both smoking initiation and bone accretion, the objective of this study was to address the role of smoking and second-hand-smoke on adolescent bone mass in China.

Methods

We measured cortical (forearm) and trabecular (os calcis) bone mineral content (BMC) and density (BMD) using dual energy x-ray absorptiometry (DXA) in 466 girls and boys (ages 12-16 yr).

* Afrooz Afghani, PhD, MPH; Associate Professor; College of Health Sciences; Touro University International; 5665 Plaza Drive, Third Floor; Cypress, CA 90630; E-mail address: aafghani@tourou.edu; Phone: (714)226-9840 ext. 2009; Fax: (714)226-9844

Results

In 166 girls, forearm BMC was best predicted by BMI (24%), age (5%), and menarche (2%) for a combined variance of 31%, while 8% of the variance in os calcis BMC was predicted by BMI alone with no contribution by age or menarche. In 300 boys, a total of 24% of the variance in forearm BMC was explained by BMI (18%) and age (6%); os calcis BMC was only predicted by BMI (21%). The addition of cigarette smoking and second-hand-smoke into the multiple linear regression models did not make significant contributions to the variances in either girls or boys.

Conclusion

The reasons may have been due to the low levels and duration of tobacco use and exposure among the adolescents we studied. Selecting an older sample of adolescents who smoke more frequently and for a long duration may have uncovered a different relationship. Nevertheless, this was the first study that investigated the role of smoking and second-hand-smoke on bone mass during adolescence.

Introduction

Numerous studies [5,21,37,40] indicate that over 90% of peak bone mass is achieved by about 15 to 18 years of age. In the United States and other Western countries [9,32,39] as well as in China [10,28,46], the first upswing in tobacco use occurs in the late pre-adolescent and early adolescent years (ages 10-13). The influence of smoking and second-hand-smoke on bone mass has not been previously investigated in children or adolescents.

In adults, smoking has been found to be associated with an increased risk for bone fractures and osteoporosis. Smoking has been shown to increase the risk for hip fractures in women by about 1.2 to 1.5 [15-17], and vertebral fractures in men by about 2.3 [34]. Krall and Dawson-Hughes [25] have found bone mineral density of the radius of postmenopausal women to be inversely related to pack-years of smoking (r= -0.18, p=0.05, n=125). The rates of bone change at the radius were significantly different between smokers (-0.914 ± 2.6 percent/year, n=34) and nonsmokers (0.004 ± 2.6 percent/year, n=278). The same trend was seen at the os calcis, the femoral neck, and the spine. Hopper and Seeman [18] studied the bone density of female twins (ages 27 to 73) discordant for tobacco use. They found that for every 10 pack-years of smoking, the bone density of the twin who smoked more heavily was 2.0% lower at the lumbar spine (p=0.01), 0.9% lower at the femoral neck (p=0.25), and 1.4% lower at the femoral shaft (p=0.04). These investigators conclude that women who smoke one pack of cigarettes each day throughout adulthood will, by the time of menopause, have an average deficit of 5 to 10 percent in bone density, which is adequate to increase the risk for fractures. In men, Valimaki et al. [42] showed inverse correlations between bone mineral density of the lumbar spine and self-reported smoking (r range of -0.18 to -0.46) when they controlled for weight. Inverse relationships also emerged between bone mineral density of the hip and smoking prevalence (r range of -0.10 to -0.63).

The mechanisms by which tobacco effects bone mass in adults are not well elucidated. However, epidemiological data suggest that women who smoke cigarettes behave physiologically as though they are relatively estrogen-deficient and that cigarette smoking affects the absorption, distribution, or metabolism of estrogen [19-20,30-31]. Studies by Barbieri and colleagues [2] suggest that nicotine, cotinine, and anabasine inhibit the conversion of androstenedione to estrogen in a dose-dependent fashion. When supraphysiological doses of androstenedione were applied to human choriocarcinoma cells and placental microsomes, the inhibition of aromatase was blocked by these tobacco products. These investigators conclude that the mechanisms underlying the anti-estrogenic role of tobacco probably involve inhibition of the aromatase enzyme system. In men who smoke, alterations in hormone levels have also been reported [35]. A number of studies [4,13,23-24] have found that male smokers have higher levels of testosterone and adrenal androgen and possibly higher levels of estradiol compared to non-smokers. The data in men reinforces the fact that constituents of cigarette smoke can effect the production and metabolism of steroid hormones, which will perhaps influence bone mass attainment during adolescence or bone loss during adulthood.

The proven adverse influence of tobacco exposure on adult bone density, the high prevalence of smoking among adult males [46] living in China, the early onset of smoking among Chinese youth [10,41], and the adolescent period being a critical time for both bone accretion and smoking initiation, raised questions about the potential impact of cigarette smoke on bone development in Chinese youth. In this chapter, we examined the hypothesis that cigarette smoking and second-hand-smoke are inversely related to cortical (forearm) and trabecular (os calcis) bone mass in Chinese adolescents.

Materials and Methods

Study Cohort/Sampling Procedure/Subject Description

The Wuhan metropolitan area is a city of 7.25-8.25 million people consisting of 3 geographic regions: Hankou (a commercial region), Hanyang (an industrial region), and Wuchang (a cultural region), as well as 4 rural counties. The urban regions are divided further into 7 administrative districts. Each urban district and rural county serves as an independent administrative unit directly under the city administration and is responsible for schools within its administrative boundary.

One school was randomly selected (by a coin toss) from each of the 7 urban districts and 4 rural counties in the Wuhan area. An additional school in each district/county was randomly selected among all schools in the same district/county that were similar to the first selected school in terms of school size, teacher/student ratio, type of school (best-rated, intermediate, low-rated), and functional zone. A total of 22 schools were randomly selected. Four classes in each of the selected schools were randomly chosen for survey data collection.

A total of 4703 students in 22 randomly selected middle schools completed a paper-and-pencil questionnaire in their classrooms. Each student was given a 10-digit ID code. Based on the prevalence rates of smoking in this cohort and the results of a power analysis, 696 students from 15 schools were identified and invited to participate in this study. All adolescents were between 10 and 16 years of age. Participation required signed parental consent as well as signed child assent. Consent/assent forms and questionnaires were first compiled in English and then translated to the Chinese language by professional translators at USC. These forms were then translated back into English for the purpose of validating the translation. Consent/assent forms and research protocols were approved by the USC and Wuhan Institutional Review Boards. Additionally, subjects suffering from any conditions known to influence bone, including diabetes, pregnancy, polycystic ovarian disease, hyper- and hypo-thyroidism, hypercortisolism, amenorrhea and any other hormonal or metabolic disorders were excluded from this study.

A total of 206 subjects (30%) refused to participate in this study. Another 16 were lost due to electrical failure on the day of bone scans, five had transferred to another school, and three were absent on the day of data collection. Table 1 shows the breakdown of participants based on gender and smoking status.

Table 1. Subject Characteristics

	Non Smokers	Passive Smokers	Active Smokers
Girls			
N	59	57	50
Age (years)	14.1 ± 0.37	14.3 ± 0.37	14.3 ± 0.62
Weight (kg)	46.5 ± 7.00	49.5 ± 7.36[*]	48.9 ± 5.96
Height (cm)	156.8 ± 5.66	158.2 ± 5.42	156.2 ± 4.85
BMI (kg/m^2)	18.9 ± 2.65	19.7 ± 2.41	20.0 ± 2.24
Pubertal (%)	83	89	98[**]
Forearm BMC (grams)	2.77 ± 0.46	3.03 ± 0.57[*]	3.03 ± 0.43[*]
Forearm BMD (g/cm^2)	0.33 ± 0.05	0.35 ± 0.05[***]	0.34 ± 0.04
Os Calcis BMC (grams)	1.63 ± 0.30	1.69 ± 0.32	1.76 ± 0.35
Os Calcis BMD (g/cm^2)	0.47 ± 0.06	0.47 ± 0.06	0.48 ± 0.06
Boys			
N	87	108	105
Age (years)	14.5 ± 0.57	14.3 ± 0.42[***]	14.5 ± 0.55
Weight (kg)	53.1 ± 11.62	53.3 ± 10.18	52.0 ± 10.10
Height (cm)	163.5 ± 8.45	164.0 ± 8.39	163.6 ± 8.08
BMI (kg/m^2)	19.7 ± 3.27	19.7 ± 2.70	19.3 ± 2.69
Forearm BMC (grams)	3.2 ± 0.67	3.13 ± 0.56	3.25 ± 0.71
Forearm BMD (g/cm^2)	0.34 ± 0.06	0.34 ± 0.04	0.35 ± 0.06
Os Calcis BMC (grams)	2.4 ± 0.63	2.4 ± 0.55	2.41 ± 0.65
Os Calcis BMD (g/cm^2)	0.53 ± 0.09	0.53 ± 0.07	0.53 ± 0.09

[*]significantly different than non-smokers (p<0.05)
[**]significantly different than non-smokers (p<0.01)
[***]significantly different than non-smokers and active smokers (p<0.05)
BMI: body mass index
BMC: bone mineral content
BMD: bone mineral density

Measurements

Forearm and os calcis scans (PIXI, Lunar Corporation: Madison, WI) were performed to provide forearm and os calcis bone mineral content (units: grams) and density (units: grams/cm^2). The non-dominant forearm was used for forearm measures. Scans of the distal radius and ulna were taken at a point 2/3 the distance from the olecranon to the styloid process. The left heel was used for os calcis measurements. Quality control was performed every day by measuring a forearm and a heel phantom. The precision error (coefficient of variation for repeated measurements) for this technique is 1.5% for the forearm and 2.0% for the os calcis.

Weight and height were measured in subjects wearing light clothing without shoes. Weight was measured in kilograms using a standard calibrated scale and recorded to nearest 0.1 kg. Height was measured using a stadiometer and recorded to the nearest 0.1 centimeters. Body mass index (BMI) was calculated as the ratio of body weight to height squared (kg/m^2).

Questionnaire

All girls answered a question regarding menarche. The question asked: "have you had your first menstrual period?" If they answered "yes", they were defined as "peri/post-menarcheal". If they answered "no", they were defined as "pre-menarcheal". Data was treated as a dichotomous variable.

Questions pertaining to second-hand-smoke included the "number of days in the last 7 days in which the subject was in the same room with someone who was smoking cigarettes", "in the same vehicle with someone who was smoking cigarettes", and whether or not the subject "was around smokers for at least 15 minutes per day". Subjects were classified as "passive smokers" if they answered "yes" to either one of these 3 questions. Passive smoking and second-hand-smoke are synonymous terms.

Questionnaire items assessed whether or not the subjects "have smoked at least 100 cigarettes in their life" and whether or not they "have smoked in the last 30 days". Subjects were classified as "active smokers" if they answered "yes" to either one of these 2 questions.

Statistical Analysis

Data was analyzed using SPSS 10.0 software (SPSS Inc., Chicago, IL). Normality was checked and the dependent variables were approximately normally distributed. Therefore, no transformations were necessary. Descriptive statistics, chi-square tests, bivariate Spearman correlations, and analysis of variance with Tukey post-hoc tests were performed. Stepwise multiple linear regression models were used to estimate the effect of variables (age, BMI, menarche, passive smoking, active smoking) on the important dependent variables, forearm and os calcis bone mineral content. Dummy variables of passive and active smokers were created to use in multiple linear regression models as well as in the correlation analysis. Statistical significance was accepted at the $p < 0.05$ level.

Results

A total of 166 girls and 300 boys participated in this study. Table 1 summarizes the means and standard deviations for age, weight, height, BMI, % menarcheal (girls), BMC and BMD of the forearm and the os calcis based on gender and smoking status. The majority (96%) of girls were 13 (30%) and 14 (66%) years of age. One girl was 12 years old, 3 girls were 15, and 2 girls were 16. In girls, there were no significant differences in age, height, BMI, os calcis BMC and BMD among the three groups of smoking status. Passive smokers were significantly heavier than non-smokers. A higher proportion of active smokers compared to non-smokers had reached menarche (χ^2=6.67; p<0.01). Forearm BMC of the passive and active smokers were significantly greater than non-smokers. Also, passive smokers had significantly greater forearm BMD than non-smokers and active smokers. The majority (89%) of boys were 13 (16%) and 14 (73%) years of age. One boy was 12 years old, 25 boys were 15, and 6 boys were 16. In boys, there were no significant differences in weight, height, BMI, BMC or BMD among the three groups of smoking status. However, passive smokers were significantly younger than non-smokers and active smokers.

Figure 1 shows os calcis BMC in 146 non-smokers, 165 passive smokers, and 155 active smokers. Although there was a trend for higher BMC with frequency of smoking, results from analysis of variance (with Tukey post-hoc testing) revealed that these differences were not significant.

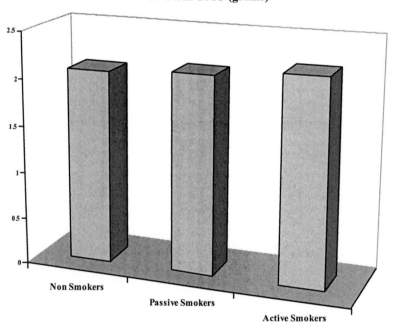

Figure 1. Os calcis BMC in non-, passive and active smokers

Table 2 presents Spearman correlations between the independent variables and measures of BMC and BMD. In girls, the following variables were significantly correlated (r range of

0.25-0.58) with forearm BMC: weight, BMI, age, menarche, and height. Significant correlations (r range of 0.34-0.52) were found between os calcis BMC and the following variables: weight, height, and BMI. Most variables (except height) tended to correlate better with forearm (cortical bone) than with os calcis (trabecular bone). In boys, the following variables were significantly correlated (r range of 0.25-0.54) with forearm BMC: weight, BMI, height, and age. Significant correlations (r range of 0.43-0.66) were found between os calcis BMC and the following variables: weight, height, and BMI. Age correlated better with forearm (cortical bone), while weight and height correlated better with os calcis (trabecular bone).

Stepwise multiple linear regression analyses were performed to determine the best regression model for BMC, believed [11,45,47] to be a better measure in growing children than BMD. Collinearity diagnostics were used to test for multicollinearity among the independent variables. Multiple regression coefficients, and partial/total R^2s according to site (forearm and os calcis) for girls and boys are presented in table 3.

In girls, a total of 31% of the variance in forearm BMC was attributed to BMI (24%), age (5%), and menarche (2%). Passive and active smoking did not make significant contributions to forearm BMC. A total of 8% of the variance in os calcis BMC was attributed to BMI with no contribution by age, menarche, passive and active smoking. In boys, forearm BMC was best predicted by BMI (18%) and age (6%), accounting for 24% of the variance. A total of 21% of the variance in os calcis BMC was explained by BMI. The addition of passive and active smoking in the models did not make significant contributions to the variance in forearm or os calcis BMC.

Table 2. Spearman Correlations

	Forearm		Os Calcis	
	BMC	**BMD**	**BMC**	**BMD**
Girls				
Age	0.35[*]	0.28[*]	0.09	0.16[**]
Weight	0.58[*]	0.52[*]	0.52[*]	0.53[*]
Height	0.25[**]	0.09	0.46[*]	0.23[**]
BMI	0.53[*]	0.55[*]	0.34[*]	0.46[*]
Menarche	0.29[*]	0.26[*]	0.03	0.13
Passive Smoking	0.11	0.18[**]	0.02	0.02
Active Smoking	0.15	0.04	0.08	0.09
Boys				
Age	0.25[*]	0.22[*]	0.04	-0.06
Weight	0.54[*]	0.55[*]	0.66[*]	0.58[*]
Height	0.36[*]	0.30[*]	0.65[*]	0.37[*]
BMI	0.50[*]	0.54[*]	0.43[*]	0.51[*]
Passive Smoking	-0.06	0.05	-0.03	0.03
Active Smoking	0.05	0.04	0.05	0.00

[*]$p<0.001$
[**]$p<0.05$
BMI: body mass index
BMC: bone mineral content
BMD: bone mineral density

Table 3. Multiple Linear Regression Models

	Forearm BMC (grams)		Os Calcis BMC (grams)	
	b ± SE	R^2	b ± SE	R^2
Girls (n=166)				
Intercept	-1.9 ± 0.95		0.90 ± 0.19	
Age (years)	0.20 ± 0.07[**]	0.05	NS	NS
BMI (kg/m^2)	0.08 ± 0.01[*]	0.24	0.04[*] ± 0.01[*]	0.08
Menarche	0.23 ± 0.11[***]	0.02	NS	NS
Passive Smoking	NS	NS	NS	NS
Active Smoking	NS	NS	NS	NS
Total R^2	0.31		0.08	
Boys (n=300)				
Intercept	-3.1 ± 0.91		0.47 ± 0.21	
Age (years)	0.31 ± 0.06[*]	0.06	NS	NS
	Forearm BMC (grams)		Os Calcis BMC (grams)	
	b ± SE	R^2	b ± SE	R^2
BMI (kg/m^2)	0.09 ± 0.01[*]	0.18	0.10 ± 0.01[*]	0.21
Passive Smoking	NS	NS	NS	NS
Active Smoking	NS	NS	NS	NS
Total R^2	0.24		0.21	

b: multiple regression unstandardized coefficient
SE: standard error
[*]significant at the p<0.001
[**]significant at the p<0.005
[***]significant at the p<0.05
NS: non-significant
BMI: body mass index
BMC: bone mineral content

Discussion

Peak bone mass is a key determinant of skeletal health throughout life. Bachrach and colleagues [1] studied an American-born Asian cohort and found that Asian girls and boys tend to reach a plateau in bone mineral density earlier than other ethnic groups. Therefore, the fact that we investigated the role of tobacco smoke use and exposure in Asian girls and boys living in China who are at an age critical for bone accretion and smoking initiation and who can potentially be exposed to different environmental factors, makes our study and our findings imperative.

The frequency and duration of tobacco use are critical determinants of its physiological influences on bone density [14]. We speculate that the reasons we did not find significant inverse relationships between smoking and bone mass may have been due to the low levels of tobacco smoke use and exposure among the adolescents we studied. Past-30-day and 100-lifetime-cigarettes were the measures that determined active smoking status. Smoking levels among those classified as "smokers" were quite low. Thirty eight percent of the girls inconsistently answered questions regarding smoking frequency and duration. Forty eight percent of the girls classified as "smokers" indicated that they had smoked less than one cigarette in the last 30 days. Ten percent had smoked one cigarette in the past 30 days and 4 percent had smoked between 2-5 cigarettes in the last 30 days. Fourteen percent of the boys inconsistently answered questions regarding smoking frequency and duration. Fifty one percent of boys indicated that they had smoked less than one cigarette in the last 30 days; 19% had smoked one a day; 14% had smoked between 2-5; 1% had smoked between 6-10; 1% had smoked more than 20. These rates were quite low compared to the frequencies and durations reported in tobacco-using adult men and women living in China [46] as well as in the US [8].

Although there was no evidence that smoking and environmental tobacco smoke adversely effect the bone health of youth in the early adolescent years, a few questions remain unanswered. Since peak bone mass is not achieved until the later adolescent years and smoking increases with age [41], determining the role of tobacco use and exposure on bone mass during late adolescence might prove beneficial in drawing conclusions regarding the matter. Does tobacco adversely effect bone mass of the more mature smoker? If so, does tobacco exert a greater effect on cortical bone or on trabecular bone? Studies have shown that trabecular bone has high turnover and responds to factors such as body composition [29,37-38], hormones [3,7,33,37], and smoking [18,38] to a greater extent than does cortical bone, which has a slower turnover rate and is more influenced by exercise; studies [27,36] have shown positive associations between bone mineral density in the radius and the hip and most types of physical activity in children. Therefore, we expected smoking to relate more closely to os calcis than to forearm bone mass. Future research should shed light on the influence of tobacco smoke on these two different bone tissue sites and types.

It is also critical to determine whether frequency and duration of cigarette smoking are determining factors for bone mass during adolescence. Cornuz et al. [12] have shown that the risk for bone fractures in adults rises with greater cigarette consumption. Grainge and colleagues [16] have shown that bone mineral density is more strongly related to the number of months spent smoking than to pack-years of smoking. On the other hand, Vogel et al. [43] concluded that the magnitude of the smoking effect on bone mineral density of 1303 Japanese-American men participating in the Hawaii Osteoporosis Study was linked to the duration of smoking as well as to the number of cigarettes smoked.

We recognize that investigation of the role of the Chinese diet on bone mass of the Asian youth living in China is also critically important for understanding the etiologic significance of adolescent diet on peak bone mass and its possible confounding role in the tobacco-bone density relationship in this population. Previous investigations have shown interactions between smoking and serum calcium and vitamin D levels. Krall & Dawson-Hughes [25-26] reported that the adverse affect of smoking on bone mass may be related to decreased intestinal absorption of calcium. Brot and co-investigators [6,17] have shown depressed levels of vitamin D among 510 Danish perimenopausal smokers. Therefore, understanding the influence of cigarette smoking on calcium and vitamin D levels may help scientists define other probable mechanisms responsible for the link between tobacco and osteopenia.

In conclusion, we believe that this was the first study that investigated the role of smoking on bone mass during adolescence. We are also not aware of any other study in any age group or gender that has assessed the role of second-hand-smoke on bone mass. Although the public health impact of smoking in China is undoubtedly great, its deleterious effect on adolescent bone mass was not evident in this cross-sectional study.

Acknowledgements

This study was partially supported by the National Cancer Institute / National Institute of Drug Abuse Transdisciplinary Tobacco Use Research Center grant (1 P50 CA84735-01) awarded to the University of Southern California. This work has been partially published in *Med. Sci. Sports Exerc.*, May 2003.

References

[1]   Bachrach, L.K., Hastie, T., Wang, M.C., Narasimhan, B., and Marcus, R. (1999) Bone mineral acquisition in healthy Asian, Hispanic, Black, and Caucasian youth: a longitudinal study. *J. Clin. Endocrinol. Metab.* **84**: 4702-4712.

[2]   Barbieri, R.L., Gochberg, J., and Ryan, K.J. (1986) Nicotine, cotinine, and anabasine inhibit aromatase in human trophoblast in vitro. *J. Clin. Invest.* **77**: 1727-1733.

[3]   Baron, J.A., La Vecchia, C., and Levi, F. (1990) The antiestrogenic effect of cigarette smoking in women. *Am. J. Obstet. Gynecol.* **162**: 502-514.

[4]   Barrett-Connor, E., and Khaw, K.T. (1987) Cigarette smoking and increased endogenous estrogen levels in men. *Am. J. Epidemiol.* **126**: 187-192.

[5]   Bonjour, J.P., Theintz, G., and Buckes, B. (1991) Critical years and stages of puberty for spinal and femoral bone mass accumulation during adolescence. *J. Clin. Endocrinol. Metab.* **73**: 555-563.

[6]   Brot, C., Jorgensen, N.R., and Sorensen, O.H. (1999) The influence of smoking on vitamin D status and calcium metabolism. *Eur. J. Clin. Nutr.* **53**(12): 920-926.

[7]   Cann, C.E., Cavanaugh, D.J., Scnurpfiel, K., and Martin, M.C. (1988) Menstrual history is the primary determinant of trabecular bone density in women. *Med. Sci. Sports Exerc.* **20** (Suppl. 2): S59.

[8]   Centers for Disease Control and Prevention. (1999) Cigarette smoking among adults-United States, 1997. *MMWR* **48**: 993-996.

[9]   Chen, X., and Unger, J.B. (1999) Hazards of smoking initiation among Asian American and Non-Asian adolescents in California: a survival model analysis. *Prev.* Med. **28**: 589-599.

[10] Chen, X., Li, Y., Unger, J.B., Gong, J., Johnson, C.A., and Guo, Q. (2001) Hazard of smoking initiation by age among adolescents in Wuhan, China. *Prev. Med.* **32**(5): 437-445.

[11] Cooper, C., Fall, C., Egger, P., Hobbs, R., Eastell, R., and Barker, D. (1997) Growth in infancy and bone mass in later life. *Ann. Rheum. Dis.* **56**: 17-21.

[12] Cornuz, J., Feskanich, D., Willett, W.C., and Colditz, G.A. (1999) Smoking, smoking cessation, and risk of hip fracture in women. *Am. J. Med.* **106**(3): 311-314.

[13] Dai, W.S., Gutai, J.P., Kuller, L.H., and Cauley, J.A. (1988) Cigarette smoking and serum sex hormones in men. *Am. J. Epidemiol.* **128**: 796-805.

[14] Daniell, H.W. (1976) Osteoporosis of the slender smoker: vertebral compression fractures and loss of metacarpal cortex in relation to postmenopausal cigarette smoking and lack of obesity. *Arch. Intern. Med.* **136**: 298-304.

[15] Forsen, L., Bjorndal, A., Bjartveit, K., Edna, T., Holmen, J., Jessen, V., and Westberg, G. (1994) Interaction between current smoking, leanness, and physical inactivity in the prediction of hip fracture. *J. Bone Miner. Res.* **9**: 1671-1678.

[16] Grainge, M.J., Coupland, C.A., Cliffe, S.J., Chilvers, C.E., and Hosking, D.J. (1998) Cigarette smoking, alcohol and caffeine consumption, and bone mineral density in postmenopausal women. The Nottingham EPIC Study Group. *Osteoporos. Int.* **8**(4): 355-363.

[17] Hermann, A.P., Brot, C., Gram, J., Kolthoff, N., and Mosekilde, L. (2000) Premenopausal smoking and bone density in 2015 perimenopausal women. *J. Bone Miner. Res.* **15**: 780-787.

[18] Hopper, J.L., and Seeman, E. (1994) The bone density of female twins discordant for tobacco use. *N. Engl. J. Med.* **330**: 387-392.

[19] Jensen, J., Christiansen, C., and Rodbro, P. (1985) Cigarette smoking, serum estrogens, and bone loss during hormone-replacement therapy early after menopause. *N. Engl. J. Med.* **313**: 973-975.

[20] Jensen, J., and Christiansen, C. (1988) Effects of smoking on serum lipoproteins and bone mineral content during postmenopausal hormone replacement therapy. *Am. J. Obstet. Gynecol.* **159**: 820-825.

[21] Katzman, D.K., Bachrach, L.K., Carter, D.R., and Marcus, R. (1991) Clinical and anthropometric correlates of bone mineral acquisition in healthy adolescent girls. *J. Clin. Endocrinol. Metab.* **73**: 1332-1339.

[22] Kiel, D.P., Baron, J.A., Anderson, J.J., Hannan, M.T., and Felson, D.T. (1992) Smoking eliminates the protective effect of oral estrogens on the risk for hip fracture among women. *Ann. Int. Med.* **116**: 716-721.

[23] Klaiber, E.L., Broverman, D.M., and Dalen, J.E. (1984) Serum estradiol levels in male cigarette smokers. *Am. J. Med.* **77**: 858-862.

[24] Klaiber, E.L., and Broverman, D.M. (1988) Dynamics of estradiol and testosterone and seminal fluid indexes in smokers and non-smokers. *Fertil. Steril.* **50**: 630-634.

[25] Krall, E.A., and Dawson-Hughes, B. (1991) Smoking and bone loss among postmenopausal women. *J. Bone Miner. Res.* **6**: 331-337.

[26] Krall, E.A., and Dawson-Hughes, B. (1999) Smoking increases bone loss and decreases intestinal calcium absorption. *J. Bone Miner. Res.* **14**(2): 215-220.

[27] Kroger, H., Kotaniemi, A., Vainio, P., and Alhava, E. (1992) Bone densitometry of the spine and femur in children by dual-energy x-ray absorptiometry. *Bone Miner.* **17**: 75-85.

[28] Li, X., Fang, X., and Stanton, B. (1996) Cigarette smoking among Chinese adolescents and its association with demographic characteristics, social activities, and problem behaviors. *Substance Use & Misuse* **31**: 545-563.

[29] Liel, Y., Edwards, J., Shary, J., Spicer, K.M., Gordon, L., and Bell, N.H. (1988) The effects of race and body habitus on bone mineral density of the radius, hip, and spine in premenopausal women. *J. Clin. Endocrin. Metab.* **66**: 1247-1250.

[30] MacMahon, B., Trichopoulos, D., Cole, P., and Brown, J. (1982) Cigarette smoking and urinary estrogens. *N Engl J Med.* **307**: 1062-1065.

[31] Michnovicz, J.J., Hershcopf, R.J., Naganuma, H., Bradlow, H.L., and Fishman, J. (1986) Increased 2-hydoxylation of estradiol as a possible mechanism for the anti-estrogenic effect of cigarette smoking. *N. Engl. J. Med.* **315**: 1305-1309.

[32] Najem, G.R., Batuman, F., Smith, A.M., and Feuerman, M. (1997) Patterns of smoking among inner-city teenagers: smoking has a pediatric age of onset. *J. Adolesc. Health* **20**(3): 226-231.

[33] Rubin, K., Schirduan, V., Gendreau, P., Sarfarazi, M., Mendola, R., and Dalsky, G. (1993) Predictors of axial and peripheral bone mineral density in healthy children and adolescents. *J. Pediatr.* **123**: 863-870.

[34] Seeman, E., Melton, L.J., O'Fallon, T., and Riggs, B.L. (1983) Risk factors for spinal osteoporosis in men. *Am. J. Med.* **75**: 977-983.

[35] Seeman, E. (1996) The Effects of Tobacco and Alcohol Use on Bone. In: Marcus, R., Feldman, D., and Kelsey, J. (eds), *Osteoporosis*, Academic Press, San Diego, CA, pp. 577-597.

[36] Slemenda, C.W., Miller, J.Z., Hui, S.L., Reister, T.K., and Johnston, C.C. Jr. (1991) Role of physical activity in the development of skeletal mass in children. *J. Bone Miner. Res.* **6**: 1227-1233.

[37] Slemenda, C.W., Reister, T.K., Hui, S.L., Miller, J.Z., Christian, J.C., and Johnston, C.C. Jr. (1994) Influences on skeletal mineralization in children and adolescents: evidence for varying effects of sexual maturation and physical activity. *J. Pediatr.* **125**(2): 201-207.

[38] Stevenson, J.C., Lees, B., Devenport, M., Cust, M.P., and Ganer, K.F. (1989) Determinants of bone density in normal women: risk factors for future osteoporosis? *Br. Med. J.* **298**:924-928.

[39] Swan, A.V., Creeser, R., and Murray, M. (1990) When and why children first start to smoke. *Int. J. Epidemiol.* **19**(2): 323-330.

[40] Theintz, G., Buchs, B., Rizzoli, R., Slosman, D., Clavien, H., Sizonenko, P.C., and Bonjour, J.P.H. (1992) Longitudinal monitoring of bone mass accumulation in healthy adolescents: evidence for a marked reduction after 16 years of age at the levels of lumbar spine and femoral neck in female subjects. *J. Clin. Endocrinol. Metab.* **75**: 1060-1065.

[41] Unger, J.B., Li, Y., Chen, X., Xia, J., Azen, S., Guo, Q., Tan, S., Gong, J., Sun, P., Liu, C., Chou, C., Zheng, H., and Johnson, C.A. (2001) Adolescent smoking in Wuhan, China: baseline data from the Wuhan smoking prevention trial. *Am. J. Prev. Med.* **21**(3): 162-169.

[42] Valimaki, M. J., Karkkainen, M., Lamberg-Allardt, C., Laitinen, K., Alhava, E., Heikkinen, J., Impivaara, O., Makela, P., Palmgren, J., Seppanen, R., Vouri, I., and the Cardiovascular Risk in Young Finns Study Group. (1994) Exercise, smoking, and calcium intake during adolescence and early adulthood as determinants of peak bone mass. *BMJ* **309**: 230-235.

[43] Vogel, J.M., Davis, J.W., Nomura, A., Wasnich, R.D., and Ross, P.D. (1997) The effects of smoking on bone mass and the rates of bone loss among elderly Japanese-American men. *J. Bone Miner. Res.* **12**(9): 1495-1501.

[44] Williams, A.R., Weiss, N.S., Ure, C.L., Ballard, J., and Daling, J.R. (1982) Effect of weight, smoking, and estrogen use on the risk of hip and forearm fractures in postmenopausal women. *Obstet. Gynaecol.* **60**: 695-699.

[45] Witzke, K.A., and Snow, C.M. (2000) Effects of plyometric jump training on bone mass in adolescent girls. *Med. Sci. Sports Exerc.* **32**(6): 1051-1057.

[46] Yang, G., Fan, L., Tan, J., Qi, G., Zhang, Y., Samet, J.M., Taylor, C.E., Becker, K., and Xu, J. (1999) Smoking in China: findings of the 1996 National Prevalence Survey. *JAMA* **282**: 1247-1253.

[47] Yarbrough, D.E., Barrett-Connor, E., and Morton, D.J. (2000) Birth weight as a predictor of adult bone mass in postmenopausal women: the Rancho Bernardo Study. *Osteoporos. Int.* **11**: 626-630.

Index

D

M

N

O

S

T